Science Learning, Science Teaching

Third edition

Jerry Wellington and
Gren Ireson

Routledge
Taylor & Francis Group

LONDON AND NEW YORK

First edition published 1999
Second edition published 2008
This third edition published 2012
by Routledge
2 Park Square, Milton Park, Abingdon, Oxon OX14 4RN

Simultaneously published in the USA and Canada
by Routledge
711 Third Avenue, New York, NY 10017

Routledge is an imprint of the Taylor & Francis Group, an informa business

British Library Cataloguing in Publication Data
A catalogue record for this book is available from the British Library

Library of Congress Cataloging in Publication Data
Wellington, J. J. (Jerry J.)
   Science learning, science teaching / Jerry Wellington and Gren Ireson.
   – 3rd ed.
      p. cm.
   Includes bibliographical references and index.
   1. Science – Study and teaching (Secondary) I. Ireson, Gren. II. Title.
   Q181.W4416 2012
   507.1'2–dc23   2011033713

ISBN: 978-0-415-61971-4 (hbk)
ISBN: 978-0-415-61972-1 (pbk)
ISBN: 978-0-203-13496-2 (ebk)

Typeset in Garamond
by HWA Text and Data Management, London

MIX
Paper from
responsible sources
FSC
www.fsc.org   FSC® C004839

Printed and bound in Great Britain by
TJ International Ltd, Padstow, Cornwall

Science Learning, Science Teaching

Now fully updated in its third edition, *Science Learning, Science Teaching* offers an accessible, practical guide to creative classroom teaching and a comprehensive introduction to contemporary issues in science education.

Aiming to encourage and assist professionals with the process of reflection in the science classroom, the new edition examines the latest research in the field, changes to curriculum and the latest standards for initial teacher training. With two brand new chapters, key topics covered include:

- the science curriculum and science in the curriculum
- planning and managing learning
- learning in science – including consideration of current 'fads' in learning
- safety in the science laboratory
- exploring how science works
- using ICT in the science classroom
- teaching in an inclusive classroom
- the role of practical work and investigations in science
- language and literacy in science
- citizenship and sustainability in science education.

Including useful references, further reading lists and recommended websites, *Science Learning, Science Teaching* is an essential source of support, guidance and inspiration for all students, teachers, mentors and those involved in science education wishing to reflect upon, improve and enrich their practice.

Jerry Wellington is a Professor in the School of Education at the University of Sheffield, UK.

Gren Ireson is Professor of Science Education in the School of Education at Nottingham Trent University, UK.

Contents

List of figures   vii
List of tables   ix
Preface   xi

THEME A
Science teaching and the science curriculum   I

1 The art and craft of science teaching   3

2 Becoming a teacher   25

3 The science curriculum and science in the curriculum   41

THEME B
Approaches to science learning and science teaching   59

4 Learning in science   61
   Jon Scaife

5 Planning and managing learning in science   119

6 Inclusive science education   140

7 Practical work in science education   161

8 Investigations in science   171

9 *How Science Works*   185

10 Safety in the science laboratory   191

11 Language in science teaching and learning   198

12 Numeracy in science teaching and learning   223

THEME C
Enriching science learning and science teaching   **231**

13 Using ICT in science education   233

14 Exploring the nature of science   258

15 Using out-of-school sources   282

16 Citizenship and sustainability in science education   296

    Index   305

Figures

1.1   Concept map for the topic *Earth in space*   7
2.1   Cartoons showing different models or metaphors of teaching   27
2.2   Development of subject knowledge and pedagogical knowledge in teaching   29
2.3   Factors affecting science teachers and their teaching   37
2.4   Common ground and shared meanings in science education   38
3.1   A new model or a return to pre-1968?   47
3.2   A-level entries 2001–2010   48
3.3   Gender differences at A-level   48
4.1   Variation of mean science knowledge with age   64
4.2   Piagetian stages of development   67
4.3   Current developmental profile (CDP) and zone of proximal development
       (ZPD)   70
4.4   'Would you say this was a plant?'   79
4.5   'Does the candle make light?'   79
4.6   Diagnostic question: syringe   80
4.7   Diagnostic question about electric current   82
4.8   Matchstick patterns   92
4.9   Hypothetical chunking of gas generation apparatus by (a) a teacher and
       (b) a student   93
4.10 Pre-teaching task used to elicit understanding of mass of dissolved
       substance   105
4.11 Intervention experiments   106
4.12 Student concept map before teaching   107
4.13 Student concept map after teaching   108
4.14 Circuit with two branches   111
5.1a Blank lesson planning grid   121
5.1b Alternative lesson planning grid   122
5.2   The lesson planning cycle   123
5.3   Gestures and sign language can be extremely valuable in management and
       control   132

6.1	Why do people succeed or fail? Questions to ask of individuals' differences and attributes	146
6.2	A strategy for differentiation	147
8.1	Dimensions of investigative work	173
8.2	Example ISA	175
8.3	Investigation planning sheet	177
8.4	The investigation planning cycle	178
8.5	An example 'prompt' sheet	179
8.6	Self assessment, or peer assessment, sheet for investigative work	181
9.1	Key strands in *How Science Works*	186
9.2	How scientists work	188
9.3	Real world science	188
11.1	Entries from a science dictionary	205
11.2	Readability using Word	209
11.3a	Differentiated DART activities for a Year 7 (mean age 12) group: Activity A	211
11.3b	Differentiated DART activities for a Year 7 (mean age 12) group: Activity B	212
11.4	Writing brief for alternative energy resources	216
11.5	Ways of note-making and note-taking	217
12.1	An exercise for developing graphicacy	228
13.1	Example writing frame	245
13.2	Using an electronic mark book	246
13.3	Inserting the correct formulae	247
13.4	A basic data-logging system	248
13.5	A simple data-logger	249
14.1	Nature of science scoring grid	261
14.2	Nature of science profile	262
14.3	Statements for Jenner's experiment	274
14.4	Process words	275
14.5	Example role play cards	277
15.1	Classifying informal sources of learning	284
15.2	Media science and school science as filtering systems	286
16.1	Lesson plan example	303

Tables

1.1	Bloom's taxonomy and intended outcomes	15
1.2	Dimensions of progression in a person's knowledge and understanding	15
1.3	GCE A-level entry trends	19
2.1	What should be in the science curriculum, and why?	32
2.2	What is science education for? A summary of justifications	35
3.1	Examination entries, by gender, for biology and physics, 1985	44
3.2	Big ideas in biology, chemistry and physics	49
3.3	Aligning the four ideas with biology, chemistry and physics	49
3.4	Why teach science?	51
3.5	Groups of aims in science education	55
3.6	Balanced science education	55
4.1	Seven types of memory element	73
4.2	Changes in the views of a group of 11-year-olds over time	83
4.3	Classification of question types and corresponding mental operations	97
4.4	Switch and bulb logic table	111
5.1	Headings for a scheme of work	120
5.2	Traits of different learning styles	125
5.3	Suggested activities to cater for different learning styles and intelligences	127
5.4	Guidelines for questioning	129
6.1	Some key events leading to inclusion, 1981–2011	141
6.2	Gender differences in science performance, PISA 2009	145
6.3	Planning and teaching for differentiation: basic guidelines	149
6.4	Possible teaching tactics to aid comprehension	151
6.5	A science wordbank for pupils aged 11 to 16	153
7.1	Ten possible aims of practical work	162
7.2	The role of practical work in science	164
7.3	Pitfalls and problems with practical work in science	168
8.1	A typology of investigations	173
8.2	Classification of investigations in terms of variables	174
10.1	Accidents to pupils in schools by percentage	192
10.2	Most common school laboratory accidents by percentage	192

10.3   Risk assessment index: an example   195
10.4   Example risk assessment for producing copper sulphate crystals   196
11.1   A taxonomy of the words of science   200
11.2   Watch your language: could you add to the list?   203
11.3   Some 'hard' words in science   204
11.4   Writing for learning in science; guidelines and check list   207
11.5   Four measures of readability   208
11.6   DARTS: a brief summary   213
12.1   Planning for numeracy in science education   227
12.2   An exercise for developing graphicacy   228
13.1   Uses and applications of ICT in science learning and teaching   234
13.2   Overview of uses of ICT in science teaching and learning   235
13.3   Process and ICT use in science teaching and learning   235
13.4   Feedback from teachers on the impact of ICT on their teaching   236
13.5   Questions to ask of a website: five criteria for evaluating web pages   241
13.6   Potential benefits of publishing tools in science teaching and learning   244
13.7   Internet use in UK households   255
13.8   Internet activity by age   255
15.1   Formal and informal learning in science   282
15.2   Using newspapers in science teaching and learning   287
16.1   Successful learners, confident individuals and responsible citizens   301

Preface

There is no substitute for teaching experience and classroom observation. On the other hand, time is often needed to stand back and reflect upon this experience. The aim of this book is to encourage and assist teachers (both pre- and in-service), mentors and others involved in science education with the process of reflection in the hope that it will improve and enrich their practice.

This book has been written with the current standards for initial teacher education in mind but is not geared specifically to any particular statements of standards or competencies, nor to a specific curriculum. It should therefore be of value to students, teachers and mentors in the UK, the USA, Australasia and other countries.

The book is a revised edition of *Science Learning, Science Teaching* (2008, Routledge, London). The book reflects the main changes since 2008 and reflects feedback from users regarding the structure. In addition new chapters have been added; Jon Scaife's chapter on learning (Chapter 4) considers some of the central thinking and theory as well as what might be called the current 'fads' in learning and has been fully revised in this new edition. All the references and further reading have been updated throughout the book.

The book aims both to address contemporary issues in science education which will have a direct bearing on science teaching in the twenty-first century, and to present and discuss practical approaches in science education. Many contemporary issues are also long-standing, recurring debates, such as the role of practical work, the nature of science, the place of ICT, children's prior learning, the purposes of science education, the importance of language in science, the need for differentiation, the handling of controversial issues, citizenship, and the role of 'informal' learning. These are all considered. In parallel with those discussions, practical approaches for learning and teaching are offered which, we hope, will be of value in the classroom and the laboratory. The book aims to focus on learning – and planning for learning – as much as it considers teaching and planning for teaching.

Space is limited, so none of the discussions or suggestions goes into the depth that could be achieved if a single book were written on just one of the areas. Consequently, ample references and suggestions for further reading are given throughout. This book, like science teaching for all, is designed for a mixed-attainment and mixed-motivation audience, so it provides for the possibility of special needs and interests, and offers ample scope for extension work. Some readers may not have the time or the inclination to follow up all the references and further reading but we hope that others will.

Finally, readers are bound to find something missing, even in this revised edition. Not every issue or practical approach could possibly be covered in a book of this kind. The main aim of the book is to introduce readers to the basic questions of why, what and how, which occur so frequently in the learning and teaching of science.

Comments and feedback on any points either in, or not in, the book are welcome; a number have been included from the previous edition. The authors can be contacted by post or email as follows: Jerry Wellington at the University of Sheffield (j.wellington@sheffield.ac.uk); Gren Ireson at Nottingham Trent University (gren.ireson@ntu.ac.uk); Jon Scaife at the University of Sheffield (j.a.scaife@shef.ac.uk).

Theme A

Science teaching and the science curriculum

Chapter 1

The art and craft of science teaching

Meeting high standards – a tall order

One of the premises of this book is that science teaching is an extremely demanding occupation. No other subject teacher has to cope with such a range of situations, with such a conceptually difficult subject and with a group of learners who bring all kinds of prior learning and preconceptions to it. Teaching science is a tall order. In this first chapter, we identify ten key aspects of science teaching and begin to outline some of the questions they raise and to offer some practical ways forward. Each area is developed later in the book. The ten key areas of science teaching are summarised: using language, questioning, explaining, practical work, using resources, presenting the nature of science, assessing learning, developing progression and continuity, planning and managing – and lastly, but most importantly, generating motivation and enthusiasm. A key chapter is Chapter 4, 'Learning in science', and other chapters will make reference to it. Should Chapter 4 then be read in parts when referenced? Should it be read as a stand-alone chapter? These are questions which, themselves, go to the heart of learning and only you, the reader, can answer such questions.

Using language carefully

Learning science is, in many ways, like learning a new language. In some ways it presents a greater difficulty in that many of the hard, conceptual words of science – such as energy, work, and power – have a precise meaning in science and sometimes an exact scientific definition, but a very different meaning in everyday life. Equally, many of the naming words of our lives have been commandeered by science. Consider: element, conductor, cell, field, circuit, and compound. Thinking of cell we have different meaning across the sciences and in everyday use. This is made worse because many of the terms of science are metaphors. For example, a field in science is not a field in the everyday sense.

Another category of language that science teachers (and many other teachers) use has been christened the 'language of secondary education'. The list includes: modify, compare, evaluate, hypothesise, infer, recapitulate, and so on. These are words used by teachers and in examination papers but rarely heard in playgrounds, pubs or at football matches.

What should science teachers do about their specialist language and the language of secondary education? Well, they cannot avoid it, skirt round it, or constantly translate it into the 'vernacular'. This would do a disservice to their pupils who will eventually be confronted by scientific language, certainly in test papers and examinations. The general answer is to treat language with care, to be aware of its difficulties, and to bear in mind that although pupils can and do use scientific terms in speech and writing this does not mean that they understand them. This is equally true of journalists, other writers and radio or TV pundits of course. Even the great and the good fall into this trap. Many others refer to mathematics as the 'language of science' which introduces its own issues.

Chapters 11 and 12 are devoted to language and numeracy in science and discuss directed or structured reading; note-taking and note-making; pupils' writing in science; discussion and debating; using newspapers in science and the importance of numeracy and 'graphicacy' in science and its communication. Of course, communication in science involves far more than just the spoken and the written word and this is also discussed in these chapters.

Questioning

One of the most difficult arts (or is it a science?) of teaching which involves judicious use of language is the activity of questioning, which goes on in so many classrooms (see Chapter 4). Research shows that most of the questions are asked by teachers and that most pupil responses are short answers to closed questions, involving factual recall:

TEACHER: Which element has an atomic number of 6?
PUPIL: Carbon.

At the other end of the spectrum is the art of Socratic questioning. A classic book called *Meno* describes how Socrates 'pulled out' or literally educed (from the Latin educere, 'to lead out') the principle of Pythagoras from a 'mere slave'. He did this purely by questioning-eliciting and building upon the slave's existing ideas and knowledge. This is the highest form of questioning. Cynics may argue that this may have worked for a genius such as Socrates in a one-to-one with a lowly slave – but try doing this with 24 adolescents on a wet Friday afternoon. We have sympathy with the cynics. But it is still worth examining the questioning techniques used by teachers and how they can be improved. The best teachers are often the best questioners.

> As higher-level questions require more thinking from pupils, they will be more difficult to answer. Research has shown that effective teachers use more higher-level questions than less effective teachers ...
>
> (Muijs and Reynolds 2010)

What types of question are there and what purposes do they serve?

* Closed questions have only one acceptable answer, e.g. a name, a piece of information, a specific line of reasoning (or argument);
* Open questions – a number of different answers could be accepted, e.g. an opinion, an evaluation, a belief, a pupil's own line of reasoning.

Research indicates that most teachers' questions are closed, partly because the responses are (not surprisingly) easier to handle. Also, closed questions are useful in controlling and shaping a lesson, not least in ensuring that the whole class is paying attention. Many questions can be used by a teacher to focus, guide or redirect a lesson. These are generally diagnostic questions, e.g. eliciting what pupils already know, or checking that pupils are 'on the right lines'.

One type of question that teachers use, but need to be wary of, is the 'guess what's in my head' or pseudo-question. This type of question was caricatured humorously by Peter Ustinov:

Teacher: Who is the greatest composer?
Pupil: Beethoven.
Teacher: Wrong, Bach.
Teacher: Name me one Russian composer.
Pupil: Tchaikovsky.
Teacher: Wrong. Rimsky-Korsakov.

(quoted in Edwards and Westgate 1994: 100)

In Chapter 5 we look again at the art of questioning, as part of the business of planning and managing teaching. We will, here, explore the issue of dealing with partially correct answers and matching the cognitive level of the question to the learner.

The art of explaining

One of the great arts of teaching is to be able to explain things, i.e. to put difficult ideas into terms that pupils can understand. As teachers develop, they learn a range of different ways of representing and formulating the ideas of science that make them comprehensible to pupils. Through observation, practice and experience teachers develop a repertoire of explanations and different ways of explaining things. If one does not work, then perhaps another will. This 'wisdom of practice' (Shulman 1986: 9) develops over time – teachers acquire a whole armoury of examples, illustrations, explanations and analogies. An example can be drawn from the *National Numeracy Strategy* where one finds:

> ... giving accurate, well-paced explanations and referring to previous work or methods – for example, explaining a method of calculation and discussing why it works, giving the meaning of a mathematical term, explaining the steps in the solution to a problem, giving examples that satisfy a general statement, illustrating how the statement $7 - 3 = 4$ can represent different situations.

(DfEE 1999)

The art of explaining involves the ability to convey difficult scientific ideas without distorting their meaning or telling lies. This often requires considerable intellectual effort and sound subject knowledge. It involves breaking down a complex idea, or a process, into its smaller component steps. Processes such as photosynthesis, cooling by evaporation, melting or boiling, and fractional distillation can only be understood if the simpler ideas they rely on are first identified, then put into a sequence, then explained. The business of *identifying* the underlying or prerequisite ideas, then *sequencing* them is the basis of *concept mapping*.

> The real power of concept mapping is to label the linking lines (directional arrows) with verbs.

(Ross *et al.* 2000)

Box 1.1 gives a few of the key ideas behind concept mapping and some suggested steps in making them for oneself. Figure 1.1 shows an example of a concept map for the topic of *Earth in space* produced in a resource by the Institute of Physics.

Box 1.1 Concept mapping

What is a concept map?

A concept map is a special kind of thinking (metacognitive) tool. Its purpose is to relate concepts to one another as a hierarchy which, at the same time, should display their relationships in a scientifically valid form. (Note: the word 'concept' in this case is taken to mean any word or phrase that has a scientific meaning.)

There are three very specific features that characterise a concept map.

1   It must represent a hierarchy of ideas ranging from the most general idea at the apex to the most specific ideas at the base.
2   The link between any two ideas must have a word or phrase that describes the relationship and is scientifically valid.
3   The concept map must be revised each time new information is included and when incorrect relationships are discovered.

Creating concept maps

The concept map is rooted in this idea of relationships and that is why the hierarchy and the statements of relationship are essential if the map is to function. If you cannot find words to describe the scientific relationship between two ideas then it is not valid to make the link.

Links should not be made if they cannot be justified. The relationship should be researched more deeply through texts or consultation, until either a suitable connecting phrase is found or the idea is rejected.

One danger with the process is that the map can end up as a topic web, in which case it will have neither hierarchy nor statements or relationships, and will do nothing to promote understanding of the subject matter.

Concept mapping is a dynamic process and the map should constantly be revised. The first map is merely a starting point which may contain errors and/or misconceptions. Its value, however, is that it not only challenges the author's understanding but also opens up the thinking to other people in a highly visible and accessible way.

Steps in concept mapping

1   Choose the concepts, i.e. keywords or very short phrases that you wish to use in your map. Do not choose too many at this stage. Write them out on separate small pieces of paper.
2   Rank the list of concepts from the most abstract and inclusive to the most concrete and specific to establish a hierarchy.
3   Group the concepts according to two criteria:
     i)   concepts that seem to be at similar levels of generality or specificity;
     ii) concepts that are closely related.
4   Arrange the concepts as a two-dimensional array rather like a family tree with the most general concepts at the top.

5   Try to think of words or phrases that could link the concepts together so that it makes scientific sense. If you can't make a link at this point leave out the concept for the time being.

6   When you are satisfied that the map now reflects your current understanding, draw it out on a sheet of A4 paper.

7   Link the related concepts with lines and label them with the connecting phrase or word that describes the logical connections and which makes sense when read in conjunction with the concepts.

8   Be prepared to revise your map. A concept map should allow the reorganisation and reconstruction of ideas in order to create a dynamic framework for knowledge and understanding.

Source: this is based on a set of guidelines produced by Keith Bishop of the University of Bath, partly derived from Novak and Gowin (1984).

For those happier with an ICT-based solution, excellent, free, software is available for concept mapping at: http://cmap.ihmc.us/

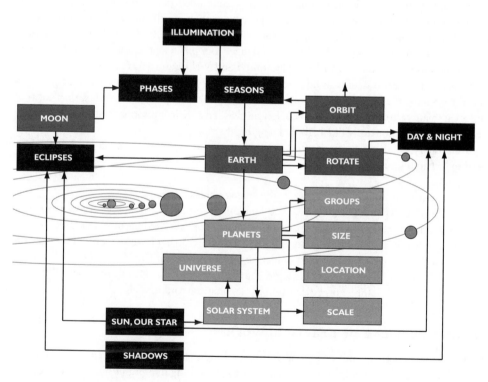

Figure 1.1 Concept map for the topic *Earth in space*
Source: Institute of Physics

Producing a concept map requires considerable mental effort. Just try doing it for any of the above processes. Similarly with a complex idea such as momentum or acceleration. 'Momentum' depends on an understanding of 'mass' and 'velocity'. Velocity requires an understanding of speed and direction. Speed is understood by … and so on. Explaining momentum requires a lot more effort than simply defining it as mass times velocity. One way to aid understanding is to use lots and lots of examples, from many different contexts. Moving objects with a large or a small momentum could be shown or talked about: a lorry, a train, a bee, the Titanic. Examples help.

Equally, analogies and metaphors are an integral part of science. Many explanations involve describing the unfamiliar in familiar terms, or explaining unfamiliar events by comparing them with familiar occurrences. Thus, electric current is like the flow of water in a pipe (the water analogy). Fractional distillation is like sorting out a pack of cards into Kings, Queens, Jacks and so on. Global warming is, in some ways, like the effect of a greenhouse on its contents. Respiration is like burning. Light is sometimes like a stream of particles, sometimes more like the waves in a tank of water. But all analogies and comparisons have their limits. If a water pipe is cut, the water leaks out – but electricity does not 'leak out' of a wall socket or a cut wire (although we often talk of 'leakage' in an electrical context). Weather forecasters often talk about the Sun *burning off* cloud or mist, whilst this would be spectacular to see, clouds obviously don't burn. Thus, analogies are valuable but must not be taken too far: this message has to be conveyed to pupils.

Similarly with both multimedia images and physical models in teaching science. Multimedia can be a powerful tool in teaching science, especially in showing the normally invisible entities that scientific explanations rely on, e.g. particles in a melting block of ice; electrons in a wire; electrons 'orbiting' the nucleus. But there is a danger if pupils take these images too literally or too seriously (see Chapter 5 of Collins, Hammond and Wellington 1997).

Similarly, physical models can be used to show things that are either very small, e.g. atoms and their bonds, the helix of DNA, or particles as marbles in a tray; and things that are very large, e.g. plate tectonics. But, like analogies, models have their limitations. Atoms, and bonds between them, are not really like balls and lengths of string.

In summary, good explanations often require illustrations, models and analogies but teachers need to be careful to:

- point out their limitations, i.e. where the analogy breaks down;
- use illustrations and examples that are familiar to pupils and take account of their own environment and personal circumstances (when one of us started his teaching career in East London we always used insulation in house lofts in discussing heat loss, until it dawned on us that 95 per cent of the school population lived in blocks of flats);
- avoid examples, illustrations or analogies that may be gender, culturally or religiously biased (see Gilbert 1998, for a good discussion of explanations and models).

Making best use of practical work

Science is about language. But it is also about doing things, seeing things happen, measuring and controlling things. This is all part of practical work – something that pupils have come to expect in secondary science ('When are we getting the Bunsens out?') and that (unfortunately) many teachers now often take for granted.

On the positive side of the balance sheet, practical work can excite, motivate, illustrate and clarify. But on the other hand it can also confuse, turn off, complicate and demotivate. Teachers need to be clear about which practicals to do, when and why, i.e. what is the purpose of each piece of practical work? So many practicals in school science have been 'passed on' from one teacher or textbook to the next that they have become 'institutionalised' into school schemes of work. They are here (and done) because they're here because they're here ...

Returning to a positive note, practical activity in science can have several important purposes:

- to illustrate a scientific law, e.g. the connection between pressure and volume of a gas;
- to demonstrate a phenomenon, e.g. expansion; or a process, e.g. rusting, photosynthesis;
- to interest and motivate pupils;
- to aid memory of events and processes;
- to develop and teach specific scientific skills and techniques, e.g. using a Bunsen; reading from meters; adjusting a microscope; taking measurements;
- to show potential dangers and safety hazards;
- to stimulate discussion, e.g. with a Predict-Explain-Observe-React (PEOR) activity (see Chapter 4).

The art (or science) of good science teaching is to match the learning objective(s) of a lesson to an activity, whether it be practical work or not. For example, theories and theoretical ideas are not best learnt by doing practical work, especially if they involve abstract, invisible entities such as particles, atoms, electrons, fields or waves.

In short, practical work is valuable in showing what happens (phenomena, events) and sometimes how (processes) but rarely in explaining why things happen (theories). Science as a subject is as much theoretical as it is practical (see Millar 1998: 29 and other chapters in Wellington 1998), and therefore hands-on work alone is not enough. 'Minds-on' activities, ones which involve thinking, doing and reaching conclusions such as PEOR activities, are needed too.

A full chapter later in this book (Chapter 7) is devoted to practical work, its value and its drawbacks, with another chapter on investigations (Chapter 8).

Choosing and using resources

One key aspect of planning and managing learning is the skill of selecting the right resources for the right teaching and learning objectives. Picture a dream world where science teachers have a range of teaching resources at their disposal: DVDs, PowerPoint or other presentation software and a data projector, often with an interactive smart board to go with it; a class set of textbooks, differentiated worksheets, an overhead projector (OHP) and transparencies, a class set of equipment for each pupil practical, a helpful and supportive technician, ready access to computers and software in labs and a bookable computer suite, the internet, a library/resource centre stocked with science materials, funding for field-trips and visits to museums or interactive science centres ...

Now wake up. In a real school, most teachers will have access to some of the above wish-list. None will have access to all of them. Even Ofsted admit that reality is far from perfect and that class teachers are not always at fault. The Ofsted review of the 1990s reported that the level of resources in 'a significant number of schools' adversely affects subject teaching, commonly in the 'teaching of practical subjects' (Ofsted 1998: 12). More recently the Ofsted report, *Success in Science* states:

Unsatisfactory accommodation hinders teaching and learning in a number of ways. For example, classes not taught in specialist rooms have limited opportunities to conduct investigations or take part in practical activities. A mixture of specialist and non-specialist accommodation can lead to problems of timetabling and make it difficult for teachers to plan lessons which ensure continuity of learning.

(Ofsted 2008)

These things are often beyond the control of the science teacher, since it is due to 'major weaknesses in the management of resources' such as 'the library and IT [information technology] facilities'.

ICT, which both new and long-serving teachers are constantly being counselled to use in supporting learning and teaching, is a classic case. Many science teachers would love to use ICT given half the chance – they may well appreciate the power of spreadsheets and databases, the value of computer simulations, the benefits of data-logging, the potential of multimedia to animate and make the invisible visible, and the new horizons opened up by the internet. But they have to work in classrooms that are located in institutions called schools. Access to ICT resources – when and where they want them – and to technical support for ICT in science teaching is a major problem for most teachers. The same Ofsted review (1998) reported that in only one-third of schools has careful management ensured 'adequacy of IT resources' and even in many schools in this small minority the available IT is not put to 'good use' (p. 148) often for lack of technical support.

So, in the real world, the task of choosing resources to match learning objectives, i.e. horses for courses, is a messy and complex business. Given their availability we can say, however, that:

- video and multimedia can capture interest and demonstrate events, processes or experiments that cannot be shown in the school lab – from volcanoes erupting to babies being born, i.e. processes that are either too fast, too slow, too risky or too costly for the school lab are often best shown with video or multimedia;
- visits to factories, power stations, museums or science centres can be a memorable part of a pupil's curriculum and relate lab science to the world outside.

Finally, it is well established that ICT is of great value in teaching and learning science. Chapter 13 in this book is devoted to ICT use in science. Using other resources (such as newspaper cuttings and interactive centres) to support school science teaching is discussed in Chapter 15.

Presenting and portraying the 'nature' of science

The job of science teachers is a tough one. Not only do they have to teach scientific knowledge, develop the skills of science and foster scientific attitudes – they also have to convey messages about the nature of science and the work of scientists. These messages have to be conveyed either overtly and explicitly, i.e. by planned activities or prepared teaching; or covertly and implicitly, i.e. by the teachers' actions during practical work or by their reactions to pupils' work or practical data.

We all know that practical work in science does not always go according to plan. Nature, especially in science labs, sometimes does not behave itself. What should teachers do when their practicals go wrong? There is evidence that some teachers 'talk their way through it', some know crafty ways of rigging or tweaking experiments, while some just cheat (see Nott and Wellington 1997). What messages do teachers' actions convey about science and scientists?

Later, a chapter is devoted to this issue and to practical ideas for teaching, or conveying messages, about the nature of science, i.e. the how. But in this introduction we consider briefly: what are the key messages about science and scientific activity that we wish to convey?

This, in itself, is highly debatable. Hence the summary below is presented in (what we call) 'Yes ... but' format:

- Science is contextualised? Science and scientists operate in a spiritual, moral and political context. Yes ... but it does cross boundaries. Viagra works on both sides of the Atlantic (not that we've tried to verify or falsify this). Genetically modified food can be imported and exported.
- Science is provisional? Its ideas and theories change over time. Yes ... but Newton's laws are centuries old and they got us to the moon and back. Theories may be tentative, but many laws are *not* (e.g. Ohm's, Boyle's, Charles'), nor are facts, e.g. expansion of metals. Copper will still conduct electricity in 100 years' time.
- Science is not value-free? Agreed ... but some scientific facts, laws and theories are independent of people and society. Newton's Second Law works in Iran as well as it does in North America. The kinetic theory of particles can be applied globally.
- Science is limited? It cannot explain everything. Yes ... but surely it deserves at least 8/10?
- Science is a double-edged sword? Yes ... it does have its drawbacks. But would you like to live (except as an aristocrat) in pre-science days? Here it is worth pausing to think over Robert J. Oppenheimer's quote 'A scientist cannot hold back progress because of fears of what the world will do with his discoveries'.
- Science deals in relative, not absolute truth? Yes ... but an iron bar will expand when it is heated. This is absolutely true: any place, any time.
- Science is determined by reality? (see Ogborn 1995 on 'Recovering reality'). Yes ... reality (not just people and their construction of it) does determine science. But a lot of good scientific theories have come from creative thinking, hunches and leaps of the imagination. Many scientific explanations depend on entities and ideas that are not real or observable, e.g. point masses, fields, frictionless surfaces.
- Science is theory-laden? Mostly ... but some research at the 'frontiers of science' may not be, e.g. on BSE, GM foods.
- Science is an objective, rational activity? Yes ... but science is not a totally objective pursuit of the truth, and not totally guided by the natural world. It is a human activity, driven by personalities, egos and funding; often done in the context of large institutions, driven by social movements; even driven by the media and public opinion; often driven by politicians and other decision-makers. Science involves competition as well as cooperation.
- Science is tentative? Yes ... but some scientific knowledge is pretty reliable. We ride in planes, we drive over suspension bridges, we take antibiotics. People, quite rightly, have some faith in science.

Assessing and evaluating learning (and teaching)

What is assessment for?

Experienced teachers are constantly assessing pupils in classrooms – whether it be from oral questioning, from overhearing their conversations during small group work, from reading their written work or from closely observing their actions during practical sessions. Assessment or (more harshly) judgement of people occurs inevitably.

Teachers might decide to assess pupils, or be forced to assess them, for a wide variety of reasons. For example, teachers might assess their students in order to:

- enable teachers to set targets for individual pupils;
- boost the self-esteem of pupils (equally, it can dampen it);
- inform higher education or employers about attainment;
- give feedback to pupils and parents on progress;
- maintain standards;
- rank pupils;
- entertain, for example, with a quiz;
- sort pupils into different sets or groups;
- motivate pupils and give incentives for learning (a stick and a carrot);
- give feedback on their own teaching effectiveness;
- identify individual weaknesses and problems;
- assist pupils in subject/career choice;
- diagnose errors and misconceptions.

Some of these purposes involve *looking forward*; some involve *looking back*; and some, perhaps the most important, are intended to *guide action*. Some writers also see a difference between *assessment* and *evaluation* with evaluation being a process of ranking learners (Scriven 1999). Some of the above examples are *summative*, some *formative* and some *diagnostic*.

Types of assessment

Summative assessment of pupils, e.g. at the end of a unit, a module or a key stage (KS) in order to give them a 'mark', is the area we often focus upon. This form of assessment also receives the most publicity in terms of media coverage (the 'league tables'), political debate and discussion on 'standards'. Summative assessment is sometimes called *assessment of learning*. But summative assessment comes, in a sense, too late. For the classroom teacher the two forms of assessment most valuable in identifying needs, planning for learning, and organising differentiation are:

- *diagnostic* assessment: to identify pupils' preconceptions or learning difficulties so that future teaching can be guided and pitched appropriately or tailored to individuals' needs;
- *formative* assessment: to assess learning as it proceeds, recognising positive achievements, and making decisions about (forming) future steps and targets.

The main purposes of both are to improve teaching and learning. These later two forms can be placed in the *Assessment for Learning (AfL) category*. Day-to-day assessment can be used: to identify very able or gifted pupils' difficulties in spoken or written English; and to become aware of the wide range of special educational needs (SEN) that a large group of learners inevitably has.

Strictly speaking, summative assessment comes at the *end* of a course or a teaching scheme and has no influence on the teaching and learning process. By contrast, diagnostic and formative assessment of individual pupils is, quite simply, the only sound basis for good teaching. To paraphrase Ausubel (discussed later), you cannot teach pupils unless you know them and 'start from where they are'. *Self-assessment* can also be valuable to pupils in assessing where they are.

Class teachers will also inevitably be involved in summative assessment, e.g. an end-of-unit test or end-of-year exam. Marking and monitoring pupils' work regularly, providing pupils with helpful oral and written feedback, and setting sensible targets for future progress are all important skills for the science, or any other subject, teacher.

How can teachers become 'good assessors' and use assessment as a *positive*, motivating tool? Thorp (1991: 101) suggests five important principles for good assessment that still apply. He argues that good assessment should:

- influence and inform future teaching and learning;
- show what learners know, understand and can do;
- measure learners' progress;
- provide feedback for learners, teachers and parents, where appropriate;
- give learners a positive sense of achievement and therefore empower them.

In order to make this happen the teacher needs to operationalise the strategy in the classroom. Muijs and Reynolds (2010) suggest the key elements of assessment for learning are:

- use of effective questions;
- giving feedback on assessed work;
- sharing the learning goals (with the learners);
- use of peer and self assessment;
- use of assessment to plan the learning.

These principles can be put into practice through three different media: what the teacher *sees*, what the teacher *reads* and what the teacher *hears*. Thus, teachers can assess and evaluate their pupils' progression in three different ways:

1   By *observation*, i.e. by observing them during classwork whether it be written work, discussion work or practical work. A teacher's observations of their actions and procedures can be an important part of assessing practical skills or the ability to investigate.
2   From their *oral work*, i.e. by listening to what pupils say in either whole-class discussion (e.g. question and answer sessions); by listening to and observing small-group work; by arranging time for oral presentation of their work, e.g. on a project or a report-back on a homework.
3   From *written work*, i.e. from written tests or examinations; from written classwork or homework; from written reports on practical work and investigations.

In practice, assessment has depended far too heavily on the written word. Teachers have, often for justifiable practical reasons in a busy classroom, been unable to use observation and oral work to assess learners. Even when they have done this informally and internally, it has not been encouraged or accepted formally and externally. This is unfortunate because the almost total emphasis on the written word has disadvantaged many pupils – many may be good at speaking and doing science but poor at writing science. There is still a huge need for differentiated assessment.

By way of an example, one of the authors investigated the science knowledge of 15 'low ability' year 9 pupils using a standard written test and a previous version of the same test which was read to each pupil, individually, and their responses recorded, hence no need to read or write. The result showed an increase of 1.5 levels per pupil on an 8-point scale.

The important activities of differentiation, questioning, feedback, marking and setting homework are discussed in later chapters.

Ensuring continuity and progression in learning and teaching

One of the key aims in teaching, given more publicity (if not prominence) by the advent of a National Curriculum, is to develop continuity and progression in children's learning. The two terms have become buzz words for something that is good and desirable. But in reality they are hard to define and even harder to put into practice.

Although the words 'continuity' and 'progression' are usually spoken or written together, they do not denote the same thing. Continuity is to do with organising and planning a curriculum or a programme of study, whereas progression is more about an individual's development or increasing complexity in a pupil's scientific ideas. Driver *et al.* (1994) express this well:

> The term progression is applied to something that happens inside a learner's head: thinking about experience and ideas, children develop their ideas. Some aspects of their learning may happen quite quickly and easily, whereas others happen in very small steps over a number of years.

Continuity on the other hand is something organised by the teacher:

> it describes the relationship between experiences, activities and ideas which pupils meet over a period of time, in a curriculum which is structured to support learning. Curriculum continuity cannot guarantee progression. Its role is to structure ideas and experiences for learners in a way which will help them to move their conceptual understanding forward in scientific terms.

On the face of it, continuity might appear easier to develop since it is somehow more 'external', 'written down' and open to checking. But research (especially the extensive work by Ruth Jarman) has shown that, except in a few outstanding cases, it is not happening. As Jarman (1999) points out, there are difficulties about what continuity is, why it is needed and how it should be achieved. Teachers offer a range of interpretations and metaphors for the term continuity, for example: 'building upon'; 'the next rung of the ladder'; 'not repeating'; 'not leaving a gap'; 'maintaining momentum'; 'no gaps, no overlaps'; 'not duplicating'; 'picking up where "they" left off'; 'a gradual transition'; 'a common thread'. These terms are used by teachers in Jarman's research and in curriculum documents, both local and national.

However, in reality teachers have found it hard to put these ideas into practice, particularly at the interface between primary and secondary education (in the UK, Key Stages 2 to 3). Some teachers treat new pupils in the secondary school as a *tabula rasa* or blank slate, imagining (as some have put it) that they are 'building on a greenfield site'. This often occurs because primary pupils come from such a variety of backgrounds (with huge differences in teaching approach, level of treatment of topics, knowledge 'input') and a wide diversity of feeder schools. True liaison and continuity require a huge investment in time and energy by teachers in both phases – teachers in the secondary phase especially question whether the benefits outweigh the costs. Not surprisingly, many prefer to start from scratch. In addition, a minority of secondary science teachers simply do not trust what their primary predecessors have done.

Progression in children's scientific ideas needs to be built *into* curriculum documents, schemes of work and, for the individual teachers, lesson plans. Genuine progression will:

- *build on* the learner's previous ideas, whether they be from outside experience or formal education;
- *extend* the learner's understanding from a narrow range of contexts, e.g. the school lab, to a broad range, e.g. the home, other planets, industrial processes;
- *enable* learners to move from explaining simple events and phenomena, e.g. magnetic attraction or falling objects, to explaining more complicated events and processes, e.g. electromagnetic induction or planetary motion;
- *proceed from* explaining things in qualitative terms, e.g. heat lost through single and double glazing, to explanations using numbers and symbols, e.g. the equation for heat 'flow' across a boundary;
- *develop* from explanations using things that can be seen, e.g. water in a pipe, to explanations based on entities that are not observable, e.g. electrons in a wire or particles in a liquid.

Some readers may, at this point, be thinking this is nothing new and indeed it can be traced back to Bloom (1956), where Bloom's taxonomy gives progression from knowledge to evaluation. Table 1.1 shows this progression alongside indicative intended learning outcomes.

Table 1.2 sums up some of the main features of progression. These are the key elements of progression in knowledge *and* understanding. Asoko and Squires (1998) offer a useful example

Table 1.1 Bloom's taxonomy and intended outcomes

Bloom's statement	Indicative outcome
Knowledge	Ability to recall factual information; list facts, label a diagram.
Comprehension	Ability to describe; describe the function of a component, classify items.
Application	Ability to apply knowledge to new situations.
Analysis	Ability to break a problem into component parts; carry out calculations, make a contrast between listed items.
Synthesis	Suggest new information; make an hypothesis, design a practical investigation.
Evaluation	Ability to question data; make a statement on the error associated with results.

Table 1.2 Dimensions of progression in a person's knowledge and understanding

From	To
narrow ... experiences and understanding in a small number of examples in a narrow range of contexts.	... broad knowledge of many examples in a broad range of situations.
simple ... understanding simple events.	... complex knowing and explaining complicated situations
using *everyday* ideas ...	... using *scientific* ideas
knowledge *that* ...	... knowledge *how and why* things happen.
qualitative explanation ...	... explanations using *numbers, formulae* and *equations*.
explanations based only on *observable* entities ...	... explanations using *unobservable, idealised* entities, e.g. rigid bodies, point masses.

of progression in ideas that gives the principles some meaning and may help the reader to contextualise the discussion:

> puddles disappear
> ⇩
> puddles disappear faster when it is windy
> ⇩
> when puddles disappear the water evaporates into the air
> ⇩
> puddles disappear faster when it is windy because the air above them does not become saturated with water vapour
>
> (Asoko and Squires 1998: 176)

Knowledge of evaporation could also progress by:

1   *seeing or discussing* it in a wider range of contexts, e.g. petrol on a forecourt or another volatile liquid in the lab; the Dead Sea, the school pond;
2   *bringing in the unobservable* entities, i.e. liquid particles, to explain why it occurs and how (for example) wind affects it;
3   *bringing in quantitative* elements, e.g. the kinetic energy ($\frac{1}{2}$ mv^2) of particles; the reasons for cooling by evaporation.

The skill of the teacher is, first, to examine the scientific ideas being taught to consider the progression in them. How can ideas or processes such as photosynthesis, nuclear fission, digestion, chemical reactions or electromagnetic induction be sequenced in the same way as evaporation above? Second, this progression in ideas must be related to the learner, e.g. at what stage are learners 'ready' for a numeric, quantitative explanation? These ideas are explored more fully in Chapter 4.

Progression in investigations

Progression can also occur, and be built into, practical and investigational work. This will occur as:

- learners develop the ability to deal with, or control, more than one variable at a time;
- scientific ideas, rather than their own everyday ideas, are brought into their predictions and their evaluations;
- analysis of their data and evaluation of its strengths and limitations is based more and more on scientific ideas and knowledge;
- the range of instruments and techniques for data collection is extended, as is their ability to make informed choices on how and what to measure, and what instruments and methods to use;
- presentation of results or data becomes more refined and employs diagrams, tables or graphs using accepted scientific conventions;
- written work employs more and more scientific language and terminology.

The issue of progression in investigations is discussed more fully in Chapter 8.

The final message for this section is a challenging one. Centrally imposed curricula have not ensured either continuity or progression. This is still the teacher's job. It requires not only hard work, e.g. liaising with others, looking at previous work, studying others' schemes of work, but also intellectual effort. Sequencing scientific ideas and concepts into a progressive order is not easy – just try a few examples.

Planning and managing lessons and schemes of work

At the heart of good teaching lies good planning and good management. Any beginning teacher will have heard, many times, *failing to plan is planning to fail*. Individual lessons need to be well planned and structured, and to some extent be self-contained. But they must also relate to previous lessons, previous knowledge and previous understanding – and connect to future lessons and future learning. This is why individual lessons need to be planned and sequenced into a scheme of work. A scheme of work covering a period of several weeks has exactly the same requirements as an individual lesson plan. Both should have:

- clear *aims* and *objectives*;
- clearly identified *keywords* and key *scientific ideas*;
- *variety*, in terms of activities, resources and teaching or learning styles;
- *connections* with previous knowledge and links to future teaching and learning;
- *links* to other areas of science, other parts of the curriculum (where possible) and to everyday life.

As for an individual lesson, there is some measure of agreement about the main components needed for 'good practice'; to this end an effective lesson should have:

- a clear *introduction*, a 'starter' or engaging context, including these elements: gaining attention; stating the purpose of the lesson, i.e. why are you teaching this?; reviewing and relating back to previous learning and teaching;
- a *variety* of activities, e.g. perhaps some listening, some questioning, some group work, some writing, but not an entire lesson of the same thing;
- appropriate supervision, *intervention* and *guidance* during classwork, i.e. knowing when to leave groups alone, when to challenge them, when to move them on; providing appropriate remedial help where needed; keeping pupils on task;
- a 'plenary', a *summary* or 'recap', at the end of a lesson: for example, reviewing and consolidating what has been learnt, looking forward to the next lesson in the scheme, and setting follow-up work when appropriate.

Most teachers would agree that these are the main components of a 'good lesson'. They certainly do not apply to every situation or circumstance nor is it always practically possible to include them all – but they offer a useful framework or aide-memoire when lesson planning.

Parkinson (1994: 75–8 and 2002: 48–51) provides a valuable discussion and a checklist of the main components of a scheme of work (SoW) which is still useful. Our adapted version of what an SoW should contain is:

- a carefully sequenced and approximately timed set of lessons;
- learners' likely previous knowledge and the degree of difficulty of the new science concepts;

- a list of teaching activities, with their learning objectives, suggested teaching strategies and risk assessments for practical work;
- ideas for differentiation in each learning activity, including extension work;
- assessment opportunities (this should include formative and summative assessment);
- suggestions for homework, where appropriate;
- resources required, e.g. ICT, books, worksheets, posters, apparatus.

One of the bonuses, but at the same time one of the drawbacks, of being a science teacher is the sheer range of classroom and laboratory situations that one is able, but also expected, to manage successfully. Situations range from didactic teaching, investigational work, teacher demonstration and class practicals to small-group discussion, note-taking, fieldwork and the use of computers. No other subject teacher, with the exception of our colleagues in Design Technology, has to plan for and manage such a range of situations.

Chapter 5 is devoted to the business of planning and managing. One situation which science teachers increasingly have to deal with is the presentation and discussion of controversial or sensitive issues (see Chapter 14). Curriculum planners and textbook writers have, rather belatedly in our view, come to realise that science is as much about values as it is about facts. Indeed, in modern science, facts and values are often inseparable. Recent issues such as cloning, BSE, genetically modified (GM) food and the current debate on aspirin as a cancer preventative have made this obvious – not least to science learners, thanks to extensive media coverage. Other controversial issues – the nuclear debate, evolution versus creationism, and the origin of the universe – have been around for decades. Presenting controversial issues in a balanced way, which is a legal requirement, and handling subsequent discussion is a skill that science teachers must now add to their repertoire. A later section puts forward practical ideas.

Generating motivation and enthusiasm for science

Probably the most important, but sometimes the most neglected, aspect of science teaching is the ability to interest a wide range of pupils in science. This is the *affective* domain of educational aims, underlying the entire *cognitive* domain: without motivation, interest and engagement there will be little achievement. For the broad range of pupils, science has a poor track record in this, the affective domain. Up to the age of 16, all pupils have to study science in some form so there is no *obvious* problem. But post-16, the lack of interest in and enthusiasm for science subjects shines clearly through the statistics. Department for Education and Skills (DfES) figures show a steady decline in the numbers taking physical sciences at Advanced Level. More worryingly, in the 1990s boys were three times more likely to opt for physical sciences than girls. Girls have been more likely than boys to choose life sciences, though the gender gap in this direction is less marked.

However since 2000 it would seem that area entries for GCE A-level sciences are on an upward trend, see Table 1.3, but the gender issues in physics are as stark as ever.

The simple statement of the Ofsted review (1998) was low-key but damning: 'Post-16, the teaching of science subjects compares unfavourably with that of most other subjects' (p. 133). The report talks of 'spoon feeding' and an over-reliance on dictated notes and duplicated hand-outs. The introduction of GNVQ Science at Advanced Level (in 1993) did extend the range and style of study available in science post-16. But there is clearly a lot more work to be done in order to interest and enthuse learners of all abilities and both sexes in science education, both pre- and post-16.

Table 1.3 GCE A-level entry trends 2001–10 (in thousands)

	2001	2002	2003	2004	2005	2006	2007	2008	2009	2010
Biology										
Female	29.2	32.1	31.7	31.5	31.9	32.3	32.0	32.6	31.8	32.6
Male	17.9	19.9	19.9	20.7	22.0	22.6	22.5	23.5	23.7	25.2
Total	47.1	52.0	51.6	52.2	53.9	54.9	54.5	56.1	55.5	57.8
M:F ratio	0.6	0.6	0.6	0.7	0.7	0.7	0.7	0.7	0.7	0.8
Chemistry										
Female	17.2	18.7	18.6	18.9	19.2	19.7	20.1	20.3	20.6	21.1
Male	17.5	17.9	17.4	18.3	19.7	20.4	20.2	21.4	21.9	22.9
Total	34.7	36.6	36.0	37.2	38.9	40.1	40.3	41.7	42.5	44.0
M:F ratio	1.0	1.0	0.9	1.0	1.0	1.0	1.0	1.1	1.1	1.1
Physics										
Female	6.0	7.3	6.9	6.4	6.2	6.0	6.1	6.2	6.5	6.7
Male	21.8	24.2	23.6	22.3	21.9	21.4	21.4	22.0	22.9	24.3
Total	27.8	31.5	30.5	28.7	28.1	27.4	27.5	28.2	29.4	31.0
M:F ratio	3.6	3.3	3.4	3.5	3.5	3.6	3.5	3.5	3.5	3.6

What can be done, especially in the context of a fairly rigid national curriculum and the dominant view of the teacher as a 'deliverer' of knowledge? Teachers can adopt a number of strategies in planning and managing lessons:

- using a variety of teaching methods;
- increasing their awareness of both sexes and all abilities;
- using topical and controversial issues as a context for teaching content and processes;
- planning for a range of learning styles and interests;
- broadening science education and connecting it with other areas and everyday experiences, i.e. making it *relevant*.

In terms of their own classroom behaviour, teachers can convey enthusiasm and increase motivation in the following ways:

- The greatest possible use of praise and rewards: punishment may be unavoidable but it certainly demotivates, as does sarcasm or humiliation.
- 'Success breeds success': ensuring some success, however small, can be a huge motivator for pupils. Continuing failure, and excessive criticism, are not.
- Self-presentation: a teacher's own body language and posture can convey enthusiasm, e.g. gestures, facial expression, posture or stance – similarly with teaching voice.

It should, however, be noted that developing interest or motivation in secondary school learners, of any age, could be difficult for the teacher. Research – see Turner and Ireson (2010) and Turner, Ireson and Twidle (2010) – shows that learners' *attitudes* to science become fixed before leaving primary school.

In summary ...

The key areas of teaching and the principles outlined in this chapter are hard to live up to, especially every day of the week. But they can all contribute to a student's enjoyment of science. Remember that teachers do have an impact – a learner's enthusiasm for (or dislike of) a subject is retained long after their memory of its facts or content. The way that science teachers present their subject is far more important than what they teach. Praise, encouragement and reward will have long-term benefits: excessive criticism, ridicule and sarcasm will ultimately rebound.

> Children learn what they live
> If a child lives with criticism,
> he learns to condemn,
> If a child lives with hostility,
> he learns to fight,
> If a child lives with ridicule,
> he learns to be shy,
> If a child lives with shame,
> he learns to feel guilty,
> If a child lives with tolerance,
> he learns to be patient,
> If a child lives with encouragement,
> he learns confidence,
> If a child lives with praise,
> he learns to appreciate,
> If a child lives with fairness,
> he learns justice,
> If a child lives with security,
> he learns to have faith,
> If a child lives with approval,
> he learns to like himself,
> If a child lives with acceptance and friendship,
> he learns to find love in the world.

Dorothy Law Nolta (date unknown)

Surely *child* could be replaced with *learner* of any age at any stage of their learning journey.

References and further reading

This list is selective. Additional suggestions for further reading are given at the end of the later chapters, which cover in depth the ten aspects of teaching introduced here.

Language

Language barriers, and some practical ideas for tackling them, are discussed in:
Edwards, A. and Westgate, D. (1994) *Investigating Classroom Talk*, London: Falmer Press.
Henderson, J. and Wellington, J. (1998) 'Lowering the language barrier in learning and teaching science', *School Science Review*, March 1998, vol. 79, no. 288, pp. 35–46.
Wellington, J. and Osborne, J. (2001) *Language and Literacy in Science Education*, Buckingham: Open University Press.

Questioning

Chin, Christine (2004) 'Students' questions: fostering a culture of inquisitiveness in science classrooms', *School Science Review*, vol. 86, no. 314, pp. 107–12.

Muijs, Daniel and Reynolds, David (2010) *Effective Teaching*, London: Sage Publications.

Selley, Nick (2000) 'Wrong answers welcome', *School Science Review*, vol. 82, no. 299, pp. 41–6; looks at ways of building on pupils' wrong answers in science lessons.

A very useful short article, focusing on the work of one science department, is:

Carr, D. (1998) 'The art of asking questions in the teaching of science', *School Science Review*, June 1998, vol. 79, no. 289, pp. 47–50.

The other source of questions, the learners, is explored in:

Watts, M., Gould, G. and Alsop, S. (1997) 'Questions of understanding: categorising pupils' questions in science', *School Science Review*, vol. 79, no. 286, pp. 57–63.

Explaining

Phil Scott's work on 'meaning making' and communication in science teaching is of great value to teachers in this area. For example:

Scott, Phil and Jewitt, Carey (2003) 'Talk, action and visual communication in teaching and learning science', *School Science Review*, vol. 84, no. 308, pp. 117–24; looks at a range of ways (a multimodal approach) of teaching the idea of magnetic fields.

Mortimer, Eduardo and Scott, Phil (2003) *Meaning Making in Secondary Science Classrooms*, Maidenhead: Open University Press; discusses in detail, with a range of examples, the way in which teachers and pupils can interact to develop meaning and enhance learning in science lessons.

Other works on 'explaining' are:

DfEE (1999) *The National Numeracy Strategy*, London: TSO.

Gilbert, J. (1998) 'Explaining with models', in Ratcliffe, M. (ed.) *ASE Guide to Secondary Education*, Hatfield: ASE/Stanley Thornes, pp. 159–67.

Kinchin, Ian (2000) 'Using concept maps to reveal understanding: a two-tier analysis', *School Science Review*, vol. 81, no. 296, pp. 41–6; describes how pupils' ideas and alternative frameworks can be explored by analysing their concept maps, thus providing a diagnostic basis for future learning and teaching.

Ogborn, J., Kress, G., Martins, I. and McGillicuddy, K. (1996) *Explaining Science in the Classroom*, Buckingham: Open University Press.

Ross, Keith, Lakin, Liz and McKechnie, J. (2010) *Teaching Secondary Science: Constructing Meaning and Developing Understanding [3rd edn]* London: David Fulton.

Shulman, L. (1986) 'Those who understand: knowledge growth in teaching', *Educational Researcher*, vol. 15, no. 2, pp. 3–14.

Practical work

Ofsted (2008) *Success in Science,* London, Ofsted.

One useful book containing 16 different perspectives on practical work, and what it is for, is:

Wellington, J. (ed.) (1998) *Practical Work in School Science: which way now?*, London: Routledge.

A particularly useful chapter is:

Millar, R. (1998) 'Rhetoric and reality: what practical work is really for', in Wellington, J. (ed.) *Practical Work in School Science: which way now?*, London: Routledge, pp. 16–31.

The nature of science

Nott, M. and Wellington, J. (1997) 'Producing the evidence', *Research in Science Education*, vol. 27, no. 3, pp. 395–409.

Ogborn, J. (1995) 'Recovering reality', *Studies in Science Education*, vol. 25, pp. 3–38.

Osborne, J. (1998) 'Learning and teaching about the nature of science', in Ratcliffe, M. (ed.) *ASE Guide to Secondary Science Education*, Hatfield: ASE/Stanley Thornes, pp. 100–9.

Thorp, S. (ed.) (1991) *Race, Equality and Science Teaching*, Hatfield: ASE.

Assessment

Black, P., Harrison, C., Lee, C., Marshall, B. and Wiliam, D. (2003) *Assessment for Learning: putting it into practice*, Buckingham: Open University Press.

Muijs, Daniel and Reynolds, David (2010) *Effective Teaching*, London: Sage Publications.

Scriven, M (1999) 'The nature of evaluation' available at http://ericae.net/digests/tm9906.pdf [accessed 9 September 2011]

School Science Review (2003) December, vol. 85, no. 311: focuses on assessment in science education with a useful range of ten articles on different aspects of assessment.

Going further back:

Black, P. (1998) 'Formative assessment: raising standards inside the classroom', *School Science Review*, vol. 80, no. 291, pp. 39–46.

Black, P. and William, D. (1998) 'Assessment and classroom learning', *Assessment in Education*, vol. 5, no. 1, pp. 7–71.

Hayes, P. (1998) 'Assessment in the classroom', in Ratcliffe, M. (ed.) *ASE Guide to Secondary Science Education*, Hatfield: ASE/Stanley Thornes, pp. 138–45.

Continuity and progression

Ruth Jarman's work stands out in this area and has resulted in a number of publications, including:

Jarman, R. (1999) 'Editorial: Primary-secondary continuity in science', *Education in Science*, February, no. 181, p. 4.

Jarman, R. (2000) 'Between the idea and the reality falls the shadow: a review of provision for primary science – secondary science curricular continuity in the United Kingdom', in Sears, J. and Sorensen, P. (eds) *Issues in Science Education*, London: Routledge, pp. 133–42.

There is a long-standing debate on the issue of transition from Key Stage 2 to Key Stage 3 in science and the so-called 'blip' in this transfer. One useful article is:

Ryan, Michele (2002) 'Tackling Key Stage 2 to 3 transition problems – a bridging project', *School Science Review*, vol. 84, no. 306, pp. 69–76.

The same issue of *School Science Review* has several useful articles on the Key Stage 3 National Strategy, one of the aims of which was to improve this 'transition problem'.

Other works on continuity and progression include:

Adey, P. (1997) 'Dimensions of progression in a curriculum', *The Curriculum Journal*, vol. 8, no. 3, pp. 367–91.

Asoko, H. and Squires, A. (1998) 'Progression and continuity', in Ratcliffe, M. (ed.) *ASE Guide to Secondary Science Education*, Hatfield: ASE/Stanley Thornes.

Driver, R., Squires, A., Rushworth, P. and Wood-Robinson, V. (1994) *Making Sense of Secondary Science*, London: Routledge.

Not forgetting:

Bloom, B.S. (1956) *Taxonomy of Educational Objectives, Handbook 1: The Cognitive Domain*. New York, David McKay.

Planning and managing

Newton, L. and Rogers, L. (2001) *Teaching Science with ICT*, London: Continuum.

Joyce, B., Calhoun, E. and Hopkins, D. (2002) *Models of Learning: tools for teaching*, Buckingham: Open University Press.

Kyriacou, C. (1992) *Effective Teaching in Schools*, Hemel Hempstead: Simon & Schuster.

Parkinson, John (2002) *Reflective Teaching of Science 11–18*, London: Continuum.

Parkinson, John (1994) *The Effective Teaching of Secondary Science*, London: Longman.

Generating motivation

Driver, R., Leach, J., Millar, R. and Scott, P. (1996) *Young People's Images of Science*, Buckingham: Open University Press.

Claxton, G. (1990) *Teaching to Learn*, London: Cassell.

Joint Council for Qualifications Available at http://www.jcq.org.uk/national_results/alevels/ [accessed 21.12.2010].

Turner, S, Ireson, G and Twidle J. (2010) 'Enthusiasm, relevance and creativity: could these teacher qualities prevent us from alienating pupils from science?' *School Science Review* 91(337), pp. 51–7.

Turner, S. and Ireson, G. (2010) 'Fifteen pupils' positive approach to primary school science: when does it decline?' *Educational Studies* 36, pp. 119–41.

General reading

Amos, S. and Boohan, R. (2002) *Teaching Science in Secondary Schools: a reader*, Buckingham: Open University Press.

Bennett, J. (2003) *Teaching and Learning Science: a guide to recent research and its applications*, London: Continuum.

Gilbert, J. (ed.) (2004) *The Routledge Falmer Reader in Science Education*, London: RoutledgeFalmer.

Ireson, G. and Twidle, J. (2006) *Reflective Reader: secondary science*, Exeter: Learning Matters.

Kind, V. and Taber, K. (2005) *Science: teaching school subjects 11–19*, London: Routledge.

Monk, M. and Osborne, J. (2000) *Good Practice in Science Teaching: what research has to say*, Buckingham: Open University Press.

Ross, K., Lakin, L. and Callaghan, P. (2000) *Teaching Secondary Science: constructing meaning and developing understanding*, London: David Fulton.

Sears, J. and Sorensen, P. (eds) (2002) *Teaching science in secondary schools: a reader*, Buckingham: Open University Press.

Going further back:

Collins, J., Hammond, M. and Wellington, J. (1997) *Teaching and Learning with Multimedia*, London: Routledge.

Ratcliffe, M. (ed.) (1998) *ASE Guide to Secondary Education*, Hatfield: ASE/Stanley Thornes.

For an overview of science education in the 1990s in the UK see:

Ofsted (1998) Seco*ndary Education: a review of secondary schools in England*, London: The Stationery Office.

A useful source of general ideas on many aspects of teaching is:

Capel, S., Leask, M. and Turner, T. (eds) (1995) *Learning to Teach in the Secondary School*, London: Routledge.

One of the best books on learning and concept mapping, which is still valuable now, is:
Novak, J. and Gowin, D. (1984) *Learning How to Learn*, Cambridge: Cambridge University Press.

Other valuable, well-written sources on science teaching and learning are:
Bishop, K. and Denley, P. (1997) *Effective Learning in Science*, Stafford: Network Educational Press.
Hodson, D. (1998) *Teaching and Learning Science: towards a personalised approach*, Buckingham: Open University Press.
Levinson, R. (ed.) (1994) *Teaching Science*, London: Routledge/Open University Press.
Parkinson, J. (1994) *The Effective Teaching of Secondary Science*, Harlow: Longman.
Whitelegg, E., Thomas, J. and Tresman, S. (eds) (1993) *Challenges and Opportunities for Science Education*, London: Paul Chapman/Open University Press.

A series of books on science teaching and learning was published in the 1990s (series editor: Brian Woolnough). These are still useful – for example:
Reiss, M. (1995) *Science Education for a Pluralist Society*, Buckingham: Open University Press.
Woolnough, B. (1996) *The Effective Teaching of Science*, Buckingham: Open University Press.

Finally, a useful and very practical source of ideas for new teachers is:
Turner, T. and DiMarco, W. (1998) *Learning to Teach Science in the Secondary School*, London: Routledge.

Chapter 2

Becoming a teacher

The process of 'becoming a science teacher' is a complex and a personal one. In this chapter we consider that process and some of the models and metaphors that have been used to gain an understanding of what it means to be a teacher and how a teacher's development can be viewed.

Metaphors for the teacher

One of the difficulties in becoming a teacher, and continuing to develop as a teacher, is in deciding what counts as a 'good teacher'. What works for one person may not 'work' for another. What one person believes is good teaching may not accord with another's beliefs or principles. There is certainly a significant amount of research evidence on 'good teaching'. A crude summary of some of the common features of the 'effective teacher' could be listed as follows:

- thoughtful planning;
- clear, restricted goals in a lesson;
- lesson clarity;
- strong structuring of lessons;
- careful and effective time management;
- use of pupils' own ideas;
- high percentage of time-on-task for the pupils;
- appropriate, varied questions, directed at a range of pupils;
- variety of teaching methods;
- frequent feedback to pupils (on their spoken and written answers);
- high expectations of pupils.

These are helpful, if a little bit daunting and certainly hard to live up to. But a list such as this does not really explore what it means to be a teacher, and what a teacher's guiding values, beliefs and principles might be.

One way of reflecting upon this is to consider what metaphors we might use for teachers and for learners. This idea was first publicised widely by some of the excellent Children's Learning in Science (CLIS) materials in the early 1990s. Consider the following:

- the teacher as a postal worker (Postman Pat);
- the teacher as an air-traffic controller (or an airline pilot) or a navigator;
- the teacher as an actor;

- the teacher as a caterer, providing either self-service or waiter-service meals;
- the teacher as a barman or barmaid;
- the teacher as a bricklayer … or maybe an architect.

Figure 2.1 illustrates some of these models or metaphors.

Metaphors like these provoke all kinds of thought and discussion. The teacher can be seen as a potter, moulding clay; a guide in hilly terrain with the pupils as travellers; a petrol pump attendant filling a car; a gardener, tending plants and giving them nutrients, and in many other ways. It is interesting to note that different models relate to different industries: the construction industry, retail and catering, agriculture, the travel industry and others.

When people reflect on their own teaching they may subscribe to more than one of these metaphors. Indeed, moving from one model to another is part of what is meant by 'a variety of teaching approaches'. Perhaps the biggest danger in educational policy and practice has been to rely, perhaps unknowingly, on one dominant metaphor. The all-pervasive model of the 1990s was 'the teacher as deliverer' – the Postman Pat model of education. The language of teachers 'delivering' things has dominated the discourse of curriculum documents, staffroom chat, parents' evenings and formal staff meetings. The metaphor of teachers delivering 'items', commodities or packages to learners has permeated our thinking to such an extent that the word 'deliver' is almost impossible to avoid in discussions about teaching.

Surely a better way forward is to recognise that teaching and learning can be likened to many different situations, from different industries. A number of metaphors can be employed for different situations. Some models or metaphors work best for one set of circumstances, ages, abilities and aims – some work best for others.

Developing, and continuing to develop, as a science teacher

As already mentioned, science must be one of the most (if not the most) difficult subjects to teach in the secondary school. Not only do science teachers need to be able to manage and control all kinds of situations such as lab work, demonstrations, small group activities, didactic teaching, discussion work, 'circuses' of experiments; they also need to be aware of, and be able to handle, all kinds of health and safety issues in their daily teaching. Their job is at stake in safely organising rooms containing gas, electricity, glass and chemicals.

In addition, their subject is a conceptually difficult one. Just having and maintaining one's own subject knowledge is a prerequisite for good science teaching but is in itself a tough requirement. Many science teachers have a subject specialism, e.g. physics or biology, and just keeping this up to date and rust-free is a tall order. For those teaching post-16 courses in science it is not unusual to find that they are teaching topics which, ten or fifteen years ago, did not figure in their degree studies. In addition, up to the age of sixteen, most science teachers are also required to teach outside their own specialism. This makes additional demands on planning, preparation and thinking time.

Finally, science teachers are dealing with learners who may not only find science difficult and uninteresting but also bring into the classroom preconceived ideas about many 'science' topics: energy, force, heat flow and plant growth are just a few examples. Their preconceptions, sometimes misconceptions, need to be considered and occasionally challenged. There is sometimes a gap between 'common sense' and scientific ideas. Indeed, some scientific ideas, e.g. Newton's laws, centrifugal force being 'fictitious', plant mass coming mainly from carbon dioxide in the air, run contrary to common sense. Arguably, this is part of the very nature of science.

Actor

Deliverer

Bartender

Gardener

Guide/navigator

Figure 2.1 Cartoons showing different models or metaphors of teaching
Source: drawn for the authors by David Houchin

In short, science teachers face considerable challenges:

* getting to grips with their own subject, sometimes outside their own specialism;
* managing and controlling a range of situations, some involving difficult safety issues;
* enthusing and motivating their pupils;
* handling pupils' prior conceptions about the natural world and presenting them with new ideas and explanations that will appear contrary to common sense.

Perhaps science teachers should be paid more than other subject specialists? This suggestion is not new but equally it is not straightforward, it may cure one ill only to generate an even bigger one!

Models of 'becoming a teacher'

Two models of teacher development and the art of teaching have been widely used in the last two decades. Like any models, they are over-simplifications and are open to criticism, but they can be useful in conceptualising what it means to become a teacher. One is from Shulman, the other from Schön.

Subject knowledge and pedagogical knowledge

Teachers have a set of knowledge that they bring to the classroom and a set of knowledge that is developed and learned from their classroom experience. These two ways of knowing our subject have been called respectively, subject content knowledge and pedagogical content knowledge (Shulman 1986 and 1987).

The two sets of knowledge interact and inform each other. At the start of a teacher's career the pedagogical content knowledge is fairly thin, but studies have shown that new teachers undergo a rapid acquisition of this knowledge (Wilson, Shulman and Richert 1987). As teachers progress through their careers the pedagogical content knowledge increases in size and importance in relationship to the subject content knowledge, and the two inform each other.

Through teaching experience, and by working with mentors and learning alongside teaching colleagues, we develop new tactics and approaches. Teachers learn new explanations for difficult concepts, and new metaphors or analogies to help them explain. As they learn this 'pedagogical knowledge' their understanding of their own subject improves – hence the old adage: 'You don't know your subject until you teach it!' The diagrams in Figure 2.2 show crudely how these two types of knowledge might change over time.

Of course, the relative sizes of these elements, and their positions relative to each other, are open to some debate. However, one would hope that knowledge of science (SK) does grow as a result of teaching, i.e. it is both brought to the classroom and developed by classroom experience. Similarly, knowledge of teaching (PK) must surely develop through observing others, coaching and mentoring, reading books like this and reflecting on one's own practice.

Reflective practice

The second model sees the effective teacher as a reflective practitioner, capable of reflecting upon and analysing his or her own teaching practices, even though they cannot always be formulated, made explicit or put into words. Schön claims (1983: 54) that teachers possess a

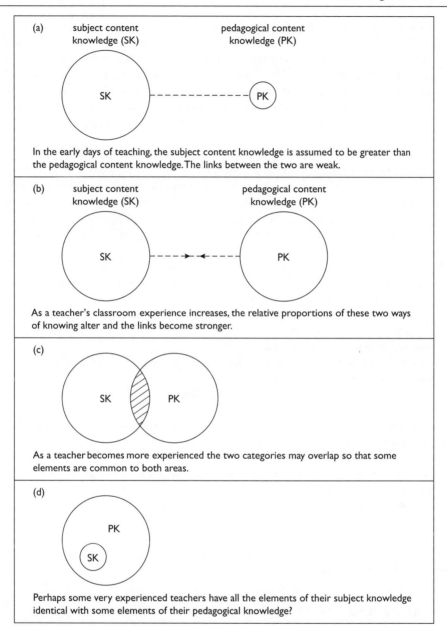

Figure 2.2 Development of subject knowledge and pedagogical knowledge in teaching
Source: Mick Nott and Jerry Wellington

type of knowledge called 'knowing-in-action', which is a form of practical knowledge (akin to Shulman's PK). This knowledge is personal and tacit in that 'we are usually unable to describe the knowing which our action reveals' (p. 54) – hence the notion that teaching is an art and a craft as well as a science.

Teachers develop by reflecting back on their own practice, especially when everyday teaching throws up 'surprises' (Schön 1987) that they have to respond to (we discuss these in Chapter 14, calling them 'critical incidents'). Teachers also reflect during the actual practice of teaching, which Schön calls 'reflection-in-action' (which relates to what we might call 'thinking on your feet'). This model has its critics. Some say that 'reflective practice' has just become a well-worn slogan, empty of meaning (Gilroy 1993: 140). It is not always clear what reflection in teaching involves, nor is there agreement about the word's meaning. Gilroy (1993: 126) cites Lucas's work in Sheffield where he reported that reflection can mean several things: 'ripping oneself to shreds', critical feedback and evaluation, a guiding principle for teaching, or a 'tough mode of active learning'.

Our own view is that the model of the teacher as a 'reflective practitioner' (and it is only a model) is a valuable one. Schön's work deserves to be read. It would be a strange thing if a good teacher did not reflect on his or her own practice. However, simply being a reflective practitioner is not a sufficient condition for being a 'good' teacher. A reflective practitioner could be an incompetent teacher. Similarly, plenty of historical figures from the past have been reflective practitioners and have not always been good people. Hitler was a reflective practitioner.

More recently Bolton (2010) writes of reflective practice as enabling practitioners 'to learn from experience about themselves' by challenging assumptions. Reflective practice, in Bolton's eyes, can enable you, the practitioner, to look into:

- what you know but do not know you know;
- what you do not know and want to know;
- what you think, feel, believe, value, understand about your role and boundaries;
- how your actions match up with what you believe;
- how to value and take into account personal feelings.

The argument is then presented that using the above will allow you to explore difficult situations, for example:

- what you can change in your context; how to work with what you cannot;
- how to value the perspective of others, however different they are from you;
- how you can counteract seemingly given social, cultural and political structures. (Bolton 2010 p. 4)

It is worth taking a moment to reflect on this. Are these ideas a formalisation of well-planned, engaging and inclusive science lessons?

Mentoring and the role of a mentor

What Shulman's and Schön's models partly neglect is that 'becoming a teacher' should not be, and rarely is, a lone process. Teachers may often be alone in the classroom but they are always part of a departmental team and a school staff. Teachers (new and old) can learn from the teaching of others as much as they can from reflecting on their own teaching.

New teachers will often have a mentor whose job it is to support, help and guide them, much as a craftsman did with an apprentice in the old apprenticeship model. The mentor is often said to be a critical friend, offering help and guidance, but also setting up challenges to allow the novice to develop and extend their teaching ability. Successful mentors will begin by acting as a role model and then as a coach, i.e. by agreeing to be observed, by giving direct assistance in planning, and classroom support during teaching. But then mentors will move on to giving feedback on teaching, suggesting new teaching strategies to try out, and encouraging new teachers to analyse and reflect upon their own teaching. Good mentors will recognise these stages in a new teacher's development and take account of them. For instance, to launch into extensive criticism and analysis of lessons in the early days would be poor mentoring. On the other hand, in the later stages, the new or student teacher should start to become more independent and autonomous, and grow into the role of reflective practitioner.

Mentoring is clearly an important and complex process in the professional development of teachers and deserves a lot more space than this book has room for. For further reading, Brooks and Sikes (1997) makes an excellent start. They argue that 'a mentor's personal characteristics and interpersonal skills are … important', that it is a skilled role and requires something more than the offering of general friendship. Among the personal qualities cited are, 'honesty, openness, sensitivity, enthusiasm, sense of humour, organisation, self-awareness and reflectiveness'; and the interpersonal skills of 'the ability to listen effectively, to give criticism constructively and to empathise'.

Brooks and Sikes (1997: 35) conclude that:

- mentoring is a collection of strategies used flexibility and sensitively in response to changing needs;
- mentoring is an individualised form of training, often conducted on a one-to-one basis, which needs to be tailored to the needs of the individual;
- mentoring is a dynamic process, aimed at propelling students forward, which needs to combine support with challenge.

In short, mentoring is an extremely difficult and greatly underestimated job.

Our own observations and experiences in schools over the last 28 years indicate that the practice of mentoring varies enormously in both quantity and quality. Some are 'born mentors', some develop into good mentors through reflective practice, while those who have mentoring thrust upon them are often the worst at practising it.

Why should anyone learn science … and therefore why teach it?

It is important for teachers to be able to articulate an answer to the question 'Why teach science?', especially when pupils pose it. This can always be a slightly embarrassing question for any subject specialist teacher in a secondary school: 'Why teach French if most pupils go to Spain for their holidays … or even Florida?'; 'Why teach history … it's all in the past?'; 'Why teach about "old" literature or Shakespeare's plays?'

We start this section with an activity devised by Robin Millar (Table 2.1). It lists twelve specific areas or topics which are taught in most science curricula around the world. On what grounds can we justify their inclusion in the secondary science curriculum? Before reading on, try the activity.

If we applied a crude criterion of relevance to the curriculum we could be left with nothing except reading and writing and perhaps some number work, though even this can be replaced by a cheap calculator. Even ICT skills boil down to reading, writing and the manipulative skill of using a 'mouse'. So if we wield 'relevance' like a huge axe to hack away any element of the curriculum which is neither practically useful nor of vocational significance, i.e. gets people jobs, there is little left standing in the secondary timetable.

Take science. What specific knowledge or skill from secondary science is of practical value to us? How many examples can you list? Wiring a plug is an obvious example (though this is hardly a science skill). It is far easier to list counterexamples. When did you last use Faraday's laws of electrolysis, the particle theory of matter, or the ability to carry out a titration? In short, justifications for teaching science based on crude, utilitarian grounds, i.e. its subsequent usefulness, are limited. This is especially true when we remember that only a small minority of our pupils will go on to use science in their working lives (they are more likely to use technology) and an even tinier minority will become working scientists.

For most learners, then, teachers will need to be able to justify why they are teaching them science on other grounds. Our own attempt to articulate some justifications is given below. Whether they will cut any ice with cynical, disaffected pupils in science is debatable. We will divide them up crudely into three areas: the intrinsic worth of learning science; its extrinsic or utility value; and the citizenship argument.

Table 2.1 What should be in the science curriculum, and why?

Consider each of the 'pieces' of scientific knowledge and understanding in the list below. For each, decide which of the following categories you think it should be

U   Everyone ought to understand this at an appropriate level – for utilitarian reasons (i.e. it is practically useful).

D   Everyone ought to understand this at an appropriate level – for democratic reasons (i.e. it is necessary knowledge for participation in decision-making).

C   Everyone ought to understand this at an appropriate level – for cultural reasons (i.e. it is a necessary component of an appreciation of science as a human enterprise).

X   It is not necessary that everyone know this. It need not be included in a science curriculum, the aim of which is public understanding of science.

'Pieces' of scientific knowledge

Science topic	Your classification
1 The germ theory of disease	
2 The heliocentric model of the solar system	
3 The carbon cycle	
4 The reactivity series for metals	
5 The electromagnetic spectrum	
6 Radioactivity and ionising radiation	
7 Newton's laws of motion	
8 Energy: its conservation and dissipation	
9 An understanding of simple series and parallel electric circuits	
10 The theory of plate tectonics	
11 Darwin's theory of evolution	
12 Acids and bases	

Source: Millar (1993)

The intrinsic value of science education

First, learning science can help us to make sense of the universe we live in – and of ourselves. It can help people to understand some of the events and phenomena which we see happening – either on television, the internet, or in everyday life. We see fossils, avalanches, droughts, thunderstorms, volcanoes erupting, oil films on puddles, tidal waves, leaves falling in autumn, skin cancer, condensation, frost and dew, blue sky (occasionally), fog, frogs and tadpoles, obesity, famine, orbiting comets, 'shooting stars' and the occasional eclipse.

We could write two more pages of examples, and any reader could add to the list. Science can help people to make sense of all these events. It may not have definitive answers on all their causes, e.g. the alleged causal connection between global warming and drought, famine or flood. But surely it is better to know that the two very bright objects which 'came together' in the evening sky in February 1999 were Venus and Jupiter rather than two UFOs making a rendezvous; or that the eclipse on 11 August 1999 was not a message from God? We can understand a lot more about the world if we add scientific sense to common sense. The latter is limited.

Second, science can actually be interesting and exciting. Not everything has to be 'relevant'. Teachers and curriculum developers have suffered under the cloud of relevance for over 25 years (we personally blame James Callaghan's famous education speech, when he was Labour Prime Minister in 1976, for launching the relevance bandwagon). Many events in science, e.g. caesium reacting with water, and many explanations, e.g. why a needle floats on the surface of water, can be interesting and intellectually stimulating in their own right. Many young (and old) people have hobbies or pastimes that are totally 'irrelevant' – except to them. Please can we have a break from the relevance criterion?

Finally, in this first category, we have the culture and heritage argument. This is an important one, even if it cuts little ice with 15-year-olds. Science is part of our past culture, and a big chunk of our contemporary culture. It is also a global activity, even if it may differ from one culture or nation to another. Our heritage, our history and many of the important stories of the past are based on science and scientists. Part of science education is about science stories or stories about scientists. Knowing these stories, and understanding science, is part of what it means to be a cultured and educated person.

The citizenship argument

The need for scientific knowledge: for individuals and key decision-makers

Participants in a democracy, it is argued, cannot make decisions and important choices without scientific knowledge and understanding. This argument becomes of clear importance when we consider past and current issues such as nuclear energy and nuclear weapons, traffic pollution, the use of drugs, animal testing, and not least many of the debates about the food we consume. (Should we eat genetically modified (GM) foods, beef from the bone, or any meat at all?)

Our individual decisions on these issues, as informed democrats, can be better reached by our knowledge of the science behind them. However, there are two limitations to this. First, the amount of science we need to know on each issue may not need to be that great. For example, with GM foods we need to know what they are, how they are created, their dangers (or advantages) and how far their pollen might spread – but detailed knowledge of DNA or genetic theory is probably not necessary. Nor is in-depth, mathematical knowledge of nuclear fission or fusion needed for all citizens in the nuclear debate, although knowledge of nuclear waste, radiation, and half-life might be useful.

Second, ultimately scientific knowledge will not make the decision for us. Knowledge of science is a necessary but insufficient basis for a decision. In the final analysis, decisions are made on the basis of values as well as knowledge and understanding of science, by a process of reflection.

A scientifically literate society would not necessarily be a 'good society'. However, some knowledge of science is essential in order for individuals to make decisions and become citizens in a democracy. Knowledge of science is even more important for those who are the key decision-makers in a democracy. This is plainly true but in practice few key politicians or other decision-makers in the past have been scientifically literate.

The need for knowledge about scientists, their work, 'scientific evidence' and the nature of science

As well as knowing some science, citizens in a democracy need to understand something about science itself and how scientists work. They need to understand that scientific evidence is not always conclusive. Evidence is messy as often as it is clear cut. This was shown throughout the 1990s with issues such as global warming, BSE, GM foods, cloning and debates over sources of energy. The days of certainty, proof and simple causality, chains of cause and effect, have long gone. We live in an age where risk, probability and correlation are more important ideas than proof, certainty and causality. A simple example is that of television advertisements; look carefully the next time you see one that says something like 91 per cent agree – the small print often says something like 'based on a sample of 103 women'.

Learners, indeed all citizens, need to know that:

- science has limits, it cannot predict and explain everything – there are other ways of understanding the world;
- science is done by people, or by groups and networks of people – it is a human activity and therefore not 100 per cent infallible;
- scientific evidence is not always conclusive – decisions are not made on scientific grounds alone. Most decisions have to be made by weighing up benefits, risks and probabilities;
- science does change over time, albeit often very slowly, and across cultures or nations;
- above all, science proceeds in a social, moral, spiritual and cultural context.

Utilitarian arguments

Actually, elements of science education can be useful, even if not to everybody. Some arguments relate to individuals, some to the economy.

a) Many students will not go on to follow careers in science, but some will. This minority should not determine the shape or content of the entire science curriculum for the majority (as may well have happened in the past). But, like any minority, they should not be forgotten – either for their own sake or for the good of the economy.

Similarly, we must not forget that a significant number of people do use science in their own work, even if very occasionally, inadvertently or unknowingly. Certainly, some civil servants and politicians, who almost seem to take pride in being scientifically illiterate, should use it.

Table 2.2 What is science education for? A summary of justifications

I	Intrinsic value
1.1	Making sense of natural phenomena and demystifying them.
1.2	Understanding our own bodies, our own selves.
1.3	Its intrinsic interest, excitement and intellectual stimulation.
1.4	Being part of our culture, our heritage.
2	Citizenship arguments
2.1	Science knowledge and knowledge of scientists' work are needed for all citizens to make informed decisions in a democracy.
2.2	Key decision-makers (e.g. civil servants, politicians) need knowledge of science, scientists' work and the limitations of scientific evidence, to make key decisions, e.g. on foods, energy resources.
3	Utilitarian arguments
3.1	Developing generic skills which are of value to all, e.g. measuring, estimating, evaluating.
3.2	Preparing some for careers and jobs that involve some science.
3.3	Preparing a smaller number for careers using science or as 'scientists'.

b) The generic skills argument: science may well develop certain general, transferable skills in people that can be of direct value in life or in the workplace. Skills such as 'problem-solving' are often quoted, though exactly what this is and whether it is really transferable is debatable. However, certain lesser skills do develop in science education and are of direct utility: measuring accurately, recording results, tabulating and analysing data, estimating, forming hypotheses, predicting, evaluating what went wrong, handling apparatus, 'troubleshooting', using a range of measuring instruments, and so on. All of these are enhanced by science education, some are central to it. All are of utilitarian value, either in everyday life or in the workplace.

c) Attitudes: science education can also help to develop attitudes or 'dispositions' which can be of direct value to life and to work: an enquiring mind, curiosity and wonder, a sense of healthy scepticism, a critical and analytical approach.

In summary, there are plenty of good reasons for teaching science, some of which can, and we argue certainly should, be conveyed to learners. Some of the arguments, e.g. the culture or heritage approach, will have little impact on young learners. But others may well convince them, if put forward both explicitly and implicitly. Table 2.2 gives a summary of the main justifications that can be used by science teachers.

However it is also worth noting that research tends to indicate that learners' attitudes to science itself are fixed at a relatively young age (Turner and Ireson 2010). It would appear that any intervention needs to be applied before pupils reach the age of ten, for after that attitudes appear to be fixed.

Principles into practice

These principles may appear somewhat academic and divorced from the classroom. But in fact, as well as determining why we teach science, they can be used to guide what we teach, and how we teach it. They have a direct bearing on classroom practice. For example, if we pursue the citizenship argument then classroom activities should involve:

- examining newspaper and other media presentation of science in a critical way;
- the presentation and discussion of controversial issues, i.e. those on which there are considerable debate and no clear-cut answers;
- some teaching and learning on the nature of science itself, the work of scientists, and the status of scientific evidence.

To neglect any of the above three strategies is to ignore the citizenship argument. Similarly, the culture or heritage argument demands that at least some science education should present the 'stories' of science, to show how science has changed and developed over time and how people have been involved. Stories might include the history of nuclear energy; beliefs about evolution or the origin of the universe; changing views about the human body; immunisation or vaccination; the short, so far, story of BSE, is it really over (Coghlan 2011)?

Third, if we are teaching science for its intrinsic value and interest, then we – and future curriculum developers – should include the 'big issues' of science rather than spending so much time on the specific detail and the nitty gritty, certainly pre-16. When selecting topics we can only include so much: why not select, unashamedly, topics and issues that are exciting, interesting and motivating? Given the current governmental focus in England of 'more facts' this may become a more political factor which takes us back to some of the earlier discussion on reflective practice.

In the same way, the classroom teacher can deliberately select methods and activities that will capture interest and induce curiosity. A simple aid such as video can succeed here and will also show phenomena, events and entities that cannot be seen in the school lab. Multimedia, invaluable, for instance, in 'making the invisible visible', and other forms of ICT can also help but not replace the more traditional.

Finally, the utilitarian arguments for science education demand that some practical work be done, in addition to some theory. Practical work can develop certain generic skills of value to all, which may transfer to other contexts. Similarly, work in science should be planned with the development of certain attitudes and dispositions in mind.

In summary, then, the various justifications for teaching science can, and should, have practical implications for what is taught and how. An individual teacher's own lessons are guided by beliefs and principles, whether they are aware of them or not.

Science teachers and the nature of science

To end this chapter we need to consider the teacher's own view of the nature of science. Our personal view of science and what science is has as great an impact on our teaching as our view of why science is important:

> As teachers we do not just act as the gateway to knowledge. We ourselves represent, embody, our curriculum. And, in our teaching, we convey not just our explicit knowledge, but also our position towards it, the personal ramifications and implications which it has for us.
>
> (Salmon 1988: 42)

There are many factors that affect the way that science teachers teach. Some are pressures, some constraints, while some will assist and enhance their teaching. Figure 2.3 gives a crude summary of some of the main factors involved.

It is generally accepted that the teacher's own view of the nature of science is one of the important factors, although there is some debate as to the level of its importance (Lederman 1992). In this book we consider various notions of science: scientists' science, children's science,

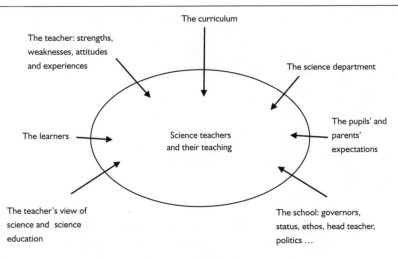

The curriculum

The teacher: strengths,
weaknesses, attitudes
and experiences

The science department

The learners

Science teachers
and their teaching

The pupils' and
parents'
expectations

The teacher's view of
science and science
education

The school: governors,
status, ethos, head teacher,
politics …

Figure 2.3 Factors affecting science teachers and their teaching

curriculum science, and of course teachers' science. These are just four of the different locations where different bodies of scientific knowledge reside (Gilbert *et al.* 1985). Imagine them as different repositories of science, all of which have importance for science education. Everybody forms their own personal construct of what science is. The activity of science teaching involves the interaction of these personal constructs. As Salmon (1988) puts it: 'Education is the systematic interface between personal construct systems.' This is an interesting definition and an important one for this book. It shows that successful teaching must achieve some shared meaning between the various parties involved, some sort of common ground between teachers' science, children's science and accepted scientific knowledge and process (see Figure 2.4 and Novak 1981).

The work of David Ausubel (1968), whilst appearing dated, offers: 'The most important single factor influencing learning is what the learner already knows. Ascertain this and teach him accordingly.' This chapter, however, is premised on the belief that what the teacher already knows is a factor affecting teaching. As Shuell puts it:

> The conceptions and assumptions we hold about the nature of knowledge, the way knowledge is represented and the manner in which new knowledge is acquired determines what we study in science education, what we teach in science classrooms and the way in which the teaching of science is carried out.
>
> (Shuell 1987)

The teacher's own image or view of what science is does have implications for the way that they present and teach science in the classroom, both on content and process.

In summary …

This chapter has attempted to encourage readers to reflect on their own view of teaching and of science within those terms.

It is often said that scientific knowledge is provisional, i.e. its ideas, laws and theories are subject to change. This is even more true of views on the nature of science. There is no general

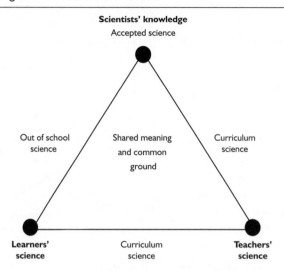

Figure 2.4 Common ground and shared meanings in science education

consensus on what science is, nor is there a commonly agreed view of what constitutes 'scientific method'. Many people argue that the way science is viewed and conceptualised varies from one discipline to another, for example, from life science to physical science (Lederman 1992). There is certainly a wide variation in views among the well-known philosophers of science from the past, ranging from Popper (1959) and Kuhn (1963) to Feyerabend (1975), with the latter arguing against the idea of there being any such thing as scientific method (see further reading). Other commentators on the nature of science such as Collins (1985) and Woolgar (1988) have focused on the way that scientists actually work. The single common message is that scientists do not have a rigid or fixed view of what science is, or of what constitutes scientific method.

In short, the message for teachers and curriculum planners is that there is no definitive view of what science and scientific method are, any more than science itself is fixed and absolute. It therefore makes no sense to accuse teachers of having an inadequate conception of science, nor to berate them for it (as has happened in the past; Lederman 1992). What can be expected of teachers, however, is that they do recognise in their teaching that science as a body of knowledge is provisional and that there is no single accepted view of scientific method. They should also emphasise that science and technology are not neutral or value-free activities. They are pursued within the context of a culture or society with its own economic and political pressures and constraints (Thorp 1991: 135).

Later in this book, we offer practical suggestions and guidelines for dealing with the nature of science in the classroom.

References and further reading

General

School Science Review (2004) June, vol. 85, no. 313; the whole issue was devoted to the 'roles of the science teacher' with articles focusing on subject knowledge, the newly qualified teacher and teachers as researchers.

Dillon, J. and Maguire, M. (2001) *Becoming a Teacher*, Buckingham: Open University Press.

Parkinson, J (2002) *Reflective Teaching of Science 11–18*, London: Continuum.

Ross, K., Lakin, L. and McKechnie, J. (2004) *Teaching Secondary Science,* London: David Fulton.

Turner, S. and Ireson, G. (2010) 'Fifteen pupils' positive approach to primary school science: When does it decline?' *Educational Studies* vol. 36, no. 2: 119–41.

Professional development and mentoring

Bell, B. and Gilbert, J. (1996) *Teacher Development: a model from science education*, London: Falmer Press.

Bishop, K. and Denley, P. (1997) 'The fundamental importance of subject matter knowledge in the teaching of science', *School Science Review*, vol. 79, no. 286, pp. 65–71.

Bolton, G. (2010) *Reflective Practice: Writing and Professional Development*, London: Sage.

Brooks, V. and Sikes, P. (1997) *The Good Mentor Guide*, Buckingham: Open University Press.

Gilroy, D.P. (1993) 'Reflections on Schön: an epistemological critique and a practical alternative', in Gilroy, D.P. and Smith, M. (eds) *International Analyses of Teacher Education*, Oxford: Carfax Press, pp. 125–42.

Schön, D.A. (1983) *How Professionals Think in Action*, London: Temple Smith.

Schön, D.A. (1987) *Educating the Reflective Practitioner: toward a new design for teaching and learning in the professions*, San Francisco, CA: Jossey-Bass.

Schön, D.A. (1988) 'Coaching reflective teaching', in Grimmett, P.P. and Erickson, G.L. (eds) *Reflection in Teacher Education*, New York: Teachers College Press.

Shulman, L. (1986) 'Those who understand: knowledge growth in teaching', *Educational Researcher*, vol. 15, no. 2, pp. 3–14.

Shulman, L. (1987) 'Knowledge and teaching: foundations of the new reforms', *Harvard Education Review*, vol. 57, no. 1, pp. 1–22.

Wilson, S., Shulman, L. and Richert, A. (1987) '150 different ways of knowing: Representations of knowledge in teaching', in Calderhead, J. (ed.) *Exploring Teachers' Thinking*, London: Cassell.

Other useful books on mentoring include:

Allsop, T. and Benson, A. (eds) (1997) *Mentoring for Science Teaching*, Buckingham: Open University Press.

Arthur, J., Davison, J. and Moss, J. (1997) *Subject Mentoring in the Secondary School*, London: Routledge.

Furlong, J. and Maynard, T. (1995) *Mentoring Student Teachers*, London: Routledge.

Tomlinson, P. (1995) *Understanding Mentoring: reflective strategies for school-based teacher preparation*, Buckingham: Open University Press.

What is science education for?

Millar, R. (1993) 'Science education and public understanding of science', in Hull, R. (ed.) *ASE Secondary Science Teachers' Handbook*, Hemel Hempstead: Simon & Schuster/ASE.

Millar, R. (1996) 'Towards a science curriculum for public understanding', *School Science Review*, vol. 77, no. 280, pp. 7–18.

Millar, R. and Osborne, J. (1998) *Beyond 2000: Science education for the future*, London: King's College: an excellent report resulting from a series of seminars funded by the Nuffield Foundation, available from King's College, London SE1 8WA.

Ratcliffe, M. (1998) 'The purposes of science education', in Ratcliffe, M. (ed.) *ASE Guide to Secondary Science Education*, Hatfield: ASE/Stanley Thornes, pp. 3–12.

Wellington, J.J. (2000) 'What is science education for?', *Canadian Journal of Science, Mathematics and Technology Education*, vol. 1. no. 1, pp. 23–39.

Teachers and the nature of science

Ausubel, D. (1968) *Educational Psychology: a cognitive view*, New York: Holt, Rinehart & Winston.

Bynum, W.F., Browne, E.J. and Porter, R. (1983) *Macmillan Dictionary of the History of Science*, London: Macmillan.

Coghlan, A. (2011) 'Mad cow disease is almost extinct globally', *The New Scientist*, vol 29, no 2797, pp. 6–7.

Collins, H. (1985) *Changing Order: replication and induction in scientific practice*, London: Sage.

Feyerabend, P.K. (1975) *Against Method*, London: New Left Books.

Gilbert, L., Watts, D. and Osborne, R. (1985) 'Eliciting students' views using an interview-about-instances technique', in West, L. and Pines, A. (eds) *Cognitive Structure and Conceptual Change*, New York: Academic Press, pp. 11–27.

Ireson, G. and Twidle, J. (2006) *Reflective Reader: secondary science, Exeter: Learning Matters*, Chapter 8.

Koulaidis, V. and Ogborn, J. (1989) 'Philosophy of science: an empirical study of teachers' views', *International Journal of Science Education*, vol. 11, no. 2, pp. 173–84; shows that teachers vary in their views of science but that few are naive inductivists.

Kuhn, T.S. (1963) *The Structure of Scientific Revolutions*, Chicago, IL: Chicago University Press.

Lakin, S. and Wellington, J.J. (1994) 'Who will teach the nature of science?', *International Journal of Science Education*: a study of teachers' views of science and the difficulties they face in teaching the nature of science.

Lederman, N. (1992) 'Students' and teachers' conceptions of the nature of science: a review of the research', *Journal of Research in Science Teaching*, vol. 29, no. 4, pp. 351–9.

Millar, R. (ed.) (1989) *Doing Science: images of science in science education*, Lewes: Falmer Press; a collection of articles on, broadly speaking, the relationship of science education to images and studies of the nature of science.

Novak, J.D. (1981) 'Effective science instruction: The achievement of shared meaning', *Australian Science Teachers Journal*, vol. 27, no. 1, pp. 5–13.

Popper, K.R. (1959) *The Logic of Scientific Discovery*, London: Hutchinson.

Salmon, P. (1988) *Psychology for Teachers: an alternative approach*, London: Hutchinson.

Shuell, T. (1987) 'Cognitive psychology and conceptual change: Implications for teaching science', *Science Education*, vol. 7, no. 2, pp. 239–50.

Thorp, S. (ed.) (1991) *Race, Equality and Science Teaching*, Hatfield: Association for Science Education (ASE).

Wellington, J.J. (ed.) (1989) *Skills and Processes in Science Education: a critical analysis*, London: Routledge.

Woolgar, S. (1988) *Science: the very idea*, London: Tavistock.

Ziman, J. (1980) *Teaching and Learning about Science and Society*, Cambridge: Cambridge University Press.

Chapter 3

The science curriculum and science in the curriculum

The school science curriculum has evolved over a period of more than a century. In that time, there have been major shifts: at the start of the twentieth century it was a subject for a privileged few, mostly male; in the twenty-first century, in many countries, science is seen as a subject for all pupils, all 'abilities' and both sexes. The saying *Science for All*, which was once a slogan, is now taken for granted in many school curricula worldwide. This chapter considers how the science curriculum has changed and yet, at the same time, how many of the key issues still remain the same. We also consider, using the example of energy, how certain key ideas can and should be considered across the science curriculum.

The science curriculum

The science curriculum in schools is a subject of debate across all countries and as such it is impossible, within a single chapter, to address this issue globally. Before 1988 school science in England could be seen as a number of incoherent interventions that often give the impression of being unplanned. It was not until the Education Reform Act of 1988 that school science became defined via the National Curriculum. The National Curriculum for science cannot, however, be taken in isolation and while it may appear that secondary schools operate several national curricula the science aspect is still part of a National Curriculum. Indeed the National Curriculum can be seen as a political intervention: 'It was part of a much wider attempt to address the question of accountability and control in the school curriculum' (Donnelly and Jenkins 2001: 97).

Recurring debates on the curriculum

Two excellent books, by Jenkins (1979) and Waring (1979) have traced the history of science education from the later nineteenth century to the 1970s and Donnelly and Jenkins (2001) extend this analysis into the 1980s and beyond. We cannot consider those histories in depth here. However, they do show that certain debates have cropped up over and over again.

Who, and what, is science education for?

Should science education be aimed at a minority? Should a science curriculum for all be shaped and designed with this minority in mind? Is the aim of science education to train future scientists and to teach them science … or is the aim to develop 'scientific literacy' and the public understanding of science for all citizens? Should the science curriculum aim to teach pupils about science and how it works? Should there be 'girl-friendly' science? Should both sexes receive the same diet? These questions have been, and will be, perennial.

Breadth v. balance

Similarly, how broad should science education be? Should it concentrate on only the three Big Sciences (physics, biology and chemistry) or should it bring in others such as geology, psychology and archaeology? Are the latter really 'science'? Where do we draw the line between a science and a non-science? What should be the balance between various components?

Integration v. separation

This is one debate that may seem to have gone away but in fact is still unresolved. Should each science be taught separately, or should the science curriculum (and science teachers) take a topic and teach it in an integrated way, bringing in all the relevant sciences? Should, indeed, this be extended further to embrace the whole STEM[1] agenda?

In the UK in 1974, the Schools Council Integrated Science Project (SCISP) was a major initiative in trying to introduce an integrated approach to science teaching. A topic such as flight, for example, can be taught using a range of sciences: physics to explore the aerodynamics, biology to consider animals in flight, chemistry to consider fuel and its by-products, and so on. Even psychology might be brought in to consider the job of the pilot or the air-traffic controller. There are many other topics that could be tackled in an integrated way: growth, movement, the air, rocks and soil, the origins of life in the universe, buildings, and the environment.

For various reasons the integrated approach of the 1970s has never caught on. It may be due to the entrenched subject specialisms of teachers, which may in turn be due to the structure of science degree courses in higher education, which are rarely integrated. It may be due to the examination boards or the way secondary education is timetabled and compartmentalised. Whatever the reason, the integrated approach of the 1970s gave way to the pleas for 'broad and balanced science' in the 1980s and, in the UK, the introduction of a statutory national curriculum with clear boundaries between the sciences.

Yet arguably the scientific issues and debates of the twenty-first century demand an integrated approach. We explore the ideas of breadth, balance, integration and separation later.

Process v. content

A fourth recurring issue has been the extent to which science education should be about the skills and processes of science, as opposed to the facts, laws and theories of science, i.e. content. At the time of writing, the National Curriculum in England is under review and the current Secretary of State for Education, Michael Gove,[2] has said: 'I'm not going to be coming up with any prescriptive lists, I just think there should be facts.'

Within the realm of content there has also been disagreement over whether values should come into science teaching or if we should just present the 'facts'. In teaching recent scientific issues it has become increasingly difficult to draw a clear line between facts and values. Many facts have become value-laden. Similarly, values have become dependent on whose facts we choose to take account of, e.g. in considering BSE, GM foods or even the use of mobile phones. Science teachers may well say 'Let us teach the facts and leave the values to the Humanities staff' – but this approach has become increasingly untenable, even if it was ever justifiable.

The place of practical work and the role of ICT

Finally, one debate that is over a century old concerns the place and purpose of practical work. Ever since the days of H.E. Armstrong (see Jenkins 1979) the idea of children doing experiments for themselves and 'learning by discovery' has been a subject of debate. Can children discover science for themselves? Does exploratory or investigational practical work motivate children and help them to learn and understand science? Or will children discover the 'wrong science'? Is discovery learning realistic in a 50-minute science lesson when history shows that it took scientists decades to discover vaccination or develop a working telescope? Can the pupil really be a scientist? (see Driver 1983).

This debate will run and run. H.E. Armstrong's notion of discovery learning was rediscovered by the advent of 'Nuffield Science' in the 1960s and 1970s with its emphasis on practical work, children's own discoveries, and the motto 'I do and I understand'. It has been given a new lease of life by the recent emphasis on Investigation in Science (a statutory part of the UK National Curriculum). But to what extent do children make discoveries in this kind of work? What happens if they discover the 'wrong answer'? In a later chapter we examine the place and purpose of practical work.

Currently some are advocating a move beyond *hands-on* practical work in science towards a *minds-on* approach which engages learners with the process of thinking about science in a way that is more realistic, *How Science Works*; see for example Ireson and Twidle (2008).

One related issue is the role of ICT. Many traditional 'experiments' can now be done using multimedia, and perhaps the internet. Should practical work be done 'virtually', or will this take away the means to develop important skills? ICT is widely used by 'real scientists', but will its widespread use in school science, e.g. for data-logging or for simulations, create a gap in science education? Again, this is discussed in the chapter on ICT later in the book.

The prelude to the National Curriculum

With the introduction of the Certificate of Secondary Education (CSE) examination in 1965, especially the mode 3 version (the mode 3 version allowed teachers, with external moderation, to set their own specification and examination criteria), science teachers in secondary schools were able to operate with a great deal of freedom in terms of accountability and control. This move gave control to teachers who, since 1907 had been driven by examinations. These examinations of School Certificate and Matriculation were set by examination boards, which in reality meant they were set by the universities who controlled the boards. Given this absence of government intervention, which allowed the elite, as universities of the time could be considered, to dictate the school curriculum, we would take issue with Young's view that: 'in spite of attempts, the politics of the curriculum has remained outside of Westminster' (Young 1971: 22). Our view is that simply by not intervening, government had handed the political control of the school curriculum to the universities; hence we argue that control was, at that time, in the hands of Westminster.

Unfortunately this teacher-centric science education, which had been made available from 1965, did not capture the minds of the pupils and their teachers. In terms of numbers entered most pupils were still prepared for the mode 1, similar to the GCE Ordinary level, examination. In particular the CSE examination did not address gender imbalance, especially in physics and biology, see Table 3.1.

James Callaghan's Ruskin College speech in 1976 heralded the entry of politicians into the previously exclusive 'secret garden' of education and started the agenda for large-scale change,

Table 3.1 Examination entries, by gender, for biology and physics, 1985

	Mode 1		Mode 3	
	Girls	Boys	Girls	Boys
Biology	128,816	57,899	13,775	6,413
Physics	31,244	107,395	1,529	5,933

Source: adapted from Donnelly and Jenkins (2001)

leading to increased measurable outcomes for education. Lawton (1980: 22) writes that this was to end the 'golden age of teacher control'. Since this time, ever-increasing demands have been made, by governments of all colours, on teachers in schools: 'all governments have tried to find ways of making education more subservient to their political goals' (Young 2006: 11).

Contrast this with Sir David Eccles, Conservative minister, speaking to the House in 1960: 'of course Parliament would never attempt to dictate the curriculum ...' (Hansard 1960). Even by 1985 this was still the view put forward: 'there is in this country little danger of central control of the curriculum by the administrators in the Department of Education and Science' (Wrigley 1985: 42).

Despite the apparent political view being that the curriculum should not be controlled by Parliament or the 'administrators in the Department of Education and Science', legislation, in the shape of the 1988 Education Reform Act, was to lead to the National Curriculum. This act began life four years earlier with Sir Keith Joseph, then Secretary of State for Education under the Thatcher government, setting out the basis of both the 1988 Education Reform Act and the National Curriculum for England and Wales.

The Education Reform Act 1988 (and the earlier 1986 Act) was intended to make schools more responsive to market forces and hence become more competitive, leading to greater productivity. It is not then a surprise that some saw it as a Conservative government's drive towards a private education system. The impact on secondary school science was manifold. Firstly it led to the creation of a school subject of science as opposed to biology, chemistry and physics, and a compulsory requirement for students to study science between the ages of 5 and 16.

The requirement that all state-school pupils study science until age 16 may be viewed as an intervention that allowed students to keep their options open and would potentially lead to a more scientifically literate society. This was the view spelled out by the then Secretary of State for Education, Kenneth Baker:

> About one-third of our young people at school give up science at the age of 14, but under the National Curriculum every boy and girl, particularly girls, will have to take it to the age of 16, along with technology. That is an enormous step forward.
>
> (Hansard 1988)

It moved science education from a teacher-centred period to one where debate was not so much concerned with how the science curriculum may be taught but what its objectives were and what its content might be, returning to a neo-conservative view based on Arnold's statement: a curriculum must 'make the best that has been thought and known in the world current everywhere' (Arnold 1960: 70).

The National Curriculum brought with it attainment targets (17 in the first version) and levels (1 to 10 in the early versions) that pupils should reach by given ages. This moved us away from Stenhouse's view of a curriculum:

A curriculum is an attempt to communicate the essential principles and features of an educational proposal in such a form that it is open to critical scrutiny and capable of effective translation into practice.

(Stenhouse 1975: 4–5)

Later in the same text Stenhouse writes of a curriculum:

It can never be directed towards an examination as an objective without loss of quality, since the standards of the examination then override the standards immanent in the subject.

(Stenhouse 1975: 95)

The Statutory Order for science in the National Curriculum began with the formation of a Science Working Group made up largely of: 'academic educationists and science teachers, the latter, with one exception, being heads or deputy heads of schools' (Donnelly and Jenkins 2001: 103). The Working Group for science, as with other subjects, was required to generate a programme of study that set out the content, skills and processes and a statement of attainment targets. For many, both then and now, the driver for the teacher became the attainment target which would appear to be contra to Stenhouse's view of a curriculum.

School science post 2007

The current state of school science is one where more power is being given back to schools, teachers and learners.

The study of science fires pupils' curiosity about phenomena in the world around them and offers opportunities to find explanations. It engages learners at many levels, linking direct practical experience with scientific ideas. Experimentation and modelling are used to develop and evaluate explanations, encouraging critical and creative thought, and to show how knowledge and understanding in science are rooted in evidence. Pupils discover how scientific ideas contribute to technological change – affecting industry, business and medicine and improving quality of life. They trace the development of science worldwide and recognise its cultural significance. They learn to question and discuss issues that may affect their own lives, the directions of societies and the future of the world.

(Qualifications and Curriculum Authority, QCA, 2007)

The curriculum is based on a number of key concepts that should underpin the study of both science and 'how science works'. Pupils will need to understand these concepts to develop their knowledge, skills and understanding. For example it is expected that learners will develop their scientific thinking by 'using ideas and models to explain phenomena and developing them to generate and test theories critically analysing and evaluating evidence from observations and experiments' (QCA 2007), or their cultural understanding by 'recognising that modern science has its roots in many different societies and cultures and draws on a variety of valid approaches to scientific practice' (QCA 2007).

At Key Stage 4 (learners aged 14 to 16) a new National Curriculum was introduced in August 2006 that also moved from the content-driven approach to a more ideas and concepts led approach in which:

students learn about the way science and scientists work within society. They consider the relationships between data, evidence, theories and explanations, and develop their practical, problem-solving and enquiry skills, working individually and in groups. They evaluate enquiry methods and conclusions both qualitatively and quantitatively, and communicate their ideas with clarity and precision.

(QCA 2005)

For learners in this age group it is now also a more flexible curriculum, in which the mandatory component for science is reduced, giving learners and their teachers the opportunity to learn and teach, for example, psychology, astronomy, electronics or geology, under the banner of 'science'. This is, we feel, giving some power back to teachers and learners, as can be seen from the diagram in Figure 3.1.

However from 2011, changes to the assessment at GCSE, aged 16, have been imposed:

- Students must take at least 40 per cent of the assessment of each specification in the final examination when they expect to gain the certificate.
- Students may only re-sit a unit of assessment once. The better of the two results will count. However, if a re-sit is part of the 40 per cent terminal requirement, then that mark will count, regardless of being higher or lower.
- Each specification will have a maximum of four units, and each unit must carry at least 20 per cent of the assessment.
- *Controlled assessment*, set by the examining group, replaces coursework.

The question to consider here is, is this a move towards greater equity of opportunity or a return to greater, centralised, control of science education?

Science in the curriculum

Introduction

Science in the curriculum can be considered to be either three or more separate disciplines, or as a coherent body of study. Some topics lend themselves more to the coherent body approach and we will develop this idea in the remainder of this chapter.

We will be taking energy as our exemplar and developing the learning and teaching across Key Stage 3 and Key Stage 4 science with the emphasis, at Key Stage 4, on the different approach taken in biology, chemistry and physics.

In our view, and one that is expressed through the Qualifying to Teach (QTS) standards [at the time of writing these standards are the subject of a governmental review], teachers of science should be confident and competent to deliver across the disciplines at Key Stage 3 but should also be specialists who can use their specialist expertise at all Key Stages, especially 4 and 5.

Teachers need to interest pupils in school science: we argue that the affective domain underlies the cognitive one. If pupils are not interested, not engaged, they will not learn. Taking this reasoning a stage further, a case can be made that compulsory science from age 5 to 16 masks the problem, since pupils cannot opt out at age 14. At post-16, the study of science is growing but gender differences are still apparent both within and between subjects, see Table 1.3 in Chapter 1 and Figures 3.2 and 3.3.

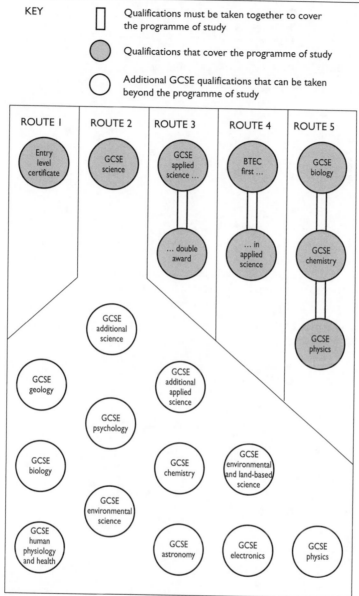

Figure 3.1 A new model or a return to pre-1968?
Source: QCA (2005)

The rigidity of the National Curriculum and the dominant view of the teacher as deliverer can be cited as mitigating factors acting as potential barriers to engaging science teaching. However, strategies to overcome this including both the planning phase and the classroom 'delivery' phase can be implemented.

It must not be forgotten that teachers do have an impact; this impact acts on the pupils' enthusiasm and success. The impact a teacher has can also be affected by their classroom management style, for example criticism, ridicule and sarcasm will ultimately rebound.

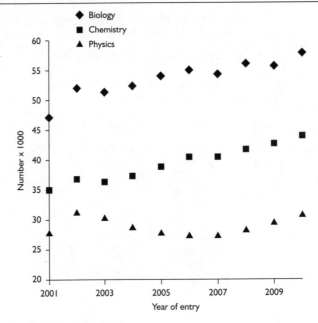

Figure 3.2 A-level entries 2001–2010

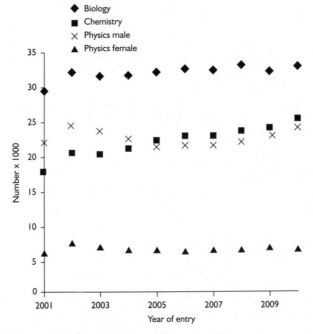

Figure 3.3 Gender differences at A-level

The National Curriculum tells us *what* to teach but not *how* to teach it and this is where we hope science teachers will become innovators of best practice.

Big ideas

What are the big ideas in biology, chemistry and physics? Do your big ideas differ when thinking of science as opposed to school science? For example, you may see particle physics, genetic modification and superconductivity as big ideas in science but are they big ideas in terms of school science?

The Key Stage 3 National Strategy (Department for Education and Skills, DfES, 2002) for science lists five key scientific ideas that underpin the Key Stage 3 programme of study:

*   cells
*   interdependence
*   particles
*   forces
*   energy.

The strategy document suggests that: 'It is important to introduce all five key scientific ideas early in Key Stage 3. Pupils need to develop their understanding steadily so that they can recognise, use and then apply each of the ideas in different contexts' (DfES 2002).

If we are to think beyond science at Key Stage 3 to science or the sciences at Key Stage 4, how do these key scientific ideas connect and do we need more? See Tables 3.2 and 3.3 for our suggestions for placing the key scientific ideas from Key Stage 3 into biology, chemistry and physics contexts at Key Stage 4 and beyond.

Energy appears to be a common theme across the three disciplines but what more do we need to convey the big ideas post-Key Stage 3? The National Curriculum for Key Stage 4 science (DfES 2004) lists four key ideas stating that: 'Pupils should be taught the knowledge, skills and understanding of how science works through the study of organisms and health, chemical and material behaviour, energy, electricity and radiation, and the environment, Earth and universe.'

Table 3.2 Big ideas in biology, chemistry and physics

Biology	Chemistry	Physics
Cells	Particles	Particles
Interdependence	Energy	Forces
Energy		Energy

Table 3.3 Aligning the four ideas with biology, chemistry and physics

Biology	Chemistry	Physics
Organisms and health		
	Chemical and material behaviour	Chemical and material behaviour (partial)
Energy, electricity and radiations (partial)	Energy, electricity and radiations (partial)	Energy, electricity and radiations
Environment, Earth and universe (partial)	Environment, Earth and universe (partial)	Environment, Earth and universe (partial)

Within the above publication the breadth of study identifies a range of scientific ideas across the three major scientific disciplines which 'provide contexts for the teaching of the knowledge, skills and understanding'. Each statement summarises a key idea in science that can form the basis of a range of learning opportunities.

As with Key Stage 3, energy is a key idea that runs across the three major disciplines. However, as we shall see, the approach taken to its 'delivery' can be very different.

Why teach the big ideas?

If we accept that school science contains key ideas, why should we teach them? More importantly, perhaps, we could ask the question 'Why these key ideas?'.

Initially we may ask, why teach science? Wellington (2000) offers three themes: the intrinsic value of science; the citizenship argument; and the utility argument.

The intrinsic value of science can be thought of as knowledge that helps us make sense of the universe we live in. It can help us make sense of topical science in the media such as, BSE, HIV, avian influenza, tsunami or dangers of nuclear power. This view allows us to think that science can just be interesting; it doesn't have to be relevant and driven by external, examination or economic, pressures. Finally it helps us see the cultural heritage in science. Knowing the history, stories and anecdotes helps us, as educators, to teach. Indeed Erwin Schrödinger wrote of the importance of history:

> History is the most fundamental of all sciences, for there is no human knowledge that does not lose its scientific character when men forget the conditions in which it originated, the questions it answered and the functions it was created to serve.
>
> Schrödinger (1956)

The citizenship argument is rehearsed in Chapter 16 and is developed there.

The utility argument stresses the fact that science education can be useful to many pupils even if not to all. While not all pupils will continue to study science and even fewer will enter a scientific career, those who do can be considered a minority and like any minority, they should be catered for.

Equally, generic problem-solving skills can be developed that are of utilitarian value for both future scientists and non-scientists alike.

Wellington summarised the justifications for the teaching of science as shown in Table 3.4. If we accept that these are sufficient reasons to teach science, why biology, chemistry and physics? Why the big ideas outlined for Key Stages 3 and 4? These are more complex questions but can also be addressed under the three headings in Table 3.4.

All three major disciplines develop generic skills, are needed for science-based careers and careers as scientists. All three major disciplines provide the knowledge needed to make decisions in a democracy; all three develop the knowledge to empower the decision makers. All three have intrinsic value especially under the subheadings 'Making sense of natural phenomena' and 'Understanding our own bodies' (QCA 2007).

Teaching energy across the curriculum

How then are we to develop a strategy for teaching the big idea of energy? The Key Stage 3 National Strategy framework for teaching science (DfES 2002) states that under the big idea of energy pupils should, in year 7 (age 12), be taught:

Table 3.4 Why teach science?

Intrinsic view	Citizenship argument	Utility of science
Making sense of natural phenomena	Knowledge of science and the work of scientists is needed to make decisions in a democracy	Generic skills are of value to all
Understanding our own bodies	Decision makers need a working knowledge of science to make key decisions	Some need to be prepared for careers in science and some for careers as scientists
Intellectual stimulation		Attitudes of curiosity and wonder can be developed which may, for example, have value in employment.
Part of our cultural heritage		

Source: adapted from Wellington (2000)

- the uses of fuels (food) by living and non-living systems;
- that the Sun is the ultimate source of energy;
- the transfer stages in a range of living and non-living systems;

and in year 9 (age 14) they should be taught about:

- the idea of energy conservation as a useful scientific accounting system when energy is transferred.

The QCA scheme of work for year 7 (unit 7I, introduction) states that in this unit pupils:

- are introduced to the concept of energy in the context of fuels as convenient and therefore valuable sources;
- consider the nature and origin of fossil fuels and renewable sources of energy and how their use has implications for the environment;
- consolidate and extend their ideas about energy resources for living things: food for people and sunlight for plants;
- link the energy resources to the role of the Sun as the ultimate source of most of the Earth's energy resources.

The Introduction to unit 7I further states that:

This unit provides an introduction to energy through the idea of foods and fuels as energy resources. The term 'resource' is used in preference to 'source' to try to encourage the idea that energy is not just a kind of stuff, like fuel. Energy transfer is associated with change, in particular changes that can perform useful tasks, as a first step towards more formal understanding. This enables pupils to make connections between apparently disparate phenomena, as contexts are drawn from across the sciences, e.g. burning fuel, movement, eating food and plant growth.

(QCA 2004)

In our view the important ideas to be taken from this are that energy is not a substance that can be consumed. Energy can only be transferred from one part of a system to another. In order to present an approach for teaching energy across the curriculum we suggest that five key points need to be addressed:

1   What is energy? Energy, especially in a physics context, can be simplified to an accounting device, which tells us what can and cannot happen in any system. This is why a ball cannot rebound to a height greater than the one it was dropped from.

2   Where does the energy come from? Energy per se cannot be created, or indeed, destroyed. However energy can be transferred from one place to another, for example from a cell or battery to a bulb. Obviously a bulb is very different to a battery so doesn't that suggest that we have different forms of energy? Isn't it just a case of having electrical energy in the cell and light energy in the bulb? But doesn't a bulb get hot (try changing one just after it 'blows') so isn't this heat energy? One way of thinking about these questions is as follows.

3   Energy as an accounting device: When a cell causes a bulb to light or a flame causes a kettle of water to boil a transfer of energy is required. We can, should we wish, measure the energy supplied, energy transferred and energy lost and we would always find that the total supplied would equal the total transferred plus the total lost. In this sense by lost we simply mean not transferred to where we want it. For example in transferring energy from a cell or battery to a bulb we don't want any to be transferred to the wires or glass – we want it all to be transferred to the filament (but this never happens).

4   Diluting energy? When energy is transferred from one part of a system to another we never seem to get as much as we started with so is not this evidence that energy can be used up or be lost? No, because while energy may become less useful as we transfer from one part of the system to another it is never lost. An analogy is to think about water. Imagine 5 litres of water in a pitcher. If this is poured into 10 glasses of 0.5 litres each, nothing is lost: we still have 5 litres, it is simply more spread out. However if we poured the glasses back into the pitcher we would get slightly less than 5 litres – the transfer process is not 100 per cent efficient but the water is not 'missing' – we simply can't recover it! Now consider pouring the pitcher into a watering can and watering the garden – again no water is lost but it is now almost impossible to recover any of it. Energy transfers are much the same, i.e. we never get 100 per cent transferred but some processes are more efficient than others and in some cases a large proportion can be recovered.

5   Energy in many forms? Many texts talk of forms of energy and indeed the students will often arrive at secondary school talking of heat, light, sound, chemical, food, spring energy etc. As teachers, using this approach, we need to be aware of its limitations, we need to realise that all of these forms can be reduced to one of two: potential or kinetic. Potential energy is stored energy, e.g. in a wound spring or chemical cell, while kinetic energy is a property of all moving objects. However even these two forms are not intrinsically different – energy is the same 'stuff' whether it be stored or due to motion. An analogy here could be money. You could have money in the form of pounds sterling, Australian dollars or euros. It is still money and you can, at a bank, *transfer* between one form or another or it can be *stored* in the bank. As above it also brings in the notion of efficiency of transfers, you always *lose* something when you change between one currency and another.

How can we build on the above key points? Recall that the QCA scheme of work suggests an approach to energy that 'enables pupils to make connections between apparently disparate phenomena, as contexts are drawn from across the sciences, e.g. burning fuel, movement, eating food and plant growth'.

First, we now approach energy from a chemistry context via the notion of burning fuel. The QCA scheme of work further states that: pupils should learn that fuels are substances that burn to release energy and suggests the following activities:

- Ask pupils 'What fuels can you name and what do we use them for?'
- This leads to a general statement that when fuels burn they make things happen. Introduce the definition of 'energy' as what burning fuels release to make things happen.

However we would contend that the phrase 'make things' happen is misleading and advocate that pupils are taught that the ability to transfer energy tells us what is possible but does not make things happen. By way of an analogy, having £1000 in your pocket does not cause you to take your 'significant other' for a long weekend in Paris but having only £100 limits your options. Similarly with the water analogy, having a litre of water does not make you drink or make coffee but having only 50 cm³ makes it more difficult.

However we need to be clear that fuels do not, in themselves, contain energy that is released but rather energy is transferred from one part of the system to another.

Consider the burning of methane as shown by the equation:

$$CH_4 + 2O_2 \rightarrow CO_2 + 2H_2O + \text{energy transfer}$$
methane + oxygen $\rightarrow$ carbon dioxide + water

The energy transfer is not from the methane but rather from the methane/oxygen part of the system to some other place in the system.

Looking at the transfer process in this way allows us to provide a plausible definition of energy as:

Energy is transferred when a fuel is used.

It is also important to make the distinction that while energy is conserved fuels are not: you can not un-burn coal or oil for example. It is better to talk of saving resources or fuels rather than energy, or to talk of making the energy transfer processes more efficient.

Finally we approach energy from a biology context via the notion of plant growth. The QCA scheme of work further states that pupils should learn that:

- plants store starch;
- new materials made from glucose produced during photosynthesis lead to an increase in biomass;
- the glucose from photosynthesis provides energy for all living processes in the green plant.

During photosynthesis, glucose is synthesised from carbon dioxide and water as shown in the following equation:

$$6CO_2 + 6H_2O \rightarrow C_6H_{12}O_6 + 6O_2$$
carbon dioxide + water $\rightarrow$ glucose + oxygen

This process requires energy from the Sun to break existing bonds in the carbon dioxide and water before new ones are formed in the products. The important issue is that energy is not used up in this process but is simply transferred from one part of the system to another.

If an animal (including a human) eats the plant material, energy is again transferred but not used; in this case the plant (food) can be considered to be a fuel and as such can be used up. However the energy cannot. It is merely transferred from one part of a system to another. In this instance published schemes, including the QCA scheme (QCA 2004), can be misleading, in fact simply wrong: 'Look at the energy ratings of food, e.g. a chocolate bar. Ask pupils to consider the question "If you ate the chocolate bar how high would you have to lift the apple before all the energy is used up?" '

In summary ... striking a balance in the science curriculum

The question that is still relevant for science education is: how should the various parts of science come together to form some sort of coherent whole, i.e. a broad and balanced science curriculum? Balance and integration are not synonymous. There are insufficient grounds for a truly integrated science or science curriculum, i.e. there is no unifying principle involving the concepts, content or processes of science that can bring about integration. We are thus faced with a mixture rather than a compound in devising a balanced science course. What should this mixture contain? Our own suggestion, which is presented as an Aunt Sally, is that it should include the following:

*   a study of the content and concepts of the sciences, giving a balanced coverage of the main sciences and some mention of the less commonly covered sciences;
*   consideration of the practices and processes of science (how science works), i.e. scientific methods and procedures (while remembering that there is no clear consensus on a single scientific method);
*   study of the links between science, technology and society;
*   consideration of the history and nature of science (again, how science works and what counts as 'ideas and evidence' in science).

It does seem desirable that science education should be presented as a balanced, coherent and concurrent mixture of these parts, i.e. various sciences taught alongside their methods, their applications, their impact on society, with some consideration of their nature and limits. Is this expecting too much? It is certainly a goal that can be achieved within the framework of a national curriculum. As for the process versus content debate, it cannot be doubted that the traditional, content-led approach to the science curriculum with an overemphasis on factual recall, inert ideas, irrelevant laws and theories and difficult abstractions has been long overdue for change. But a swing or backlash towards an exclusive emphasis on processes and skills is equally undesirable, philosophically problematic and probably as likely to fail its students as a content-led approach. Particularly dangerous is the belief that processes could and should be taught in isolation from content (Wellington 1989).

There are various ways of conceiving balance, none of which is definitive but all of which can be valuable aids to thinking about the goal of a balanced science curriculum as an entitlement for all pupils.

Table 3.5 Groups of aims in science education

Cognitive	Psychomotor	Affective
Factual knowledge Understanding Application Synthesis Evaluation	Manipulative Manual dexterity Hand-to-eye coordination	Interest Enthusiasm Motivation Involvement Eagerness to learn

Table 3.6 Balanced science education

Knowledge that	Knowledge how (to)	Knowledge why
Facts, 'happenings', phenomena, experiences	Skills, processes, abilities	Explanations, models, analogies, frameworks, theories

Another important facet to emphasise is the affective aspect of science education as opposed to the cognitive aspect. The affective element includes the pupil's attitudes and disposition towards science: interest, excitement, enthusiasm, motivation, eagerness to learn and openness to new learning. These are important dimensions of any science curriculum that are neglected at our peril (Claxton 1989). The notion of different elements or 'domains' of educational aims goes back to Bloom's (1956) taxonomy of educational objectives; this is still valuable in considering a balanced science curriculum. A summary of these three elements is given in Table 3.5.

A final framework for considering balance in both science lessons and schemes of work is offered in Table 3.6. The table presents three kinds of knowledge (Ryle 1949) as being important in science education: knowledge that, i.e. traditional factual recall and the experience of events and phenomena in science; knowledge how, i.e. processes and skills; and knowledge why, i.e. a knowledge of explanations, laws, frameworks and theories. Science teachers and curriculum planners could usefully employ these three categories in considering their teaching, science courses and curricula for the future. A 'balanced' science education will not focus on one of these three categories at the expense of the others.

Points for reflection

- What is science education for? i.e. What is its purpose?
- Who is science education for? Should everyone learn science? Why?
- Should the slogan 'science for all' be taken to imply 'the same science for all'? If not, how would you differentiate the science curriculum for different learners?
- What would you say are the 'big ideas' in science'?
- Which other areas of the school curriculum link best with science in your view?

Notes

1 STEM – commonly used acronym in the UK for Science, Technology, Engineering and Mathematics and comparable with MST – Mathematics, Science and Technology as used throughout Europe.
2 http://www.bbc.co.uk/news/education-12227491

References and further reading

General

References from the QCA website will no longer be available. Since the change of government in May 2010 the QCA, now QCDA, has been in the process of winding down:

QCDA is closing as part of the Government's education reforms. We're updating our website to reflect our reducing remit until the site closes in autumn 2011. You can find removed content in the National Archives web archive.

For example the Unit 7I Energy Resources can be found at: http://tna.europarchive.org/20040117025520/ http://www.standards.dfes.gov.uk/schemes2/secondary_science/?view=get

Arnold, M. (1960) *Culture and Anarchy*, Cambridge: Cambridge University Press.

DfES (2002) *Framework for Teaching Science: years 7, 8 and 9*, London: DfES.

DfES (2004) *National Curriculum for Science*, London: DfES.

Donnelly, J.F. and Jenkins, E.W. (2001) *Science Education: policy, professionalism and change*, London: Paul Chapman.

Driver, R. (1983) *The Pupil as Scientist*, Milton Keynes: Open University Press.

Dunne, D. (1998) 'The place of science in the curriculum', in Ratcliffe, M. (ed.) *ASE Guide to Secondary Education*, Hatfield: ASE/Stanley Thornes, pp. 23–32.

Hansard (1960) Parliamentary debate, 21 March, column 51.

Hansard (1988) Baker, K., Hansard, 20 December, column 267.

Ireson, G. and Twidle, J. (2008) 'Magnetic braking revisited: an activity for how science works?', *Physics Education*, 43, pp. 522–524.

Jenkins, E. (1979) *From Armstrong to Nuffield*, London: John Murray.

Lawton, D (1980) *The Politics of the School Curriculum*, London, Routledge.

QCA (2004) *Science at Key Stage 3, Unit 7I: energy resources*, London: QCA. Accessed on 14 March 2006, at www.standards.dfes.gov.uk.

QCA (2005) *Changes to the Curriculum from 2006 for Key Stage 4*, London: QCA.

QCA (2007) *Secondary Curriculum Review*, London: QCA. Accessed on 25 February 2007, at www.qca.org.uk/secondarycurriculumreview/subject/ks3/science/index. htm.

Schrödinger, E. (1956) *What is Life? And Other Scientific Essays*, New York: Doubleday.

Stenhouse, L. (1975) *An Introduction to Curriculum Research and Development*, London: Heinemann.

Waring, M. (1979) *Social Pressures and Curriculum Innovation*, London: Methuen.

Wellington, J.J. (2000) *Teaching and Learning Secondary Science*, London: Routledge.

Wrigley, J. (1985) 'Confessions of a curriculum man', in Plaskow, M. (ed.) *Life and Death of the Schools Council*, London: Falmer Press.

Young, M.D.F. (1971) 'An approach to the study of curricula as socially organised knowledge', in Young, M.D.F. (ed.) *Knowledge and Control: New Directions for the Sociology of Education*, London: Collier-Macmillan.

Young, M.D.F. (2006) *Government Intervention and the Problem of Knowledge in Education Policy*, London: Institute of Education.

Examining the science curriculum further

Bloom, B.S. (1956) *Taxonomy of Educational Objectives*, Cambridge, MA: Harvard University Press.

Childs, A., Twidle, J., Sorensen, P. and Godwin, J. (2007) 'Trainee teachers' use of the Internet – opportunities and challenges for initial teacher education', *Research in Science & Technological Education*, vol. 25, no. 1, pp. 77–97.

Claxton, G. (1989) 'Cognition doesn't matter if you're scared, depressed or bored', in Adey, P. (ed.) *Adolescent Development and School Science*, Lewes: Falmer Press.

Claxton, G. (1991) *Educating the Inquiring Mind: the challenge for school science*, London: Harvester Wheatsheaf.

Jenkins, E. (1989) 'Processes in science education: an historical perspective', in Wellington, J.J. (ed.) *Skills and Processes in Science Education: a critical analysis*, London: Routledge.

Millar, R. (1989) 'What is scientific method and can it be taught?', in Wellington, J.J. (ed.) *Skills and Processes in Science Education: a critical analysis*, London: Routledge.

Ryle, G. (1949) *The Concept of Mind*, London: Hutchinson.

Screen, P. (1986a) *Warwick Process Science*, Southampton: Ashford Press.

Screen, P. (1986b) 'The Warwick Process Science Project', *School Science Review*, vol. 68, no. 242, pp. 12–16.

Smail, B. (1993) 'Science for girls and for boys', in Hull, R. (ed.) *ASE Secondary Science Teachers' Handbook*, Hemel Hempstead: Simon & Schuster.

Twidle, J., Sorensen, P., Childs, A., Godwin, J. and Dussart, M. (2006) 'Issues, challenges and needs of student science teachers in using the Internet as a tool for teaching', *Journal of Technology, Pedagogy and Education*, vol. 15, no. 2, pp. 207–21.

Wellington, J.J. (ed.) (1989) *Skills and Processes in Science Education: a critical analysis*, London: Routledge.

SPT 11–14 A series of five CD-ROMs addressing the learning and teaching of physics to learners in the 11 to 14 age range, London: Institute of Physics.

Approaches to science learning and science teaching

Chapter 4

Learning in science

Jon Scaife

This chapter looks at how people learn. It examines theories (mainly so-called 'constructivist' ideas) about children's learning and their mental development. It links these to practical teaching strategies so that teaching can be targeted at known learning needs. Learning-informed teaching strategies discussed below include assessing for learning, designing constructive challenges to pupils' current ideas, harnessing curiosity through predictions, questioning for understanding, targeting thinking skills and teaching for cognitive development.

STUDENT 1:   I enjoy science.

STUDENT 2:   I hate it!

STUDENT TEACHER: Tell me why.

STUDENT 2:   It's so hard ... I got put in top group but I don't know how cos it's dead confusing – I don't understand anything we do.

STUDENT 3:   *I* don't understand it – but I still get it right.

This exchange took place during a recorded interview with some girls aged 14 and 15. The interview was carried out by a student teacher as part of a project about students' attitudes to school science. What do you make of it? Two things struck me when I watched the recording: student 2 says she hates science, finds it hard and confusing and doesn't understand it, yet is in the highest attaining group. Odd! And student 3, who had earlier declared that she liked science because, 'I don't like doing practicals' (that really is what she said!) admits that she too doesn't understand science but manages to get it right. Odder still!

These students hadn't been selected for the interview, they had volunteered to stay behind at lunchtime to take part in the project. They seemed to be speaking spontaneously and honestly about their experiences in their science lessons. Perhaps there's something to be learned from listening to their views. What are they telling us? First, it's clear that they have views about their own knowledge and understanding: two students don't think they understand the subject adequately. Secondly, they have views about what counts as success in science: success means 'getting it right'. Thirdly, their experience is that getting it right doesn't involve understanding.

If getting it right in science doesn't involve understanding, what does it involve? A clue emerged later in the interview when the students were talking about the topic of Materials. Student 3 said: 'It's something we didn't do a lot of ... we had Mr X ... we did about two lessons on it and that was it – and everything he told us we already knew anyway.' I think that last phrase is very significant. The student seems to be identifying what the teacher has told them as what counts, in terms of 'getting it right'. This, rather than what she understands, is what matters. And, ironically, he had already told them it!

The teacher could learn a great deal from listening to those students.

Introduction

This chapter is about how people learn, and about how teaching can make use of understandings about how people learn. For instance, imagine you were going to take over the teaching of the students in the interview. What do you think of what they've been learning? What haven't they been learning? What have they come to learn about learning itself?

The trouble with learning is that it isn't a 'thing'. It's hard to pin down, elusive to observe and even to think about – and perhaps that is why teaching often has a higher profile than learning in education. To illustrate, picture a science class you've been in fairly recently. Think of the teaching: what was taught, how well was it taught, was it taught scientifically appropriately? Now think of the learning and check the same three questions, substituting 'learned' for 'taught'. Hard? Virtually impossible unless you're a mind-reader because there's absolutely no guarantee that what was taught is what was learned. In fact there's a lot of research evidence that suggests the two are often distant relatives.

In this chapter the main aims are to summarise some of the longer-standing and useful perspectives and also some recent ideas about learning (some people call these 'theories') and to look at teaching in the light of these ideas. In the course of this it will be useful to settle on some working definitions for words like learning, knowledge, understanding and so on, because they are overworked in everyday language and confusions easily arise. Science teachers are used to this problem, with words like animal, chemical, power, and so on, which have everyday use but which need more precise definitions to be used scientifically (see Chapter 11). A glossary is included at the end of the chapter.

Why theories?

For quite a while 'theory' has been an unpopular word to use when talking about education (Adey, 1995b). In one respect this is odd, because every conscious human act is guided by background knowledge and by expectations – in other words by mini-theories. We live by being guided by our theories – if we didn't do this we would face every moment like a newborn baby. On the other hand there is a long history of those who deal with theories seeing themselves as superior to those who deal with action. In turn, practitioners sometimes see theorisers as elitist and untrustworthy. But there are two good reasons for science teachers not to shun the T-word. The first is that science itself is crammed full of theories. Without theory there would be stone-age engineering but no science. Science is a massive achievement in human theorising. It is an amazingly productive synthesis of thinking and doing. Science is 'living' evidence that theories and practice aren't opposites, they are jigsaw pieces that more or less fit together. The second reason for science teachers to be comfortable with theory in education is that they have written quite a lot of it themselves. As we will see, there are several 'big names' who have been both science teachers or scientists and also thinkers about learning.

Why though are some teachers sceptical, even hostile towards educational research? Perhaps this is because too little 'official' research is carried out by teachers themselves. The trouble with teaching is that contrary to some public opinion, it takes a lot of time. After planning, teaching, assessing, caring for pupils and doing everything else the job entails, most teachers have neither the time nor the energy to do any in-depth researching into the effects of their work, the nature of their job, the curriculum or anything else. Surveys, comparisons and evaluations are very difficult for teachers to carry out at the same time as holding down a full timetable. The problem with this, as Spinoza pointed out over three hundred years ago, is that those who ignore history are condemned for ever to repeat it! If teaching is to develop and change in a changing world, there must be a place for reflection and research.

> Some educators and researchers in education have come to the conclusion that, as a foundation for their activities, they must develop some theoretical ideas as to how children build up their picture of the world they experience. They believe that unless they have a model of the student's concepts and conceptual operations, there is no effective way of teaching.
>
> (Glasersfeld, 1991: 21)

What can theories offer to teachers?

The first thing is that if a theory is any good it should at least add something beyond common sense. It might do so by extending, reinforcing or even conflicting with common sense. Its perspective may be sharper or its conclusions firmer. It may spotlight differences that to the common sense view are invisible. The theoretical ideas in this chapter have things to say about children's learning. The topics include the following: How do people learn? Do students know any science before they are taught it? How can teachers find out what students have learned? How does mental maturity influence thinking? Can mental maturing be accelerated? Do students know what they're doing in science lessons? Is there more than one kind of learning? Do students learn from practical work? From discussion? From teachers' questions? Can we learn how to learn?

This chapter is based on the idea that if more could be learnt about how people learn, then pupils and teachers would both benefit. The chapter sets out to give a brief introduction to some theories of learning, to some common ideas that children have in science and to some possible approaches for teachers. If you would like to explore some of these ideas more deeply, suggestions for further reading are included at the end.

What's the problem?

Most science teachers are well qualified in science and have completed school science courses with considerable success. Does this show that science teaching and learning are on sound footings?

Consider these views:

> In general, quantitative measures of the public understanding of science from a variety of countries and, in some instances, extending over time, present a disappointing picture.
>
> (Jenkins, 1999)

> In the everyday world of the citizen, science itself emerges not as coherent, objective and unproblematic knowledge, but as uncertain, contentious and often unable to answer many important questions with the required degree of confidence. In some instances, expert scientific knowledge is marginalized or ignored as irrelevant to the problems being addressed.
>
> (Jenkins, 1999)

never … has there been a time when the public at large, or even its highly educated segment, could be considered literate in science

(Shamos, 1995)

the average citizen's knowledge of science is far less today than at any other time since science became a part of the school curriculum … science educators have not been successful in transcending school science literacy to adult science literacy

(Kyle, 1995)

Unfortunately we must face the bitter truth that most students in schools all over the world do not understand. In other words, given situations in which they must apply their 'school knowledge', they do not know what to do.

(Gardner, 1993a)

Although the statements above date from a decade or more ago I have found no clear indication in the current science education research literature that they no longer apply.

Imagine all the children born in Britain, for example, in 1980. Figure 4.1 illustrates what I think has happened to their average level of science knowledge over about 30 years. It improved during schooling and peaked at school leaving age, at about GCSE grade E or equivalent. Since then it has declined steadily. If you doubt this, select a few adults more or less at random and ask them about some science from Key Stage 3 of the national curriculum. It costs a fortune to educate the nation in science as ineffectually as this! There is plenty of scope to make science teaching more effective in terms of people's long-term learning.

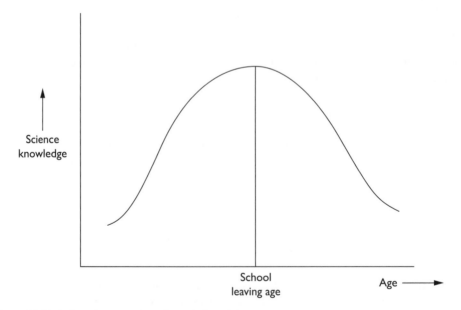

Figure 4.1 Variation of mean science knowledge with age

Why learning: why not focus on teaching?

Teachers' concerns about teaching tend to change and develop with increasing experience. We could think of them as moving through the following developmental stages:

- *Stage 1*: surviving in the classroom;
- *Stage 2*: teaching: acting like a teacher, covering the curriculum, managing the classes;
- *Stage 3*: learning: what are they learning? how do they learn well? how can I improve their learning?

What would you say are your dominant concerns currently? The most common concern shared by student teachers in the early stages of their qualification courses is survival in the classroom. 'Will they (children) listen to me? Will they do what I tell them? What if they don't?' If you are in the grips of this stage, take heart, it usually wears off quite early in the first teaching placement. The second stage in the development of new teachers focuses strongly on the acts of teaching: 'Am I doing what I'm supposed to? Am I covering the curriculum? Is the class properly controlled?' This is the stage where the curriculum and teaching performance take over from survival as the main concerns.

In the third developmental stage the teacher is concerned with the effects of her/his teaching on the students' learning: 'What are they learning? What do I want them to learn? How can I enhance their learning?' Now, isn't this the main point of teaching? The first two stages of teacher development are means to an end – and learning is the 'end'.

The more we know about learning the better we can teach. This view even has 'official' support: in the British Training and Development Agency for Schools' professional standards for teachers in England it is stated that in order to qualify, student teachers should:

- Understand how children and young people develop.
- Build on prior knowledge, develop concepts and processes, enable learners to apply new knowledge, understanding and skills and meet learning objectives.
- Assess the learning needs of those they teach in order to set challenging learning objectives.
- Support and guide learners to reflect on their learning, identify the progress they have made and identify their emerging learning needs.
- Evaluate the impact of their teaching on the progress of all learners, and modify their planning and classroom practice where necessary.

In addition, after qualification teachers should:

> Use assessment as part of their teaching to diagnose learners' needs, set realistic and challenging targets for improvement and plan future teaching.
>
> (Training and Development Agency for Schools, 2007)

If you come across a teacher who is a star performer, a great character, a bundle of energy, an excellent story teller, a dynamic manager, and/or a charismatic leader, ask yourself: do her/his students learn fruitfully? If they do, well and good. If not, then the teacher's qualities are wasted, because teaching is not an end in itself.

How do people learn?

Some data

Let's start right here. Can you think of something that you're reasonably, or even very, good at – anything at all, not just school work. How did you get that way? How come your learning in that field has been successful? What would you pick out as the key factors that have contributed to your successful learning? You might be able to come up with responses to these questions in a matter of seconds. Do your responses have anything to say about teaching? In other words, can anything be learned about effective teaching from your own successful learning?

If you respond to these questions, you're actually carrying out research into learning. Don't get carried away though, because the data you have obtained from 'introspection' is highly personal. Much more research would be needed before generalisations were justifiable. But self-reflection is a good start.

Learning and mental development: Piaget

As people grow they develop intellectually as well as physically. Their powers of reasoning and their capacity to experience ranges of emotions increase. As they grow they are able to learn new ideas. What kinds of tasks and problems can children solve at different ages? This question was studied in detail by Jean Piaget (see note 1). He drew inferences about the cognitive processes employed by individual children as they attempted to solve various kinds of problems. The result of this experimental work, together with Piaget's view of intelligence as an adaptively favourable characteristic in natural selection, led him to propose a theory of children's cognitive development. The impact of Piaget's ideas on teaching in Britain has been very considerable.

According to Piaget, children make meaning for themselves; they learn by actively constructing knowledge. The process of learning helps the individual to navigate through the world of their life experiences. A new experience might be *assimilated* by a person into her or his current cognitive structures. 'Assimilation' in this context means treating the experience as similar to other ones which the person has experienced. Assimilation provides us with a huge mental economy – we don't have to keep inventing new solutions to new experiences, we try old ones first. For instance, if you went into a room in which you had never been before, you would almost certainly have no difficulty identifying a door by which to leave the room, even though you had never seen it before. You would simply assimilate the experience into a 'cognitive structure' or category of 'doors' in your memory and treat it as a door. Most of the time assimilation works well enough. But sometimes it doesn't: an experience might not fit with a person's current cognitive structures. One possibility in that case is that the structures might change or *accommodate* to the new information. Piaget saw these processes of assimilation and accommodation as helping to bring about 'equilibrium' between the person's cognitive structure and their experiences.

Piaget believed that although cognitive development in children is a continuous process, it does not take place smoothly, at a steady rate. He identified three principal *stages* of development, which occur in a definite order, as illustrated in simplified form in Figure 4.2. Children of secondary school age have normally reached either the concrete operational stage or the formal operational stage.

Concrete operational thinking involves processes such as classifying, sorting and ordering objects. The child has developed ideas of conservation and reversibility; when a ball of plasticene

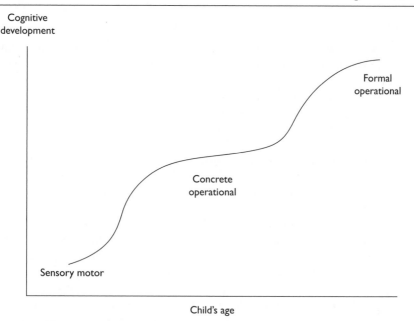

Figure 4.2 Piagetian stages of development

is moulded into a new shape and then rolled back into a ball, the child may know that the amount and weight of plasticene remain unchanged through the cycle. Driver (1983: 55) illustrates the type of inferential logical problem that might be solved at this cognitive stage: If water in beaker A is hotter than water in beaker B, and water in beaker B is hotter than water in beaker C, which beaker has the coldest water in it?

Formal operational thinking is associated with the use of hypothetical models for the purpose of explaining things. It is characteristic of situations involving several variables and also of the use of abstract notions like ratio and proportion.

The significance of these cognitive stages of development for science teachers is that some forms of learning cannot be achieved until children reach the formal operational stage. Piaget's experimental work led him to believe that formal operational thinking can take place in 12-year-olds but subsequent research (Shayer *et al.*, 1976; Lawson and Renner, 1978) indicates that most children develop formal thinking much later than this and some do not develop it at all.

It has been argued that familiarity with the idea of stages of cognitive development will allow teachers to devise approaches to the science curriculum with greater insight (Shayer and Adey, 1981). A science scheme, 'Thinking Science', which has been designed with explicit reference to Piaget's model, will be described later in this chapter.

Piaget was educated as a biologist and his view of knowledge as adaptively useful to an individual clearly draws on his science background. The idea of knowing as adapting has been extended by Glasersfeld; this is explored in the following section. But this is not the only direction in which the connection between biology and thinking has developed. Indeed, it has been predicted that, just as the twentieth century has witnessed an 'explosion' in physics, the twenty-first century will see an equivalent process in neurobiology and the study of the mind/brain. I will return to this topic in a section on 'brain-based learning' later in the chapter.

Learning as knowledge construction: constructivism

A major scientific debate took place during the late nineteenth and early twentieth centuries. The question was: Is outer space full of a stuff called aether? Aether was an attractive idea because it gave a sense of absoluteness to space and it helped to overcome difficult puzzles such as how light travelled through space from the Sun to the Earth: light waves were thought to travel through aether a bit like sound waves travel through air. A famous experiment by Michelson and Morley in 1887 was designed to show the effect of the Earth moving through the aether. No effect was found. Within 20 years Einstein proposed that we cannot detect *absolute* physical properties of space; the only properties we can detect are *relative* ones – people's views of the physical universe depend on their relative circumstances (such as whether they are moving relative to each other). The aether is a property of absolute space; Einstein's ideas imply that we cannot know if aether, or absolute space, exists.

There are some similarities between the evolution of these ideas in physics and those in some fields of psychology and philosophy. For a long time, a dominant cultural view in the West has been that there is a universe 'out there' and that scientists are gradually uncovering fragments of truth about it. This perspective is sometimes called 'inductive realism' (see, e.g., Selley, 1989 and other chapters in this volume). At the same time, the dominant model of science teaching has been that teachers draw their pitchers from the wells of truth and pour knowledge from them into the empty vessels which are their pupils' minds. Another name for this model of teaching is the 'tabula rasa' or blank slate approach (it used to be commonplace in undergraduate lectures). The inductive realist view has been seriously challenged by numerous writers for many years. So far, in this field there is no equivalent of the Michelson–Morley aether experiment but this has not stopped people from questioning the relevance of the idea of an *absolute* universe: 'I have never said (nor would I ever say) that there is *no* ontic world, but I keep saying that we cannot *know* it' (Glasersfeld, 1991: 17).

In the view of Glasersfeld, Piaget and others who are described as 'constructivists', people do not acquire knowledge about an independent reality; rather they *construct* knowledge to fit what they experience: 'the world we come to know [is] assembled out of elements of our very own experience' (Glasersfeld, 1991: 19).

Glasersfeld's version of constructivism, known as 'radical constructivism', is based on the following premises:

1 Constructivism is about knowing (Glasersfeld, 1991: 17).
2 Knowing is a state of adaptation of an individual to the individual's environment (Glasersfeld, 1989: 125; 1991: 16). ['Environment' is intended here to include social, cultural and physical aspects and also the self.]
3 The individual's state of adaptation, and knowledge, are dynamic and ever-changing.
4 New knowledge is learned through the construction of new states of adaptation of the individual to the environment (Glasersfeld, 1989: 128).
5 New knowledge is constructed by the knower from the interaction of experiences and current knowledge, beliefs and emotional states.
6 Knowledge is not something that is 'out there', in the environment. Nor is it something that is passed about in immutable form.
7 We can have no certain knowledge of an absolute, objective reality. This includes scientific knowledge.

Radical constructivism has both strong supporters (myself included) and vigorous critics. Its opponents have accused it of implying that:

* all learning is discovery learning;
* no-one can be taught anything;
* learning is an individual, not a social, process;
* knowledge can only be constructed through the experience of the senses;
* my knowledge is the equal of your knowledge in terms of truth and merit;
* there is no absolute objective reality.

Constructivism is a contemporary view of knowing, distinct from the traditions of realism and rationalism. As with any serious challenge to tradition, it has prompted a range of reactions from curiosity and excitement to anxiety and hostility. Despite this variety, constructivism has undoubtedly established a place in science education:

> The view that knowledge cannot be transmitted but must be constructed by the mental activity of learners underpins contemporary perspectives on science education.
>
> (Driver *et al.*, 1994)

To sample the views of both supporters and critics of constructivism, see the journal *Science and Education*; the whole of volume 6, numbers 1 and 2 (January 1997) is devoted to the topic.

Vygotsky and Bruner: Learning with a little help from friends

> No man is an Island, entire of it self; every man is a piece of the Continent, a part of the main.
>
> (Donne, 1634, Meditation XVII, p. 3)

If John Donne were writing today, I'm sure he would include women and children too. Up to now in this chapter intellectual development and knowledge construction have been considered from the point of view of the individual. But we are a social species, the more so by virtue of our possession of language. Is this significant? Do *interpersonal* processes influence how and what we learn? The biologist and constructivist Humberto Maturana (1991: 30) certainly thinks that they do: 'Science is a human activity. Therefore, whatever we scientists do as we do science has validity and meaning, as any other human activity does, only in the context of human coexistence in which it arises.' Central to this coexistence is language. For Maturana, we exist in language, experience takes place in language and we know what we know through its constitution in language.

Maturana may be regarded by some as holding a radical view but the underlying point, that knowledge is constructed by individuals through interpersonal processes, is now shared by many people. Jerome Bruner (1964) stressed the importance of language in cognitive development nearly 30 years earlier. Around this time, the work of L.S. Vygotsky began to appear in the West, having been suppressed for two decades in Russia. Vygotsky (1978) believed that, 'children undergo quite profound changes in their understanding by engaging in joint activity and conversation with other people'. This view is shared by Edwards and Mercer (1987) who regard knowledge and thought as 'fundamentally cultural, deriving their distinctive properties from the nature of social activity, language, discourse and other cultural forms'. The implication is

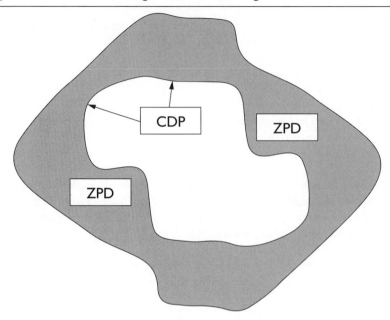

Figure 4.3 Current developmental profile (CDP) and zone of proximal development (ZPD)

that *meaning* is constructed not only through processes operating on individuals – such as the stimulation of senses or the mediation of prior knowledge – but also through processes of social communication (see note 2).

Vygotsky worked extensively with people with learning difficulties. He used to test their capabilities by asking them to attempt various tasks. Similar practices continue today: a familiar case is the production of data about students' 'reading ages'. This measure compares a child's reading with the average reading performance of each year group. Imagine carrying out a large number of such measures, each assessing the child's performance at different tasks, in different cognitive domains. The result would be a 'profile' of the child that is indicative of the current development of the child. This 'current developmental profile', or CDP, is shown in Figure 4.3. Now suppose that a teacher sat with the child, offering well-judged prompts as he/she attempted the tasks. The prompts don't solve the child's tasks but provide limited guidance to help the child solve them her/himself. The result of this would be another profile, with generally higher values in the measured domains than when the child worked without guidance. Vygotsky described the relationship between the two profiles, using an expression which translates from Russian as 'zone of proximal development'. Some authors have shortened this to ZPD or 'zee pee dee'. One account of this (Vygotsky, 1978: 86) is that the ZPD represents 'the distance between the actual developmental level as determined by independent problem solving, and the level of potential development as determined through problem solving under adult guidance or in collaboration with more capable peers'. Interpreted in this way, the ZPD is an *extra* amount of constructing that can be done by the child, and its 'size' depends on:

- the child's current level of development;
- the child's current mental constructions;
- the discourse between the child and her or his environment.

The ZPD concept lends itself to application in education. Imagine you were in a learning environment in which all you have to do is work within your CDP; the result will probably be initial comfort followed by boredom. Alternatively suppose a teacher expected you to think beyond the ZPD; you would be lost, unable to make sense of what was being taught. Optimal teaching challenges the learner to think and act within the ZPD. The message to teachers from Vygotsky's account is to design teaching so that it presents learners with achievable challenges.

The adult's action in guiding the child's learning has been likened by Bruner (1985, p. 25) to the construction of scaffolding: 'the tutor in effect performs the critical function of "scaffolding" the learning task to make it possible for the child … to internalize external knowledge'. A word of caution is appropriate here, because the word 'scaffolding' can conjure up a variety of images. One image which is sometimes implied in discussion of Bruner's scaffolding idea is that of a temporary structural support; a 'buttress' would be a more accurate term for this. The purpose of scaffolding in the building trade is to support the process of construction, not to support the structure itself. Bruner's choice of word suggests a process, but who does the building – the child or the adult?

Newman and Holzman (1993) are fiercely critical of 'pragmatic' interpretations of the ZPD. They argue that, 'the ZPD is not a zone at all' (p. 88) but rather that it is 'a reorganising of environmental scenes to create new meaning and a learning that leads to development' (p. 147). This is a much broader notion than the functional object described above: e.g., 'Speaking (verbalizing, using a language) is, perhaps, the single human performance that best exemplifies … the form and substance of the life space of everyday human performance, the ZPD' (p. 112). According to these authors the school by no means necessarily contributes constructively to development through learning:

> Traditional schools are not ZPDs; they teach children and adults alike to devalue and even destroy ZPDs. In the typical classroom children are taught to view the major activities in the ZPD – working together, imitating that produces something other than mere repetition, collectively changing the total determining environment into something that is not predetermined, reshaping the existing tools of language and play into new meanings and discovery – as illegitimate.
>
> (Newman and Holzman, 1993, p. 195)

Vygotsky's view is that learning *leads* development in the ZPD. When teaching aims to bring about learning that is ahead of development it: 'impels or wakens a whole series of functions that are in a stage of maturation lying in the zone of proximal development' (Vygotsky, quoted in Newman and Holzman, p. 60). This contrasts sharply with the idea that learning can take place until it reaches limits imposed by the current level of development, a view sometimes ascribed to Piaget. However as Shayer (2002) points out, Piaget's main interest was in the child's current level of development, whereas Vygotsky was interested in the effects of intervention. Looking at Figure 4.3, Piaget focused on the CDP and Vygotsky on the ZPD and their ideas can be seen to be complementary rather than contradictory.

The ZPD represents current *potential* learning, leading to new development (Vygotsky referred to it as containing 'buds' of development). It is not a characteristic of the child alone but rather it is an aspect of the large, complex *system* consisting of the child and her or his environment. 'Environment' is used here in the most general sense, including the child's peers, parents, teachers and school, the physical environment and also the social context, its history and the history of the child. Whether the child's potential learning is actually realised depends on the operation of the system as a whole.

Like Piaget, Vygotsky is a constructivist. Both stress the significance for learning of what a person already knows. In Vygotsky's account learning occurs in the ZPD and the ZPD starts from current knowledge. He emphasises social interaction and for that reason some writers refer to him as a 'social constructivist'. This term can be misleading, because there are others who take a radically different position from Vygotsky or Piaget, e.g. Gergen (1995) and Shotter (1995), who describe their perspectives as forms of 'social constructionism'. In those accounts learning and knowing are seen as qualities in social space, including the space between people. In contrast, the psychological accounts of Piaget and Vygotsky, as well as current neuroscientific and evolutionary views, regard learning and knowing as 'embodied'. Plotkin (1994) expresses this position unequivocally: 'When we come to know something, we have performed an act that is as biological as when we digest something.'

Ausubel: rote/meaningful and reception/discovery learning

The educational psychologist David Ausubel made a helpful distinction between two extreme types of learning. What he labelled as 'rote learning' is sometimes referred to as learning parrot fashion. Occasionally a mental catalyst (a mnemonic) is used to help rote learning, such as 'Richard of York gave battle in vain' for the colours of the visible spectrum (which inevitably prompts children to ask about indigo!). 'Meaningful learning' contrasts with this because it results in knowledge that is not superficial or arbitrary but is well connected with other knowledge.

> [M]eaningful learning takes place if the learning task can be related in non-arbitrary, substantive (non-verbatim) fashion to what the learner already knows ... Rote learning, on the other hand, occurs if the learning task consists of purely arbitrary associations ... if the learner lacks the relevant prior knowledge necessary for making the learning task potentially meaningful, and also (regardless of how much potential meaning the task has) if the learner adopts a set merely to internalize it in an arbitrary, verbatim fashion (that is, as an arbitrary series of words).
>
> (Ausubel, 1963: 27)

Ausubel's distinction between rote and meaningful learning is complex. Learning can, for example, be both meaningful and rote, depending on context. In school, children sometimes learn to use technical language in skilful, socially meaningful ways, without having any technical understanding of the words. John Holt described this as 'right-answerism': it gets teachers off pupils' backs. In a study of 16-year-olds who had been taught about 'the living cell', Dreyfuss and Jungwirth found that pupils had invented a variety of explanations for the scientific phenomena in question, irrespective of the technical plausibility of the explanations:

> such pupil explanations of 'abstract' biological phenomena are usually never discussed by the teachers ... Pupils then adopt them because of their efficacy, not in the solving of scientific problems, but in satisfying the teachers
>
> (Dreyfuss and Jungwirth, 1989: 51)

There are traps for the unsuspecting teacher here. I fell into one when my daughter announced that her class was 'doing buildings next term' and could I tell her something about them? Over the next few days we had stories and drawings of bridges, walls, portal frames, triangles and arches. Finally I suggested we finish off with doors, windows and lintels. I drew a brick wall with a hole in for a window. We agreed that the window probably couldn't hold up the weight of the bricks above it. I drew another wall with a window hole and a space above for a lintel. 'What shall we do to hold the bricks up?' I asked. 'Use a lintel!' was the confident answer. I was in the process of congratulating myself about my teaching when came the question, 'Dad … what's a lintel?'

Another distinction drawn by Ausubel concerns the situations in which people learn. One extreme is 'reception learning', where people are completely passive in a social sense, that is, they just 'sit there'. Ausubel contrasted this with 'discovery learning' where in order to learn anything of substance, the person has to do something. Both of these learning situations have been sharply criticised. After a period in the 1960s and 1970s when discovery learning was fashionable in science education, it has gone out of vogue. The trouble was that it clashed with the curriculum: students didn't always discover what they were supposed to. There is little educational support for reception learning but it may be thought to have an economic advantage: mass lecturing, or computer-based alternatives to lecturing save on teachers' pay.

Memory: Gagné et al.

Robert Gagné (I pronounce his name 'Gan yay') developed a model of how human memory functions, with a corresponding model of how 'bits' of knowledge get remembered. Memory is essential: without it there can be no learning. If we can theorise about how we remember, some useful implications for teaching may arise.

Gagné (1977) and later, Gunstone, White and others suggested that we remember knowledge in the form of various types of memory elements. White's (1988) version is given in Table 4.1. In his richly informative book *Learning Science*, White explored this model and its implications for teaching. White and Gunstone (1992) developed this approach further.

Table 4.1 Seven types of memory element

Element	Brief definition	Example
String	A sequence of words or symbols recalled as a whole in an invariate form	'To every action there is equal and opposite reaction'
Proposition	A description of a property of a concept or of the relation between concepts	The yeast plant is unicellular
Image	A mental representation of a sensation	The shape of a thistle funnel; the smell of chlorine
Episode	Memory of an event one took part in or witnessed	An accident in the laboratory; the setting up of a microscope
Intellectual skill	The capacity to perform a whole class of mental tasks	Balancing chemical equations
Motor skill	The capacity to perform a whole class of physical task	Pouring a liquid to a mark
Cognitive strategy	A general skill involved in controlling thinking	Perceiving alternative interpretations; determining goals; judging likelihood of success

Engage and connect

If I want to learn about something, I focus my attention on it. Attention seems to me to be necessary for learning. (The question of just how much attention is needed is interesting. While asleep we learn how to cope with the edge of the bed so as not to fall out; this suggests a minimum level of attention for learning.)

Why don't students pay attention to teachers all the time? I think the answer is because it would be unnatural to do so. Curiosity is a human characteristic. We inherit a roving attention, which is adept at scanning the environment. Particular things capture our attention naturally: movement, change in environment, unusual or surprising things, attractive and interesting things, and so on. The teacher is part of the student's environment and the teacher's actions compete with many other things, external and internal to the student, for the student's attention and engagement. It sometimes surprises me how much attention some teachers manage to get, given the competition!

Attention may not be enough. People obviously pay attention when driving or riding a bike but they can rarely provide much detail about a completed journey. If, say, you knew you were going to be asked how many traffic lights you stopped at or whether there was a post box on a particular corner, you would focus your attention on that particular issue. You would be 'engaging' with the issue. In the cognitive domain (which includes much of school science) for anything more than superficial learning to occur, engagement is necessary. How is engagement different from attention? I see the difference in terms of action – action on the focus of engagement. Attention is needed in order to navigate traffic lights but engagement is needed in order to count them. Piaget stressed how vital action is for learning. This is sometimes interpreted as implying physical activity but I am sure he was referring to mental activity, or 'operating' on the focus of the learning. This has an implication for teaching. If engagement is important for learning and action is important for engagement, teaching should be more than just 'show and tell'. It should include 'doing'. One way is to set learners tasks of applying ideas. Many student teachers will have first-hand experience of this, as it is often said that you learn something best when you have to teach it – in other words, when you apply your knowledge.

It was remarked earlier in this chapter that learning is now widely regarded as a process of constructing. New knowledge is sometimes said to be constructed by synthesising current experiences and current knowledge. I don't think this is quite right, since it looks like mixing apples and pears. I prefer to think of the new knowledge as emerging from thinking about current experiences and about current knowledge, with the thinking itself influenced by current knowledge. I'm including conscious and non-conscious thoughts in this. If this all seems rather abstract, hold on to the central point: learning arises from making constructions between the present and the past. We learn all the time. We're always making meaning of the present in terms of what we know – is it familiar, or is it novel? It is in our biology to do this.

The affective domain

Mental activity is sometimes described in terms of knowledge, feelings and emotions. The first of these is the 'cognitive domain' and the other two constitute the 'affective domain'. Educational research and classroom teaching have both tended to focus attention on cognition. But there are those who argue that the affective domain cannot be ignored. 'Affect', a person's emotional and intentional state, is a gate-keeper to cognition. A familiar example is motivation – a person's will or intention to act or think.

We can explore this now. You're reading this text: do you sense any influences, acting on you right now, competing with each other to determine what your mind dwells on next? I am aware of several current influences: I want to finish this chapter, I am thinking rationally about what I'm writing and I would like another mug of tea! Are children's thoughts in the classroom all that different? In the vividly-titled paper, 'Cognition doesn't matter if you're scared, depressed or bored', Guy Claxton (1989) describes a set of pupil 'stances' which determine not only the 'amount' of learning that takes place but also the direction or domain in which it takes place. Claxton's labels are deliberately evocative: swot, thinker, boffin, socialite, dreamer, rebel and sinker. This classification is not based on any empirical data; nonetheless the stances have some 'chalk-face' appeal and they lend support to the argument that 'attitude' and 'motivation' are key elements in determining learning.

The idea that people have different intelligences in different fields such as maths, art, personal interaction, sport and so on has been around for several years (e.g. Gardner, 1993b). Schools have focused on cognitive intelligence, however, rather than other fields. As the view has grown that the affect strongly influences cognition, there have been calls for greater attention to be given to emotional intelligence, motivation and student self-image. There is 'an incontrovertible link between how pupils perceive themselves as learners and their subsequent capacity to achieve' (Broadfoot, 1998). In one study described by Salmon (1995), some children were asked to attempt some school-type tasks. After doing some of the tasks the children were asked to pretend that they were 'boffins', or high flyers. The standard they achieved while pretending was markedly higher! A strong influence on students' self-image is the expectations that the teacher holds for them. This conclusion is supported in many studies, one of which led to it becoming known as the 'Pygmalion effect' (Rosenthal, 1968).

'Learning styles'

During the last third of the twentieth century the learner has moved from the periphery to a central position in educational discourse. With this shift, interest has grown in attempts to describe the learner so that he or she is less of a 'black box' to teachers and other education professionals. What makes learners tick? Why do they learn well sometimes and not at all at other times? These are important questions, well worth asking. In the face of 'big questions' like these there is pressure to come up with answers of some kind. Two that have emerged involve 'learning styles' and 'brain-based learning'. The learning styles account argues that people have their own dominant ways of approaching learning tasks. One of the most widely found versions is that there are three distinguishable styles: visual, auditory and kinaesthetic. This scheme is often abbreviated to VAK. While writing this I did a web search with the phrase 'VAK learning' and received over 300,000 hits. (That's up 400 per cent in the last three years.) You might like to try looking at some of the hits yourself. My guess is that it won't be long before you start feeling a little sceptical.

Inevitably, students have begun to latch on to the idea of fixed learning styles. Coffield et al. (2004, p. 137) report a member of their research team overhearing a student say, 'I learned that I was a low auditory, kinaesthetic learner. So there's no point in me reading a book or listening to anyone for more than a few minutes.' Most teachers wouldn't be taken in by that but there is a serious underlying point, namely that the VAK movement propagates the idea that each person has their own learning style as part of their makeup, a part of who they are. This is to ignore the fact that we humans appear to be the most versatile and resourceful learners on Earth. We are champions at adapting to the situations we find ourselves in. This is just as well because we don't seem to have many other outstanding attributes. Compared with other animals with whom our ancestors would have had to compete to survive we are not exceptionally strong, fast or fertile – we are just extremely flexible learners. We cope well with visual experiences – although not as well as birds. We are good with auditory experiences – though dogs are better. And we can dance and catch cricket balls, though monkeys are generally nimbler. Robert Leamnson (1999, p. 90) rejects the proposal that people have fixed learning styles. He argues that, 'learning styles map properly onto topics or subjects and not onto people' (p. 91). Leamnson argues that we have learning *preferences* that are context dependent – that is, we learn in particular ways in particular contexts.

A further problem with learning styles accounts is that if someone is labelled as, say, a visual learner, what are the implications? Should they look for opportunities to learn in visually rich contexts or should they look to develop other 'styles'? Labelling, especially in a dynamic context like learning, risks closing down one's willingness to engage with events and processes that lie outside the scope of the label. The risk is that the label becomes a new reality.

VAK is just one of many schemes that claim to describe and categorise people's learning styles. Are there other schemes, perhaps with a stronger research basis? In a substantial research report on the field of learning styles, with particular reference to post-16 teaching, Coffield *et al.* (2004) gave little cause for optimism. Their evaluation 'showed that some of the best known and widely used instruments have such serious weaknesses (e.g. low reliability, poor validity and negligible impact on pedagogy) that we recommend that their use in research and in practice should be discontinued' (p. 138). Ironically the instrument found to have the best psychometric credentials, the Allinson and Hayes 'Cognitive Style index', was designed for organisational and business applications.

A positive feature of the learning styles discourse is that it is at least partly driven by, and has helped to drive, interest in the learner. But as Coffield *et al.* (2004, p. 137) put it, 'the status of research in this field is not helped by the overblown claims of some of the developers and their enthusiastic devotees'.

I agree with Leamnson that it is more useful to think of learners' preferences than learning styles. Preferences are behaviours that can change and develop. Learning styles can too easily be taken as labels that limit people's expectations. More fruitful than labelling learners is to watch and listen to them, so as to diagnose their current learning needs. Diagnostic teaching, which we examine in depth in later parts of this chapter, focuses on learning but doesn't attach labels to learners.

'Brain-based learning'

Have you ever wondered where you are? Or whether you actually even exist? René Descartes solved the first problem by inventing Cartesian coordinates, a three-dimensional map reference system. He solved the second too, well before *Blade Runner* or *The Matrix*. He concluded he must exist because he knew he was thinking. He wrote (in Latin), 'I think therefore I am'. He was deeply interested in the mind and because he was clever and famous his ideas were influential. One of his big ideas was that the mind and the body are two quite separate things. This is an example of 'dualism'. Mind–body dualism has made a lasting impression on western thought. It quietly underpins many people's 'worldviews' – assumptions that are taken for granted and are normally unstated. Contemporary scientists, on the other hand, usually subscribe to 'monism', the view that there is just physical stuff and nothing else, or at least nothing else that science can describe. Not surprisingly, then, contemporary neuroscientists are generally monists, which means that they regard the mind as arising, somehow, from properties of matter, and in particular the matter that makes up the body. This 'embodied mind' view is economical and simple, in that it doesn't invent anything mystical to try to explain things, which dualist accounts tend to do. On the other hand it doesn't explain everything. For instance, nobody has yet explained how electrochemical processes in the brain result in conscious experience. You can look up from this sentence, notice something, think about it, look back to this sentence and be aware of doing all of that, without any of it feeling like electrochemistry. But then again, what *does* internal bodily electrochemistry feel like? At least one philosopher (Colin McGinn, 1989) has argued that the problem of accounting for conscious processes in terms of brain processes is too complex for us ever to solve!

To say that the brain is complex is probably the biggest understatement you will find in this chapter. There are more possible neuronal combinations in a single human brain than there are atoms in the known universe. An additional complication is that it is very difficult to do experiments to find out how human brains work – there are some appropriately impenetrable ethical boundaries in the way. At present neuroscience can point to correlations between some patterns of brain activity and some types of conscious experience. This is a very long way from talking about neurons for doing maths or for playing the guitar. Does this mean that neuroscience has nothing to contribute to current understandings about learning? I think the answer to this, with one exception, is yes. I haven't seen a 'brain-based learning' course or resource that has offered any credible neuroscientific justification for the claims they have made. Yes, if kids improve their fitness or do interesting group projects their school performance may well improve. That is probably because they feel better about themselves than before, which is great. But claims about brain processes such as 'X stimulates the brain to think better' or 'brains do well in conditions of Y' are little more than pseudoscientific 'just so' stories for marketing purposes. A recent example is that Mozart's music is good for babies' brains before they are born. Although I like Mozart's music I'm highly sceptical that it can be identified as a causal factor in the development of a foetus. Is there a chance that a home environment in which Mozart is heard might have other features that are conducive to healthy development?

There is, though, one area where neuroscience can be related to learning: 'neuronal selection'. There are two key points. First, it is widely believed that the phrase 'use it or lose it' applies to synapses, the connections between neurons. That fits with the commonsense observation that practice leads to improvement. Secondly, it has been forcefully argued by Gerald Edelman (1992) that, 'neurons that fire together wire together'. This process can be related to several aspects of learning. One of the most basic, one that we have all done automatically since soon after birth, is to construct our knowledge of the objects that we experience around us. Picture a baby in her chair with a new coloured toy on a tray in front of her. As far as we can imagine it, look at this from the baby's perspective. The toy doesn't come with labels telling the baby, 'I am blue, smooth, squashy, round, I make a noise when shaken, I'm called a ball'. Instead the baby looks, reaches, grasps, squeezes, shakes, sucks, drops – and in the process has a whole spectrum of experiences from her senses of vision, touch (surface texture, temperature, hardness, weight), hearing and perhaps taste. Many of these experiences are simultaneous, presumably involving neurons firing together. Through repetition of simultaneous experiences like these, Edelman argues, a particular neuronal activity pattern will come to be established in the baby's brain that correlates with the particular combination of seeing, touching and hearing sensations. It seems plausible that the establishment of this pattern corresponds to the baby's construction of her 'conceptual scheme' (as Piaget might have called it) of the toy. In other words, the embodiment of the baby's conceptualisation of the toy is the neuronal activity pattern.

This account proves nothing about the relationship between learning (in this case learning about the nature of a toy) and brain processes. We are a long way from that. But it may convince you that a neuroscientific account and a constructivist view of learning may in some respects be compatible with one another, and that's a start. For further reading in this fascinating field see Zull (2002) for a broad biological perspective, Edelman and Tononi (2000) and Frith (2007) for accounts from neurobiology, Plotkin (1994) for an evolutionary psychologist's view and Dennett (1991) and Searle (1997) for philosophers' perspectives.

Is that it on learning?

No, for two reasons. Firstly, this chapter contains my selection of significant theoretical views on learning and other people may have made other selections or may view mine differently; secondly this is a rapidly developing field and new ideas are currently emerging. As Edelman puts it:

> We are at the beginning of a neuroscientific revolution. At its end, we shall know how the mind works, what governs our nature, and how we know the world. Indeed, what is now going on in neuroscience may be looked at as a prelude to the largest possible scientific revolution, one with inevitable and important social consequences.
>
> (Edelman, 1992)

Children's ideas in science

One of the main themes of this chapter so far is that a person's current knowledge and ideas strongly influence what they will learn. When applied to science teaching, this prompts the following questions: do children have any ideas in science and if so, what are they like?

In an investigation of their understanding of the word *plant,* children were asked: Would you say any of these pictures are of plants? (Osborne and Freyberg, 1985: 6); see Figure 4.4. This response from a 9-year-old is not atypical: 'Grass is a plant; a seed is a plant – well it'll grow into a plant. Definitely not a carrot – it's a vegetable. And not an oak tree; it's a small tree then it's a big tree, not a plant.'

A response like this indicates that the child has definite ideas about the scientific topic (classification, in this case) and further, that these ideas are not the same as the scientific community's views.

Another study reported by Osborne and Freyberg used cards like those shown in Figure 4.5 to investigate children's views about light. Concerning card (a) students were asked: Does the candle make light? What happens to the light? Where it was relevant the children were then asked: How far does the light from the candle go?

Following the last question, four students said: 'One metre at the most'; 'About one foot'; 'Just stays there and lights up'; 'Stays there'. Two of these responses came from 10-year-olds and two from 15-year-olds. The 15-year-olds had studied light as a science topic and they could define terms like refraction and reflection reasonably well!

Commonality of alternative ideas

In the course of a major survey in England, Northern Ireland and Wales (see note 3), the Assessment of Performance Unit asked 15-year-olds of all attainment backgrounds the following

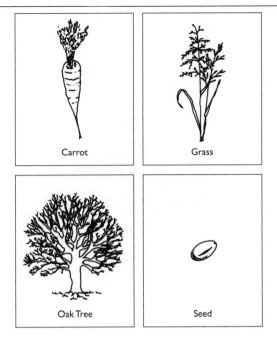

Figure 4.4 'Would you say this was a plant?'
Source: Osborne and Freyberg (1985)

Figure 4.5 'Does the candle make light?'
Source: Osborne and Freyberg (1985)

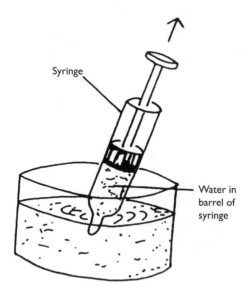

Figure 4.6 Diagnostic question: syringe
Source: Holding *et al.* (1990)

question (see Figure 4.6): 'When the plunger of this syringe is pulled up, water goes into the barrel of the syringe. What makes the water go into the syringe? Explain as fully as you can.'

Here is a sample of students' written responses (including original spellings, emphases etc.), reported in Holding *et al.* (1990: 42):

- The water goes up into the syringe because of two reasons: (1) atmospheric pressure pushing down on the water; (2) *the suction* and less atmospheric pressure inside the syringe.
- The sucktion of the handle and the vaccum caused makes the water travel up the syringe.
- Air pressure on the surface of the water forces the liquid in to the barrel of the syringe.
- As the syringe is drawn up it creates a vacume thus somthing has to fill the vaccume. The watter is therefore sucked in.

Again, these responses show different views from those held in the scientific community but this time there is evidence of a clear, coherent alternative idea, namely that *suction* is an active causal agency.

Commonality between some of the alternative views held by students about science has been revealed regularly in research carried out by the Children's Learning in Science (CLIS) team at Leeds University (see, e.g., Brook *et al.*, 1984). The team found, for example, that:

- many children use 'heat' and 'temperature' synonymously;
- the sensation of coldness is due to transfer of 'cold' towards the body;
- particles swell: this explains pressure change and expansion;
- the word 'mixture' is often used for 'compound';
- 'food' for plants is anything taken in from the outside, e.g. water, minerals, air.

Some of these more commonly occurring ideas will be familiar to teachers. But sometimes the ideas seem so disconnected from the teacher's that their origins appear to be a complete mystery: 'They focus on things I would never dream of looking at!' said an experienced teacher about children's practical work.

Useful summaries of research into children's ideas can be found in Driver *et al.* (1985 and 1994), and Osborne and Freyberg (1985). The journal *School Science Review* is another good source.

What children make of science lessons

In a short, informative paper Ross Tasker (1981) reported the findings of a series of classroom observations of 11–14-year-old children in typical science lessons. The aim of the study was to learn about children's perceptions and interpretations of practical work. Tasker found that there was often a large mismatch between teachers' and children's views about what was taking place.

- Teachers saw connections between lessons but students saw them as stand-alone events.
- Students tended not to connect the work they were doing with other science they had met. Teachers, on the other hand, referred to such connections as if they were self-evident.
- Students often have completely different ideas from the teacher about the purpose of a lesson or an activity.
- Two common purposes from the students' viewpoint are 'to follow the instructions' and 'to get the right answer'. When asked why they are following instructions, students are likely to reply 'because he/she told us to'.
- Teachers may wrongly assume that students understand experimental procedures and have appropriate skills, such as how to use a balance. Tasker noted that this particular mismatch was liable to lead to off-task and possibly disruptive behaviour.
- Teachers may wrongly assume a level of conceptual knowledge of science in students.
- Students see things differently from teachers. Something that the teacher regards as trivial may be regarded as highly significant by the students and vice versa. (One instance from my own teaching arose with the use of digital ammeters. I wanted to show the same current on either side of a bulb and I duly got readings such as 0.123 A and 0.124 A. Some students saw the difference and concluded that current is indeed used up in the bulb! I have used analogue meters ever since.)

Retention of understanding

As infants, we learn a few words and then our vocabularies go on growing through to old age. Many people learn to crawl, then walk, then swim, and then perhaps ride a bike. By the time we might learn to drive a car we have constructed and retained much knowledge about movement. Such knowledge has proved stable; once learnt it tends not to be lost. Is this also the case with learning in formal science?

Consider the following account of Vanessa, an 11-year-old whose science lessons had included a topic on electric current. Vanessa was interviewed some months after the topic had been taught. She was asked to connect up a bulb to a battery, which she achieved quickly and correctly. She was then presented with the question shown in Figure 4.7, which she had previously encountered during the teaching of the topic.

A battery is connected to a torch bulb as shown in the diagram:
The bulb is glowing.

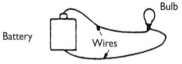

In the way you think about it, the electric current in the wires is best described
by which diagram?

There will be no electric
current in the wire attached
to the base of the battery.

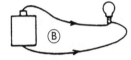

The electric current will
be in a direction towards
the bulb in both wires.

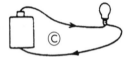

The direction of the electric
current will be as shown. The
current will be less in the
'return' wire.

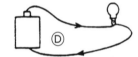

The direction of the electric
current will be as shown. The
current will be the same in
both wires.

Figure 4.7 Diagnostic question about electric current
Source: Osborne and Freyberg (1985)

VANESSA: At first I thought it was Model B, because I didn't realise that if it was B the battery
would go flat very soon. So now I think Model C is best … quite a bit of current
comes into the bulb, and some of it wasted up. It can't take it all at once so some
of it takes it back.

INTERVIEWER: Did you do things with meters? (Experimentally test which model is valid)

VANESSA: Yeah, we found that Model D worked with the meters. But I don't understand D.
I know it works but I don't understand how it works.

INTERVIEWER: Did your teacher discuss it?

VANESSA: Yes, and I kind of knew how that went … it made sense a little bit … but afterwards
I thought of some other ideas … How did that work? … What happened? and,
How did he explain …? I got muddled up. If you are not using any power in the
bulb how is it going on? But I understand C.

                               (Osborne and Freyberg, 1985: 25 and 96–97)

Vanessa's description of her thinking is revealing. She remembered that Model D was the
official answer and indeed at the time of teaching 'it made sense a little bit'. But despite this she
has chosen Model C. This is not arbitrary; her reasoning is that some of the current is 'wasted
up'. It is evident that she has compacted the notions of current and energy into something that
has properties of both. The very reasonable view that: 'If you are not using any power in the
bulb, how is it going on?' has been made equivalent to current getting used up. Perhaps the

Table 4.2 Changes in the views of a group of 11-year-olds over time

	A (%)	B (%)	C (%)	D (%)
Before lessons	0	7	86	7
After lessons	0	0	14	86
One year later	0	13	40	47

Source: Osborne and Freyberg (1985)

key to Vanessa's selection is in the last sentence. She was able to answer Model D during the teaching, knowing that this was the appropriate answer for the formal context of the science class. But her belief in C, stemming from her construction of an adequately consistent rationale for understanding it, has resulted in Model C being retained in the longer term.

This trend of regression towards intuitive or internally consistent knowledge is also evident in the data in Table 4.2 (Osborne and Freyberg, 1985: 122) from a group of fifteen 11-year-olds who were given the same question as Vanessa.

Science teachers' ideas in science

In the national curriculum of England and Wales, science is a very broad subject. It contains strands of astronomy, biology, chemistry, earth science and physics. In contrast with this, the typical degrees held by science teachers and student teachers are narrow. I have yet to meet a student teacher who has been justifiably confident in all strands of the Key Stage 3 science curriculum (for most 11–14-year-olds). Many experienced science teachers have gaps in their curriculum knowledge. Knowing about the gaps is half the battle. From 1999 onwards, newly qualified science teachers in Britain have been required by the Department for Education (DfE; see note 4) to have found and filled their gaps at Key Stage 3 during their initial teacher education courses. Responsibility for this falls in large measure on the student teachers themselves, because of the short time they spend in university or college and because of the teaching commitments of staff in schools.

One way of identifying gaps that has been used successfully by student teachers is to use the sort of diagnostic questions described in the previous section. These were devised for researching children's ideas but they have also proved very handy for probing adults' understanding of science at this level. Here are some for you to try.

1   A ball is thrown up into the air. As it travels up, what do you think happens to: its speed? its acceleration? the force on it?
2   When water boils in a pan or kettle, big bubbles appear. What do you think is in the bubbles? (a) air; (b) nothing; (c) water vapour; (d) a mixture of hydrogen and oxygen gases?
3   Vanessa's question, in Figure 4.7.

For several years I have given student teachers a set of diagnostic physics questions and asked them to rate their confidence in their responses. These are the results:

•   The most problematic topic was mechanics.
•   The topic in which they were least confident was current electricity.
•   The average of the men's and women's scores were similar.

- The men rated their knowledge much higher than did the women; relative to their performance scores the men tended to be over-confident and the women under-confident.

In some cases, before tackling the diagnostic questions the student teachers had self-assessed their knowledge by going through the national curriculum. Compared with the self-assessment, the diagnostic survey was far more informative and useful in highlighting the gaps that the students needed to address.

Assessing for learning

'Assessment for learning', diagnostic and formative assessment

Together with learning, teaching and curriculum, assessment is a core aspect of education in schools and colleges. The phrase 'assessment for learning', or 'AfL', has gained considerable currency in Britain and beyond in recent years, as a web search readily shows. Much of the credit for this is owed to Paul Black and Dylan Wiliam through the impact of their 'black box' research work (see Black and Wiliam, 1998a and 1998b, and Black *et al.*, 2004). Their review has been highly influential, not least in informing UK government policy on assessment in schools in the first decade of the twenty-first century. Black and Wiliam discussed 'assessment for learning' not simply as three familiar words joined in a phrase but as a new concept – a new focus for assessment in classrooms. By 2004, AfL was a recurrent theme in government publications on school improvement.

Black and Wiliam's work was commissioned by the Assessment Reform Group (2005). This group provided a practical definition of AfL by describing 'assessment that promotes learning' as follows (Assessment Reform Group, 1999):

- It is embedded in a view of teaching and learning of which it is an essential part.
- It involves sharing learning goals with pupils.
- It aims to help pupils to know and to recognise the standards they are aiming for.
- It involves pupils in self-assessment.
- It provides feedback which leads to pupils recognising their next steps and how to take them.
- It is underpinned by confidence that every student can improve.
- It involves both teacher and pupils reviewing and reflecting on assessment data.

Other assessment-related terms can also be heard in schools: summative, formative and sometimes diagnostic assessment. How do these differ from AfL and from each other? I have found it very useful to distinguish different types of assessment activities according to the *purpose to which the activity is put*. In other words, it's not the method or arrangement that I'm highlighting but the aim behind the assessment. Here are three distinct types and purposes:

- Formative assessment: to enhance the learning of those being assessed, through informing them about their assessed performance.
- Diagnostic assessment: to enhance the teacher's understanding of the learning needs of the learners.
- Summative assessment: to inform third parties about the assessed performance of the learners, possibly leading to grading by an external body.

The term AfL is 'teacher-friendly' and its introduction has highlighted that there is more to assessment than just the summative variety. I think it makes sense to regard diagnostic and formative assessment as types of AfL. It is, though, valuable to distinguish between them so that they can be used under the teacher's design in practical teaching. Formative assessment (FA) is intended to put learners in the picture – to inform them about how they are doing and where they need to focus their efforts. FA can be done by the teacher, by the learner or by the learner's peers. FA is compatible with a constructivist view of learning because in that view learning is not 'done to' learners but can only be done by learners themselves. It is helpful, therefore, for them to find out about their learning needs and also about the knowledge that they have already successfully constructed. It may also be argued that formative assessment contributes to the development of a sense of responsibility in learners for their own learning. In addition, effective formative assessment can counter the unfortunate view that learning is, in the 'real world', just about making the right impression.

The direct beneficiary of diagnostic assessment is the teacher. The indirect beneficiaries are the learners. Diagnostic assessment fits well with constructivism because constructivists (such as Piaget and Vygotsky) hold that people's current knowledge and ways of learning are highly influential on their future learning and development. A teacher who teaches without diagnostic information is forced to rely on habit and guesswork. Diagnostic assessment enables the teacher to tune their teaching to the current knowledge and ways of learning of the learners.

When teachers first encounter the idea that learning is strongly influenced by what the learner already knows, they are understandably bothered about coping with up to 30 different learners, each with their own starting points. This would be impossible to deal with if all of the children had strikingly different ideas. Fortunately for class teaching however, there are often just a few commonly occurring alternatives amongst children's ideas. Some examples were discussed earlier in this chapter. Research into children's pre-teaching or 'prior' ideas has provided a platform on which science teaching can build. It has shown that it is worthwhile for teachers to diagnose children's prior ideas and that the results of the diagnosis are manageable: they can be used by the teacher. A teacher summed this up neatly to me like this: 'I take my starting point from the kids'.

There are at least three other good reasons for diagnosing students' knowledge:

1 To evaluate learning after teaching. This gives the teacher feedback on the effectiveness of her/his teaching;
2 To be able to map progression in the students' ideas;
3 To check for retention: in other words, to check whether new understandings have been retained weeks or even months after the teaching.

The value to teachers of diagnostic information about learners has been forcefully emphasised by Hattie (2009). In a synthesis of an enormous number of studies about factors influencing learning, Hattie concluded that, 'The most powerful single influence enhancing achievement is feedback … the most important feature was the creation of situations in classrooms for the teachers to receive more feedback' (p. 12). The interesting thing about this is that the feedback that Hattie is referring to is not given by teachers to learners. It is diagnostic feedback *to* teachers. 'When teachers seek … feedback from students as to what students know, what they understand, where they make errors, when they have misconceptions, when they are not engaged – then teaching and learning can be synchronised and powerful. Feedback to teachers helps make learning visible' (Hattie, 2009, p. 173).

The combination of diagnostic assessment plus teaching response is known as diagnostic teaching. An example of diagnostic teaching and some practical ways of diagnosing students' ideas are included later in this chapter.

Assessing pupils' progress (APP) and the Assessment for Learning Strategy (AfLS)

The origins of APP and AfLS in schools can, I think, be traced to three roughly simultaneous developments: Black and Wiliam's 'black box' research on assessment and learning, concern about standards of attainment in Key Stage 3 leading to publication of the National Strategy for Key Stage 3, and the death of a child, Victoria Climbié, in tragic circumstances. I will briefly expand on the latter two:

1   At the same time as Black and Wiliam's work, official concerns began to surface about the academic progress that children were making during Key Stage 3 (from ages 11 to 14). The government response to this was to publish a National Strategy for Key Stage 3, the aim of which was explicit: school improvement. The National Strategy began in schools in 2001 in English and maths, with science being added in the following year. The KS3 Framework for teaching science (Department for Education and Skills, 2002) included 'suggestions and advice' on assessment and target setting. This contained implicit reference to diagnostic assessment, diagnostic teaching and formative assessment (p. 49) and explicit reference to APP (p. 51). APP was described as teacher assessment to be 'made against the relevant yearly teaching objectives for each year for the unit of work' (p. 51).

2   In September 2003, 'Every Child Matters' (ECM) was published as part of the government's response to the Laming report into the death of Victoria Climbié. One of Laming's messages was that the social, health and education services were not adequately joined up; they were not talking to each other and as a result there were gaps in support for children in need. Victoria Climbié fell into a gap between the services. On the back of ECM the government committed itself to an educational initiative called 'personalised learning' (PL). The subtitle of a Department for Education and Skills (2004) publication makes the intention clear: 'How can we put the learner at the heart of the Education system?'

APP, AfL and PL continued to be prominent in DfE publications to the end of the first decade of the twenty-first century. The change of UK government in 2010, however, brought about an official cooling towards PL. By January 2011, the 2008 DCSF document, 'Personalised Learning – a practical guide' was archived and its webpage warned that the publication 'should not be considered to reflect current policy'. No such relegation has befallen AfL or APP. Perhaps this is no surprise; the PL initiative was overtly political, with explicit reference to the need for learning support for children from economically and socially disadvantaged contexts. In contrast, the scope of AfL and APP is very much confined to the classroom.

The main aim of the introduction of AfL was to encourage teachers to adopt new assessment practices. These practices were intended to be part of normal lessons. How has it turned out? With the help of cooperating teachers, Black and Wiliam successfully piloted AfL techniques such as question–answer sessions with 'no hands up'; 'traffic lights' in which pupils feed back to the teacher about work they've been doing using red, yellow or green cards or voters; 'comment-only marking' and 'show me' boards (mini-whiteboards) on which pupils can give brief individual responses to a question. A very simple, quick (and free!) way to get basic diagnostic information from pupils that has become popular in schools is 'thumbs': put your thumb up if you feel confident about what we've just done, thumb down if you're not happy about it and sideways if you're in between. Why 'no hands up'? It's because a problem with whole-class questioning is that some pupils tend to put their hands up every time a question is asked – and some never do. (An excerpt showing some pupils' views on putting hands up can be viewed here: http://www.bbc.co.uk/programmes/p00b1yc7.) One way to avoid the problem is to select pupils at random by having their names on lollipop sticks and picking a stick from a tin without looking at the name. The value of Black and Wiliam's work can be seen from the fact that these techniques can now be found in use in many classrooms. Video clips of AfL techniques in action are carried on www.teachers.tv which is available from a number of online distributors. For instance, using the distributor site www.teachersmedia.co.uk the search term 'lollipop' will take you here: http://www.teachers.tv/videos/effective-inclusion-bringing-special-school-experience-into-the-mainstream-classroom. Between 1'40 and 2'40 of this clip a teacher can be seen using and talking about the lollipop sticks questioning method.

These AfL practices are well worth trying out to see how they work for you. However, a note of caution is in order. When one of the authors of the CASE thinking skills programme, described later in this chapter, was asked how just 30 CASE lessons could have brought about big improvements in pupils' grades, he explained that it was unlikely that the 30 lessons were the direct cause. It was much more likely that the participating teachers had come to understand the basis and purposes of the CASE approach. This understanding had probably permeated all of their teaching and it was that that had produced the impressive outcomes. I suspect exactly the same applies to AfL. When teachers have an understanding of the basis and purpose for AfL it is likely that they will 'get it right' more often than not. But if the practices become detached from their underlying rationale they risk becoming little more than performances of currently fashionable teaching practices. (An inoculation against this is to keep asking oneself and colleagues, 'what are we doing this for?') Swaffield (2009) is also worried about this. She sees the AfL Strategy (though not AfL itself) as permeated by implications of, and references to, summative aspects of APP, and in particular by testing using 'convergent' assessment criteria for judging whether pupils match prescribed objectives, as opposed to finding out (using 'divergent' assessment) what they *can* do.

What about APP? One difference between APP and AfL is their timescales. AfL occurs within lessons whereas APP is described in government guidance as 'medium term assessment', taking place in cycles of weeks or months. When APP was introduced teachers were reassured that it didn't involve any additional testing: good news! Instead, teachers were to gather evidence of pupils' performance from multiple sources on an occasional basis. Since the aim of APP is 'school improvement' and specifically the raising of standards of progress during a key stage, APP requires teachers to synthesise the data they have generated and match it to national standards in curriculum-based themes. That's no small task. The national curriculum level descriptions are relatively coarse, which can be useful for summative statements but is not so useful if a profile of pupil progress is wanted. This is where 'assessment focuses' (AFs) come onto the scene. The AFs for science 'are linked to the National Curriculum programmes of study and the level descriptions, and are designed to give a detailed, analytic view of pupils' attainment across all the key stages and in all areas of science' (Department for Children, Schools and Families, 2010). There are five AFs in science: thinking scientifically, understanding the applications and implications of science, communicating and collaborating in science, using investigative approaches, and working critically with evidence. It is tempting to read that list and think: 'these are educationally valuable things to emphasise: it's a good idea to make them focuses for assessment'. On the other hand they represent a big conceptual and administrative challenge for teachers. What the teacher has to do is select episodes in a range of lessons that lend themselves to assessing pupils' performance using detailed statements in the AFs. This results in a profile for each pupil consisting of five levels, one for each AF. The profile is then condensed into a single statement. Let's see how it might look: if Anna's work over a period of time was judged to have been at levels 5, 5, 6, 5, 5 in the five AFs then Anna would be reported to be at 'high level 5'. If Ravi's profile was 6, 5, 6, 6, 6 he would be at 'secure level 6'. For the purpose of supporting learning the teacher's detailed judgements against the AF statements are likely to be more helpful than the overall level. This is because the detail can be used diagnostically (by the teacher) and formatively (by the pupil) to target learning needs in specific areas.

Swaffield (2009) can see a time when APP will fall out of favour, 'like every other standards driven strategy'. She is concerned that AfL may then slip away too, tainted by association with APP. I think there is an alternative and more positive future, in which AfL is practised by teachers who are clear about its purposes and connections with learning. Perhaps in that scenario APP might evolve to become a medium-term version of AfL that enables teachers to acknowledge diverse learning achievements.

Progression

One of the DfE requirements for new teachers is that they should, 'Evaluate the impact of their teaching on the progress of all learners, and modify their planning and classroom practice where necessary' (Teacher Development Agency, 2007). This is easier to say than do. Most science departments rely on published courses to present curriculum material in an appropriate sequence and at a suitable depth. A common approach is a 'spiral curriculum' in which topics are periodically revisited during a child's schooling, each time at a higher level. This ensures that the curriculum is organised sensibly for teaching but it cannot guarantee anything about children's learning. Some forms of assessment are needed to check that students' knowledge is progressing at a reasonable rate and to check the match between the curriculum and the students' capabilities. Ordinary pen-and-paper end of topic tests give some indication, but of what? A colleague and I have argued that traditional assessment tends to reward factual recall and low-level thinking in science (Abdullah and Scaife, 1997). A different approach to checking progression is to use student interviews before and after teaching a topic. Interviews can be time consuming and it would only be practical for a teacher to survey a sample of students in a class. Nevertheless interviews can provide rich and detailed information about students' knowledge and understanding. We used semi-structured interviews, designed to keep students talking about the science topic but leaving them otherwise unconstrained. Interviews were recorded and the responses were analysed using a framework derived from White and Gunstone (1992). Students' propositions (assertions and factual statements), episodes (usually autobiographical) and images were listed. They were then evaluated in terms of: 1) the total number of propositions, episodes and images; 2) their precision or correspondence with scientific ideas appropriate for the age group; and 3) their self-consistency. We called these measures extent (E), precision (P), and consistency (C). A student's E score appeared to us to be a good indicator of the breadth of her/his knowledge, whereas the quality of that knowledge, in other words the student's understanding of the topic, was indicated by a combination of the P and C scores.

Data were generated from samples of students before and after topics were taught. This yielded indications of progression, not only in factual knowledge but also in understanding. Four distinct types of progression emerged from the various groups of students interviewed: 1) all three scores increased; 2) P and C increased but E decreased; 3) E increased but P and C decreased; 4) E and P increased but C decreased (Abdullah, 1997). Students who showed progression of types 1 and 2 have improved their understanding, though over a narrower knowledge base in type 2. Those showing type 3 have learned some new scientific vocabulary but, in Piaget's terms, they have not accommodated the new experiences and they are 'disequilibrated', or confused. The students in this group need time to consolidate their new experiences and ideas. Those in group 4 are inconsistent. They have more scientifically precise ideas than before teaching but they are also holding on to other inconsistent views.

Armed with detailed knowledge such as this about the students' progression, the teacher is in a good position to judge what to do next. Clearly it is unlikely that a single whole-class approach will suit all the students.

Teaching: what learning about learning teaches about teaching

Anything that is known about learning has potential implications for teaching. That is the subject of this section. The basic question is this: how can knowledge about learning help make teaching more effective? In this section I will take the constructivist view that learning involves constructing connections. Glasersfeld points out the benefits of this:

> The most widespread effect has been achieved by the very simple constructivist principle that consists in taking whatever the student produces as a manifestation of something that makes sense to the student. This not only improves the general climate of instruction but also opens the way for the teacher to arrive at an understanding of the student.
>
> (Glasersfeld, 1991: 24)

Driver and Bell (1985), working in the context of the school science curriculum, identified a set of key points which they referred to as a *constructivist view of learning*. These points are:

- Learning outcomes depend not only on the learning environment but also on the prior knowledge, attitudes and goals of the learner.
- Learning involves construction of knowledge through experience with the physical environment and through social interactions.
- Constructing links with prior knowledge is an active process involving the generation, checking and restructuring of ideas and hypotheses.
- Learning science is not simply a matter of adding to and extending existing concepts, but may involve their radical reorganisation.
- Meanings, once constructed, can be accepted or rejected. The construction of meaning does not always lead to belief.
- Learning is not passive. Individuals are purposive beings who set their own goals and control their own learning.
- Students frequently bring similar ideas about natural phenomena to the classroom. Some constructed meanings are shared by many students.

For a short, readable discussion of this constructivist view of learning see Scott (1987).

Active construction, active learning and activity

The previous section put forward the view that people actively construct new knowledge of their own, rather than being passive recipients of someone else's knowledge. This apparently simple idea could have very significant implications for teaching (and also for parenting and for some of the ways in which we try to persuade people to change their views). How is the notion of active construction related to 'active learning'?

If the job of a science teacher were simply to *transmit* knowledge to a class, then the teacher might rate the following lesson characteristics highly:

- quiet, attentive class;
- a lot of work 'got through' in each lesson;
- efficient coverage of the syllabus;
- students able to demonstrate knowledge in written tests.

Such a teacher would tend to operate in 'transmission mode' and would cast her or his students into the role of 'passive learners'. Clive Carré (1981) lists several reasons why a teacher might choose this mode of teaching:

- Time: if the teacher talks and the students listen the curriculum appears to be covered much more quickly;
- Tradition: transmission mode was often 'good enough' for the teacher so it is good enough for the students;
- Student pressure: many students indicate that they prefer the teacher to do the work – and in particular, the thinking;
- Security: transmission mode allows the teacher to keep tight hold of the reins and feel secure in what is going on in the lessons;
- Status: transmission mode allows the teacher to maintain the role of 'expert'.

Contrast the 'passive learning' environment with what Bentley and Watts (1989) described as a necessary set of requirements for 'active learning':

- a non-threatening learning environment;
- pupil involvement in the organisation of the learning process;
- opportunities for learners to take decisions about the content of their own learning;
- direct skill teaching;
- continuous assessment and evaluation;
- relevance and vocationalism.

Contrasted above are two types of learning *environments*. I do not believe that these environments create two types of learning *processes*, one active and one passive, because I think that learning is essentially an active process. But different environments can and, I believe, inevitably do result in the construction of different kinds of new knowledge. An appropriately designed learning environment can stimulate engagement, help to focus learning, help to concentrate the energy of curiosity and knowledge construction towards a particular domain of thought and experience. In an inadequately designed learning environment, children still have intellectual energy and they still construct new ideas, but the focus is uncertain – it *could* be the carbon cycle but it could equally be determined by any of a whole spectrum of personal needs, goals and interests of each individual child.

Neither of the environments described above can be guaranteed to bring about meaningful science learning, because this depends on more than the environment. As to which is the better designed, each will have its supporters.

In much the same way, *activity* is not, in itself, any guarantee of meaningful science learning. Students may be on their feet in a laboratory, handling scientific apparatus, talking and listening to each other, writing observations and so on but this guarantees very little about the nature of the learning that is taking place, as Tasker (1981) observed. Activity may be necessary for some forms of knowledge construction but it is by no means sufficient. In particular, as is pointed out by Driver and elsewhere in this volume, science practical activity is rarely an end in itself:

> Many … practical lessons end abruptly when the prescribed task is complete and little, if any time is given to the interpretation of the results obtained, although this is just as important as the activity itself. Pupils need time to think around and consolidate the new ideas presented to them. After all, they may have developed their own ideas as a result of many years of experience. It is unlikely that they will easily adopt new ways of thinking as a result of one or two science lessons … perhaps the time has come to help children make more sense of those practical experiences. What is being suggested is not a return to a more didactic teaching, but an extension of the range of types of activities in science classes.
>
> (Driver, 1983: 83)

In one respect, the currently established practical approach to school science in Britain stands out for having legitimised learning through social interaction, since pupils usually carry out experimental work in small groups and it is generally accepted that they will talk to each other in the process. Whether this talk results in meaningful learning in science depends greatly on the design of the practical task and its context in the lesson. Practical tasks which are designed on a recipe basis, or with the principal aim of simply occupying the class, are likely to result at best in rote learning – and if that is what is wanted then there are surely better ways of promoting it (see Chapter 7 on practical work).

Would you agree that there is more than one way to cook a potato? One way may suit one person and another may suit another. Some may like chips today and mash tomorrow. Forgive the obvious – but it's rather similar in teaching. The approaches outlined below are not meant to be seen in competition or opposition, any more than chips are in opposition to mash. They are alternative teaching approaches, all based on understandings about learning. Of course, if teachers were teaching two or three students at a time, it would be possible to 'tune' the approaches to suit the needs of the people concerned. But in school-sized classes this isn't feasible. The solution in school is to provide a 'balanced menu', in other words to mix and vary the teaching approaches.

Cognitive conflict

This is a teaching strategy that links well with Piaget's ideas. The psychological background is that if somebody experiences a surprise or a novelty, they may try to make sense of it in terms of what they know already. That would be known as 'assimilation'. But if they cannot manage this, they may amend their knowledge to make new sense of the novelty. In this process of change, known as 'accommodation', they are learning something.

Here is an illustration: some children connect an electric bell to a battery. They can hear it ringing loudly and see that the arm of the bell is moving. The teacher then produces a second, similar bell inside a glass jar. Everyone can see that the bell is connected to a battery and that its arm is moving like the first bell, but it can only just be heard. Why is this? (first cognitive conflict). Pupils might assimilate the experience by suggesting that the glass is stopping the sound or that the arm is not hitting the sounder. The teacher, who has earlier pumped air from the jar, opens a valve to let air back in and the bell can now be heard clearly (second cognitive conflict). This is harder to assimilate! The intention is that pupils will accommodate a new idea, in this case that air can carry sound.

Scott *et al.* (1991) list several varieties of teaching approaches that use cognitive conflict. Cognitive conflict is a good strategy but it is not infallible. Some students presented with a surprise may just want to switch off. The teacher's skill is then to keep them engaged. Some students may have their ideas shaken but not stirred enough for them to make an instant switch to a new conceptual belief. They may need time to digest and reflect on what they have experienced. They may need further evidence to persuade them to adopt a new belief. Other students, especially those used to struggling with science, may feel threatened by the uncertainty of cognitive conflict. This may cause them to entrench, to cling firmly to a position, not because of its scientific plausibility but because it is there, something to hold on to. Clearly this calls for a degree of sensitivity and 'mind-reading' from the teacher. Despite these possible difficulties, well-managed cognitive conflict can be a highly effective teaching strategy in terms of promoting changes in students' concepts and beliefs.

Chunking

How many 'bits' of information can you hold simultaneously in your short-term memory? Here's a test: in a moment, look at the first letter in this line of text, and the first of the line below (or above) and the first of the line below that. Then look away. Can you remember the three letters? Easy! Try it again with more. What is your short-term memory capacity?

In a study which is famous for the simplicity of its conclusion, Miller (1956) found that most people can cope with roughly 7 bits at once. Above that, errors creep in. So how do we recognise complex things, with many more than 7 bits? The answer is that we 'chunk'. We learn how to make mental economies. Consider the two patterns in Figure 4.8. They are drawn from

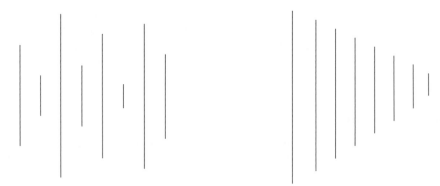

Figure 4.8 Matchstick patterns

exactly the same elements, 8 lines of different lengths. Why is the second pattern so much easier to recall? It's because we only need a few bits of information to conceptualise it. We chunk information about it into a few bits.

There are very many connected ideas in science. Teachers find it much easier than children to take overviews of topics. That is because teachers have learned to use bigger chunks. But when it comes to teaching, the skill is to find learner-sized chunks. This can be tricky: make the chunks too small and there are too many of them to join together; make them too big and errors creep in. Figure 4.9 illustrates how the teacher may think in big chunks but needs to rethink in smaller chunks for the students.

Teachers do not normally set out to teach students to chunk, either directly, or implicitly through presenting materials and ideas with gradually increasing complexity. As White (1988) notes, there is much potential here for teaching to improve learning.

Starters and closings

If students are asked what they like about science lessons many of them will pick out practical science activities as a positive feature. However as Tasker found (see above) the learning outcomes from practical work can be far removed from the teacher's intentions. Students, especially younger ones, will be able to report on events and episodes that they have experienced but find it much more difficult to locate those experiences in a conceptual framework. A combination of Piaget and a well-known idiom sums it up: they struggle to see the abstract wood for the concrete trees! There is only one person who can help in this situation – the teacher. He/ she can help the learners to organise their experiences and link bits of knowledge that would otherwise be isolated fragments. It would be a mistake to try to do this while students are actually experiencing the science activities. The start and the end of a lesson are usually good opportunities to do this vital 'gathering together' of ideas and experiences. Teachers can use the start of a lesson to:

* Direct or reorient learners' attention on to the topic or process in hand;
* Help learners to engage;
* Generate interest and curiosity in what is to come;
* Diagnose current ideas, skills and learning needs.

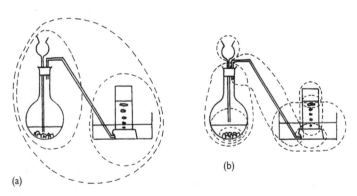

(a)   (b)

Figure 4.9 Hypothetical chunking of gas generation apparatus by (a) a teacher and (b) a student
Source: White (1988)

The close of a lesson is at least as important for learning as the start. It is a big opportunity lost if a practical activity is allowed to over-run at the expense of the last few 'golden minutes'. A useful thought for the teacher is: 'If after school someone asked one of these students, "What did you learn in science today?" what would I hope they'd say?' The last few minutes can then be focused on this intended learning. For instance, whole-class questions could be used to:

- Diagnose understanding;
- Select, emphasise and reinforce key observations, arguments and conclusions;
- Generate interest in what's to come, and connect it with today's themes.

Acknowledging learners' ideas: 'Development of ideas' and 'dialogic' teaching approaches

Learners don't arrive in class with empty heads. They have all sorts of ideas prior to being taught, including about science topics. Traditional transmission teaching ignores learners' prior ideas and aims to swamp them with textbook science delivered by the teacher. The trouble is that what the teacher 'delivers' isn't what is 'received' by learners. A common outcome is that learners learn that one story about science makes sense in everyday life but another one is needed for school. As mentioned above, it is often the first of these 'schemas' that lasts into adulthood. In this section we look at three teaching approaches that make a point of taking learners' ideas about science into account.

In the development of ideas approach (DoI), the aim is to teach children about the scientific ideas without requiring them to reject their own. In this sense DoI contrasts with the use of cognitive conflict. One version of DoI described by Brown and Clement (1989) contains four stages. First the students' ideas are elicited, using a 'target question'. Suppose for example that the teacher is trying to convince students that there is a downward force on a ball which has been thrown in the air, even when it stops at its highest point. (Students often find it hard to accept that a stationary object can be accelerating.) The second stage is to find an analogous situation which is more plausible to the learners. This is called the 'anchor'. In the example, the teacher might ask a student to hold the ball near to where it reached its highest point and ask: 'Do you need to use any force to keep the ball there?' If the students are unable to connect the anchor with the target, the teacher uses intermediate or 'bridging' analogies to help them. 'What if you take the force away by letting go?' 'We could keep the ball stationary at its top point by attaching a string to it and tying it to the ceiling. Does the string hold the ball up?' and so on. The teacher is working towards the fourth stage, which is to get the student to compare the anchor or bridging cases with the target.

Another version of DoI is to provide a concrete example before students meet a related but more abstract problem. Stavy (1991) gives the example of students observing evaporation of iodine and then attempting to understand the evaporation of acetone. The key is that iodine is visible after evaporation. This is the 'concrete' experience that helps students to cope with the additional abstraction caused by the acetone vapour's invisibility. The concrete case acts as a bridge from students' prior knowledge to their knowledge of the abstract case.

A more radical version of DoI has been described by Niedderer (1987). As far as science concepts and language are concerned, students often seem to inhabit two worlds: an everyday world and a world of science lessons (Solomon, 1987 and 1989). In the everyday world they (and the rest of us) talk about 'using energy', 'keeping the cold out', a football 'having a curl on it', the sun 'going down', ' not behaving like an animal' and so on. Solomon argued that children learn the appropriate words and propositions in science classes (e.g. 'energy cannot be created or destroyed') but these do not replace everyday ideas. Instead, they linger temporarily alongside and eventually fade away. Niedderer's aims are to encourage students to see the scientific view, to acknowledge differences between this and everyday views and to understand where both views came from. This final aim is strikingly distinct from traditional science teaching. However, since the traditional approach has failed in terms of public scientific literacy, it may be worth trying something radically different.

Building on the work of Vygotsky and others, Mortimer and Scott (2003) suggest another teaching approach that works with learners' ideas. They call this a 'dialogic communicative approach'. That's quite a mouthful so I'll call it dialogic teaching. They use 'dialogic' to refer to any classroom talk that acknowledges more than one view about the topic in question. Scott and Ametller (2007) have classified different types of communicative approaches that a teacher could use in class. In an 'interactive' approach the teacher's intention is that both teacher and students will contribute substantively to discussion. When the approach is also 'dialogic' the teacher purposefully asks students for their views, with the intention of using them to make judgements about what to do or where to steer the discussion next. The teacher is using the discussion to diagnose students' current knowledge and understanding. Interestingly this means that the lesson can't be planned in final detail. If it was it would be too rigid to respond to the learning needs revealed by the dialogue. Instead the teacher needs to have a 'landscape' of possible routes forward – something that can be built up over time and with the help of more experienced colleagues. In my experience interactive dialogic teaching is not widely found in classrooms. Far more common is the 'IRE' exchange, in which the teacher initiates an enquiry, a student responds by replying directly to the teacher and the teacher evaluates the response, while the rest of the class spectate or switch off. I would certainly support Scott, Mortimer and Ametller's case that interactive dialogic communication has considerable untapped potential as a questioning approach in class.

The exploration phase is followed by more interactive teaching, in which learners are expected to take part in class talk, but where the teacher's scientific views have a higher profile. This is 'interactive authoritative teaching' – authoritative because the teacher is the main 'author' of the ideas being talked about. Mortimer and Scott call this the 'work on' phase. Finally there is a 'non-interactive authoritative' phase in which the exploratory and developed work is reviewed and key conclusions are expressed. This is the 'review' phase.

Mortimer and Scott comment that this three-part scheme isn't rigid. What it does is to highlight the value of teachers seeking learners' beliefs and ideas and working with them. An interactive classroom isn't enough, they argue, because too often the questions are actually pseudo questions and the talk is dominated by the teacher's views of science. The learners may be contributing but they're not airing their own scientific views. Because of that those views will remain unchallenged.

A slightly different angle on dialogic teaching has been promoted by Osborne (2009). He is concerned that science teaching can carry the message that learners are expected to accept scientific ideas just because they are branded 'scientific'. It's a bit like saying, 'Trust me, I'm a science expert.' Osborne argues that alternative ideas should be brought into science teaching so that they can be weighed up critically alongside scientifically accepted ideas. It's just as important, he says, for learners to know why scientifically wrong ideas are wrong as to know what ideas are acceptable in science. An obvious source of ideas, both scientifically right and wrong, is the pupils, so starting with what they bring fits Osborne's strategy. As well as helping pupils to construct stronger foundations for learning in science, this 'argumentation' approach could also develop good habits in making critical judgements. That is an increasingly useful skill in our 'information age'.

Questioning

Questioning is one of the most widely used teaching devices. It can take many forms. Even very young children quickly learn to decode peculiar-sounding teacher enquiries such as 'Are you a packed lunch?' A general way of classifying teachers' questions is this: open, closed, pseudo. Pseudo questions are not questions in an everyday sense. In these examples: 'Shall we start?' and 'John! What do you think you're doing?' either everyone knows that the teacher already knows the answer, or no answer is required. Some pseudo questions are actually instructions: 'Question 1. Use the table to complete a graph of length against time.'

Questions that ask simply for the recall of information rarely evoke deep thinking. On the other hand, questions looking for explanations, especially in the students' own words, can prompt 'higher level thinking'. Compare these: '1. Does the sun set in the east or the west? 2. Why does the sun appear to set in the west?' And: '1. Which drink cooled fastest? 2. How did you decide which drink cooled fastest?' In each case question 1 simply asks for a statement whereas question 2 is looking for a connected thread of ideas. Connections are a hallmark of deeper thinking.

In research involving observation of 35 science lessons, a colleague and I classified the teachers' questions as shown in Table 4.3. The table indicates that low level thinking is prompted by requests to recall, describe or identify. If we want students to think beyond the superficial, our questions should ask them to justify, explain, hypothesise, predict, reframe and sum up.

Whether a question is closed or open depends on the expected response. If the question presupposes an either/or option or a small range of possibilities it is closed: e.g. 'Is lithium a metal?' and 'Can you tell us the name of a halogen?' Open questions can have a wider range of possible responses: e.g. 'What do you think might happen if I put the sodium into the water bath?' and 'Where do you think plants get their food from?'

All three of these general types of questions have their uses and, as is often the case in teaching, a mixture is probably a sound approach.

Study of children's reactions to questions reveals a surprising difference between open and closed questions (Waterman, 1999). If children are asked questions that they can't make sense of, or they think are silly, they will tend to respond if the questions are closed but not if they are open. In the former case the child is not able to connect with the teacher's intended meaning, but produces a response that may hide the depth of misunderstanding from the teacher. In the latter case the teacher will not be so misled.

Mini teaching strategies using questioning

The ideas below have come from observations of teaching in which questioning appeared helpful to students' learning. They come from too many teachers and student teachers to acknowledge!

PAUSING

A 13-year-old said to me: 'If you want to answer in our class you've got to be quick.' Nothing obviously wrong with that, is there? Then she went on: 'The trouble is it's the same few boys who shoot their hands up first and the teacher always lets them answer.' White (1988) comments on how widespread this is in teaching. We fret about gaps in discussion, perhaps out of a concern not to lose momentum. But short pauses, (typically one second) are unhelpful. They encourage superficial impulsive thinking; they deny access to the discussion to students who prefer to think before speaking, and they may broadly suit boys more than girls. When the pause is longer, say

Table 4.3 Classification of question types and corresponding mental operations

	No.	Description of questions	Types of mental operations	Examples of questions
LOWER-LEVEL THINKING	1	Recalling facts/events or remembering and repeating definitions from previous lessons.		
		Included are questions that usually begin with what; when, where.	Recalling episodes	'Do you remember what we did two weeks ago?'
	2	Describing the elements of an experiment situation, identifying variables and providing simple relationships.	Judging	'How do these tubes vary?' 'Which bulb is the brightest?'
HIGHER-LEVEL THINKING	3	Questions that basically begin with 'how'. Description of the procedure and the establishment of fair testing through a controlled experiment.	Justifying judgements (justification of procedures)	'How did you test whether the length of a tube affects the pitch of the note?' 'How did you establish a relationship between . . .?'
	4	Questions seeking proof/ evidence.	Justifying judgements (justification of judgements)	'Does this prove that width makes a difference?' 'What evidence have you got for that?'
	5	Recognising the pattern in a dataset or describing the trend of a graph. (This category refers only to visual representations of data.)	Judging	'Can you see a pattern in the runs of heads?'
	6	Questions beginning with 'why', seeking a reason behind the procedure followed.	Justifying judgements (justification of arguments or explanations)	'Why is this a wise decision?' 'Why is this fair?'
	7	'What-if' questions.	Hypothesising	'What would be the problem if . . .?' 'If I already have two heads in a row, then what is the chance of getting another head on the third throw?'
	8	Giving predictions.	Hypothesising	'Having in mind the previous results, could you tell me how far the next roller ball would go?'
	9	Getting to conclusions.	Reframing	'What is the whole point of sampling?' 'What did we learn about the fair test today?'

Source: Koufetta-Menicou and Scaife (2000)

three seconds, the message to the class is 'everyone think about this'. This is one of my favourite mini strategies because it is so simple to try out. Some researchers who were investigating the effects of three-second pausing suggested that after asking a question the teacher could mentally recite: 'Mary had a little lamb, its fleece was white as snow' because this takes about three seconds to do! I tried it and found it worked so now I'm trying to make pausing a habit.

BOUNCING

The 13-year-old above added a final comment: 'And then [the teacher] assumes the rest of the class have got it.' There are several ways round this problem. One fruitful way is to take a student's answer and 'bounce' it around the class: 'Do you agree with Jane's idea Carl? Who else agrees? Vinod, what do you think? Why don't you think Jane is right Sandra?' As these examples indicate, bouncing often leads to further development of ideas. It also provides the teacher with useful diagnostic information.

WRONG ANSWERS

I don't believe that it is educationally sound for teachers always to correct wrong answers. Most answers mean that the student has given some attention and perhaps even some deep thought to the question. Teachers can turn wrong answers into learning experiences:

TEACHER: Which do you think is denser, the water or the ice?
STUDENT: The ice.
TEACHER: Who agrees?
TEACHER (to someone who agrees):   What's your reasoning?
STUDENT: Because ice is a solid and molecules pack closer together in solids.
TEACHER (to someone who disagrees):   Why do you think the water is denser?
STUDENT: Because the ice is floating on it.

In the first exchange the initial (wrong) answer has been used by the teacher to diagnose a misconception (that ice molecules are closer packed than liquid water molecules). The teacher's questioning has also led to a challenge to the faulty view from a peer. The challenge will be strengthened when the teacher's own views are introduced. The emphasis in this exchange was on learning; judgements about rightness and wrongness were used to support learning through reasoned thinking.

THIRD PARTY IDEAS

An alternative to asking questions of a class directly is to ask them to judge other people's ideas. They may be more willing to do this than to risk putting forward their own ideas. This can be especially fruitful when the teacher picks topics from the list of common science misconceptions (see earlier in this chapter). Teacher: 'Some people think that there's no gravity on the moon because there's no air. What do you think of this?' 'Andie says green plants would die without light and water. Brett says they need food as well. Chelsea says they make their own food. Dean thinks they have to have air but he's not sure. Who do you agree with?' Questions like these would suit whole-class or group work. 'Concept cartoons' software (Naylor and Keogh, 2000) contains a wide selection of third party scenarios like these.

DIAGNOSTIC QUESTIONING

The aim in using diagnostic questions is to obtain as clear a picture as possible of the students' ideas about a topic. (Reasons for diagnosing were discussed earlier.) The trouble is that students often assume that questions are being used to grade them and that they have to try to get the right answers. We don't want this in diagnostic teaching – we want the students' beliefs about science, not their beliefs about what we want. First, the students need to know that a diagnostic survey is not a test and their scores will not be identified. Secondly the questions need wording in ways that elicit students' beliefs and don't stress the importance of being right. The question in Figure 4.7 is a good example. Contrast that with the following: 'Draw a circuit diagram of a bulb lit by a battery and use arrows to show the current flow.' This may be adequate for testing students but it certainly is not suitable for diagnosing their ideas. A useful strategy in making up diagnostic questions is to include words like 'you' and 'your'. This helps to communicate your aim of finding out about the students' authentic beliefs.

TURNING TELLING INTO ASKING: SOCRATIC QUESTIONING

Two and a half millennia ago, the Greek philosopher Socrates demonstrated to his companion Meno that an uneducated slave boy could construct a solution to a quite difficult geometric problem. The point Socrates made to Meno was that the boy had accomplished the solution without being told anything. He was guided on the way only by Socrates' questions. Teaching using well-judged leading questions is sometimes known as Socratic questioning. Is this more effective than 'transmission teaching' in which the teacher lectures and tells things to the students? Some people argue that it is more effective because the students have to engage more deeply than in lectures in order to be able to answer the questions. And the answers to the questions are 'owned' by the students which may mean that they are highly plausible to them. Because ideas in science are strongly linked by causal connections there is much scope for Socratic questioning in the subject.

CURIOSITY

I would like to conclude this survey of questioning in science teaching with a single simple notion that can act as a guide. If questioning is fuelled by a teacher's *curiosity* about students' learning then it is highly likely to enhance learning.

PEOR: predict, explain, observe, react

Asking students to make predictions can be highly effective in promoting learning. This is especially so in science, where predictions linked to practical activities can be confirmed or confounded by the outcome. In the 'PEOR' cycle (Bonello and Scaife, 2009) students are first asked to make a prediction about a science demonstration or activity. Predictions (P) generate interest; someone who has committed themselves to a prediction becomes, through their curiosity and through social forces in the group, a stakeholder in the outcome. It is important to follow predictions with questions asking for explanations (E). This discourages guessing and promotes higher level thinking. Students next observe (O) the activity and then they are asked for their reactions (R). There is plenty of scope in PEOR cycles for teacher-managed peer discussion, adding further stimulus to engagement and learning.

The potential of good ICT to generate new, rich learning experiences

You may have been wondering when ICT was going to appear in this chapter. In a way it already has, because it can be used just like any other resource to enhance teaching in the various ways described above. But ICT has some distinct characteristics of its own (see Chapter 13 on ICT for further discussion). It is well suited to self-managed learning, such as project and investigative work, although students probably benefit from 'scaffolding' – Bruner's term describing light-touch guidance – without which there may be a risk of them touring superficially through software. Another general advantage is that ICT is 'cool', at least in comparison to most science equipment. It may motivate students, some of whom would not otherwise be interested in science. Opportunities for peer teaching are likely to arise. Some students are more competent and confident than their teachers with ICT and if they are given support by the teacher this has the potential to be very good for their self-esteem and motivation.

As well as these broad learning opportunities, ICT offers some particular advantages. Here we consider two specific areas where it has considerable potential to enrich learning.

Data-logging

Current technology has the capability to sense, process and display data so quickly that it appears to human senses to be instantaneous. Helen Brasell (1987) investigated the effect of differing delay times in the display of feedback to students who were experimenting with a motion sensor. The sensor recorded how far away the students were and the data were displayed graphically for the students to see. They were given instructions that required them to connect physical (concrete) and graphical (abstract) frames of reference. Brasell found longer-lasting, deeper learning when the delay times were short (below 25 seconds). The actual delay time in normal use is virtually zero; this was an impossibility prior to the arrival of ICT in science teaching. In this sense, ICT has opened up a new possibility for learning: it has reached parts of the mind that older technologies could not reach!

The motion sensor can be used to teach about position and movement but it can also be used to teach generic understanding of graphs, certainly a useful skill to learn in science. At an even more fundamental psychological level it can be used to help learners 'bridge' between concrete experiences and abstract representations. Used in this way the ICT is contributing to a process known as 'cognitive acceleration'. This is discussed further in the next section.

There are various brands of motion sensor, of which I have used several. Irrespective of brand, it is one of my favourite and most frequently used ICT resources. It offers the following pedagogic advantages:

- Everyone can join in and participate.
- Everyone can gain some positive achievements to show from the lesson.
- The activities are motivating and fun.
- Cooperative group work occurs.
- Students can gain confidence in using ICT.
- During the activity students work in an increasingly self-managed way.
- All students can be challenged a bit.
- The practical 'overheads' are low, giving ample time for experimenting. A large proportion of students' time is spent on 'authentic' learning (Scaife and Wellington, 1993).

- The conceptual overheads are low, allowing the teaching strategy to be used with a wide range of students, from junior school to post-graduate.
- Learning and retention are significantly improved (Thornton and Sokoloff, 1990).
- The strategy is 'constructivist': students start with familiar, 'concrete' phenomena and ideas and build on them towards more abstract concepts.
- The strategy is 'Vygotskian': a powerful ZPD is constructed through the PEOR cycle (see above), peer interactions and Socratic questioning.

I am not the only one who likes this particular ICT resource: here is part of an email from a student teacher, Mike Bingham, who used the sensor during his school placement: 'Hi Jon, Just thought I'd let you know that I used the LogIt Ranger today for the first time (yr 12) and it was a resounding success! My lessons with year 7 and the sensor were also a success!'

Electronic voting systems

A different kind of ICT resource that appears to have considerable potential to enhance learning-focused pedagogy is the electronic voting system, or EVS. These systems are increasingly appearing in schools and colleges. Typically they use a PC or laptop, a receiver and a set of handsets. Responses from the handsets are shown on the PC and can be projected for class viewing if required. They do not need an interactive whiteboard. Draper (2007) claims that EVSs, 'engage the students i.e. not only to wake them up and cheer them up, but to get their minds working on the subject matter, and so to prompt learning'. He identifies three particular applications of EVSs in teaching:

1 Using simple questions to check understanding and give students formative feedback;
2 Diagnostic assessment: using responses (such as the proportion who got a question right) to decide whether it is appropriate to spend time on a sub-topic or to move on;
3 Introducing challenges and puzzles to generate opinions, differences, discussions, argument and cognitive conflict.

I am particularly impressed by the diagnostic potential of EVSs. Draper agrees:

> there are powerful benefits not just for learners but also for teachers. Both need feedback, and both do much better if that feedback is fast and frequent – every few minutes rather than once a year. So the other great benefit of using EVS is the feedback it gives to the lecturer, whether you think of that as like course feedback, or as allowing 'contingent teaching' i.e. adapting how the time is spent rather than sticking to a rigid plan that pays no attention to how this particular audience is responding.
>
> (Draper, 2007)

Thinking skills, cognitive development and 'CASE'

On average, 12-year-old school children have learnt more science than 11-year-olds. Does it follow that 12-year-olds are any better at learning science than they were a year earlier? As well as learning curriculum material, have they learnt anything about learning? There is an argument that there should be room in teaching for focusing on learners' thinking skills rather than exclusively on curriculum content. The idea is that if learners become better at learning, then anything they are subsequently taught will probably be learnt better.

According to the DCSF Standards Site (Department for Children, Schools and Families, 2007b), 'Interest in the teaching of thinking skills has burgeoned in the UK'. This site contains a link to a short history of thinking skills development from the middle of the twentieth century. In one strand of that history Michael Shayer built on the work of another psychologist, Reuven Feuerstein, and applied his ideas in the field of Piagetian assessment and then, along with the science educator Philip Adey, in science learning. Shayer and Adey were not just interested in thinking skills but in the possibility that the teaching of these skills could speed up children's mental development. This is the cognitive equivalent of the idea of an athletic training regime speeding up a child's physical development, something we can see in the emergence of young tennis and swimming stars.

'CASE'

Shayer and Adey adopted the premise that children's cognitive development does not necessarily take place at an inexorable rate, uninfluenced by external factors. They proposed that not only learning, but also the rate of cognitive development, is dependent on the child's social and physical environment. Included in the child's environment, of course, is the school and the influence of teaching. The Cognitive Acceleration through Science Education (CASE) project has grown from research which compared the stages of cognitive development typically found in secondary aged children with the cognitive demands of various attainment standards in science courses, including the national science curriculum. The research examined, among other things, the extent to which science curricula matched students' current capabilities. Materials from the project have been published as a teaching package known as 'Thinking Science' (Adey et al., 2001). This package has been designed explicitly to encourage 'the development of thinking from concrete to formal operational'. One reason for wanting to do this, according to the authors, is because students will be unable to achieve standards equivalent to GCSE grade D or above unless they can use formal operational thinking. The themes of the activities in the package are control of variables, proportionality, probability, compensation and equilibrium, combinations, correlation, classification, formal models and compound variables (see also Adey, 1987a). As can be gathered from this list, the emphasis is on 'content-free' processes. The authors describe this approach in teaching as 'intervention', as opposed to 'instruction'.

The CASE materials were trialled in several schools by dedicating approximately one science session per fortnight to the project, for a period of two years. This amounted to approximately a quarter of the science curriculum time. Pupils from project and control classes were followed up to GCSE, to investigate the nature of any effects arising from the intervention. At the end of the two-year intervention programme, there were no significant differences between the two groups, which at least indicated that the programme had not disadvantaged the project group through disruption to their science courses! After this, however, the project students began to out-perform the control students, gradually drawing ahead up to and including their GCSE year. More intriguing still was a 'far-transfer' effect reported by the CASE team. Not only was there evidence of the project students' attainment advancing more rapidly than the control students in science but also in mathematics and in English.

Some people are sceptical about any claims of long-term and far-transfer effects. On the other hand, the point has been made elsewhere that if the potential payoff is big enough, even the highly improbable would be worth exploring! This argument seems to have been persuasive, since increasing numbers of school science departments have adopted 'Thinking Science' alongside their Key Stage 3 science courses. Observations of 'CASE lessons' in action have suggested that it is a challenging and demanding scheme of work, both for students and for teachers. There are indications, however, that there is a potential payback, not only in terms of improved student attainment but also in increased interest in learning in both students and teachers. For a detailed description of the CASE project and associated research see Adey (1987b) and Adey and Shayer (1994).

Learning to learn: 'metacognition'

Compared with other animals, human beings are not only expert learners, we are also capable of metacognition. I am using this term to refer to learning and knowing about learning, understanding oneself as a learner, and making judgements – whether consciously or automatically – about what and how to learn. In evolutionary terms, metacognition is like having a cognitive turbo-charger. We are born into a culture and we immediately learn from and within it. Culture directs us to take enormous short cuts. We don't bother learning how to use a flint tool because it's more useful to learn how to use the internet. And it is easier to do that if someone guides us to take further short cuts. Learning like this is not arbitrary, it is tuned to help us get along successfully in our world. We don't have to think much about this ('Shall I learn flint-sharpening today?') because we have some inherent knowledge about what is useful to learn. (For a current neurobiological perspective on this see Edelman's discussion of 'value categories': Edelman, 1992, chapters 9 and 11.) Is it possible to go further than this inherent capacity for metacognition? It certainly is: we can not only learn to learn better, we can be taught to do so. White (1988) argues strongly that if students were taught to use appropriate 'cognitive strategies', their learning would accelerate apace. He states though, on page 99, that, 'revolutionary changes should occur in the organisation of schools, in curricula and in teaching methods' in order to achieve this, but that, 'if it should prevail it will bring about the major change to occur in the practice of teaching since the 19th century'. How can these cognitive strategies be taught? White makes several practical suggestions:

- *Student-generated questions.* The act of asking questions requires engagement and creative thought, two core cognitive strategies.
- *Purpose.* Tasker's study (1981) illustrated how students may embark on activities in an unthinking, recipe-following fashion. White argues that students should be taught to ask: 'What is this all about? What does it relate to? What am I supposed to do?'
- *Planning.* Some strategies for solving problems in science are better than others. Can students be taught how to plan problem-solving strategies?
- *Paraphrasing.* It is well known that you find out how well you know something when you try to teach it. Teaching involves re-phrasing sets of ideas. Students can be taught how to do this: how to paraphrase a scientific argument or the solution to a problem. In my view this is a particularly valuable cognitive strategy to teach.

In my experience CASE is less common in schools than it was a decade ago. However CASE and other thinking skills innovations have definitely influenced national curriculum design. Much of the curriculum strand, 'How science works', targets thinking skills, as can be seen from the titles of the two main sub-strands: 'Explanations, argumentation and decisions' and 'Practical and enquiry skills'.

The CLIS project

The Children's Learning in Science Project based at Leeds University was responsible for much valuable research into children's ideas in science. The project built on these findings to devise teaching approaches that are broadly compatible with a constructivist viewpoint (see earlier in this chapter). The example that follows makes use of several teaching approaches outlined above, including diagnosing students' prior ideas, the PEOR teaching cycle and cognitive conflict.

Conservation of mass

Three year 8 classes had been working on the topic of dissolving. They had explored whether salt and sugar are still there when they dissolve. Most students had come to the view that salt and sugar *are* still there, even though they cannot be seen. The next topic, conservation of mass, was introduced with a worksheet (Figure 4.10) which asks for students' views about whether dissolving affects mass.

Of 66 students, 27 held the scientific view (B), while 34 expected the side with dissolved sugar to be lighter. Now aware of these views, the teachers devised an activity to help move students' ideas from their current positions towards the scientific view. (Rosalind Driver likens this to someone phoning you for directions; you would probably say first: 'Where are you now?') The activity used the 'Balance' worksheet (Figure 4.11) to take pupils through a PEOR sequence.

Groups of students discussed and recorded their predictions and then watched the four demonstrations. After this they wrote down and attempted to explain what they had seen. These events were recorded by CLIS researchers. Here is a short extract from pupils' discussion during one of the pre-publication trials. The demonstration involved the addition of red ink to the water and the discussion took place before pupils saw the outcome of the mixing:

S1:   No, it won't balance.
S2:   I think it will.
S3:   It will balance because, er…
S1:   It won't.
S4:   Maybe because it's a liquid.
S3:   So? It'll still be the same amount of liquid, won't it?
S4:   No, because the level will go *up* on that one there.
S3:   Yeah, I know, but you don't add owt!

These pupils are evidently engaged with the scientific issue. The comments show perception and thought, and they are challenging each other's views. The key question, though, is this: can the PEOR sequence result in learning in science? In order to test this, the students were asked, after the demonstrations, to reconsider the 'Liz and Rob' worksheet (Figure 4.10). If they wanted to change their view they were asked to explain why. One student who did change wrote: 'The four experiments we did it came to same because it is the same amount of sugar and it got dissloved it is the same. And that means norfing has been substracted or added so it is the same.' After this stage, almost unanimous agreement was reached that when salt or sugar dissolved, there was no change in mass.

An anxiety sometimes expressed by teachers about the approach described above is that it is time consuming. Would it not be better for the teacher just to do a simple demonstration, showing that mass is conserved? If such a demonstration were a reliable and effective way of promoting desired learning then it would indeed be hard to justify the constructivist approach. On the other hand, observations which seem unequivocal to teachers may be interpreted quite differently by pupils. As Asoko *et al.* (1993) point out, 'pupils do not always "see" what they are intended to see, and even minute movements of the balance pointer may be taken as evidence

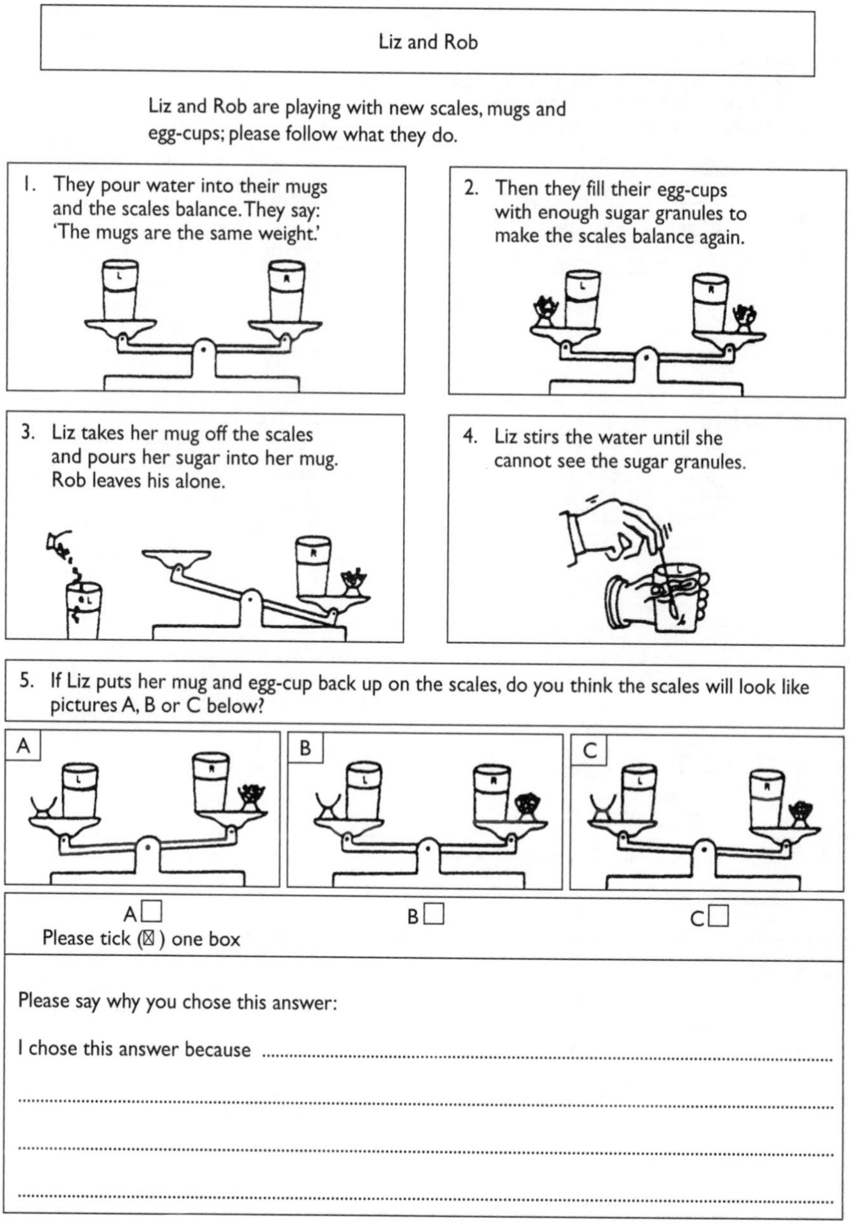

Figure 4.10 Pre-teaching task used to elicit understanding of mass of dissolved substance
Source: Holding *et al.* (1990)

that supports their view and refutes the science idea'. When people are deciding whether or not the meaning of an observation is significant, they base their judgement on prior knowledge. This prior knowledge is generally different for each of us and so it is no wonder that we reach different conclusions about the meanings of the observation (see notes 5 and 6).

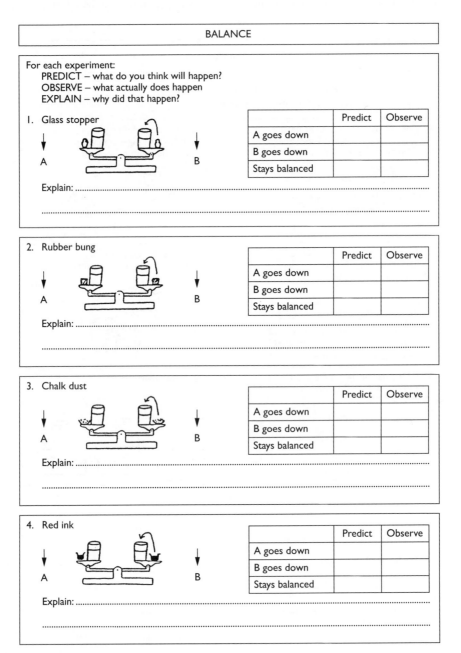

Figure 4.11 Intervention experiments
Source: Holding *et al.* (1990)

Concept mapping

A concept map is a picture, showing, and hopefully clarifying, concepts and relationships between them (see Chapter 1 of this book and also, e.g., Novak and Cañas, 2006). Concept mapping is often used synonymously with 'mind mapping'. Richard Gunstone has made extensive use of concept mapping in science education (see, e.g., Gunstone, 1995). His explanation of their use is this: 'students are given a number of related terms and asked to (a) show those they see as linked by drawing lines to link them, and (b) writing on these lines the nature of the link they see'. A selection of concept mapping software is now available but for classroom use hand-drawn maps are quick, easy and potentially fruitful. Figure 4.12 shows a concept map on the topic of plant growth that might be produced before the topic is taught at lower secondary level.

As can be seen, the map makes only a modest writing demand on the student, which is an advantage in terms of student engagement. Other positive features are:

- They can give a sense of achievement to the student by making her/his ideas explicit and presented in a structured way;
- They can be done individually or in groups, the latter case bringing in peer learning;
- They provide diagnostic information to the teacher;
- They encourage imagination, lateral thinking, deeper thinking, curiosity and tentativeness;
- They bring out an overview of a topic, which students often find hard to see;
- If used before and after the teaching of a topic they can be used to demonstrate progression and attainment.

Figure 4.13 illustrates the last point by showing the sort of concept map that might be produced at the end of successful teaching by the student who produced Figure 4.12. Other examples of the use of concept mapping in science can be found in Prain (1995) and Lovejoy (1995).

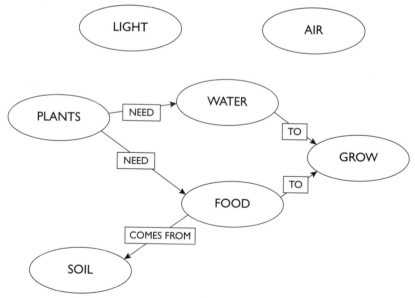

Figure 4.12 Student concept map before teaching

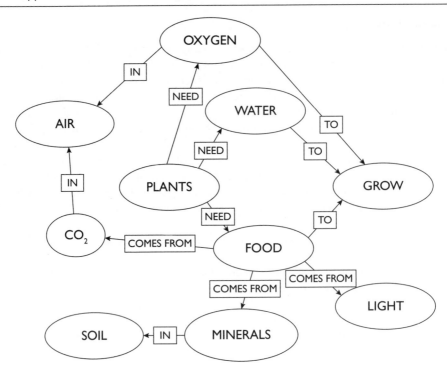

Figure 4.13 Student concept map after teaching

A behavioural approach

A behavioural approach in teaching focuses on *training*. Behavioural theories emphasise the significance of *observable actions* rather than private consciousness. Behaviour is modified through a process known as conditioning, and change can be accelerated or inhibited by *reinforcement*.

Learning, in a behavioural context, is defined as an observed *response* to particular *stimuli*. This is the type of learning that is assessed in British schools by tests such as 'SATs' (Standardised Assessment Tasks). The aim in behavioural teaching is therefore to identify and manage appropriate stimuli so as to bring about desired behaviour. Wheldall and Merrett (1989: 5) list what they call 'the five principles of Positive Teaching':

1   Teaching is concerned with the observable.
2   Almost all classroom behaviour is learned.
3   Learning involves change in behaviour.
4   Behaviour changes as a result of its consequences.
5   Behaviours are also influenced by classroom contexts.

They argue that good teaching involves the maintenance of an appropriate environment for desired learning to take place, a sentiment strongly supported by Marland (1975), Rogers (1991) and others: 'We have been concerned with methods of encouraging pupils to behave in ways which will maximise their opportunities for learning appropriate academic skills and knowledge' (Wheldall and Merrett, 1989: 18). Wheldall and Merrett describe how teachers can set about systematically categorising their pupils' behaviour as either desirable or undesirable. Potential stimuli and reinforcers for these behaviours can be identified and ultimately teachers' own behaviours can be modified so as to bring about desired changes in their pupils. A brief illustration, frequently found during initial teaching experience, is that of pupils repeatedly interrupting the teacher while he or she is carrying out a demonstration to the class. This is readily identifiable as undesirable behaviour! On closer observation it becomes apparent that whenever the teacher is interrupted in this way, he or she responds there and then to the pupil concerned. The teacher's response is acting as a reward to the pupil to continue behaving in the same way; the teacher is inadvertently 'reinforcing' the pupil's behaviour. As a result of this analysis, the teacher's action can be modified to prevent the reinforcement from taking place. Student teachers have found analysis such as this to be helpful because it offers a way forward, out of a difficult classroom problem. (I don't think that there is any single 'right' response in the situation described. Which of a range of alternative actions would be the most appropriate could only sensibly be judged in the teaching context.)

John Holt (1964) warns strongly that if undue emphasis is placed on desired behavioural outcomes, students will find it worthwhile to learn responses simply to please, so as to get the teacher off their backs. However, a behavioural approach in teaching could complement many of the approaches described earlier. It may be attractive in circumstances in which the applicability of the 'cognitive' approaches seems limited. Safety procedures in laboratories, maintenance (as opposed to negotiation) of social rules for class discussion and training in the use of equipment are examples which might benefit from this approach.

Punishment, used as a tool for managing pupils' behaviour, can be wearing and stressful for teachers. It can become a routine response, which does little, ultimately, to bring about the change for which it is nominally employed – that of improving the quality of the learning environment. As an alternative to punishment Wheldall and Merrett's approach is likely to be less stressful, both to teachers and pupils, because it emphasises *positive reinforcement* of desired behaviour as a baseline teaching approach, rather than punishment of unwanted behaviour. Teachers who find themselves constantly repeating commands to pupils might, by reflecting on their actions in behavioural terms, be able to bring about significant improvements not only in their pupils' learning but also in the quality of their professional lives.

Planning for learning: an example

In this example the teacher is in the middle of a topic on current electricity with a mixed attainment class of 12-year-olds. We will take a detailed look at a lesson plan, focusing on the decisions the teacher has made to influence students' learning. The curriculum aims for the lesson are to promote learning about current flow, single-loop circuits, circuits with two branches, switches and the use of circuit diagrams. The teacher also wants to use the lesson to improve students' skills of logical thinking and their procedural skills in setting out and connecting circuits. In terms of class management the group is typical for its age.

Before the lesson the teacher will draw two large circuit diagrams on the board: one very simple and one containing branches and switches. He knows (from Piaget) that this abstract representation will be difficult for many of the students to grasp. To help their learning he needs to make as many links as possible with 'concrete' experiences. His plan is to start with a demonstration of a very simple circuit and to use questions and discussion to assess the collective ZPD (Vygotsky) of the class.

The electrical components are fairly small, which is problematic for demonstrating. He wants the students to be able to identify all of the components in the demonstration circuit and to see how they are joined together. He will then be able to 'bridge' between the concrete experience of seeing the circuit and the abstract circuit diagram. To make the demonstration more concrete the teacher has prepared some coloured cards, labelled with the names of electrical components on them. He plans to lay the cards out on the demonstration table in exactly the same configuration as in the first diagram on the board. When he puts the components on the cards he will put the battery the same way round as in the diagram – he learned this idea originally from some students who were having difficulty sorting out the plus and minus connections between battery holders and meters. The teacher also noticed that because the battery holders were opaque it would not be obvious that batteries were inside them. To reduce students' guesswork he wrote 'BATTERY' in large letters on the sides of the holders. The other components (bulbs, switches, wires) were easy to identify.

When the teacher has laid the components on the cards he will check a sample of students by bouncing questions to see whether they are satisfied that the arrangement matches the layout of the diagram. He will then connect up the wires, pointing out practical matters on the way: 'to unplug, pull on the plug not the wire'; 'it doesn't matter what colour wires you use'. He has done enough electricity teaching to know that it is worth having some spares handy, especially bulbs. This will help give the students confidence in him. He has also requested a multi-meter with the equipment.

After connecting the simple circuit, he will give a concrete demonstration of the flow of current by tracing a path round the circuit with his finger. He will tell the students to use this method when they set up their own circuits later.

Next he plans to progress to the more complex circuit (Figure 4.14). However, he can't be sure in advance that the students will be ready to make this leap, so he will use questions and discussion to assess their new ZPD. If necessary he will set up an intermediate demonstration. He will use cards again and lay out the components until the students are satisfied that the arrangement matches the second diagram. The new circuit contains three switches so he has made up three coloured cards labelled ON and OFF on either side. This is because he wants the students to make deductions about the bulbs in terms of the switches and it will not be obvious from the switches themselves whether they are on or off. He is going to use a PEOR cycle with this circuit. For each on-off arrangement of the switches the students have to predict which bulbs will be on. The teacher plans to draw a logic table on the board, to be filled in by a volunteer during the PEOR discussion (Table 4.4). He then plans another PEOR cycle in which they have to predict which switches need to be on to obtain various arrangements of lit bulbs.

In the PEOR cycles he will use various types of questions and questioning: Socratic, looking for explanation, highlighting cognitive conflict, exploiting wrong answers, bouncing. All the time he will be trying to assess the students' ideas and judging how to respond.

Parts of this account involve formal planning such as preparing the cards and the blackboard. Other parts come from habits that the teacher has learned, like seeing through the students' eyes and continually checking their knowledge, using what he knows about learning.

Finally, a daft question: which is the best?

We live in a culture which celebrates being 'best', especially when being best is said to accord with common wisdom or current values. Complex systems like human beings, however, do not readily lend themselves to such a simplified measure. It is one thing to try to answer: Which is

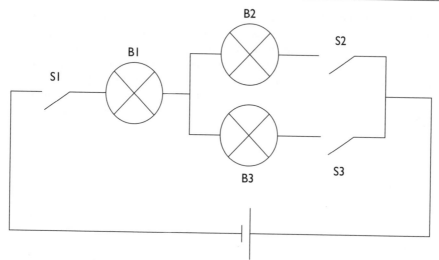

Figure 4.14   Circuit with two branches

Table 4.4   Switch and bulb logic table

S1	S2	S3	B1	B2	B3
Off	Off	Off			
Off	Off	On			
Off	On	Off			
On	Off	Off			
On	On	Off			
On	Off	On			
Off	On	On			
On	On	On			

the best size for the print in this book? and quite another thing to address the question: Who is the world's best author?

None of the approaches described above is claimed to be the best. It has not been an aim of this chapter to come to a judgement of a 'best buy', because that would have been an artificial and a misleading simplification. The approaches have been included because there is merit in each and each merits consideration. My guess is that there will be times when each is highly effective in promoting learning.

In summary

This chapter began with the view that even though there isn't a universally accepted explanatory theory of learning, theoretical ideas can still contribute very usefully to teaching (see Note 7). In education, learning is a 'new kid on the block' compared with teaching, assessment and curriculum and there is much still to learn about it. The chapter argued that teaching based on knowledge about learning is surely better than teaching based on habit or guesswork.

Constructivist ideas about learning from Piaget, Vygotsky and others were introduced. Two of the more significant ideas are 'cognitive conflict' and the 'zone of proximal development'. Both of these show how children's pre-teaching ideas are important influences on their learning. The chapter described ways of finding out about children's pre-teaching ideas and about their learning needs. We explored strategies for guiding children's knowledge and understanding towards the science curriculum. We also looked at ways of influencing their cognitive development and thinking skills so that they are equipped to deal with the abstract conceptual demands of science.

Points for reflection

- Do you think that a teacher could teach without having any theory, whether conscious or unconscious, about learning?
- When you plan your next science lesson, what will influence your planning? Can you make connections between this question and the ideas of *assessment for learning* and *cognitive conflict*?
- A teacher might say, 'I don't have time for finding out about learners' pre-teaching ideas. What's the point?' What would you say to this? Do you think there could ever be advantages in *not* knowing about learners' prior ideas?
- In the PEOR teaching cycle (predict, explain, observe, react) do you think any of the four stages lend themselves well to pairs or small group discussion, as opposed to individual work?

Glossary

This is not a list of dictionary definitions, it is an attempt to clarify the sense in which certain important words have been used in this chapter.

Ability. When used to describe a person as a whole this is a defunct and unhelpful notion. No such single word reliably predicts a person's future accomplishments. It may be useful though when used in specific contexts, e.g. 'Jo has musical ability'. Note that if we don't *show* ability, it doesn't mean that we have low (or even no) ability. The two are often confused. The claim for example, that, 'Albert has little mathematical ability' is actually an admission that so far nobody has seen Albert attain much mathematically. It's said that something like that was once said of the young Einstein! To sum this up, *absence of evidence isn't the same as evidence of absence.*

Affective domain. Mental activity associated with feelings and emotions (sometimes also includes intentions).

Development. A result of changes that tend to occur over longer time-scales than in learning. Developmental changes tend to be more reliably permanent than changes resulting from learning. But learning and development are not clearly distinct: do birds learn to fly or develop to fly?

Knowledge. In this chapter I have taken knowledge to refer to something that a person has: I have knowledge by virtue of the way my neurons or neuronal groups interconnect. These connections depend on my entire life history. One of the things that influenced them was my education. Not everyone shares this view however, and this is one of the richly developing areas on the boundaries between education, psychology, philosophy, neuroscience, sociology and artificial intelligence! Further reading: Bickhard (1997), Churchland (1994), Dennett (1991), Edelman and Tononi (2000), Harré (1986), Laland and Brown (2002), Piaget (1972), Phillips (1997), Searle (1997), Vygotsky (1978).

Learning. The process by which changes occur in knowledge, skills, understanding, beliefs, behaviours, values and attitudes.

Ontology. To do with the idea of *being*, or of *what is*. A branch of metaphysics concerned with being in the abstract. Radical constructivism explicitly excludes claims about 'what exists' and confines itself to what we know or can know (Glasersfeld, 1991, p. 17).

Pedagogy. The science, art and craft (and sometimes the guile) of teaching.

Teaching. Lecturing, instructing or telling ('transmission teaching'); also listening, modelling, questioning, diagnosing, facilitating, coaching, supporting and more.

Understanding. I am taking a person's current understanding to be their current capacity to apply knowledge and skills appropriately in various contexts. Understanding is not separate from knowledge and skills; to comment on someone's understanding is to comment on the quality, and particularly the connectedness, of their knowledge and skills.

Notes

1 For a short summary of Piaget's theory of intellectual development see Donaldson (1978). Donaldson argues that children's thinking may be less constrained by stages of development than was proposed by Piaget. She suggests that a crucial factor is the set of interpersonal contexts in which children's thinking develops. See also Smith, Cowie and Blades (1998, chapter 11).

2 *Common Knowledge* by Edwards and Mercer (1987) contains detailed instances in which classroom discussion is analysed in terms of what the authors describe as the 'common meaning' made of it by teacher and pupils.

3 Large samples of children have been surveyed by the Assessment of Performance Unit (APU) to investigate, among other things, the knowledge and understanding that children had in science. Summary reports, describing main findings and implications for teaching, are available from the Association for Science Education, College Lane, Hatfield, Herts AL10 9AA.

4 The Department for Education has had many names in the last few decades. When referring to departmental publications I have used the name that was current at the time of publication. In other cases I have used 'Department for Education' or 'DfE' for simplicity.

5 Rosalind Driver's paper (1989) takes a broad-based and pragmatic look at the implementation of a constructivist teaching scheme. She adds flesh to the bones described above, in the section on teaching models.

6 The generative learning approach to teaching described in Osborne and Freyberg (1985: 109) is based on Wittrock's 'generative' model of learning. There is much in common between this and the constructivist model of learning described by Driver and Bell (1985) and summarised above. For a summary of the generative learning model see Osborne and Freyberg (1985: 83).

7 For a comprehensive summary of recent accounts of learning in general, not only in science, see Bransford *et al.* (2000).

References and further reading

Recommended references on ideas about learning in Science and their applications in teaching

Osborne, R. and Freyberg, P. (1985) *Learning in Science*, Auckland: Heinemann. A wide-ranging and very readable account about learning in science from teachers and researchers.

White, R.T. (1988) *Learning Science*, Oxford: Blackwell. A rich source of theoretically grounded ideas about learning and teaching science.

White, R.T. and Gunstone, R. (1992) *Probing Understanding*, London: Falmer. A resource of diagnostic strategies.

General references

Abdullah, A.T.S. (1997) *Learning science in primary school: An investigation of children's knowledge and understanding of science concepts*, Unpublished PhD thesis, University of Sheffield.

Abdullah, A.T.S. and Scaife, J.A. (1997) Using interviews to assess children's understanding of science concepts, *School Science Review*, 78(285), 79–84.

Adey, P. (1987a) Science develops logical thinking – doesn't it? Part 1. Abstract thinking and school science, *School Science Review*, June, 622–630.

Adey, P. (1987b) Science develops logical thinking – doesn't it? Part 2. The CASE for science, *School Science Review*, September, 17–27.

Adey, P. (1995) Barmy theories, *School Science Review*, 76 (276), 95–100.

Adey, P. and Shayer, M. (1994) *Really Raising Standards*, London: Routledge. The background to the design and implementation of the 'CASE' project.

Adey, P., Shayer, M. and Yates, C. (2001) *Thinking Science*, (3rd edition) Cheltenham: Nelson Thornes. Materials for teaching 'CASE' lessons.

Asoko, H., Leach, J., and Scott, P. (1993) 'Learning science', in R. Hull (ed.) *Association for Science Education Secondary Science Teachers' Handbook*, Hemel Hempstead: Simon and Shuster.

Assessment Reform Group (1999) *Assessment for Learning: Beyond the Black Box*. Cambridge: University of Cambridge School of Education. Retrieved 17-09-07 from: http://arg.educ.cam.ac.uk/publications.html.

Assessment Reform Group (2005) *The Assessment Reform Group*. Retrieved 18-04-07 from http://arg.educ.cam.ac.uk/.

Ausubel, D.P. (1963) *The Psychology of Meaningful Verbal Learning*, New York: Grune and Stratton.

Bentley, D. and Watts, M. (1989) (eds.) *Learning and Teaching in School Science: Practical Alternatives*, Milton Keynes: Open University Press.

Black, P. and Wiliam, D. (1998a) Inside the Black Box: Raising standards through classroom assessment, *Phi Delta Kappan*, 80, 2, 139–148.

Black, P. and Wiliam, D. (1998b) Assessment and classroom learning, *Assessment in Education: Principles, Policy and Practice*, 5(1) 5–75.

Black, P., Harrison, C., Lee, C., Marshall, B. and Wiliam, D. (2004) Working inside the black box: assessment for learning in the classroom, *Phi Delta Kappan* 86, 1.

Bonello, C. and Scaife, J.A. (2009) PEOR – engaging students in demonstrations. *Journal of Science and Mathematics Education in Southeast Asia* 32 (1) 62–84.

Brasell, H. (1987) The effect of real-time laboratory graphing on learning graphic representations of distance and velocity, *Journal of Research in Science Teaching*, 24(4), 385–395.

Broadfoot, P. (1998) Don't forget the confidence factor, *Times Educational Supplement*, Nov. 6, p. 25.

Brook, A., Briggs, H., Bell, B., and Driver, R. (1984) *Aspects of Secondary Students' Understanding of Heat: Summary Report*, Leeds: CLIS Project.

Brown, D.E. and Clement, J. (1989) Overcoming misconceptions by analogical reasoning: abstract transfer versus explanatory model construction, *Instructional Science*, 18, 237–261.

Bruner, J. (1964) The course of cognitive growth, *American Psychologist*, 19, 1–16.

Bruner, J. (1985) 'Vygotsky: a historical and conceptual perspective', in J. Wertsch (ed.) *Culture, Communication and Cognition: Vygotskian Perspectives*, Cambridge: Cambridge University Press.

Carré, C. (1981) *Language, Teaching and Learning: Science*, London: Ward Lock.

Champagne, A.B., Gunstone, R.F. and Klopfer, L.E. (1985) 'Effecting changes in cognitive structures among physics students', in West, L.H.T. and Pines, A.L. (eds.) *Cognitive Structure and Conceptual Change*. Orlando, FL: Academic Press.

Claxton, G. (1989) 'Cognition doesn't matter if you're scared, depressed or bored', in P. Adey (ed.) *Adolescent Development and School Science*, London: Falmer.

Coffield, F., Moseley, D., Hall, E. and Ecclestone, K. (2004) *Learning Styles and Pedagogy in Post-16 Learning*, London: Learning and Skills Research Centre. Also available on the internet via www.LSRC. ac.uk.

Department for Children, Schools and Families (2007a) *Personalised Learning*. Retrieved 3-3-2011 from: http://nationalstrategies.standards.dcsf.gov.uk/node/83151.

Department for Children, Schools and Families (2007b) *Thinking Skills in Primary Classrooms*. Retrieved 3-3-2011 from: http://webarchive.nationalarchives.gov.uk/20100612050234/http://www.standards. dfes.gov.uk/thinkingskills/.

Department for Children, Schools and Families (2008) *Personalised Learning – a practical guide*. DCSF-00844-2008. Retrieved 3-3-2011 from: http://www.education.gov.uk/publications/standard/ publicationdetail/page1/DCSF-00844-2008.

Department for Children, Schools and Families (2010) *The National Strategies: Science Assessment Focuses*. Retrieved 2-2-2011 from http://nationalstrategies.standards.dcsf.gov.uk/node/259801.

Department for Education and Employment (1998), *Teaching: High Status, High Standards*, Circular Number 4/98.

Department for Education and Skills (2002) *Key Stage 3 National Strategy Framework for Teaching Science: Years 7, 8 and 9*. DfES 05/2002.

Department for Education and Skills (2004) *Learning About Personalisation: How Can We Put the Learner at the Heart of the Education System?* DfES 0419 2004.

Donaldson, M. (1978) *Children's Minds*, reprinted 1985, London: Fontana. A very readable account of children's mental development, also containing a concise account of some of Piaget's key ideas.

Donne, J. (1634) *Devotions upon emergent occasions, and severall steps in my sicknesse*, London: Printed by A.M. and to be sold by Charles Greene, 1634.

Draper, S. (2007) *Electronic Voting Systems and Interactive Lectures: Entrance Lobby*. Retrieved 18-4-07 from: www.psy.gla.ac.uk/~steve/ilig/.

Dreyfuss, A. and Jungwirth, E. (1989) The pupil and the living cell: a taxonomy of dysfunctional ideas about an abstract idea, *Journal of Biological Education*, 23, no. 1, 49–55.

Driver, R. (1983) *The Pupil as Scientist?*, Milton Keynes: Open University Press. A pioneering book on constructivist-informed science teaching.

Driver, R. (1989) 'Changing conceptions', in P. Adey (ed.) *Adolescent Development and School Science*, London: Falmer.

Driver, R. and Bell, B. (1985) Students' thinking and the learning of science: a constructivist view, *School Science Review*, March, 443–456.

Driver, R., Guesne, E. and Tiberghien, A. (1985) *Children's Ideas in Science*, Milton Keynes: Open University Press. A useful source of common pre-teaching conceptions in science.

Driver, R., Squires, A., Rushworth, P. and Wood-Robinson, V. (1994) *Making Sense of Secondary Science*, London: Routledge. Another useful source of common pre-teaching conceptions in science.

Edelman, G. (1992) *Bright Air, Brilliant Fire: On the Matter of Mind*, London: Penguin. Human mental life from the perspective of a Nobel prize-winning neurobiologist. Brilliant, though a challenging read.

Edwards, D. and Mercer, N. (1987) *Common Knowledge*, reprinted 1993, London: Routledge. A Vygotskian perspective that looks closely at classroom talk.

Gagné, R.M. (1977) *The Conditions of Learning* (3rd edn.), London: Holt, Rinehart and Winston.

Gardner, H. (1993a) Lost youth, *The Guardian (Education)*, Oct. 12, p. 6.

Gardner, H. (1993b) *Frames of Mind: The Theory of Multiple Intelligences* (2nd edn.), London: Falmer. Gardner is widely known for his view that intelligence may be usefully thought of as made up of many distinct components, or 'intelligences'.

Gunstone, R. (1995) 'Constructivist learning and the teaching of science', in Hand, B. and Prain, V. (1995) *Teaching and Learning in Science: The Constructivist Classroom*, London: Harcourt Brace.

Hattie, J. (2009) *Visible Learning: A Synthesis of Over 800 Meta-analyses Relating to Achievement*, London: Routledge.

Head, J. (1982) What can psychology contribute to science education?, *School Science Review*, June, 631–642.

Head, J. (1989) 'The affective constraints on learning science', in P. Adey (ed.) *Adolescent Development and School Science*, London: Falmer.

Holding, B., Johnston, K. and Scott, P. (1990) *Interactive Teaching in Science: Workshops for Training Courses*, Workshop 9: Diagnostic teaching in science classrooms, CLIS project, Hatfield: Association for Science Education.

Holt, J. (1964) *How Children Fail*, revised edn. 1990, London: Penguin. This remains a classic from the early stages of child-centred educational thinking.

Howe, A.C. (1996) Development of science concepts within a Vygotskian framework, *Science Education* 80(1), 35–51.

Jenkins, E.W. (1999) School science, citizenship and the public understanding of science, *International Journal of Science Education*, 21, 7, 703–710.

Koufetta-Menicou, C. and Scaife, J.A. (2000) Teachers' questions – types and significance in science education, *School Science Review* 81, 296, 79–84.

Kyle, W.C. Jr. (1995) Editorial, *Journal of Research in Science Teaching*, 32, 9.

Lawson, A. and Renner, J. (1978) Relationships of science subject matter and developmental levels of learners, *Journal of Research in Science Teaching*, 15, 465–478.

Leamnson, R. (1999) *Thinking About Teaching and Learning*, Stoke-on-Trent: Trentham Books. A biologically-oriented perspective on learning, focusing on Key Stage 5 and college aged learners, from a college teacher.

Lovejoy, C. (1995) 'Using students' conceptual knowledge to teach a junior secondary topic of circulation and respiration', in Hand, B. and Prain, V. (1995) *Teaching and Learning in Science: The Constructivist Classroom,* London: Harcourt Brace.

Marland, M. (1975) *The Craft of the Classroom*, London: Heinemann.

Millar, R. (1993) 'Science education and public understanding of science', in R. Hull (ed.) *Association for Science Education Secondary Science Teachers' Handbook*, Hemel Hempstead: Simon and Shuster.

Mortimer, E. and Scott, P. (2003) *Meaning Making in Secondary Science Classrooms*, Maidenhead: Open University Press.

Naylor, S. and Keogh, B. (2000) 'Concept cartoons in science education'. Available from www.angelsolutions.co.uk/products/concept-cartoons.htm. Versatile cartoon resources that can be used for identifying learners' pre-teaching understandings.

Needham, R. (1987) *Teaching Strategies for Developing Understanding in Science*, Leeds: CLIS Project.

Newman, F. and Holzman, L. (1993) *Lev Vygotsky: Revolutionary Scientist*, London: Routledge.

Niedderer, H. (1987) 'A teaching strategy based on students' alternative frameworks – theoretical conceptions and examples', in *Proceedings of the Second International Seminar. Misconceptions and Educational Strategies in Science and Mathematics* 2, 360–367, Cornell University.

Novak, J.D. and Cañas, A.J. (2006) *The Theory Underlying Concept Maps and How to Construct Them*. Retrieved 1-10-06 from: http://cmap.ihmc.us/Publications/ResearchPapers/TheoryUnderlyingConceptMaps.pdf.

Osborne, J. (2009) An argument for arguments in science classes. *Phi Delta Kappan* 91, 4.

Piaget, J. (1972) *The Principles of Genetic Epistemology*, London: Routledge and Kegan Paul. Going back to the original author gives direct, rather than second-hand, access to their ideas, though Piaget isn't the easiest author to read.

Prain, V. (1995) 'Writing for learning in science', in Hand, B. and Prain, V. *Teaching and Learning in Science: The Constructivist Classroom,* London: Harcourt Brace.

Rogers, B. (1991) *You Know the Fair Rule*, Harlow: Longman.

Rosenthal, R. (1968) *Pygmalion in the Classroom: Teacher Expectation and Pupils' Intellectual Development.* London: Holt, Rinehart and Winston. Classic accounts about the impact of expectations.

Salmon, P., (1995) *Psychology in the Classroom*, London: Cassell.

Scaife, J.A. and Wellington, J.J. (1993) *Information Technology in Science and Technology Education*, Buckingham: Open University Press.

Scott, P. (1987) *A Constructivist View of Learning and Teaching in Science*, Leeds: CLIS Project.

Scott, P.H. and Ametller, J. (2007) Teaching science in a meaningful way: striking a balance between 'opening up' and 'closing down' classroom talk, *School Science Review*, 88 (324) 77–83.

Scott, P.H., Asoko, H.M. and Driver, R.H. (1991) 'Teaching for conceptual change: A review of strategies', in Duit, R., Goldberg, F. and Niedderer, H. (eds.) *Research in Physics Learning: Theoretical Issues and Empirical Studies*. Proceedings of an International Workshop. Available on the internet: http://www.physics.ohio-state.edu/~jossem/ICPE/TOC.html.

Selley, N.J. (1989) 'Philosophies of science and their relation to scientific processes and the science curriculum', in J.J. Wellington (ed.) *Skills and Processes in Science Education*, London: Routledge.

Shamos, M.H. (1995) *The Myth of Scientific Literacy*, New Brunswick, NJ: Rutgers University Press.

Shayer, M. and Adey, P. (1981) *Towards a Science of Science Teaching*, London: Heinemann.

Shayer, M., Kuchemann, D.E. and Wylam, H. (1976) The distribution of Piagetian stages of thinking in British middle and secondary school children, *British Journal of Educational Psychology*, 46, 164–173.

Shotter, J. (1995) 'In dialogue: social constructionism and radical constructivism', in Steffe, L.P. and Gale, J. (eds.) *Constructivism in Education*, Hove: Lawrence Erlbaum Associates.

Smith, P.K., Cowie, H. and Blades, M. (1998) *Understanding Children's Development* (3rd edn.) Oxford: Blackwell.

Solomon, J. (1987) Social influences on the construction of pupils' understanding of science, *Studies in Science Education*, 14, 63–82.

Solomon, J. (1989) 'Social Influence or Cognitive Growth?', in P. Adey (ed.) *Adolescent Development and School Science*, London: Falmer.

Stavy, R. (1991) Using analogy to overcome misconceptions about conservation of matter, *Journal of Research in Science Teaching*, 8(4), 305–313.

Swaffield, S. (2009) 'The misrepresentation of Assessment for Learning – and the woeful waste of a wonderful opportunity', *Association for Achievement and Improvement through Assessment National Conference*. Bournemouth, 16–18 September 2009. Retrieved 3-3-2011 from: http://leadershipforlearning.org.uk/hcdimages/LFL/swaffield_aaia09.pdf.

Tasker, R. (1981) Children's views and classroom experiences, *The Australian Science Teachers' Journal*, 27(3), 33–37. Science practical work through the eyes of pupils, written by a teacher.

Thornton, R.K. and Sokoloff, D.R. (1990) Learning motion concepts using real-time microcomputer-based laboratory tools, *American Journal of Physics*, 58(9), 858–867.

Training and Development Agency for Schools, (2007) 'Professional standards'. Retrieved 11 October 2011 from http://www.tda.gov.uk/teacher/developing-career/professional-standards-guidance.aspx

Vygotsky, L.S. (1978) *Mind in Society: The Development of Higher Psychological Processes*, London: Harvard University Press.

Waterman, A. (1999) *Private communication*, 19.11.1998, University of Sheffield Psychology Department.

Wheldall, K. and Merrett, F. (1989) *Positive Teaching in the Secondary School*, London: Paul Chapman.

Further reading on current ideas about learning and knowledge

Bickhard, M.H. (1997) Constructivism and relativisms: A shopper's guide, *Science and Education*, Vol. 6, Nos. 1 and 2, 29–42.

Bransford, J.D., Brown, A.L. and Cocking, R.R. (eds.) (2000) *How People Learn: Brain, Mind, Experience and School*, Washington DC: National Academy Press. Written with teachers and other practitioners in mind.

Churchland, Paul M. (1994) *Matter and Consciousness* (revised edn.), London: Bradford Books.

Dennett, D.C. (1991) *Consciousness Explained*, London: Penguin. A contemporary philosopher's vibrant account about human mental processes.

Edelman, G.M. and Tononi, G. (2000) *Consciousness: How Matter Becomes Imagination*, London: Allen Lane/Penguin Press.

Frith, Chris (2007) *Making up the Mind*, Oxford: Blackwell.

Gergen, K.J. (1995) 'Social construction and the educational process', in Steffe, L.P. and Gale, J. (eds.) *Constructivism in Education*, Hove: Lawrence Erlbaum Associates.

Glasersfeld, E.von (1989) Cognition, Construction of Knowledge and Teaching, *Synthese*, 80, 121–140.

Glasersfeld, E.von (1991) 'Knowing without metaphysics: aspects of the radical constructivist position', in F. Steier (ed.) *Research and Reflexivity*, London: Sage.

Glasersfeld, E.von (1995) *Radical Constructivism*, London: Falmer. A fascinating and rich account of a major strand of contemporary constructivist thinking.

Harré, R. (1986) 'An outline of the social constructionist viewpoint', in Harré, R. (ed.) *The Social Construction of Emotions*, Oxford: Blackwell.

Laland, K.N. and Brown, G.R. (2002) *Sense and Nonsense: Evolutionary Perspectives on Human Behaviour*, Oxford: Oxford University Press.

Maturana, H. (1991) 'Science and daily life: the ontology of scientific explanations', in F. Steier (ed.) *Research and Reflexivity*, London: Sage.

McGinn, C. (1989) Can we solve the Mind-Body Problem? *Mind*, 98, 349–366.

Miller, G.A. (1956) The magical number seven, plus or minus two: some limits on our capacity for processing information, *The Psychological Review*, 63, 81–97.

Phillips, D.C. (1997) Coming to grips with radical social constructivism, *Science and Education*, Vol. 6, Nos. 1 and 2, 85–104.

Plotkin, H. (1994) *Darwin Machines and the Nature of Knowledge*, London: Penguin. An evolutionary perspective on knowledge and learning.

Searle, J. (1997) *The Mystery of Consciousness*, London: Granta.

Shayer, M. (2002) 'Not just Piaget, not just Vygotsky, and certainly not Vygotsky as an *alternative* to Piaget', in Shayer, M. and Adey, P. (eds.) *Learning Intelligence*, Buckingham: Open University Press. A constructive counter to earlier accounts that set Piaget and Vygotsky in opposition to each other; Shayer shows how their ideas may be understood as complementary.

Zull, J.E. (2002) *The Art of Changing the Brain*, Sterling, VA: Stylus.

Chapter 5

Planning and managing learning in science

In a sense, the whole of this book is about planning and managing learning in science. This chapter, however, is aimed solely at offering practical ideas, frameworks and guidelines on preparing for and managing learning in science. They are presented for readers to consider, with a minimum of discussion: suggestions for further reading therefore are important and lengthy.

Planning and preparing

Schemes of work

The first task for many teachers is to prepare a scheme of work to cover perhaps from a half-term's to a year's work in science. This is usually a broad outline stating in brief what is to be taught lesson by lesson and often how it is to be taught, with perhaps additional notes on the resources needed (see the suggested checklist in Chapter 1). Creating schemes of work is often a shared activity in a science department that achieves several aims:

- a shared, co-ordinated approach to the curriculum for a given year group;
- a division and saving of labour among staff;
- on a practical level, a guide which can help in the case of staff absence;
- a record of the coverage of the curriculum (which should form the basis of the scheme);
- a record which can be used in liaison between schools, for example junior to secondary.

What might a scheme of work for secondary science look like? Our view is that it should be clear and concise with the detail coming in the lesson plans. The starting point is to examine the relevant curriculum area and then to divide it into convenient themes, topics or areas of study. A possible format is shown in Table 5.1, but readers are encouraged to look around at other ideas and formats in order to develop their own, which they and the school they work in are happy with.

Planning individual lessons

Planning each lesson within a scheme of work is the next stage – a somewhat enigmatic activity in that beginning teachers find it extremely time consuming and demanding whereas experienced teachers are able to give the impression that there is absolutely nothing to it. Appearances are misleading: lesson planning is a vitally important part of good teaching, not only in producing

Table 5.1 Headings for a scheme of work

Area/theme of study (for example, the environment, energy, force, health and diet)

LESSON ONE
(for example, Your surroundings, What is energy? Feeling forces, Eating for health, etc.)

Lesson aims:

Content/activity Learning and teaching ideas, for example, demonstration, circus, role-play
Resources needed (special notes on safety) Assessment plans and opportunities Links to other
parts of the curriculum

LESSON TWO . . . and so on.

a well-structured, varied, carefully paced, well-timed and scientifically correct lesson but also in ensuring good management and control. Good lesson planning is the first step to good control and discipline. Pupils can see for themselves if a lesson has been carefully thought through, clearly structured and pitched at the right level – indeed, it is a good teaching ploy to outline the what, the why and the how of a lesson at the outset. Surely teachers should tell pupils what they are about to do, how, why and for how long?

There are almost as many schools of thought on lesson planning as there are schools. This section offers a fairly traditional view and format for lesson planning for readers to consider. In another chapter an alternative view is offered from a 'constructivist' perspective, in which the lesson begins with the pupils' own conceptions of a concept or topic and the lesson is based upon that foundation. This obviously demands much greater flexibility and spontaneity on the part of the teacher. The ideas offered below take a much more content- and teacher-led perspective.

From this perspective, a lesson plan should include at least the following ten elements:

1   Basic information, for example, the class, time, room, etc.
2   The aims of the lesson, i.e. what the pupils should know/be able to do/understand at the end of the lesson which they did not know/were not able to do/did not understand when they walked in. These might be phrased in terms of cognitive aims, for example, recall, explain, understand, calculate, interpret, classify, etc.; or affective aims, for example, appreciate, enjoy, be aware of, gain a liking for, etc.; or 'doing' aims, for example, measure, observe, carry out, choose, etc.
3   The resources needed: what equipment will be needed? which visual aids? how will they be organised and distributed in the room?
4   Safety notes – more on this later.
5   The overall structure for the lesson itself, for example, introduction, development, conclusion.
6   Detail (greater or lesser depending on preference) within that structure. Some people like to write virtually a script; others confine themselves to listing the questions they will ask; others use the briefest of notes.
7   Indication of timing, perhaps in a margin at the side.
8   Notes indicating what the teacher and the pupils are doing in any given part of the lesson, for example, 'teacher activity/pupil activity'. This can be valuable in ensuring the variety and pacing of a lesson.
9   Homework ideas: homework must be planned and not set simply because *it is homework night*. It needs to carry some validity with the learners.

10 Space for evaluation (to be done after the lesson): a short section is needed to consider the progress of the lesson, and whether it achieved its aims, to list points to remember for next time, how you would do it differently if you taught it again!

Two possible formats or proformas for constructing lessons are presented in Figures 5.1a and 5.1b.

Name: Class: Date: Time:	**LESSON PLAN**

Administration	NC reference

Pupil learning objectives	Trainee-teacher objectives

Time	Teacher/pupil activity	Feedback strategy	Organisation

Prompts: Equal Opps   Cross-curricular links   Continuity and progression

Homework   Safety   Differentiation

Figure 5.1a Blank lesson planning grid

A   *Basic information*

Class ....   Date and time ....

Number of pupils ....   Place ....

Memo, e.g. homework reminder

....

Topic

....

B   *Resources needed*

[NB Safety points: ....]

C   *Aims and objectives*

Skills? Knowledge? Attitudes?

D   *Lesson summary* (main section)

TIME	ACTIVITY	NOTES AND COMMENTS	AIMS
0–5 mins	Introduction/ appetiser	Space for notes	
5–10	Development	(further expansion on separate pages if necessary)	
	Summary or conclusion		
e.g. 50 mins	Trailer for next lesson		

E   *Evaluation and reflection*

How did it go? Did you achieve your aims? Feedback from pupils/other teachers?

....

....

Figure 5.1b Alternative lesson planning grid

Readers may wish to use such proformas and gradually adapt them for themselves – lesson planning is quite rightly an activity that will vary from one teacher and school to another. What is unacceptable, in our view, is not to plan at all. Finally, in Figure 5.2 we show a lesson planning cycle that should be useful in linking lesson plans to schemes of work.

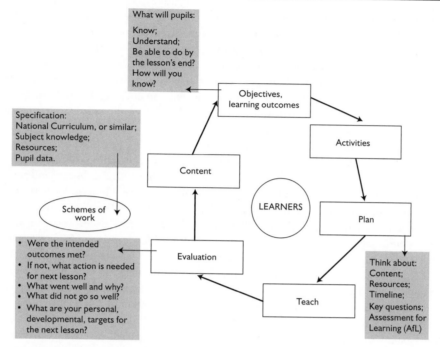

Figure 5.2 The lesson planning cycle

Keeping a lesson file

One of the things that student teachers on school experience are widely expected to do, and yet experienced teachers are strangely reluctant to be seen with, is to keep a lesson file as a necessary part of professional teaching, even if seasoned teachers pretend that they don't have one or don't need one (in reality, they are either subtle or they have a filing cabinet instead of a folder). Lesson files can usefully contain at least the following:

- schemes of work for each year/class;
- class lists and records, with essential information, for example on very special needs;
- seating plans (if used); schools also now offer photo-sheets for the class – these really help the learning of names;
- plans for individual lessons, and evaluations;
- photographic records, for example, of posters produced, wall displays, practical work, problem-solving activities, etc.;
- samples of pupils' work;
- PowerPoint slides;
- worksheets, Directed Activities Related to Text (DARTs), etc.

Planning and managing for different 'learning styles' and the notion of 'VAK'

As was discussed in Chapter 4, the concept of learning styles and preferences is not new nor is it universally accepted. But it has gained momentum in recent years and is commonly promoted in schools. The premise underlying learning styles is that different students have different preferences for the way they learn. For example, some prefer to learn visually, some by hearing (auditory learners) and some prefer to learn by doing, moving, touching or feeling (kinaesthetic). These three styles are usually abbreviated as VAK.

There are many other ways of labelling and categorising learning styles and preferences, dating back over 30 years. Some of these involve a 'Learning Styles Analysis' (LSA) or a 'Learning Style Inventory' (LSI) which allegedly tells you what kind of learner you are by asking you to answer a range of questions (see websites below).

One of the early authors (Pask 1975) argued that some people are 'serialist' learners (they learn by taking one element at a time) while others are 'holist', preferring to gain an overview first. Some learners prefer to move from specific, concrete examples to the abstract and general – others prefer to move the other way, from the abstraction and general rule or theory to the specific instances that come under it. Another LSI came from Kolb (1984) who talked about 'divergers' and 'convergers' on one dimension, and 'accommodators' versus 'assimilators' on another. Gregorc (1982) talked of different mindsets or 'mindstyles' for learning: concrete sequential, abstract sequential, concrete random and abstract random. A later analysis came from Riding and Cheema (1991) who distinguished 'wholist' learners from analysts. The wholist uses a top-down approach and prefers to grasp the whole concept or idea first before concentrating on the specifics and the details. The 'analyst' prefers to process information in a step-by-step sequential manner, building up from the concrete instances to the general rule.

Strong supporters of learning styles argue that students learn most effectively when they are taught in a style that best matches their preferred style of learning. Hence, they stipulate that all lesson plans should incorporate reference to learning styles, even to the extent of marking V, A or K in a column alongside the plan to denote the style of learning at that point in the lesson. More moderate approaches suggest that teachers should openly introduce variety into their lesson planning (e.g. by using a VAK checklist) in order to recognise the wide range of learning styles present in any one class, on any one day. In 2004, the DfES went as far as to make explicit the different 'traits' that V, A and K learners might exhibit (see Table 5.2).

More radical approaches have involved introducing a wide range of physical and other environmental conditions into a classroom, for example: different types of seating – some hard, some soft, with cushions or without; different types of lighting – brighter for some, dimmer for others, some fluorescent and some not; the use of music to enhance some holistic learners' progress, but quiet for others; different temperature levels; drinking water for those who want it; different groupings, with some students allowed to work on their own, others in peer groups.

The concepts of learning styles and its close relation, multiple intelligences, are in many ways very appealing – but there are numerous questions that teachers could and should be asking about learning styles and learning inventories:

- What is the validity of the tests that indicate whether you happen to be one type of learner or another? With the proliferation of instruments and tests, how reliable are they? How well do the different tests correlate with each other?
- Can the same person have a different learning style according to mood, time of day, inclination, subject matter and so on? Is it something a student is 'stuck with' over time?
- Is it dangerous to label learners as being of a certain type so that they carry that label and almost begin to believe in it? e.g. 'I'm a kinaesthetic learner?' Will these result in further labelling for 'under-achievers' and stereotyping of certain categories of student?
- Does the learning style label become a self-fulfilling prophecy?

Table 5.2 Traits of different learning styles

Visual	Auditory	Kinaesthetic
Prefers to read, see the words, illustrations and diagrams	Likes to be told, to listen to the teacher, to talk it out	Likes to get involved, hands on, to try it out
Talks fast, uses lots of images	Talks fluently, in a logical order and with few hesitations	Talks about actions and feelings, uses lots of hand movements, speaks more slowly
Memorises by writing repeatedly	Memorises by repeating words out loud	Memorises by doing something repeatedly
When inactive, looks around, doodles or watches something	When inactive, talks to self or others	When inactive, fidgets and walks around
When starts to understand something says, 'that looks right'	When starts to understand something says, 'that sounds right'	When starting to understand something says, 'that feels right'
Is most distracted by untidiness	Is most distracted by noises	Is most distracted by movements or physical disturbances

Source: DfES (2004)

- What should teachers actually do about learning styles in the classroom, faced with a range of learning preferences and styles?
- Should learners and teachers play to the learner's strengths – or should they work on improving a learner's weaknesses? If learning how to learn is an aim of education, then surely each student should learn how to improve their learning in their least favoured style?

Recent years have seen the learning styles approach become both a bandwagon and an industry, with in-service training days, paid consultants, websites and books on the topic proliferating (rather like the related ideas of 'brain-based learning' and 'brain gym'). In some ways it is welcome and admirable in that the learning styles movement shifts the focus onto the learner and highlights the importance of diversity. But in other ways it needs to be closely watched so that it does not become a dogmatic and rigid straitjacket for classroom management and lesson planning.

In a recent study (Coffield *et al.* 2004) over 70 different learning style frameworks were identified but little evidence was produced to suggest any impact on pupil achievement! Stahl (1999) writes:

> ... five research reviews, published in well regarded journals found the same thing. One cannot reliably measure children's learning styles and even if one could, matching children to reading programs by learning styles does not improve their learning.

We have even seen the situation in a school where children in a class were given coloured badges (V, A or K) according to how they answered a 'learning styles' inventory. They were asked to wear them in the classroom. Being naturally subversive, of course, they later swapped them around (once they were out in the corridor) and happily wore the mixed-up labels to the next lesson. Our view is that healthy scepticism is the best, only scientific, way forward.

Asking questions

One of the activities that teachers engage in whatever their view of learning or lesson planning is that of asking questions. Indeed there is probably no other context in life, except perhaps the Houses of Parliament, where so many questions are asked by so few of so many. One estimate is that teachers ask questions for one-third of their classroom time with a total, on average, of 30,000 questions per year. Some teachers ask sensible, useful, probing questions of pupils spontaneously and naturally – we would suggest that these Socratic people are few and far between. Most of us need to plan and prepare our questioning even to the extent of writing them into the lesson plan. Time spent on this can avoid embarrassment and disruption in the classroom. A question such as 'Where can I find sea water?' is likely to lead to either dumb disbelief that any adult could ask such a thing, or worse still loud shouts of 'Skegness', 'Blackpool', or 'Hastings', depending on the region. Teachers need to examine carefully four aspects of questioning:

1   Why they should ask questions at all?
2   When are the best times to ask them?
3   How should questions be posed and presented, i.e. what makes for a good questioning technique?
4   What types of question can teachers ask?

The four aspects are closely interrelated: for example, the time and reason for asking a question will determine the technique and tone used – this should be remembered as we take each aspect in turn. A large amount has been said and written about questioning and what follows below should be regarded as a brief, potted summary.

Why ask questions?

There are many good reasons for asking questions in a classroom, including the following:
•   to gain and keep attention, i.e. as a means of control;
•   to get pupils to think;
•   to keep them active and attentive, i.e. to avoid spoon-feeding;
•   to stimulate curiosity and interest;
•   to test/confirm their knowledge or understanding;
•   to identify/diagnose any problems in learning, recall or understanding;
•   to lead a class step-by-step through a topic or an experiment, i.e. Socratic questioning, 'bringing things out';
•   to elicit pupils' prior knowledge or conceptions, i.e. finding out where they are already;
•   to revise a topic, for example at the end of a lesson or at the start of a new one;
•   to gain feedback on what they have learnt, to evaluate the lesson, for example 'Have the aims been achieved?'

When to ask questions?

The reasons for asking questions are connected with the best times to ask them, for example:

1   At the start, during the starter or introduction, for example, to give a link with the previous lesson, to revise and reinforce earlier learning, to elicit pupils' ideas;

2   During the development of the lesson, for example, using key questions to guide pupils' thinking or to formulate a problem, working out the right steps, procedures and sequence for a practical instead of simply giving instructions;
3   During class activity, for example, to sort out problems in small groups or with individuals;
4   At the end of a class activity, for example, to pool results, to consider results, to work towards a conclusion;
5   At the end of a lesson or the plenary, for example, to go over, revise, reinforce, evaluate, or lead up to the next lesson.

What kind of questions can be asked?

There are two important ways of classifying questions. First, questions can be grouped according to whether they are open or closed.

Closed questions usually have one correct, often short, answer – for example, 'What is the symbol used for sodium?' or 'What is the capital of England?' The teacher usually wants pupils to give an answer that she or he already knows. If there is a particular correct answer that the teacher is seeking, such as trachea rather than windpipe, then closed questions often become a 'guess what's in my head?' exercise.

Table 5.3 Suggested activities to cater for different learning styles and intelligences

Visual, auditory, kinaesthetic	Multiple intelligence	Learning experience
Visual	Visual-spatial	Diagrams, charts, video, films, graphs, posters, maps, pamphlets, textbooks, drawing, creating mental pictures, collages, colour highlighting
Auditory	Linguistic	Discussion, group work, pair work, debates, interviewing, expositions, presentations, improvisations, listening to speakers, mnemonics, writing notes, essays and poems, sketches, stories, reading
Kinaesthetic	Bodily-kinaesthetic	DARTs, role play, dance, model making, simulations, 'show me' cards, freeze-frames, improvisation, associating ideas with movements, human graphs, sentences or timelines, field trips, games, competitions
	Logical-mathematical	Puzzles, problem solving, predicting or hypothesising, investigations, sequential tasks, summaries, pattern spotting
	Musical	Chants, rhymes, songs, mnemonics, raps, poems, musical interpretations
	Interpersonal	Collaborative group, pair or team work, interviewing, teaching or coaching others
	Intrapersonal	Individual research, learning journals, reflection on own learning, identifying own questions, self-evaluation, diaries

Source: (DfES 2004)

With open questions a variety of responses can be acceptable, such as 'Why did London become the capital of England?' They often ask what the pupils are thinking, and there will be more than one correct answer. However, for many teachers, some answers are more correct than others! In other words, except perhaps in a genuine brainstorming session, few questions are genuinely totally open. Thus a question such as 'What did you notice about the copper as we heated it?' may invite many responses whereas the teacher may be seeking only one.

Second, questions can also be grouped by the intellectual demand made by the question. It may require any of the following:

- Factual recall, for example, 'Which gas makes up 0.03 per cent of the air?' or 'Which ore does iron come from?' This will obviously involve asking closed questions.
- Understanding and application of a formula, a rule, a law, a theory, etc., for example, 'If a person lifts a weight of 50 newtons from the ground onto a shelf two metres above it, how much work has she done?' (These are generally closed questions.)
- Analysis and evaluation of, for example, a process, a material and its use, an energy source, or a set of data. Analysis may sometimes have one correct answer, for example, in analysing data from a table, but evaluation may invite several 'correct' responses, provided they are based on careful consideration and analysis, such as, 'What are the benefits and drawbacks of using nuclear fission to provide energy?'
- Predicting and hypothesising, for example, 'What do you think will happen if … ?'
- Interpreting and explaining, for example, 'Why did the wire become hot?'
- Inferring, for example, 'If we add more weights to this spring what will happen?' (cf. predicting).

These are just some of the ways of classifying questions; such a classification is not definitive and there is also much overlap between the categories. Often we cannot tell if we are predicting, hypothesising or inferring – the three go together. But a classification of this kind is useful for two reasons. First of all, in lesson planning and evaluation, teachers can prepare and examine their questions to see if they are balanced. Are all their questions of the closed, factual-recall kind? Do they ask pupils to speculate, predict and hypothesise? Do they give opportunities for weighing up pros and cons, analysing points of view and assessing benefits and drawbacks, i.e. evaluation? These are all essential features of the science national curriculum.

Thus a classification of questions asked, in both spoken and written form, is useful in lesson planning and in ensuring coverage of the curriculum. It is also vital in considering assessment of students' learning.

Having looked at the teacher's planning for questioning, what is the learners' view? Research by Pratt (2006) suggests two points:

1 Pupils see listening for the 'right answer' to memorise as more important than engaging with the lesson;
2 Pupils see listening to, rather than talking to, the teacher as more important.

What this tells us, we argue, is the need for planning strategies to engage all pupils in the questioning process, which leads us to ask how should questions be prepared and presented in a classroom? Table 5.4 offers a set of guidelines on preparing and phrasing questions, and on presenting them to a class.

Table 5.4 Guidelines for questioning

Preparing and phrasing questions

- Prepare key questions in advance, using the categories above.

- Relate the questions to the aims of the lesson.

- Phrase the questions clearly and at the right language level.

- Avoid ambiguous wording.

- Beware of 'nonsense' questions, for example 'Why does a pig have four legs?'; general questions, for example 'Where can we find seawater?', and other questions that invite stupid answers, for example 'What do you all do at least once a day?'

- Make sure that questions are carefully sequenced.

Presenting and delivering questions

- Position yourself and the class carefully – ensure that you can see and be seen.

- Insist on the use of hands rather than shouting out.

- Spread questions around the class – look for a balance, such as back and front, male and female.

- Use pupils' names in directing and responding to questions.

- Draw ideas out from the pupils – don't give too much too soon.

- If the classroom situation allows it, keep probing and prompting in order to extend pupils' thinking, for example 'What do you mean by that . . . ?', 'And then what might happen . . .?', 'What makes you say that . . .?', and so on.

Accepting and dealing with responses

- Be ready to record responses. This is a form of reward as well as a useful record, for example, of predictions.

- Use body language, such as nods, hand gestures, smiles, to encourage pupils to respond.

- Praise responses even if the answer to a closed question is incorrect – don't condemn answers to open questions purely because they don't coincide with what's in your head.

- Give leads and hints if responses are not forthcoming, perhaps by rephrasing and redirecting the question.

- Don't embarrass or humiliate by waiting too long for a response.

- Don't allow others to ridicule a pupil for an incorrect answer to a closed question or a strange answer to an open one.

- Open questions, although educationally desirable, lead to responses which can be far harder to manage and control than closed ones, such as long monologues from pupils or totally unexpected or zany replies. Developing a good questioning technique that includes asking and responding to open questions takes time and reflection.

Safety issues

Safety in the lab is not just an important issue – it is the issue which overrides all others. In other words, whatever good reasons, educational, motivational or any other there are for doing an activity or a demonstration, IF IT IS UNSAFE OR UNHEALTHY IN ANY WAY THEN DO NOT DO IT! This is the simple and cardinal rule. Given the importance attached to safety matters, *safety in the laboratory* has its own chapter, Chapter 10.

Management and control

The subject that perhaps most concerns all beginning and many practising teachers, and that relates to lesson planning, asking questions and safety, is the management and control of pupils during the lesson. This topic is another on which a vast amount has been said and written, some of which is useful and practical, part of which is too vague to be of value, and an element of which is pure scaremongering. Let us therefore start by putting classroom management issues into perspective. An important report back in 1989 (HMSO 1989) showed that, in its sample of over 2,000 teachers, the five behaviours most commonly reported as a difficulty, in the order shown below, were:

- pupils talking out of turn;
- work avoidance or idleness;
- pupils hindering other pupils;
- pupils not being punctual;
- pupils making unnecessary, non-verbal noise.

Take a careful look at these, the top five, which our experience of working with trainee and practising teachers indicates are the same twenty years on. They do not include swearing at the teacher, acts of vandalism or physical attack, all of the incidents which a gullible reader of the popular press would infer are common in schools. The Elton Report and other published studies since have shown clearly that those 'newsworthy' types of behaviour may sell newspapers but are relatively rare in the real, non-tabloid world. Thus we start here from the premise that the most common management goals for the teacher are quite simply to organise and control pupil talk in the classroom, and to keep pupils to task.

As mentioned earlier, a large number of books have been written about classroom management, and although they can never be a substitute for experience and observation they can give teachers at all stages useful frameworks for analysing their own practice. Many of the books (listed at the end of the chapter) offer practical advice on class management: Robertson (1989), for example, gives a useful checklist for 'successful teaching'; McManus (1989) provides a summary of 'teaching skills for classroom management'; Marland (1975), in one of the most widely read books in initial training, offers a guide to all aspects of the classroom component of a teacher's job, as do Kyriacou's books (1986 and 1991). It would be impossible to distil all the practical wisdom from the wide range of books in this area. However, we have offered below a checklist that might be valuable to teachers to consider before and after a lesson. These points are a summary of much of the agreed wisdom on planning, preparing, presenting and managing lessons. They are offered to readers in a clear and direct style, but please do look carefully and critically at them.

Planning

- Plan a varied, interesting lesson.
- Make sure the pupils are busy throughout, according to your lesson plan, i.e. give them plenty to do.
- Plan some time-fillers, such as a quiz, spelling test, word-search or crosswords.
- Plan a lesson that makes sense and has some sort of logical pattern, sequence, or structure to it. Make it clear to the pupils what you are trying to teach them, and why!

Preparation

- Try all experiments and demonstrations before the lesson.
- Prepare some visual material beforehand, if possible.
- Check all the apparatus before and after each lesson. Count it all out – count it all back in again.
- Ensure that ventilation and lighting are adequate.

Self-presentation

- Try to look confident and professional: don't slouch, mumble, look at your feet or stare out of the window.
- Speak clearly, at a sensible speed.
- Project yourself.
- 'Scan' the group and make eye contact. Don't just talk to the front row.
- Put some life into it, for example, move your lips, don't stand in one place like a statue, appear enthusiastic.
- Be aware of what's going on ('with it'); look for feedback, such as yawns, glazed looks.
- Do use gestures and body language as well as spoken language, especially in a large and busy lab. Develop your own 'sign language' which can be extremely valuable during practical work (see Figure 5.3 for examples of useful sign language).

Relationships

Good relationships are both a cause and an effect of good classroom management. Also, they do take time:

- Be pleasant but never friendly – it's totally false.
- Be firm but not 'stroppy'. Pupils hate teachers who shout and moan at them all the time.
- Occasionally show that you're human (this is probably safest outside the classroom, such as on the games field).
- Don't court popularity.
- Try to enjoy what you're doing, but don't smile too much (don't spend two minutes getting the class quiet, then tell them a joke).
- Start learning names immediately (by studying the class list in advance and using mnemonics, even silly ones; when handing out books; as pupils answer questions; using a seating plan, etc.).
- Use names as soon as you can, i.e. don't use 'You at the back' or 'Yes, you', again a seating plan can help here.
- Use praise, both public and private.
- Respond positively to correct answers – don't just grunt or nod imperceptibly, for example, 'Very good' or 'Yes, well done'.
- Insist on silence when you are talking to the whole class – but don't overdo it (perhaps five minutes at a stretch).
- Pick the right moment to address the class (for example, not while they're trooping out of or into the room).
- Give clear, positive starting signals to gain attention according to some sort of 'hierarchy' ranging from pleasant to curt. For example: pleasant, non-verbal signals, such as standing

'Make it much
wider/larger.'

'Turn it up
a little.'

'Just a tiny bit
(chemicals cost money you know).'

Figure 5.3 Gestures and sign language can be extremely valuable in management and control
Source: drawn by David Houchin

waiting for quiet, or 'Can I have your attention please?', 'Will you all listen now?', 'Be quiet
everybody'; curt: 'John – be quiet' (i.e. focus on individuals) or 'Shut up'.
• Don't start the lesson until you have complete silence, even if you have to work through this
range and repeat these signals.
• If spoken words won't settle the class, try written words or a definite task, such as: 'Copy
these notes off the blackboard …'; 'Draw this diagram …'; 'Copy this slide/ transparency'.

Keeping control

• Don't expect a class to follow the same activity (for example, note-taking) for an hour, or to
listen to you endlessly. Variety is the spice of a lesson.
• Try to decide in your own mind what standards and norms you want to enforce – this is
half the battle. (Commands are obeyed in direct proportion to how much you mean them.)
• Stick closely to the school norms whenever you can – it's easier.

- Be determined in enforcing these norms.
- There is no need to insist on silence during class or practical work but you can, for example, insist that pupils only talk to the person next to them.
- Be consistent and predictable over what you want and what you expect.

Starting and ending a lesson

- Stand near the door and look at each pupil as he or she comes into the room. (Don't, for example, write on the whiteboard, fiddle with apparatus, engage in deep conversation with a pupil or the lab technician, or sort out books as the class comes in.)
- You may wish to make brief individual remarks as they enter, such as 'You're sitting on the front row today' or a similar witticism.
- Don't try to start a lesson too quickly (for example, don't explain Einstein's theory of relativity while they're still taking their coats off). Give them one to two minutes to settle down and get in the right frame of mind, with the occasional salutary remark from you (such as 'Put him down', 'Spit the chewing gum in the bin', etc.).
- On the other hand, don't start a lesson ten minutes late.
- Try to sum up and round off every lesson, then tell them what they're doing next time.
- Don't dismiss the class until they are all sitting in silence. Dismiss one row at a time.
- Stand by the door and watch each pupil as he or she leaves. Save long conversations, and reprimands, until others have gone.

If things go wrong ...

- Avoid one-to-one confrontation. It's very difficult to win.
- Use other staff, for example, to supervise one or two (at most) miscreants outside the classroom (extracting one or two pupils can save a lesson for the other 26).
- If you send a pupil out, send him or her to somebody specific, such as the Head of Department, with a specific task to do.
- Don't make empty, 'unkeepable' threats, such as 10,000 lines, 90 minutes' detention.
- You can make small, keepable threats, such as 50 lines, 10 minutes' staying in.
- Don't be afraid to make pupils move seats.
- Don't get physical in any way.
- Raise your voice to the roof if necessary, but above all don't overdo it – it soon loses its impact.
- Do seek advice. Talk over your lessons with staff and other students.
- Above all, don't take it personally.

Your worst class

If all the above fail:

- Try a totally different tactic, such as individualised learning instead of class teaching, lots of colourful worksheets, video, slides, … anything!
- Find out how other teachers cope with them, if at all.
- Have a cup of tea, drink, walk or run before you carry out a post mortem (evaluation) on your lesson.

Every professional benefits from their colleagues' help. Teachers are no exception.

Even if teachers do follow all the rules, tips, dos and don'ts, and handy hints dished out to them by everyone from their mentor in school, to parents, press and politicians, there will be lessons that do not go according to plan. It is worth returning briefly to the Elton Report to see what teachers in their sample did when dealing with difficult classes or individuals. The most common strategies and sanctions used were, in this order:

- reasoning with a pupil or pupils inside the room;
- reasoning outside the room;
- setting extra work of some kind;
- detaining a pupil or pupils;
- sending a pupil or pupils out of the room;
- referring a pupil or pupils to another teacher;
- sending a pupil or pupils to a more senior teacher.

These are still likely to be the most common sanctions that teachers will continue to employ – it is unlikely that caning, hanging, drawing and quartering in return for deviant behaviour will make a comeback.

Feedback and marking

One of the clearest messages from studies of behaviour in classrooms is that although punishment has little effect in improving the behaviour of those punished (although it may have a deterrent effect on those who observe it), the use of praise can be extremely effective. Pupils like teachers who are well organised, interesting and humorous – there is also extensive evidence that they respond well to praise. Praise can be a tool for classroom control in encouraging pupils, keeping them to task, motivating them, and generally improving their self-esteem. Its value cannot be overstated.

In general, the feedback that pupils receive from the teacher is vitally important. Humiliation and condemnation are not productive – praise and encouragement are. This is also true of marking pupils' written work. More will be said on pupils' writing and marking in Chapter 11 on language in science education, but it can be said briefly here that feedback on written work is as important as it is in the oral, classroom context. What guidelines can be offered on marking work? A short summary is given here which will be developed in the language chapter:

- Always mark pupils' work at frequent intervals, even if there is not time to mark it thoroughly, word by word, on every occasion. Some feedback, comment or praise is better than nothing. At least it shows pupils that the teacher cares and is keeping an eye on things.
- Use praise and encouragement as well as criticism. Find something positive to say about the work, however small. If appropriate, praise the work as you hand it back.
- The correction of spelling is a thorny and contentious issue. Spelling is important for at least three reasons: poor spelling inhibits the writer's fluency and distracts the reader from the content; the reader judges the content to be of lower quality, not least in a scientific context; spelling is seen in society as important, rightly or wrongly. For these reasons a teacher has a duty to consider a pupil's spelling when marking work in science and to use whatever strategy is best for that pupil in order to improve it. This is the nub of the issue. With pupils who make perhaps two spelling errors in a piece of work, correction of each is

both practical and not too damning. With a pupil whose work is riddled with misspellings the situation requires tact. One strategy is to single out the more important errors and correct those tactfully but clearly. There may be persistent errors which a teacher can look for and attempt to remedy. Special help may be needed, for example through the use of IT. The process of correction and redrafting is far easier to handle and far less painful if a simple wordprocessor is used, perhaps with a spell-checker. Presentation and self-esteem can be greatly enhanced by using a computer system to reveal the true extent of a pupil's writing. Teachers should not be misled into assuming that a poor speller, or a person with unsightly handwriting, is a poor writer.

There are many issues connected with marking and giving feedback to pupils that could be considered; the main message here, though, is that it should be based on reward, praise and encouragement rather than on negative criticism or condemnation.

Homework

The final job that falls to teachers at the end of the lesson is very often the setting of homework. Not only are teachers responsible for the learning and behaviour of pupils during school hours, they also extend their influence outside these hours by the tradition of homework! Like it or not, most secondary schools have a policy of setting and monitoring homework. It can be set for a variety of reasons:

- to finish work started in the lesson, such as finishing written work, writing up a practical;
- as a new piece of work relating to the lesson;
- as an assessment of the learning in a lesson, for example, a set of questions based on the lesson content;
- as an extension to the work in the lesson, for example, a worksheet of information, reading and questions;
- as an open, flexible piece of work that can be undertaken almost independently at home, such as a piece of mini-research, a project, an exploration (this will obviously depend to a large extent on a pupil having access to resources at home or nearby);
- it should be clear and manageable within a realistic time span;
- it should not make too many demands upon or assumptions about the home environment; for example: 'Look up the following words in *Encyclopaedia Britannica* ...'; or 'Use the internet to explore ...';
- it should be clearly connected to the lesson and the overall scheme of work;
- the purpose behind it should be clear to the pupil, i.e. the reason why this demand is being placed upon them in their out-of-school time should be understood.

Homework can be valuable, and there might well be an outcry from certain quarters if the tradition of British homework disappeared. However, there are problems with it that have surfaced both in the everyday experience of teachers and in research studies of attitudes to it. The main, most common problems seem to be:

- pupils being unclear about what they had to do or how much, with no opportunity to seek clarification (this may arise from poor instructions in the lesson, not writing it down, not listening, not remembering, etc.);

- pupils not having the resources, such as secondary sources, or the equipment, such as a protractor or calculator, to carry out the work;
- pupils unable to obtain secondary sources, for example, from the public library;
- poor working conditions at home;
- badly written, unclear or poorly reproduced worksheets;
- homework set via the school's Virtual Learning Environment (VLE) assumes that pupils have access to an internet connection.

These are all problems that the teacher needs to be aware of, even if they are not all within the teacher's sphere of influence. Remember, the pupil who could not cope with the work in class, with your support, is even less likely to be able to cope at home. Chapter 15 considers the important and connected issue of children's out-of-school learning in science. Work by Hallam (2004) indicates that the efficacy of homework has a much smaller impact on achievement than the pupils' social background. Finally research by Dettmers *et al.* (2009) points to the finding that whilst time spent on homework, in this case mathematics, correlates with greater achievement at the school level, individuals who spend more time on homework do no better than those who spend less.

In summary ...

This chapter has looked at a wide range of issues connected with the important business of planning for learning in science. Management and control are uppermost in the minds of most new teachers – but these go hand-in-hand with organisation, preparation, lesson planning, appropriate assessment, praise and feedback. In the next chapter we consider the importance of planning for learning for the whole range of pupils that might be encountered in a truly comprehensive school.

Points for reflection

- In constructing a lesson plan, how should teachers plan for different learning styles in the classroom, faced with a range of learning preferences? How literally should they take the 'VAK' framework?
- In teaching and planning, should teachers play to the learner's strengths – or should they work on improving a learner's weaknesses?

References and further reading

General

A widely used source is:
Cohen, L., Manion, L. and Morrison, K. (2004) *A Guide to Teaching Practice*, London: RoutledgeFalmer (5th edition).
For a variety of classroom strategies and very practical ideas, see:

Ginnis, Paul (2002) *The Teacher's Toolkit: Raise classroom achievement with strategies for every learner*, Carmarthen: Crown House Publishing.

Muijs, D. and Reynolds, D. (2010) *Effective Teaching Evidence and Practice*, London, Sage.

Management and control

There is a wide range of books on classroom management and control. Here is a brief list showing a selection of those books with short notes on some. Although they cannot be a substitute for classroom practice and experience, they can help to provide a framework for analysing and reflecting upon them. There is nothing as practical as a good theory. One author who seems to be popular with new teachers is:

Cowley, Sue (2001) *Getting the Buggers to Behave*, London: Continuum.

Going back further:

Cheesman, P. and Watts, P. (1985) *Positive Behaviour Management: a manual for teachers*, London: Croom Helm, pp. 80–4; a discussion of the background to behaviour problems and ways of assessing them. Puts forward practical advice on intervention and a 'step-by-step' guide to positive behaviour management. The summary of suggestions for 'teacher behaviour' may be particularly useful.

HMSO (1989) *Discipline in Schools: the Elton Report*, London: HMSO.

Kyriacou, C. (1986) *Effective Teaching in Schools*, Oxford: Blackwell.

Kyriacou, C. (1991) *Essential Teaching Skills*, Oxford: Blackwell.

Marland, M. (1975) *The Craft of the Classroom*, Oxford: Heinemann; reprinted many times, this book is a short, well-organised and very practical classic covering all aspects of the new teacher's job; valuable if a little dated.

McManus, M. (1989) *Troublesome Behaviour in the Classroom – a teacher's survival guide*, London: Routledge; a detailed account of troublesome behaviour, its causes and remedies; draws extensively on research findings, but also has many practical activities to try. Useful for students and experienced teachers alike.

Neill, S. (1991) *Classroom Non-verbal Communication*, London: Routledge; illustrates, with text and numerous drawings, the use of body language, facial expression and posture in the classroom. Very practical discussion and advice, based on recent research, offering suggestions for teachers on conveying enthusiasm, gaining attention, using space and interpreting pupils' body language.

Neill, S. and Caswell, C. (1993) *Body Language for Competent Teachers*, London: Routledge.

Robertson, J. (1989) (2nd edition) *Effective Classroom Control – understanding teacher–pupil relationships*, London: Hodder & Stoughton; short but detailed, with much good advice on teacher–pupil relationships; over half of the book is devoted to analysing and dealing with unwanted behaviour in the classroom.

Rogers, C. (1983) *Freedom to Learn*, Ohio: Merrill; a compendium of Rogers' research on person-centred learning, how to manage it and set it up so that pupils' curiosity and enthusiasm are not stifled. A stimulating and challenging book.

Smith, C. and Laslett, R. (1993) (2nd edition) *Effective Classroom Management*, London: Routledge.

Thorp, S. (ed.) (1991) *Race, Equality and Science Teaching*, Hatfield: ASE; has several useful activities involving looking at schemes of work, page 57, 'Looking at my classroom', pages 15–17 and reflecting on 'Groupings in the classroom', page 51.

Planning

Baxter, M. (1998) 'Planning for teaching and learning', in Ratcliffe, M. (ed.) *ASE Guide to Secondary Education*, Hatfield: ASE/Stanley Thornes, pp. 127–37.

Dettmers, S., Truatwein, U., and Ludtke, O. (2009) The relationship between homework time and achievement is not universal: evidence from multilevel analyses in 40 countries, *School Effectiveness and School Improvement*. Vol 20, no 2, pp. 1–31.

Hallam, S. (2004) *Homework: The Evidence,* London: Institute of Education.

Pratt, N. (2006) Interactive teaching in numeracy lessons: what do children have to say? *Cambridge Journal of Education* vol 36, no 2, pp. 221–35.

Learning styles, 'VAK' and multiple intelligences

For fuller discussion on learning styles, brain-based learning and multiple intelligences see Chapter 4 in this book and:

Coffield, F., Moseley, D., Hall, E. and Ecclestone, K. (2004) *Learning Styles and Pedagogy in Post-16 Learning. A Systematic and Critical review,* London: Learning and Skills Research Centre.

DfES (2003) *Teaching and Learning in Secondary Schools: unit 10: learning styles,* London: DfES.

DfES (2004) *Pedagogy and Practice: teaching and learning in secondary schools: unit 19: learning styles,* Norwich: HMSO.

Stahl, S. (1999) Different strokes for different folks? A critique of learning styles, *American Educator* vol 23, no 3, pp. 27–31.

Wellington, J. (2006) *Secondary Education: the key concepts,* London: Routledge.

Some of the early texts are:

Gardner, H. (1993) *Intelligence Reframed. Multiple intelligences for the 21st century,* New York: Basic Books.

Gregorc, A. (1982) *An Adult's Guide to Styles,* Maynard, MA: Gabriel Systems.

Honey, P. and Mumford, A. (1982) *Manual of Learning Styles,* London: P. Honey.

Kolb, David (1984) *Experiential Learning: experience as the source of learning and development,* Englewood Cliffs, NJ: Prentice-Hall.

Pask, G. (1975) *The Cybernetics of Human Learning and Performance,* London: Hutchinson.

Riding, R. (2002) *School Learning and Cognitive Style,* London: David Fulton.

Riding, R. and Cheema, I. (1991) Cognitive style: an overview and integration, *Educational Psychology,* vol. 11, pp. 193–215.

White, J. (1998) *Do Howard Gardner's Multiple Intelligences Add Up?* London: Institute of Education, University of London.

Questioning

Chin, Christine (2004) Students' questions: fostering a culture of inquisitiveness in science classrooms, *School Science Review,* vol. 86, no. 314, pp. 107–12.

Selley, Nick (2000) Wrong answers welcome, *School Science Review,* vol. 82, no. 299, pp. 41–6; looks at ways of building on pupils' wrong answers in science lessons.

Mortimer, Eduardo and Scott, Phil (2003) *Meaning Making in Secondary Science Classrooms,* Maidenhead: Open University Press.

Going further back:

Brown, G.A. (1975) *Microteaching,* London: Methuen; this book has been around for some time but has many useful points.

Brown, G.A. (1984) 'Questioning', in Wragg, E.G. (ed.) *Classroom Teaching Skills,* London: Croom Helm.

Carr, D. (1998) The art of asking questions in the teaching of science, *School Science Review,* vol. 79, no. 289, pp. 47–50.

Kerry, T. (1982) *Effective Questioning,* London: Macmillan Education.

Sands, M. and Hull, R. (1985) *Teaching Science: a teaching skills workbook,* London: Macmillan Education; a useful collection of practical ideas on not only questioning but also management, control, marking and safety.

Wellington, J.J. (1998) 'Dialogues in the science classroom', in Ratcliffe, M. (ed.) *ASE Guide to Secondary Education,* Hatfield: ASE/Stanley Thornes, pp. 146–58.

Assessment

See the references in Chapter 1 and Chapter 4 and:

Gipps, C.V. (1995) *Beyond Testing: towards a theory of educational assessment*, London: Falmer Press.

Gipps, C.V. and Murphy, P. (1994) *A Fair Test? Assessment achievement and equity*, Milton Keynes: Open University Press.

Gipps, C.V. and Stobart, G. (1993) *Assessment: a teacher's guide to the issues*, London: Hodder and Stoughton.

Hayes, P. (1998) 'Assessment in the classroom', in Ratcliffe, M. (ed.) *ASE Guide to Secondary Education*, Hatfield: ASE/Stanley Thornes, pp. 138–45.

Sutton, R. (1992) *Assessment: a framework for teachers*, London: Routledge.

Chapter 6

Inclusive science education

Meeting the needs of all children in science

An inclusive science education implies that all pupils, not least those with learning or communication difficulties, should be given the opportunity of some sort of 'scientific experience'. This statement applies to all pupils with special educational needs (SEN), whether the difficulty they have in learning is general or specific, severe or less severe. Indeed, we should remember that we all experience difficulty of some kind or another in learning, whether it is due to tiredness, saturation or simply that it 'won't go in'. All pupils should receive a broad and balanced curriculum, relevant to their individual needs. The idea of 'inclusive education', and a discussion of how this might be achieved in mainstream schools, is the subject of this chapter.

The drive towards inclusion: a brief history

A mainstream schoolteacher starting her career in 1960 and ending it in the 1980s will undoubtedly have met a range of pupils with different needs and interests. There is no such thing as a homogenous group. However, the range of needs that teacher would have encountered is certain to have been narrower than someone starting a career in 2011. There has been a succession of legislation in the UK which has driven the policy of inclusion (see Table 6.1).

It began with the Warnock report (1978) and the subsequent Education Act of 1981. This encouraged local education authorities to integrate children with special needs into mainstream schools. Subsequent policy statements and legislation have reinforced the Warnock view and effectively widened the range of pupils in mainstream classes as, in particular, the 1997 Green Paper, *Excellence for all children* (DfEE 1997) accelerated the move towards inclusive education.

Since 1994, every school has been obliged to have a 'SENCO' (special needs coordinator). They perform a valuable role but their presence does not remove the need for classroom teachers to have their own awareness of the new range of pupils or knowledge of how to aid their teaching and learning. Science teachers will meet a wide range of potential 'difficulties', from physical disability to visual and aural impairment.

One of the prevalent areas of special need that teachers are likely to encounter is that of 'communication and interaction difficulties'. Estimates vary as to the extent of language and communication difficulty in the 'average' classroom. As long ago as the early 1990s, Beech (1992) estimated that at least two children in every mainstream class were experiencing marked difficulty with some aspect of communication. More recent estimates of prevalence suggest a similar figure of around 7–8 per cent of children with language difficulties of varying severity (Dockrell and

Table 6.1 Some key events leading to inclusion, 1981–2011

Event or publication	Effect
1981 Education Act (based on Warnock Report)	Supported right of all pupils to attend local mainstream school. Proposed abolition of 'categories of handicap' established by 1944 Act – in practice many categorisations e.g. EBD, moderate learning difficulties are still used. Led to definition and widespread use of term 'Special Educational Needs' (SEN).
1988 Education Reform Act	Introduced National Curriculum as a 'legal entitlement' for all pupils.
1994 Code of Practice on the Identification and Assessment of SEN (DfEE)	Introduced to regulate and formalise the identification of SEN through the statementing procedure. Led to some schools and parents demanding that children should be statemented as a means of increasing resources for support of that individual.
1997 DfEE green paper, Excellence for all children: Meeting SEN	Affirmed the desirability of all children attending their local school in principle.
1998 DfEE paper Meeting SEN: a programme for action and 'inclusion'.	1998 DfEE paper Meeting SEN: Rekindled long-running debate about 'integration'.
2001 Code of Practice from 1994 revised	Aimed to speed up process of identification and assessment of special needs by reducing number of stages involved from five to three.
2002 The SEN and Disability Act	Strengthened rights of parents to insist on a mainstream place for a disabled child.
2003 Every Child Matters, Green Paper 2004 Children Act	Established inter-agency working to ensure children's 'well-being' according to five identified 'outcomes' (health, safety, enjoyment, achievement etc.).
2011 SEN and Disability Green Paper	We want to put in place a radically different system to support better life outcomes for young people; give parents confidence by giving them more control; and transfer power to professionals on the front line and to local communities. (DfE, 2011)

Lindsay 1998) with some estimates as high as 10 per cent (Law *et al.* 2000). On this evidence, every school in the UK will have (on average) at least one child in every class with a language and/or communication difficulty, and this number will certainly be higher in areas of social disadvantage.

To sum up, the drive towards inclusion has increased the range and variety of needs that teachers are likely to encounter in the mainstream science classroom. Improved diagnosis, and perhaps the wider publicity given to, for example, autism and dyslexia, has also heightened general awareness of the issue.

Every Child Matters (ECM)

Probably the major initiative in the early twenty-first century relating to the well-being of all children, and thereby inclusion, has been the 'Every Child Matters' development. This can be seen as a high-profile government response to certain tragic events in that period, such as the death of a young child, Victoria Climbié, at the hands of her carers. The main thrust of the ECM programme was to create inter-agency cooperation to ensure children's 'well-being'. The main emphasis in the Green Paper (2003) leading up to the Children Act (2004), and the Act itself, has been on five aspects or 'outcomes' of well-being:

1   being healthy;
2   staying safe;
3   enjoying and achieving;
4   making a positive contribution;
5   achieving economic well-being.

These five outcomes, said to be those that matter most to children and young people, form the central thrust of the act. The Children Act 2004 provided the legal underpinning for 'Every Child Matters: Change for Children' – this is the programme aimed at transforming children's services so that they are coordinated, cooperative and 'joined-up', to use government speak. This should include representation from a number of agencies, including:

•   health, which may be via clinical psychology;
•   behavioural support services;
•   the police;
•   social services, which may include representation for looked-after children;
•   local authority services, e.g. housing services.

One of the key phrases used in the ECM documents is the idea of a 'personalised approach' to children's learning, an area where the teacher will be key.

A wide range of documents on the ECM agenda and programme have been published, many of which are accessible on the world wide web. Teachers' TV also contains some useful material on the ECM programme.

What makes individuals different?

> ... special needs can best be met when a general concern for individual differences is uppermost in teachers' thinking.
>
> (Postlethwaite 1993: 21)

> Not only do pupils differ in all sorts of ways, but you, their teacher, will have differing expectations of them from your previous knowledge of pupils. What is a science teacher to do with all this diversity?
>
> (Reiss 1998: 34)

Everyone is different. This is a tautology, but it is worth emphasising before spelling out the differences that science teachers need to be aware of. The differences that matter can be divided and summed up as follows.

Educational differences

Children bring different preconceptions (alternative frameworks), different abilities, knowledge, understanding and skills into science education. There is extensive evidence that children have a wide range of preconceptions on notions such as force, pressure, heat, energy, plant nutrition, animals, burning and indeed most of the concepts that are the concern of the secondary science curriculum. The important point for teachers is that these 'alternative conceptions' (so-called in that they differ from the accepted view of normal science) have served children in their life outside of the science classroom and are strongly held on to.

Children also have a huge variety of past experiences from home, parents, cubs or brownies, holidays, visits, etc., which leads to a wide and rich range of scientific experience, knowledge and understanding in any classroom of 20-plus people.

As for abilities, the Assessment of Performance Unit (APU 1989) studies of secondary pupils showed that pupils varied enormously in their ability to:

- observe;
- interpret observations;
- interpret information;
- plan investigations, including controlling variables.

The APU studies revealed many other important differences, of course (see APU 1988 and 1989).

Perhaps the most important difference, however, is the huge range of linguistic ability that pupils bring to the science room. Science teaching takes place almost exclusively through the medium of language, both written and spoken, see Chapter 11. Hence teachers need to recognise the pupils' differences:

- in writing ability, for example, in reporting practical work, taking notes, or written assessment;
- in speaking and listening ability, for example, when answering oral questions or reporting by speech; in group or class discussion;
- in reading ability, for example, in reading instructions for a practical or an account in a textbook or worksheet;
- in organisational ability, for example, in sequencing tasks or instructions, even in organising their own time.

Psychological differences

It is a statement of the obvious to any practising teacher that pupils exhibit psychological differences. However, it can be helpful to divide them up according to three general categories:

1 General intelligence: there are dangers, however, in taking too much account of IQ scores, as Postlethwaite warns: 'an unfavourable score on an IQ test may alert us to the need to deal with a pupil in a different way, but it is not a trap which condemns that pupil to poor levels of performance' (Postlethwaite 1993: 31).
2 Motivation, personality and attitude.
3 Self-image and self-esteem: how many pupils shrug and say 'Well, I'm just no good at *this subject*? This seems to be more common in the science area than in other subjects, and more true of girls than of boys. Past experience of failure in science will further lower self-esteem.

Different people have different learning styles, see Chapters 2 and 4. Some are 'holists', looking for overviews and connections among different parts; some are 'serialists', preferring to take an element at a time (Pask 1975). Pask argued that people learn most effectively if they are taught in a style that matches their preferred mode of learning, not an easy task for the teacher when actually teaching, but the difference should be borne in mind when arranging learning activities. We should question whether it is, in fact, better to challenge learners to develop other *learning styles*. From another perspective, it seems that some prefer to learn by moving from concrete specific examples to the abstract and the general; others prefer to start from the abstract and the general before meeting concrete examples. Both strategies are necessary for learning the powerful abstractions that make science important.

Similarly, some learners will experience difficulty of one or more kinds in learning science. Various types of difficulty will be encountered that cannot be discussed fully here, but they may include difficulties in remembering, e.g. figures, abstractions, science knowledge; classifying; gathering information systematically; generalising from one situation to another; or sustaining concentration. Postlethwaite (1993) gives a useful discussion of these difficulties and sensibly points out that they apply to most people at some time or another!

Physical differences

Examples include physically challenged pupils, for example pupils in wheelchairs and pupils with specific impairments such as visual or aural. There will be a wide range of physical differences between pupils in any secondary class. Perhaps the important point for science teachers is that practical work will need special attention, for example while giving instructions or in providing special resources/apparatus.

Social differences

Shyness, ability to listen to others, respect for fellow learners, willingness, enthusiasm, social skill, ability to work in a group, leadership quality – these are all important 'social differences' between pupils. They do relate to the four types of difference already listed, but there is not always a clear one-to-one connection (for example, 'not contributing to class discussion' may be attributable to a number of causes including shyness or introversion, lack of confidence, low self-esteem, or lack of knowledge).

Socio-economic differences

These include social class, family background, etc. Different values, religious views, moral standpoints, attitudes to education, differing educational goals and aspirations – these are all factors that will affect science teaching and learning, not least in the treatment of controversial issues such as evolution, the origin of the universe, contraception and sex education.

Gender differences

Pupils' attitudes to the sciences appear to be gender-related (Postlethwaite 1993), and hence gender affects choices they might make at crucial stages in schooling. There has been some evidence (APU 1988) that boys are more competent than girls in some areas, such as using apparatus, and that girls are better than boys in others, such as making and interpreting observations, but these generalisations are wide open to debate.

Table 6.2 Gender differences in science performance, PISA 2009

Country	Mean point score	
	Girls	Boys
Finland	562	546
New Zealand	535	529
Great Britain	509	519
Ireland	509	507
France	497	500

The 2009 Programme for International Student Assessment (PISA) results show boys having a mean score of 519 against girls 509. This can be seen in perspective as shown in Table 6.2.

All the differences listed above are interrelated, for example prior experiences and socio-economic background, but it can be useful to separate them out and summarise them in order to be aware of them and to attempt to address them.

Responding to differences

How can teachers respond to all these individual differences, characteristics and prior experiences that students of all ages and abilities bring to the class or lecture room? First, it needs to be recognised that every group is a mixed-ability group. Teachers who are heard to make comments such as 'I don't hold with this mixed-ability teaching' ignore the truism that every group of every age presents different abilities, potential, experience and motivation. The only variable is the range of those differences in a given group.

The second factor for both teachers and learners is to decide how controllable and how pervasive these individual differences are (Postlethwaite 1993: 44–5). In plain terms, the learner and the teacher can pose these two questions:

1   Which differences affect all aspects of a pupil's work, whatever the context? In contrast, which differences affect only some aspects of work, in some contexts?
2   Which of the differences can be controlled, altered and influenced, i.e. which factors can teachers and learners themselves actually do something about?

Within these two questions there are two further questions:

1   Internal or external? If the difference can be controlled, altered or influenced is it something internal to the learner, for example the effort they put in? Or is it something external, such as economic status? Is the problem that of the child or a problem of the context and background?
2   Stable/permanent or unstable/temporary? Is the difference something which is constant, unchanging or permanent, or is it short-term or temporary, such as a broken leg?

These are all questions that can be asked of individuals, often in connection with their success or failure at certain tasks or activities. The basic questions are summed up in Figure 6.1 as a kind of continuum.

We often do this with ourselves when we consider our own successes and failures and the reasons for them. Is your sheer brilliance due to pure innate ability (internal, stable, not controllable), or is it a result of your drive, motivation and dogged hard work at crucial times (internal, controllable and unstable)? If, like me, you are totally incapable of writing poetry, is it your English teacher's fault because she killed it stone dead for you as a teenager (external, stable and uncontrollable), or is it your own lack of creativity and insight (stable, internal and possibly pervasive)?

Postlethwaite (1993: 35) explains that 'advantaged pupils' often attribute their own success to internal, stable and pervasive factors such as 'high ability' and those who often fail may attribute that failure to 'low ability' – 'I'm just thick' (internal, stable). They therefore expect to fail again, leading to a downward spiral of self-esteem. Thus the attributions that pupils make of themselves and those that teachers make of them are vitally important in deciding on future action.

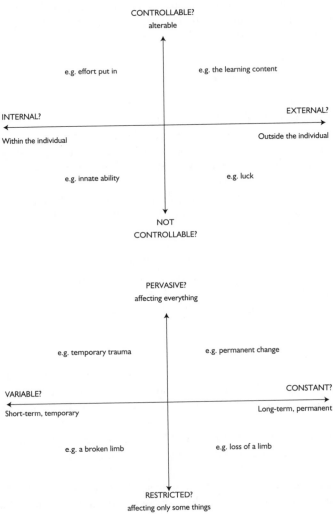

Figure 6.1 Why do people succeed or fail? Questions to ask of individuals' differences and attributes

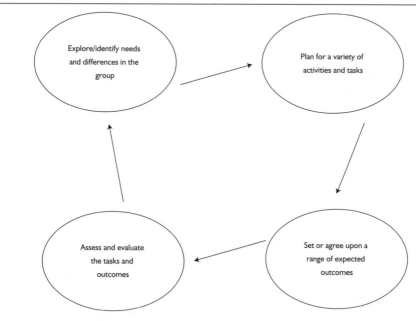

Figure 6.2 A strategy for differentiation

It seems to us that an understanding of these attributions is vitally important in the science and ICT areas. How many adults (few children) simply shrug and say 'I just can't use a computer'? How many children claim that they are 'just no good at science' without looking in detail at the reasons for saying that? It is hoped that the framework for analysing differences and causes in Figure 6.2 can be useful both for teachers and for pupils in considering action. It could also be a valuable tool in personal and social education, as well as in science.

When considering why pupils are good, or not, at learning science, or any other subject, we cannot do so without reference to their social and emotional development.

Social and Emotional Aspects of Learning (SEAL)

In 2007 the then Department for Education and Science published guidance on the implementation of SEAL within secondary schools (DfES, 2007). Here the guidance argues that attention to social and emotional aspects of learning can help pupils to:

- be effective and successful learners;
- be self-motivated;
- make and sustain friendships;
- deal with and resolve conflict effectively and fairly;
- solve problems with others or by themselves;
- manage strong feelings such as frustration, anger and anxiety;
- be able to promote calm and optimistic states that promote the achievement of goals;
- recover from setbacks and persist in the face of difficulties;
- work cooperatively;
- recognise and stand up for their own rights and the rights of others;
- understand and value differences and commonalities between people, respecting the right of others to have beliefs and values different from their own.

It could be argued that the above list is going beyond what the most able of science teachers can accomplish. However the SEAL guidance highlights the place of science within the agenda:

- examining emotional changes in adolescence;
- understanding how the brain works, centrality of emotion to how we think, learn, behave and experience the world;
- emotion and social bonding in animals;
- debating the benefits and drawbacks of scientific developments including those linked to environment, health and quality of life.

In the same way that the Every Child Matters agenda needs *whole-school involvement* so does the development of SEAL.

Inclusion and differentiation

How can teachers ensure that access to the science curriculum is appropriate for all pupils?

One of the answers to coping with individual differences is to plan for differentiation. This term is widely used but rarely defined. The term is not new but is more topical than ever because of the levels, assessment and progression built into the formal curriculum. Differentiation can be of two kinds:

- by task or activity, i.e. by providing different tasks to meet the individual differences and needs of a group;
- by outcome, i.e. by allowing different results or outcomes from activities or tasks.

The former, by task, suggests that certain activities – such as on a worksheet or in a practical session – should be made special and different for some pupils in order to cater for all needs. The latter implies that different outcomes, such as submitted work, can be planned for and accepted for (say) assessment. Thus differentiation involves first identifying needs, then planning a variety of activities or tasks to meet those needs, then agreeing and setting a range of outcomes from the activities that can be evaluated or assessed, see Figure 6.2.

The NCC (National Curriculum Council) Curriculum Guidance 10 (NCC 1992b) gave a number of suggestions to teachers on planning for differentiation. The guidance suggested two main principles that are indisputable and indeed apply to any lesson planning:

1   Teachers should define their objectives, taking into account knowledge, understanding and skills, i.e. in a given lesson what do they hope to achieve in terms of those three areas and what knowledge, experiences and skills will pupils leave the room with that they did not have when they entered?
2   Teachers should plan activities appropriate to the class, to groups within it, and to individuals. This is easier said than done, of course.

Practical suggestions are given for achieving this key feature of successful teaching: appropriateness. Table 6.3 gives a summary of guidelines on planning, pacing and communicating.

One of the problems, of course, is to put these guidelines into practice in the classroom. Differentiation by task is in many ways more of a challenge in the secondary school than in the primary. Primary teachers are experienced in organising and managing a classroom where a

Table 6.3 Planning and teaching for differentiation: basic guidelines

Planning and preparing

- Provide a range of activities that ensure the participation and involvement of all pupils (differentiated by task); and/or

- Provide similar work for the whole group but allow different outcomes for different individuals (differentiation by outcome).

- Plan for the possibility of pupils' work being recorded in different ways to suit their capabilities, such as using computers or video or audio tape.

- Plan for and make effective use of teaching assistants, support teachers and laboratory technicians where possible.

- Organise some work to be done in small groups so that pupils can demonstrate to each other what they can do.

Pacing

- Use a clearly defined, step-by-step approach that promotes a gradual development of skills, knowledge and understanding, i.e. break the lesson down into a series of small, achievable steps.

- Ensure that the pace of the lesson takes account of the differing work rates of individual pupils.

- Allow sufficient repetition to consolidate skills, knowledge and understanding.

Communicating

- Communicate in a range of different ways, i.e. speech, writing, pictures and diagrams, to give all pupils the opportunity to learn in a way that best suits them.

- Adapt communications for particular special educational needs, such as enlarged print, clear uncluttered illustrations, worksheets on audio tape.

- Use a consistent presentation for written material and a format for practical work that will avoid anxiety and encourage confidence and participation.

- Break down class worksheets into clearly itemised small steps.

- Use jargon-free, simple, unambiguous language; start from the pupils' own language and introduce words as needed.

- Explain new words to pupils so that they understand them and can then use them; display words in regular use so that they can be copied accurately.

Source: adapted from NCC Curriculum Guidance 10 (NCC 1992b)

number of different tasks, practical, oral and written, are going on at the same time. In contrast, the norm for the secondary classroom is a group of children engaged in roughly the same activity, such as a practical task, following a worksheet or taking notes. The challenge for the secondary teacher is to introduce differentiated tasks that do not create resentment, jealousy, distraction or obvious streaming within the classroom.

Some practical possibilities for the classroom

Working with the Special Needs CoOrdinator (SENCO)

All schools will have a SENCO and it is the science teacher's role, we argue, to ensure they work collaboratively with the SENCO, and other support staff, including teaching assistants, to achieve the differentiation and access discussed above (Dyson 1991; King 1989). Such teachers must first be regarded by the science teacher as more than just an extra resource in the room, or a non-teaching assistant. They should be seen as someone who can be a consultant and collaborator at all stages of providing access to the mainstream science curriculum:

- in planning and preparing lessons, i.e. in producing lesson plans and schemes of work for individual teachers and for the science department; in preparing materials, such as worksheets or DARTs, or resources, such as equipment or activities for class practicals;
- in achieving differentiation both of task and outcome, for example, in building differentiation into curriculum planning;
- in teaching the lesson itself and supervising classwork;
- in post-lesson or post-scheme-of-work evaluation;
- in joint assessment and recording of pupils' progress in both written and practical work.

This collaboration is necessary whether the 'support' teacher gives in-class support or withdraws pupils, such as unusually able or timid pupils, for special work. Whatever the strategy, cooperation/collaboration needs to be handled sensitively. The support teacher will often not be a science specialist and may often hold his or her science background in low esteem. Moreover, collaboration in the class will not work if the teaching style and environment is a purely didactic one, dominated by the 'scientist', the 'real teacher'. Collaborative teaching will work best in a resource-based, individualised learning approach in the classroom. But this in turn presents problems; problems of reading, for example of worksheets or instruction cards, and of writing, for example responses or write-ups, are often the most important source of learning difficulties in the laboratory. Collaborative teaching will need to find ways of making this approach work.

Nicholls and Turner (1998) suggest that not only should all pupils have access to a science education but that science education itself has unique benefits for pupils with learning difficulties, for example:

- the links between science and everyday experience;
- activities and phenomena that capture the imagination, enhancing motivation;
- knowledge and skills acquired through practical activity.

Reducing language barriers

Difficulties with language in some form or another are almost certainly the most common problem for learners and teachers in the mainstream, comprehensive school science curriculum (see Chapter 11 on language). Most of the suggestions below are therefore connected with practical ways of trying to overcome language barriers in science learning.

Giving instructions: the need for a multi-sensory approach

So many teachers are guilty of the 'I've told you, so now you know' approach. This is not acceptable for learners with a variety of special needs, not least those with hearing impairment, and is poor practice anyway. Instructions should be given using a variety of visual or aural support materials, including:

Table 6.4 Possible teaching tactics to aid comprehension

1.	Try to give explicit information and instructions in short manageable chunks.
2.	Try to give a 'mental' set for the lesson by outlining what the whole lesson is about. Review the lesson at the end. This allows the child to tune in and pull everything together as a whole.
3.	Structure your lessons around a number of 'main ideas' and put these (and a list of keywords) on a handout.
4.	Help structure the pupil's listening by giving questions at the beginning.
5.	Encourage students to read the questions before reading a passage so they are aware of what points are important to mention and of what they should take special note.
6.	Discuss subject-specific vocabulary and give a written list so the pupil does not have to spend time thinking about these spellings but can concentrate on the content of the lesson, these can be selected from the wordbank.
7.	Use illustrations/diagrams wherever possible, rather than just talking.

- drawings, diagrams and pictures as support for the spoken word;
- written instructions on a workcard/worksheet, the whiteboard or via a data projector;
- for certain practicals, an example set up on the front bench that can be referred to;
- in some cases, especially for those with specific needs, instructions in the form of audio file can be an extra help – this is now relatively easy via an MP3 player or even a mobile telephone;
- for some practicals, prepared pictures with words of different stages in an experiment can be given and pupils asked to sequence them correctly and perhaps label them – obviously the sequence will need to be checked before starting. This works well for pupils with English as an additional language.

A separate chapter, Chapter 11, gives guidelines on producing written material for pupils. These apply to any group of mixed ability. With specific needs extra provision may have to be made, for example:

- Visually impaired children may need a Braille version of text and special aids for diagrams – if facilities are available *tactile diagrams* can be produced which allow partially sighted or blind pupils to *feel* the diagram. An audio file version of the sheet will be a useful aid for both visually impaired and poor readers. Support may often be available to the science teacher in preparing these.
- Poor readers may need additional symbols and visual prompts to complete a task, such as filling in missing words. A symbol (for example, from the Rebus system) or simple diagram next to the blank may be a sufficient prod.

Table 6.4 gives a list of possible teaching strategies for aiding comprehension by pupils, produced with the help of a communication therapist with an interest in helping the dyslexic student. However, they apply equally well to all science teaching situations.

Variety in submitted work

As discussed earlier, differentiation by outcome implies that a range of submitted work will be accepted for, say, assessment. As well as handwritten work, teachers can consider more emphasis on diagrams and pictures; work printed from a computer that has been checked and corrected; audio file accounts or descriptions, such as of a process or an experiment; photographic records, such as of a practical or a product; video of, say, a group project on a topic or issue, or of an investigation.

Support with writing and spelling

Spelling is an issue that seems to generate more hot air than most. Spelling in science needs to be attended to and corrected but not in such a way that pupils are totally discouraged from attempting writing for fear of making spelling mistakes – a page of writing covered in red ink will not encourage. Certain guidelines can be followed by teachers and pupils in gradually improving spelling in science:

- If a large number of errors are made, teachers can select those which pupils are most likely to be able to correct and learn successfully.
- Such errors can be identified with an 'Sp', or whatever agreed convention is used in your school, in the margin and underlined. The pupil should then look along the line, find the error, and then either use a dictionary, ask a reliable friend or ask the teacher so that it can be corrected.
- Other errors can be identified with an 'Sp', and the correct spelling written in the margin or at the end, such as specialist terms in science. These can be added to a student's 'Science Wordbank', see Table 6.5 in the next section. The whole of the correct word can then be written above the mistake; teachers should avoid altering the word.

The main idea is to get pupils to try to find their own errors, to learn from their mistakes, and to correct misspellings themselves, not have the teacher do it for them.

Word lists and wordbanks

A list of 'important', commonly used words in science could be produced and displayed in large lettering on the laboratory wall. These could be of great help to those who have difficulty in 'finding words' as well as those who need help with spelling. The word list could include common items of apparatus used in practicals, such as Bunsen burner, flasks of different kinds; important labelling words, such as parts of a device, parts of the human body; words for important concepts and processes, such as photosynthesis, electrolysis, evolution; difficult nomenclature, such as for chemicals; the common units, for example joule, newton, metre, etc. These keywords could be referred to whenever pupils are doing a written task. For home use they could be written in a 'Science Wordbank' at the end of the pupil's book. For some lessons with especially new and difficult language, a sheet could be given out at the start with a clear list of all the words, terms, etc. which will be used during the course of the lesson.

Table 6.5 shows an example of a wordbank with a collection of about 300 words. This is a list formed from examining the science curriculum and a sample of recent science textbooks and from talking and listening to pupils and teachers. In our estimation, this rather daunting list contains most of the words and terms pupils will encounter in their linguistic journey to science examinations at age 16.

Table 6.5 A science wordbank for pupils aged 11 to 16

A	catalyst	ecosystem	glucose
absorption	cathode	effervescence	gravity
acceleration	cell	efficiency	
accommodation	cellular	electrolysis	H
accurate	Celsius	electrolyte	habitat
acid	charge	electromagnet	haemoglobin
adolescence	chemical	electron	half-life
aerobic	chlorine	electrostatic	halogen
alcoholic	chlorophyll	element	herbivore
alimentary canal	chloroplasts	embryo	homeostasis
alkali	cholesterol	emulsion	hormone
alkane	chromatography	endothermic	hydrocarbon
alkene	chromosome	energy	hydrogen
allele	circuit	environment	hygiene
alloy	clone	enzyme	
alpha	coil	equation	I
alternating	combustion	equilibrium	igneous
aluminium	compound	erosion	immunization
ammeter	compression	evaporation	indicator
ammonia	concave	evidence	induction
amplitude	conclusion	evolution	inertia
animal	condensation	excretion	inference
anode	conduction	exothermic	infra-red
antibiotic	conductor	expansion	insulation
aorta	conservation	extinction	insulin
artery	constant		invertebrate
asexual	contraction	F	ion
atmosphere	control	fermentation	ionic lattice
atom	convection	fertilisation	ionosphere
audible	convex	fertiliser	isotope
	corrosion	field	
B	covalent	filter	J
bacteria	crystal	filtration	joule
barometer	crystallisation	fission	
base	current	flammable	K
battery	cytoplasm	foetus	Kelvin
beta		food chain	kidney
biceps	D	food web	kilogram
bile	decompose	formula	kinetic
biodegradable	decrease	fossil	
biomass	density	fraction	L
biosphere	diabetes	frequency	larva
Brownian motion	diaphragm	fuel	ligament
	diffraction	fuse	liquid
C	diffusion		longitudinal
camera	digestion	G	loudness
capillary	dilute	galaxy	luminous
carbohydrate	diode	gamete	lung
carbon	dispersion	gamma ray	lymph
carbon dioxide	dissolve	gas	
carbonate	distillation	generator	M
cardiac		genes	magma
carnivore	E	genetics	magnesium
cartilage	echo	germination	magnetic

Continued...

Table 6.5 continued

mass	oxide	reproduction	tendon
measurement	oxygen	repulsion	terminal
meiosis	ozone	resistance	thermistor
membrane		resistor	thermometer
menstruation	P	resonance	thorax
metabolism	parallel	respiration	thyroid
metallic	parasite	result	tissue
metamorphic	particle	retina	tract
metamorphosis	penicillin	reversible	transfer
meter	periodic table		transformer
metre (length)	peristalsis	S	transpiration
microbe	phloem	saliva	transverse
microscope	photosynthesis	salt	triceps
microwave	pitch	satellite	triopism
mineral	placenta	saturated	troposphere
mixture	planet	sedimentary	
molecule	plasma	sensitivity	U
moment	pollen	series	ultrasound
monohybrid	pollution	skeleton	ultraviolet
motor	polymer	sodium	unsaturated
mucous	positive	solar system	urine
mutation	potential	solenoid	uterus
	precipitate	solid	
N	predator	solubility	V
negative	prediction	solute	vacuole
neurone	pressure	solution	vacuum
neutral	prey	solvent	valency
neutron	prism	species	vapour
newton	product	spectrum	variable
nitrogen	propagation	sperm	variation
nucleus	proportional	stimulus	velocity
nutrient	protein	stomata	vertebrate
nutrition	proton	stratosphere	vibration
	pyramid	sublimation	virtual
O		sulphate	virus
observation	R	suspension	vitamin
oesophagus	radiation	symbiosis	volume
ohm	radioactive	symbol	
omnivore	reaction	synapse	W
ore	reactivity	synthesis	watt
organism	reduction		wavelength
osmosis	reflection	T	weight
ovary	refraction	tectonics	
oxidation	renewable	temperature	

Using ICT, for task and for outcome

Using computers for writing can be of enormous benefit not only to reluctant writers and poor spellers, but also to good writers whose handwriting is unreadable. The use of a word-processor can completely change attitudes to writing, correcting, redrafting and presenting written work, see Chapter 13. Laptops, tablets and even some mobile telephones can be versatile and valuable tools for all pupils in the science laboratory. The use of computers in data-logging, again, see Chapter 13, can also be of great help to all pupils, including those with special needs. Learners who are slow and untidy at recording and presenting data can be helped by a simple system that collects data, for example on light levels or temperature, records it and presents it graphically. Although these skills still need to be developed manually, the occasional use of data-logging systems can show the way, sometimes relieve the drudgery and also raise self-esteem for many pupils.

Using laminated cards to help and enrich reading

Science textbooks have certainly improved in the last decade, thanks partly to the research which showed that the language level of most common texts was far too high. But a page of text on science can still be a daunting prospect to many pupils. One practical strategy for making reading more active, more sociable and less daunting is to use cards of various kinds to go with a piece of text. This can involve a lot of preparation and adaptation by the teacher but can pay off not just for pupils with 'special needs' but for all learners of the written word! The following examples should help to explain:

a) *True/false cards*: statements from the text are either transcribed straight onto laminated cards or adapted slightly so that they are false. Using the text, such as a page from a book, students have to sort the cards into two categories – true or false. They discuss these and then perhaps compare their results with another group or present them to the teacher.

b) *Agree/disagree cards*: on a more value-laden, sensitive or controversial topic, statements from, for example, different pressure groups or parties can be made into cards and then, during group discussion, placed into disagree/agree/not sure categories.

c) *Matching pairs*: A variety of activities can be done with cards that form matching pairs. The pairs might be:
   - a part of a body and its function;
   - part of any device, such as a car, and its function;
   - types of teeth and the job they do;
   - a picture and a word;
   - a common name and its scientific name;
   - a material and a common use for it;
   - a chemical name and its symbol – use with elements or compounds.

   There are many other possibilities in science. The activity can then involve lining the cards up as a group, or it could be done as a memory game often called 'Pelmanism'. This involves placing all the cards face down on the table in two separate groups, such as names in one group, chemical symbols in another. By gradually uncovering cards, players form pairs that they then keep if they form a pair but replace, face down, if they don't.

c) *Putting words or terms into groups*: words can be placed onto cards, such as names of a range of animals, and then sorted into classes or groups with a heading on another card (underlined or in upper case) at the top of each group, for example mammals/non-mammals. This could be done with metals and non-metals; solids, liquids and gases; conductors and insulators; vertebrates and invertebrates, and so on.

d) *Sequencing*: sentence cards describing, for example, a process or an experiment are jumbled up. They are placed by groups into their version of the correct sequence.

There are many other examples of reading activities that can be done with cards, such as finding the 'odd one out' and explaining why. They are all specific examples of Directed Activities Related to Text (DARTs), which are discussed further in Chapter 11 on language.

Realising the goal of inclusion

Exclusion

One way of considering inclusion is to look at its opposite, exclusion. In looking at the evidence on exclusions it is the case that some groups are excluded disproportionately when compared with others:

- four times as many boys as girls are excluded;
- black pupils experience six times the rate of exclusion of white pupils;
- children with statements of special educational needs experience exclusion six times more than their proportion in the school population;
- travellers, young carers, pregnant schoolgirls and teenage mothers are known to be vulnerable to exclusion.

But inclusion involves, in our view, a lot more than the absence of exclusion. Inclusive education received strong support from both UNESCO (1994) and the UK Human Rights Act (1998), which both argued that the notion of inclusion and participation in education are essential to human dignity:

> The fundamental principle of the inclusive school is that all children should learn together, wherever possible ... Inclusive schooling is the most effective means for building solidarity between children with special needs and their peers.
>
> (UNESCO 1994)

So what should inclusive education involve? Booth and Ainscow (2002) suggest the following:

- valuing all students and staff equally;
- increasing the participation of students in, and reducing their exclusion from, the cultures, curricula and communities of local schools;
- restructuring the cultures, policies and practices in schools so that they respond to the diversity of students in the locality;
- reducing barriers to learning and participation for all students, not only those with impairments or those who are categorised as 'having special educational needs';
- learning from attempts to overcome barriers to the access and participation of particular students to make changes for the benefit of students more widely;
- viewing the difference between students as resources to support learning, rather than as problems to be overcome;
- acknowledging the right of students to an education in their locality;
- improving schools for staff as well as for students;
- emphasising the role of schools in building community and developing values, as well as in increasing achievement;
- fostering mutually sustaining relationships between schools and communities;
- recognising that inclusion in education is one aspect of inclusion in society.

Why is science important for inclusion and inclusion important for science?

Why should science educators take time to plan for inclusion and special needs? Ross *et al.* (2000) suggest that science education 'by its nature, includes a whole range of characteristics' that proffer unique benefits, i.e.:

- a practical approach, nurturing first-hand experiences;
- potential for group or collaborative work and peer support;
- conceptual development in sequential steps affording opportunities for success;
- development of understanding of the big ideas in science – those broad conceptual areas which allow for internal differentiation and individual progression.

It can be seen from the above that science can impact on pupils via increased motivation and the development of social skills. In addition these benefits contribute to the whole school and the wider community by giving value to the notion of inclusion and by helping pupils avoid exclusion.

If we accept that inclusive education is desirable and that school science can make a meaningful contribution to it, how can this be achieved? We offer the following aspects which we consider important for the process of moving from policy to practice in inclusion and special needs education:

- leadership, in terms of senior leadership commitment to inclusion and training of staff;
- access, in terms of physical and environmental barriers as well as access to the curriculum and learning;
- differentiation of work and support given. To facilitate access and include all pupils the work set has to be appropriate to individual needs, i.e. make the work fit the pupil and not vice versa;
- equality of practice, local children included in local provision;
- active participation of pupils, parents, the local community and other professionals.

Much of this is simply *good teaching* and moreover it is enshrined in both *Every Child Matters* and *Social and Emotional Aspects of Learning*.

Of the above, one that trainee or newly qualified teachers sometimes feel most able to have an impact on is differentiation. We consider differentiation to be a vital component of inclusive education in science and a first step towards providing for those with special needs. Remember that it could be argued that all pupils have some special need at some point in their school career.

In summary ...

And now to repeat the point made earlier: the guidelines and practical examples listed above allow for individual differences in teaching a group. But in truth, what is 'good practice' for some is good practice for all; the strategies are useful for all pupils. To sum up: 'There is nothing special about teaching pupils with special needs ... Good teaching for them is simply good teaching' (Postlethwaite 1993: 39).

Full inclusion in mainstream schools is now widely recognised as a desirable goal. But in practice it requires enormous energy, commitment and resources to fully attain. Key factors for inclusion to be realised would seem to be:

- the ethos, atmosphere or climate of the school, including its non-teaching staff;
- the attitudes of teachers, non-teachers, parents and pupils – and the local community;
- full classroom support for children with 'special needs' – from teaching assistants, learning support assistants (LSAs) or similar;
- a common curriculum for all, but with appropriate differentiation;
- a collaborative learning and teaching atmosphere, i.e. children working together; teachers, classroom assistants and other professionals such as speech and language therapists and educational psychologists collaborating and cooperating.

In reality, this has proved hard to achieve, not least due to lack of adequate funding and other, often conflicting demands on teachers and schools, e.g. to raise their ranking in the examination and test result 'league tables'. This will not be any easier given the current British government's push for an English Baccalaureate (see, for example Mansell 2011). But the difficulty of achieving it in practice should not detract from the importance of inclusion as a goal that schools and teachers should continue to strive for.

Points for reflection

- One of the terms that became a buzzword in the 1990s was 'entitlement'; to what extent do you think that all pupils, regardless of their needs, are entitled to a science education?
- What is your own view on inclusion as a principle? Do you feel it is being achieved in practice? What might be the barriers to full inclusion?
- How many of the 'key factors' for inclusion listed above are being put into practice in schools that you have experienced?

References and further reading

General

The June 2002 issue of *School Science Review* (vol. 83, no. 305) focuses on Social Inclusion, with many articles offering ideas and strategies for teaching science to pupils with 'special educational needs'.

Booth, T. and Ainscow, M. (2002) *Index for Inclusion: developing learning and participation in schools*, Bristol: CSIE.

Booth, T., Ainscow, M., Black-Hawkins, K., Vaughan, M. and Shaw, L. (2000) *Index for Inclusion: developing learning and participation in schools*, Bristol: CSIE.

DfE (2011) *Support and Aspiration: A New Approach to Special Educational Needs and Disability - A Consultation*, London: DfE.

DfEE (1997)*Excellence for All Children*, London: DfEE.

DfES (2007) *Social and Emotional Aspects of Learning for Secondary Schools*, London: DfES

Harrison, C., Simon, S. and Watson, R. (2000) 'Progression and differentiation', in Monk, M. and Osborne, J. (eds) *Good Practice in Science Teaching*, Maidenhead: Open University Press.

Hartas, D. (2004) 'Special Educational Needs and inclusive schooling', in Brooks, V., Abbott, I. and Bills, L. (eds) *Preparing to Teach in Secondary Schools*, Maidenhead: Open University Press.

Mansell, W. (2011) The English bac causes fury in Schools, *The Guardian* 11 Jan.

Nicholls, J. and Turner, T. (1998) 'Differentiation and Special Educational Needs', in Turner, T. and Dimarco, W., *Learning to Teach Science in Secondary School*, London: Routledge.

Peterson, S., Williams, J. and Sorensen, P. (2000) 'Science for all: the challenge of inclusion', in Sears, J. and Sorensen, P. (eds) *Issues in Science Teaching*, London: Routledge.

Reiss, M., J. (1998) 'Science for all', in Ratcliffe, M. (ed.) *ASE Guide to Secondary Science Education*, Cheltenham: Stanley Thornes.

Ross, K., Lakin, L. and Callaghan, P. (2000) *Teaching Secondary Science: constructing meaning and developing understanding*, London: David Fulton.

Taber, K. (ed.) (2007) *Science Education for Gifted Learners*, London: Routledge; contains a collection of chapters by different authors on strategies and practical ideas for challenging 'gifted learners' in science.

UNESCO (1994) *The Salamanca Statement and Framework for Action on Special Needs*, Paris: UNESCO.

Going further back:

APU (Assessment of Performance Unit) (1988) *Science at Age 15: a review of APU findings*, London: HMSO.

APU (1989) *National Assessment: the APU science approach*, London: HMSO.

Borrows, P. (2000) 'Teaching science to pupils with special needs – health and safety issues', *School Science Review*, vol. 81, no. 296, pp. 37–40.

Dickinson, C. and Wright, J. (1993) *Differentiation: a practical handbook of classroom strategies*, Coventry: National Council for Educational Technology (became known as BECTA but disbanded by the current government).

Ditchfield, C. (ed.) (1987) *Better Science for Young People with Special Educational Needs*, Secondary Science Curriculum Review, Curriculum Guide 8, London/ Hatfield: Heinemann/Association for Science Education.

Duerden, B. and Jury, A. (1993) 'Pupils with special needs in mainstream schools', in Hull, R. (ed.), *ASE Secondary Science Teachers' Handbook*, Hemel Hempstead: Simon & Schuster.

Duerden, B., Fortune, D. and Johnson, M. (1992) Access and progress in science, *British Journal of Special Education*, vol. 19, no. 12, pp. 59–63.

Dyson, A. (1991) Special needs teachers in mainstream schools, *Support for Learning*, vol. 6, no. 2, pp. 51–60.

Hall, S. (1997) The problem with differentiation, *School Science Review*, vol. 78, no. 284, pp. 95–8.

Hoyle, P. (1993) 'Race, equality and science teaching', in Hull, R. (ed.), *ASE Secondary Science Teachers' Handbook*, Hemel Hempstead: Simon & Schuster.

King, V. (1989) Support teaching: the practice papers: 11, *Special Children*, October 1989.

NCC (National Curriculum Council) (1989) *A Curriculum for All – Special Needs in the National Curriculum*, NCC Curriculum Guidance 2, York: NCC.

NCC (1992a) *The National Curriculum and Pupils with Severe Learning Difficulties*, NCC Curriculum Guidance 9, York: NCC.

NCC (1992b) *Teaching Science to Pupils with Special Educational Needs*, NCC Curriculum Guidance 10, York: NCC.

Naylor, S. and Keogh, B. (1998) 'Differentiation', in Ratcliffe, M. (ed.) *ASE Guide to Secondary Education*, Hatfield: ASE/Stanley Thornes, pp. 167–74.

Pask, G. (1975) *The Cybernetics of Human Learning and Performance*, London: Hutchinson.

Postlethwaite, K. (1993) *Differentiated Science Teaching*, Milton Keynes: Open University Press.

Reid, D.J. and Hodson, D. (1987) *Science for All: teaching science in the secondary school*, London: Cassell Education.

Robertson, J. (1990) *Effective Classroom Control*, London: Hodder & Stoughton.

Smail, B. (1993) 'Science for girls and boys', in Hull, R. (ed.) *ASE Secondary Science Teachers' Handbook*, Hemel Hempstead: Simon & Schuster.

Stradling, R., Saunders, L. and Weston, P. (1991) *Differentiation in Action: a whole school approach for raising standards*, London: HMSO; gives strategies for raising the attainment of all pupils by a whole-school approach. It also gives practical guidance for a range of learning needs of secondary school pupils.

Thorp, S. (ed.) (1991) *Race, Equality and Science Teaching*, Hatfield: ASE.

Tunnicliffe, S.D. (1987) 'Science materials for special needs', *British Journal of Special Education*, vol. 14, no. 2.

Westwood, P. (1993) *Commonsense Methods for Children with Special Needs*, London: Routledge.

Widlake, P. (ed.) (1989) *Special Children's Handbook*, London: Hutchinson Education/ Special Children.

Wood, K., Lapp, D. and Flood, J. (1992) *Guiding Readers Through Text: a review of study guiders*, London: Delaware International Reading Association; a practical guide to ways of encouraging active, structured reading.

The National Association for Special Educational Needs (NASEN, Stafford ST17 4JX) produces a range of useful publications, including:

Barthorpe, T. and Visser, J. (1991) *Differentiation: your responsibility*.

The ASE manual, *Race, Equality and Science Teaching*, contains a number of ideas and activities for teaching science to pupils with different needs.

Language and communication difficulties

Beech, M. (1992) 'Children who fall through the gap', *Human Communications*, vol. 1, no. 3, pp. 13–15.

Botting, N., Crutchley, A. and Conti-Ramsden, G. (1998) 'Educational transitions of 7 year old children with SLI in language units: a longitudinal study', *International Journal of Language and Communication Disorders*, vol. 33, no. 1, pp. 177–97.

Dockrell, J. and Lindsay, G. (1998) 'The ways in which speech and language difficulties impact on children's access to the curriculum', *Child Language Teaching and Therapy*, vol. 14, no. 2, pp. 117–33.

Dockrell, J. and Lindsay, G. (2001) 'Children with speech and language difficulties: the teachers' perspective', *Oxford Review of Education*, vol. 27, pp. 369–94.

Farmer, M. (2000) 'Language and social cognition in children with specific language impairment', *Journal of Child Psychology and Psychiatry*, vol. 41, no. 5, pp. 627–36.

Feasey, R. (1998) *Primary Science and Literacy*, Hatfield: ASE.

Law, J., Boyle, J., Harris, F., Harkness, A. and Nye, C. (2000) 'Prevalence and natural history of primary speech and language delay: findings from a systematic review of the literature', *International Journal of Language and Communication Disorders*, vol. 35, no. 2, pp. 165–88.

Lewis, M. and Wray, D. (1998) *Writing Across the Curriculum: frames to support learning*, Reading: University of Reading Language Information Centre.

Dyslexia

There is a huge range of literature on dyslexia – four books that explore the issues and offer practical approaches are:

Broomfield, H. and Combley, M. (1997) *Overcoming Dyslexia: a practical handbook for the classroom*, London: Whurr.

Hulme, C. and Snowling, M. (eds) (1994) *Reading Development and Dyslexia*, London: Whurr.

Riddick, B. (1996) *Living with Dyslexia*, London: Routledge.

Snowling, M. and Stackhouse, J. (eds) (1996) *Dyslexia, Speech and Language: a practitioner's handbook*, London: Whurr.

Chapter 7

Practical work in science education

... teachers need to be aware of the goals, potential, merits and difficulties of the school laboratory.

(Tamir 1991: 20)

Practical work is one of the distinctive features of science teaching and one of the great expectations of pupil learning. How best should practical work be organised and conducted? What types of practical work can and should be done? Why do we do practical work at all in the science curriculum? These questions are all interwoven. We start with the most fundamental but least asked: why do practical work?

Why do practical work in science lessons?

An enormous amount of time and money is invested in making practical work an element of secondary school science. Schools employ lab technicians, consume consumables of all kinds and invest large sums in pieces of apparatus that most pupils have never seen elsewhere and are never likely to encounter again after school. In the current era of local management and devolved budgets, it is inevitable that the traditional expense of practical work will be questioned by someone running the school. Science teachers need to be able to justify the time and money spent on practical work not only for this reason, but also in order to answer the two further questions of 'what?' and 'how?'

In 1963, Kerr organised a survey of 701 science teachers from 151 schools in order to find out why they did practical work in school science. He suggested ten aims or purposes which those in the survey were asked to rank for importance in relation to three different age ranges: lower secondary, upper secondary and 'sixth form'. The aims presented to teachers are shown in Table 7.1.

It is interesting to note that those aims are still largely relevant today, even though we are almost five decades on. Before reading further, consider each of those aims carefully and rank them for yourself for different ages of pupils. Jot down your own ranking for: years 7, 8 and 9; years 10 and 11; years 12 and 13 or post-sixteen.

The analysis of results is well worth reading in full (Kerr 1963). Here is our own potted summary of the responses:

* There was a change in emphasis in practical work as pupils move through the secondary school, for example, away from the arousal of interest towards careful recording.
* However, observation and scientific thinking were ranked highly throughout.

Table 7.1 Ten possible aims of practical work

1. To encourage accurate observation and careful recording.
2. To promote simple, common-sense, scientific methods of thought.
3. To develop manipulative skills.
4. To give training in problem-solving.
5. To fit the requirements of practical examinations.
6. To elucidate the theoretical work so as to aid comprehension.
7. To verify facts and principles already taught.
8. To be an integral part of the process of finding facts by investigation and arriving at principles.
9. To arouse and maintain interest in the subject.
10. To make biological, chemical and physical phenomena more real through actual experience.

Source: used by Kerr (1963)

- Aim 9 was highest for years 7–9.
- Aim 1 was highest for years 12–13.

Taking all teachers and all age groups into account, the overall ranking of aims was: 1 (first), 2 and 8 (joint second), 6, 10, 9, 7, 3, 4, 5 (last). How do these compare with your own ranking?

The role and potential of practical work

The place of practical work in science needs to be justified; fortunately, there are many useful discussions which help by giving us a framework for practical work by outlining its purpose and potential. These can be summarised only briefly here.

Woolnough and Allsop (1985), in an excellent discussion on practical science, suggest that in the past four types of aim have been given by teachers and curriculum developers for small-group practicals:

1   motivational, i.e. that practical science can motivate and interest pupils (cf. Kerr 1963);
2   the development of experimental skills and techniques, such as observation, measurement, handling apparatus, etc.;
3   simulating the work of a real scientist – 'being a real scientist for the day', a phrase from the early Nuffield days;
4   supporting theory, i.e. using practicals to 'discover', elucidate or illuminate theory; and improving retention in line with the other catchphrase of practical work: 'I hear and I forget, I see and I remember, I do and I understand.'

The latter two groups of aims are wide open to criticism, as Woolnough and Allsop themselves point out, and their problems will be considered shortly. They go on to examine and discuss their own view of the purposes of practical work and then put forward their own three 'fundamental aims':

1   developing practical skills and techniques;
2   being a problem-solving scientist;
3   getting a feel for phenomena.

The types of practical work in school science associated with these aims are discussed in detail by Woolnough and Allsop, who label the three types Exercises, Investigations and Experiences, respectively. Their full description of each type is well worth reading (Woolnough and Allsop 1985: 47–59), but examples would include:

- Exercises: using a microscope, estimating, measuring, heating, manipulating, performing standard tests, e.g. food tests, setting up apparatus and equipment, e.g. a cathode ray oscilloscope, an electric circuit.
- Investigations: often of the what, which or how variety, e.g. what causes rusting? which material is best for X? how do shampoos affect hair strength? (investigations are given a whole section later).
- Experiences: studying, observing, handling, holding, exploring, watching, growing, e.g. plants, crystals; pushing and pulling, feeling etc.

This is still a useful classification for classroom teachers, it will not only enable them to plan practical work for range and variety, but also help them to consider why they are doing a practical.

In a later discussion, Millar writing in Woolnough (1991: 51) unpicks the idea of 'practical skills'. He divides the skills that he feels can be taught and improved into:

- Practical techniques: e.g. measuring temperature to within certain limits, separating by filtration or other 'standard' procedures.
- Inquiry tactics: e.g. repeating measurements, tabulating data and drawing graphs in order to look for patterns, identifying variables to alter, control, etc.

By developing these skills, pupils will develop their 'procedural understanding' of science, in contrast to their conceptual understanding. Millar argues that pupils can progress in practical science by increasing their competence in a wider range of techniques and by enlarging and extending their 'toolkit' of tactics for investigational work. These are the dual aims of practical science.

We only have space to consider a third framework for practical work. This is the Predict-Observe-Explain (P-O-E) pattern suggested by Gunstone, in Woolnough (1991: 69). He offers as a framework for demonstrations a constructivist approach to practical work which includes P-O-E tasks. Gunstone offers it as a framework for demonstrations but we have adapted it as a possible scheme for work with small groups too:

1 Predict: students are shown a particular situation and asked to predict what they believe will happen. They are asked to give reasons for their prediction, preferably in writing.
2 Observe: the demo or class practical is then performed and all students write down what they observe.
3 Explain: the third is to consider the P and O stages and to attempt to explain, or reconcile, any conflict between prediction and observation.

The latter stage is, in our view, by far the most difficult stage to handle, especially if this framework were used for a class practical! Gunstone elaborates fully on this interesting approach and other strategies that he has suggested in Woolnough (1991) and previous work cited there.

Table 7.2 The role of practical work in science

1 To develop skills:
• practical techniques
• procedures
• tactics
• investigation strategies
• working with others
• communicating
• problem-solving
2 To illuminate/illustrate ('first-hand' knowledge):
• an event
• a phenomenon
• a concept
• a law
• a principle
• a theory
3 To motivate/stimulate:
• entertain
• arouse curiosity
• enhance attitudes
• develop interest
• fascinate
4 To challenge/confront
• e.g. 'What if . . .?', Predict-Observe-Explain, 'Why . . .?'

The POE approach, see Chapter 4, can also be thought of as being what we will call *minds-on* rather than simply *hands-on* science where it is not enough just to develop the skills of a scientist but students learn to think like a scientist.

These frameworks for practical work are a selection of many offered regarding the purpose of practical work. We offer our own summary of the reasons for practical science in Table 7.2. Readers are invited to look critically and carefully at this table before we move on to the issue of organising practical activity.

Types of practical work and how to organise them

Different types of practical activity will be appropriate for the different aims shown in Table 7.2. There are at least six possibilities for organising and carrying out practical work in the average school situation with its usual constraints:

1   demonstrations;
2   class experiments, all on similar task, in small groups;
3   a circus of experiments, i.e. small groups on different activities in a 'carousel' spread over chunks of a lesson or over several lessons;
4   simulations and role-play;
5   investigations;
6   problem-solving activities.

The latter three are given special treatment in separate chapters. Aspects of the first three are considered briefly here.

Demonstrations

Why use demonstrations?

Demonstrations can be useful in meeting aims 2, 3 and 4 of Table 7.2. They can be used to illustrate events or phenomena, e.g. chemical reactions, especially if those events are too expensive, or too dangerous or too difficult or too time-consuming to be done by all. There is still a valuable place in science teaching at all levels for the interesting, sometimes unforgettable, demonstration that may form an important episode in a pupil's learning. Thus a good demo can excite, intrigue, fascinate and entertain, especially if it has the advantage of scale, i.e. bigger, better, more visible, clearer and with more impact than a class experiment.

How should demonstrations be used and carried out?

All good demonstrations need a framework so that pupils are active and can participate – in short, learners need to be occupied during a demo. Passive entertainment is not enough. The Gunstone framework of Predict-Observe-Explain is one excellent possibility, especially in achieving aim 3 of Table 7.2. At a simpler level pupils could engage in just one of these stages, using a pencil and 'jotter'. They could be asked to record results and begin to tabulate them. In short, there needs to be an activity, preferably involving writing and recording, to structure every demo. This is essential not only on educational grounds but also for management and control. Finally, as said before, demonstrations need to go for impact. This means, to state the obvious, that every pupil needs to be able to see what is happening. Careful management of seating and/ or standing is well worth the investment in time.

Whole-class practical work

Why?

The reasons for class activity in small groups relate closely to almost all the aims of Table 7.2: to develop practical skills and techniques, to illuminate and illustrate, to give a feeling for sizes and orders of magnitude, to generate results for analysis, to entertain, and to challenge.

How?

There are several aspects to managing and organising whole-class practicals, most of which can only be learnt adequately from observation and experience. But there are certain key points to be remembered: apparatus needs to be carefully distributed around the lab if pupils are to fetch it themselves – this will avoid bottlenecks; the teacher is in a supervisory role at all times and needs to be in a position to see the whole room – discussing the finer points with a small group with his or her back to the rest of the class is not good practice; always allow more than enough time for clearing away.

In planning for and structuring class practicals there are several important, necessary stages in addition to the actual activity:

- setting the scene, i.e. the pre-experiment discussion, discussing and giving instructions, arranging groups and managing the room;
- gathering results: are the pupils given a free hand or a set results table?; will the results of everyone be recorded centrally, such as on an interactive whiteboard (IWB) or spreadsheet

and data projector?; or will they record individually or as a small group without sharing widely?;

- discussing the experiment and its results;
- interpreting and concluding: this is the most problematic and widely discussed aspect of practical work;
- should conclusions be elicited from pupils or given to them?; who should interpret their data, the pupil or the teacher? This element of practical work relates very closely, of course, to the initial aim of the activity in the first place;
- writing up and reporting: this is another area of science activity that has caused great debate, see Chapter 11 on language in science. Indeed, should practicals always be written up? Can they not be recorded and stored for posterity in other ways, such as MP3 files, video, photograph or picture? Using solely written work for reporting strongly disadvantages those who may be good at practical science but poor at writing, for whatever reason.

A circus of experiments

Why use this way of organising a practical?

A circus can be useful in allowing hands-on activity for all when the number of certain pieces of apparatus or other resources, such as computers and software or specialised equipment is limited. By arranging a carousel, every pupil or group can see and use the resource in turn. It can also be valuable in providing a fairly quick, highly varied set of experiences relating to one topic, such as energy or forces. Thus circuses often fulfil the experiential aim of practical work.

How can a circus be organised?

Initially it requires a great deal more preparation from teacher and technician to provide a carousel of, say, ten different activities labelled A to J for a group of 25 pupils than planning a single task which all do at the same time. But this initial planning and organisation can pay dividends and save time in the long term. Additional preparation is needed to ensure:

- all workplaces/activities are prepared, set out and labelled before children enter;
- each activity occupies roughly the same amount of time;
- the change-over from one activity to the next is carefully planned and the sequence written down for all to see;
- consumables can be restocked as time goes on;
- instructions for each stage are clear and readable – a work card or sheet at each station will be invaluable;
- each activity is self-contained, as the sequence through which pupils go through the carousel will be different for every group;
- extension activities are given at each station to allow for time differences between activities and pupils, and the ability range.

Simulation as part of practical science

Active work in science need not always involve the 'real thing', indeed much of real science involves experiments with models and simulations of real events, for example, river flow in tanks, study of flight in wind tunnels. Pupils should therefore learn that in order to study and understand reality we often need to model it and simplify it. Thus the use of models, analogies and simulations is not only a valuable way of learning but also an important part of scientific exploration. Simulation can involve:

1   the use of ICT, for example a computer simulation or even the use of an APP on a smartphone;
2   physical models, for example a ripple tank, marbles in a tray, molecular models, an orrery, a planetarium, analogues of electric current, such as water flow or a loop of string;
3   secondary sources, e.g. tables of data, graphs and charts, news cuttings, scientific articles, DVDs, photographs, images from remote sensing;
4   role play, for example of processes such as melting and boiling or conduction, convection and radiation, molecular movement, etc.

These four types of simulation can achieve many of the aims outlined in Table 7.2, such as illustrating phenomena and clarifying theory. Indeed they can often be more effective than the 'real thing' because of increased clarity and simplicity.

The usual rules for all practical work apply to all the types listed above:

•   The activity must be SAFE. Use whatever is necessary to ensure safety, such as goggles for heating, a safety screen for some demos, etc.;
•   Always try out the class practical, circus, or demo in advance;
•   Give a clear list of all requirements to technical/support staff well in advance;
•   Manage any movement around the room carefully and safely;
•   Give clear instructions for the activity, using different approaches.

Possibilities are: oral, just telling from the start, or oral instructions arising from a class discussion; a worksheet; an interactive whiteboard or an overhead transparency; pupils rearranging a jumbled list of instructions into the correct order, which is then checked before starting! A variety of approaches is needed both for reinforcement, to avoid the 'I've told them, so now they know' syndrome and to cater for all needs and styles in a mixed class.

Oh ... by the way, remember to count everything out and count it all back in again in as visible and systematic a way as possible. Certain bits of science kit, like magnets and crocodile clips, have a habit of sticking to people!

Health, safety and risk assessment in practical science education

The issue of health and safety in science should never be underestimated. Equally it should never be used as an excuse for not including correctly risk assessed practical work from being done.

The importance of and strategies for managing health and safety in science are discussed in a dedicated chapter, Chapter 10.

In summary ... general issues and debates about the role of practical work in science

Practical work in science has enormous potential for exciting pupils, giving first-hand knowledge (almost unique to science as a curriculum subject) and supporting theory. However, we would

Table 7.3 Pitfalls and problems with practical work in science

1.	Can we mimic 'real science'?
	• Can scientific method be broken down into a set of discrete processes?
	• Can scientific processes be caught and taught?
	• Is 'discovery learning' a con?
2.	Does practical work illuminate or confuse learning in science?
3.	The observation problem: Which comes first – the theory or the practical? Can children observe without a framework?
4.	Does an insistence on (and a pupil expectation of) practical work limit and restrict the range of topics covered in science and the teaching strategies used?
5.	Group work: what are the consequences if we simply put pupils into small groups and let them get on with it?

like to finish with a summary of some of the pitfalls and problems of practical work, which is very brief simply because so much has been written on it elsewhere. Table 7.3 provides a summary: each issue is considered in turn below with an indication of further reading.

First, science teachers may create problems for themselves if they suggest that pupils in school science are really behaving like 'real scientists'. Few scientists can make explicit the processes that they themselves are engaged in:

> Ask a scientist what he conceives the scientific method to be and he will adopt an expression that is at once solemn and shifty-eyed: solemn, because he feels that he ought to declare an opinion; shifty-eyed because he is considering how to conceal the fact that he has no opinion to declare.
>
> (Medawar 1969: 11)

What chance then do science teachers have of accurately mimicking or assessing the processes of scientists, even if such an aim were desirable? (see Driver 1983, on the pupil as scientist; several contributors to Wellington 1989, and a critique of the 1970s and 1980s enthusiasm for discovery learning in Wellington 1981 and Atkinson and Delamont 1977).

Second, it may be the case that practical work, especially if things go wrong, can actually confuse rather than illuminate laws and theories. This has led to the tweaking, fiddling and stage management that has become one of the unwritten skills of the science teacher (see Nott and Wellington 1997).

This links to the third point – observation, like the truth, is rarely pure and never simple. Learners often need to be told what to look for, i.e. the framework precedes the practical. This is as true for looking down microscopes as it is for 'observing' magnetic fields or viewing convection currents in air or water. There are at least three points about observation that emerge from current views on the nature of science:

- observations rarely form the starting point for a practising scientist;
- observations are theory-dependent, i.e. theory normally precedes observation;
- if more than one person (be it pupil or scientist) observes the same phenomenon, their observations may well be different, i.e. people see through their theories (see Hodson 1986).

The practical point for teachers is that it makes little sense either to teach or to assess observation in isolation.

The fourth point is that an insistence on practical work as an essential feature of school science can actually restrict the science curriculum: 'We won't teach that topic because we can't do practical work in it.' This has led to an often hidden reluctance among science teachers to include a topic in a scheme of work because they cannot find a way of including a traditional practical. Thus topics like cosmology, earth science and astronomy, and many of the controversial issues that involve science, have often been neglected. This has led in turn to the use of a very restricted range of teaching strategies among science teachers (see Woolnough and Allsop 1985; Wellington 1998).

The final problem considered here is the issue of group work. Teachers commonly place pupils in small groups and assume that the group will work. Close observation shows that this is often not the case, especially in groups of three or more. One pupil may dominate while others play little part, e.g. in planning, predicting or carrying out a practical. Pupils may willingly adopt different roles, some of which may have nothing to do with the science: for example one member may simply record and tabulate results with no clue as to what they mean or where they came from. There are many other issues connected with group work – our general point here is that we cannot assume that groups are teams or that pupils share or rotate their roles in a group. In short, group work must be managed, it cannot be taken for granted.

Points for reflection

- In your own view, what is the value of practical work in science education? What purposes does it serve?
- Can practical work sometimes confuse science concepts and ideas for children rather than clarify them?
- Could we teach science without practical work? What would be 'lost' by doing this? What are the alternatives to practical work?
- In your view and experience, are all pupils motivated by practical work?
- Should the practical work done in school science attempt to mimic 'real science'? Can it be used to show pupils 'how real science works'?

References and further reading

General

The March 2004 issue of *School Science Review* (vol. 85, no. 312) contains a range of articles on practical work in schools, including a piece arguing that too cautious an approach to health and safety can 'inhibit' practical work and rule out a lot of 'good science'.

A collection of 16 chapters which looks at different types of practical work, justifications for it, the use of ICT, and alternatives to practical work is:
Wellington, J. (ed.) (1998) *Practical Work in School Science: which way now?*, London: Routledge.

See also:
DfEE (1999) *The National Curriculum for England: science*, London: DfEE.
Ireson, G. and Twidle, J. (2006) *Reflective Reader: secondary science*, Exeter: Learning Matters.
Sang, D. and Wood-Robinson, V. (2002) *Teaching Secondary Scientific Enquiry*, London: John Murray.

Discussions on the aims and conduct of practical work

Bentley, D. and Watts, M. (eds) (1989) *Learning and Teaching in School Science*, Milton Keynes: Open University Press; especially pp. 21–41.

Driver, R. (1983) *The Pupil As Scientist*, Milton Keynes: Open University Press.

Gunstone, R.F. (1991) 'Reconstructing theory for practical experience', in Woolnough, B. (ed.) *Practical Science*, Milton Keynes: Open University Press.

Kerr, J. (1963) *Practical Work in School Science*, Leicester: Leicester University Press; a classic enquiry into the nature and purpose of school science practical work, based on a study of 701 teachers in 151 schools.

Medawar, P. (1969) *Induction and Intuition in Scientific Thought*, London: Methuen.

Millar, R. (1991) 'A means to an end: the role of processes in science education', in Woolnough, B. (ed.) *Practical Science*, Milton Keynes: Open University Press.

Solomon, J. (1980) *Teaching Children in the Laboratory*, London: Croom Helm.

Tamir, P. (1991) 'Practical work in school science: an analysis of current practice', in Woolnough, B. (ed.) *Practical Science*, Milton Keynes: Open University Press.

Woolnough, B. (ed.) (1991) *Practical Science*, Milton Keynes: Open University Press; a range of useful chapters on school practical work.

Woolnough, B. and Allsop, T. (1985) *Practical Work in Science*, Cambridge: Cambridge University Press.

Critical comments on the value of school science practicals

Atkinson, P. and Delamont, S. (1977) 'Mock-ups and cock-ups: the stage management of guided discovery instruction', in Woods, P. and Hammersley, M. (eds), *School Experience*, London: Croom Helm.

Hodson, D. (1986) 'The nature of scientific observation', *School Science Review*, vol. 68, no. 242, pp. 17–29.

Hodson, D. (1990) 'A critical look at practical work in school science', *School Science Review*, vol. 71, no. 256, pp. 33–9.

Millar, R. (1989) 'What is scientific method and can it be taught?', in Wellington, J. (ed.) *Skills and Processes in Science Education*, London: Routledge.

Nott, M. and Wellington, J. (1997) 'Producing the evidence: science teachers' initiations into practical work', *Research in Science Education*, vol. 27, no. 3, pp. 395–409.

Osborne, J. (1997) 'Practical alternatives', *School Science Review*, vol. 78, no. 285, pp. 61–6.

Wellington, J. (1981) 'What's supposed to happen, Sir?: some problems with discovery learning', *School Science Review*, vol. 63, no. 222, pp. 167–73.

Wellington, J. (1989) (ed.) *Skills and Processes in Science Education*, London: Routledge; various chapters.

Alternatives to practical work

The March 2007 issue of *School Science Review* (vol. 88, no. 324) contains a range of articles on discussion, argumentation, talking and dialogue in science lessons which can form the vitally important enrichment and addition to (or sometimes substitute for) traditional hands-on practical work.

Fox, Katrina (2006) 'Authentic alternatives to practical work', *School Science Review*, vol. 88, no. 322, pp. 45–52; standard practical work does not always engage every pupil and attempts to provide 'authentic' and complex activities are not always possible or realistic. This article shows how activity involving discussion activities (she uses examples on the spread of disease and infection) can be a motivating alternative.

Chapter 8

Investigations in science

Click, click, click (the school clock). We were supposed to be reading the instructions for an experiment we were going to perform in class that day. Now there's another stupid thing. Year after year, this same teacher makes his students perform the same experiments. Well, if the experiments have been done so many times before, how can they still be experiments? The teacher knows what is going to happen. I thought experimenting meant trying new things to see what would happen. We weren't experimenting at all. We were playacting.

(*Claudia and the Great Search*, by Ann Martin, New York: Scholastic)

What are 'investigations'? Are they the same as problem-solving? What types of investigations are there? How should they be carried out and organised? What help can we provide to pupils to guide them and to structure the investigation? Do they present any problems in the classroom? Can they really reflect the way that science and scientists work? These are the questions that this chapter raises.

What are investigations?

Examples of investigations

Below are listed some examples of investigations that we have seen, used, read or heard about:

- How much rainfall do we get in each month throughout the year?
- What conditions do wood lice like best?
- Design an instrument to make the best spectrum.
- What are the best conditions for yeast growth?
- Which kind of paper is best for mopping up water?
- Design a machine for exercising a dog.
- Design a machine for weighing an elephant.
- Which ball is most bouncy?
- Which surface is best for bouncing a ball on?
- What makes sugar dissolve faster?
- Which factors affect the frequency of the note from a stretched string?
- Study the reaction times of different people.
- How do people's reaction times vary with different stimuli and conditions (for example, after drinking coffee, late in the day, etc.)?

- Which is the best detergent/washing powder?
- Investigate the composition, structure and strength of local soils.
- Which trainer sole is best?
- What factors determine how fast a car can travel?
- What happens to the boiling/melting point of water if you add solvents?
- Can people tell the difference between margarine and butter?
- Separate a mixture of iron filings, salt, sand, and polystyrene chips.
- Design and make a device for enabling an egg to fall 3 m without breaking.
- Build a tower to a height of 1 m, using drinking straws, which can support an egg/coin/ marble.
- Which factors affect the speed at which different things dry?
- Which fuel, from a safe selection, produces the most heat?
- Which insulating material is best for keeping hot water hot?
- Imagine a village is threatened by an erupting volcano. Devise ways of protecting it.

Different types of investigation

These are all investigations that have been suggested for, or tried in, the classroom. Varying degrees of structure and guidance will have been given. Some have a 'correct' answer; some don't. Some will take weeks or even months; some a few minutes. Some involve imaginary situations but most involve real situations. Some contexts are 'everyday' but some will be new to pupils. Some involve design-and-make (technological?) skills, some do not. Some are 'problem-solving activities', but clearly not all investigations need be of a problem-solving kind.

In an attempt to make some sense of the wide range of investigations now being used or suggested, we suggest a 'typology of investigations', which is shown in Table 8.1. This classification can be helpful in considering suggested ideas for investigations and published examples; it can also be useful in considering a department's policy and planning for investigational work.

Open and closed, pupil-led and teacher-led

A second framework for reflecting on the types of investigational work done in science lessons is given in Figure 8.1.

The three axes shown are not independent, of course. The first, teacher-led to pupil-led, indicates a continuum from one extreme at which pupils pose the questions to investigate to the other, in which all the questions are set, posed and restricted by the teacher. In practice, different work at different times will lie at different points along this axis – indeed, it must do if teachers are to meet the requirements of their curriculum.

The second axis, open to closed, shows a second continuum from one extreme in which an investigation or a problem-solving activity will have only one 'correct' answer and only one route for reaching it, to the other in which many possible solutions are equally acceptable, with many routes to them. In between these extremes lie many permutations and possibilities.

The third axis (obviously not independent of the others but still worth separating), is from undirected and unstructured to directed and structured. At one extreme, pupils will be given guidance, constraint and structure all along the way, i.e. in planning, designing, carrying out and evaluating. At the other, no guidance, structure and restriction will be placed on them. Neither extreme is very likely to occur in practice.

Table 8.1 A typology of investigations

'Which' type investigations
- Which factors affect X?
- Which design is best for ...?
- Which X is best for . . .? (for example, insulator, sole of trainers, floor covering, paper towel for absorption, soil, washing-up liquid, hamster food . . . This can often involve critically testing manufacturers' claims!).

'What' type investigations
- What happens if . . .?
- What is the connection between X and Y? (for example, shape and strength, aperture of a pinhole camera and image, length of pendulum and period time, temperature and dissolving etc.).

'How do' investigations
- How do different Xs affect Y?
- How does X vary with Y?
- How does X affect Y?

General investigations
- A survey, for example historical (nuclear energy, the chemical elements); local (pond study).
- A long-term project, for example local stream pollution, air quality, soil or path erosion. (These will often involve secondary sources, such as books, the media, extensive research and reading.)

Problem-solving activities
- Design-and-make, for example a dog-exercising machine, a desalination device.
- Solve a practical problem, for example bridge a gap, build a structure, make an alarm system.
- Simulations.

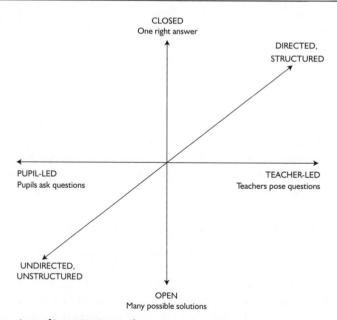

Figure 8.1 Dimensions of investigative work

Table 8.2 Classification of investigations in terms of variables

Question	Example
A single categoric variable	Which is the best type of insulation for a hot water tank?
A single continuous variable	Find out how the rate at which the water cools is dependent on the amount of water in the tank
More than one independent variable	Is it the type of insulation material or its thickness that is keeping the water hot?
Constructional activities	Make the best insulated hot water tank

Source: Gott and Duggan (1995)

The main purpose of this framework is to help teachers in planning for and reflecting on the type of investigational work they do in schools. It should help to increase variety and to clarify assessment.

Another way of categorising investigations was put forward by Watson *et al.* (1999: 105). They suggest six categories with certain key features: classifying and identifying; fair testing; pattern seeking; exploring; investigating models; and, finally, making things or developing systems.

Finally, Gott and Duggan (1995) offered a classification of investigations in terms of what type of variables, discussed later, they deal with, see Table 8.2.

Why do investigations?

There are many good reasons for using an investigational approach to science teaching, in addition to the pragmatic one of 'it's in the curriculum'. For many pupils it can be a great motivator, particularly if they really 'get into' a long-term investigation. Many pupils who are not successful in or motivated by other aspects of science work, such as learning content or written work, can sometimes be surprisingly successful at and therefore 'turned on by' investigational work. It can also be extremely enjoyable, perhaps leading more pupils to choose science once they reach the age of choice and consent. It can lead to teamwork and cooperation in science learning, which may be difficult to develop quite so actively in other ways. For many teachers of science, the introduction of investigational work can change entirely the way they approach the teaching of science generally: for example, the teaching of content (conceptual understanding) and process (procedural understanding) can be geared entirely towards an investigation as the end point or motivator. Certain critics of the investigational approach argue that it will leave 'less time for content', but this need not be the case – on the contrary, it could provide the motivation for learning content.

The 14–16 curriculum and Investigative Skills Assessment (ISA)

Within the 14–16 curriculum in England, Key Stage 4, pupils are assessed on their investigative skills using several ISAs.

An ISA is to be seen as an integral part of the teaching and learning within science. They are set by an examination group but administered and marked by the science teacher using a detailed set of assessment criteria. The aim of the ISA, amongst others, is to enable pupils to demonstrate the use of scientific language, in particular:

Revised Specimen ISA Physics 3 – Transformers

This ISA relates to: Unit P3 Physics (4451) section 13.9

Area of investigation
This work should be carried out during the teaching of the section relating to:
How do transformers work?

RISK ASSESSMENT
It is the responsibility of the centre to ensure that a risk assessment is carried out.

The Practical Work
For this part of the investigation candidates may work individually or in groups.

A suggested method is described below but centres may adapt this method to suit their own needs.

Figure 8.2 Example ISA

- dependent and independent variables;
- validity and reliability;
- precision and accuracy.

The use of ISAs also feeds into the *How Science Works* agenda, see Chapter 9. A section of an ISA from the AQA examination group is given in Figure 8.2.

Coping in the classroom

Pitfalls and problems to watch for

We have already seen that investigational work can have a number of benefits in learning and teaching science. But there are, of course, a number of pitfalls and problems that teachers (and pupils) need to be aware of:

- What is an investigation? There is little agreement or clarity in the use of words such as 'investigation', 'experiment', etc. among teachers or pupils. 'Investigation' and 'experiment' are best seen as lying on a continuum, rather than as separate activities. The framework and typology shown in Figure 8.1 and Table 8.1 respectively may help.
- Who does what in a group? Group dynamics must be considered because most practical work is carried out collectively. What is the role of each team member? Do they contribute equally or do some assume minor subsidiary roles? Do they all learn equally or are some participating within a clerical role, with little or no understanding of the underlying principles? If plans are produced individually, whose plan is followed in a group investigation?
- How should the 'process' of investigational work relate to learning 'theory' or content? Process skills interact closely with children's prior knowledge and understanding – they cannot be separated from them. This has implications for the type of investigation that children can be expected to carry out and is important in considering progression, assessment, and the linking of investigations with work on content.
- What is progression? Progression in investigation work is difficult to identify, observe and measure.

- When and how should the teacher interfere? How much input should a teacher make in an investigation? When and how should she or he intervene – at the planning stage? At the interpretation stage?
- 'Right' and 'wrong' answers: How should teachers deal with 'incorrect answers', i.e. scientifically unacceptable, to a closed-ended investigation? Pupils will often look for the 'right' answer to certain kinds of investigation.
- Planning: The planning part of an investigation is one of the most difficult aspects for pupils.
- Evaluating: This seems to be an even more difficult activity for students to do well.

Investigational work rarely reflects the 'true nature of science', indeed, how could it possibly be expected to?. It may promote the 'data first, theory second' view of science, i.e. the 'Sherlock Holmes in a white coat' notion. In addition, assessment of investigations is, to put it mildly, not easy even when provided with ISA guidelines.

For pupils to carry out investigations successfully in the classroom, most teachers feel that they will need guidance and structure of some sort, the only difference of opinion is to what degree. The next section offers some practical possibilities that have been put forward.

Giving guidance and help

When investigational work first became commonplace, many schools and education authorities designed and used structured sheets with questions for pupils to follow and fill in at different stages. See Figure 8.3 for an example. In other cases, schools provide guidance outlining the main steps in investigation under a framework of Planning, Doing and Reporting. For example:

Planning:

- Think of the question you are trying to answer.
- What do you predict will happen?
- Have you a reason or hypothesis for your prediction?

Doing:

- You must look closely (observe) what happens.
- Make careful measurements using the right instruments.
- Say what you need to change and keep the same – the variables.

Reporting:

- Say what your results mean.
- Try to explain or interpret them.
- Could you have done better?
- How might you change your plan?
- Evaluate your work.

The above suggestions also need to be read alongside the PEOR cycle discussed in Chapter 4 and, if you are undertaking formal assessment, the current examination criteria, e.g. for an ISA.

St. Cuthbert's School – A Specialist Science College Investigation Planning Sheet	
In this investigation I will investigate	
This is what I think will happen	
The reason(s) for thinking this are	
What I am going to do is	
What I will measure (or look for) is	
The apparatus I need is	
The things I will keep the same are	
The things I will vary are	
I will record my results by	
I will display my results by	
I will make the investigation safe by	

Figure 8.3 Investigation planning sheet

In order that pupils may come to better understand their learning, it is important that they feel confident in their planning and assessment. One possibility is to show the investigation planning in the form of a cycle, such as the one in Figure 8.4.

The planning cycle grid is used with the pupils by asking them to discuss what should go in each box, pooling the results and then producing a final version based on this guided discussion. By giving ownership to the pupils and writing in their language, pupils are better equipped to carry out investigations and act on the teacher's feedback.

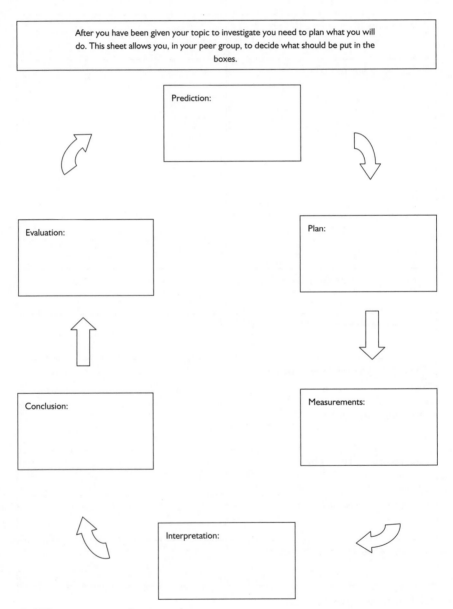

Figure 8.4 The investigation planning cycle

St. Cuthbert's School – A Specialist Science College
Investigation Data Sheet

Example data for the 'make a clock' investigation.

1. Keeping the length of the pendulum fixed and varying the mass.

Length fixed at 0.50m

Mass (kg)	Time for 10 oscillations (s)				Time period (s)
	Run 1	Run 2	Run 3	Average	
0.050	13.1	13.0	13.1		
0.055	12.9	13.0	13.0		
0.060	13.0	13.0	13.1		
0.065	13.0	13.1	10.7		
0.070	13.1	13.0	13.0		

2. Keeping the mass fixed and varying the length.

Mass fixed at 0.15 kg

length (m)	Time for 10 oscillations (s)				Time period (s)
	Run 1	Run 2	Run 3	Average	
0.50	13.6	13.8	13.9		
0.60	15.3	15.5	15.4		
0.70	16.7	16.9	16.7		
0.80	17.8	17.9	17.8		
0.90	16.3	18.8	18.8		

Figure 8.5 An example 'prompt' sheet

It is important that when a pupil makes a mistake, for example in carrying out an investigation, they are not penalised in other assessment categories. To this end we suggest that 'prompt sheets' be used, see Figure 8.5. The example given is a data set that could be given to a pupil who failed to collect their own – notice the rogue result, not to be highlighted on the pupil copy, which gives opportunity for discussion.

Many other frameworks and guidelines for pupils have been produced – the above selections are a small sample. They will certainly help to overcome at least some of the pitfalls and problems outlined above. The main general feeling is that pupils will need guidance and structure for at least part of the time during their investigational work. What does seem to vary from one school to another is the amount of guidance given to pupils, which of course has implications for assessment. In particular you, as the teacher, must be happy with any level of guidance you give when assessment is being done: carefully check the guidance given by the examination groups and, we would argue, always stay within the rules.

Developing a model/structure for investigational work: three levels

One of the aims of doing investigational work in the classroom, of course, must be to develop in pupils some sort of understanding of science procedures as well as the more specific 'toolbox' of skills and techniques. The latter can be taught almost as rules of thumb and can quite rightly involve training as much as education. Thus pupils can be taught how to read a range of measuring instruments, how to set up data-logging equipment, how to record results manually, and how to set up certain common types of apparatus, such as for distillation. This is all part of basic practical science education, verging on training.

At a slightly higher level pupils can be taught the importance of accuracy, the limitations of certain measuring instruments and the need to repeat measurements, i.e. take lots of readings. They can also learn the ideas of identifying and controlling variables and therefore the notion of a 'fair test'.

One of the ways in which they can be encouraged to do this is by assessing their own investigational work. A possible framework for encouraging pupils to do this, at different levels, is given in Figure 8.6.

Eventually, the aim must be to develop a general model of 'investigational work' that pupils can use and apply in a number of different situations. Some curriculum models imply a linear approach to investigation, i.e. Plan, Do, Observe, Analyse, Evaluate … finish. This is often forced upon teachers and learners by the constraints of an external curriculum, the school timetable and laboratory organisation. The impact of the external curriculum is greater, in our view, since the introduction of ISAs to the assessment.

In an ideal world, however, a model of investigational work, and the practice of 'real science', should follow a cyclic approach, as we indicated in Figure 8.4 earlier. The process of interpreting and evaluating results should not be the end-point. Rather it should lead back to the first activity of asking new questions, making revised plans and revisiting predictions.

The ultimate aim in investigational work, therefore, must be to encourage, or even inculcate, a generalised pattern or model of such work. To develop this, pupils must be able to see each investigation task at some level of abstraction. They must be able to pay attention to the general, structural features of the task as well as its context-embedded, surface, specific features. This must be the justification or rationale for expecting thousands of pupils to spend thousands of hours on investigations in science, i.e. to develop a pattern or model for tackling investigations and problems. How else could we justify the time spent?

This has implications for teaching. As well as providing pupils with interesting investigations in exciting, often everyday contexts, teachers also need to spend time on the general features of each task. The notion of *How Science Works*, HSW, should also be built on under the guise of investigative work; HSW is covered in Chapter 9. However you, as the teacher, should be asking and helping pupils to ask of themselves:

- What are the pupils doing and why?
- What types of variable are they controlling?
- What is this idea of a 'fair test'?
- Why is it important to repeat measurements?
- What limits does their experiment and others like it have?

Only by considering the general structural features of each specific task will the model develop, a model which might then be transferred to other contexts and other tasks, including

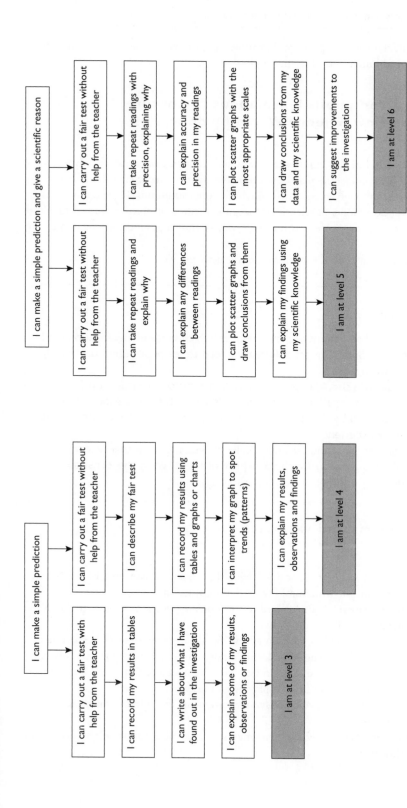

Figure 8.6 Self assessment, or peer assessment, sheet for investigative work

perhaps those outside the science classroom. In this way pupils may also learn something about the nature, purpose and limitations of science itself.

In summary ... can pupils learn about the nature of science and How Science Works by doing investigations?

Our view is that they can, but curriculum statements and guidelines often reflect only one view or model of science. These guidelines may be a reasonable mirror or representation of how some scientists actually work, although certain critics might not even admit this. However, it is certain that there could never be a model of scientific procedure, method or practice that mirrors 'real science' in all its forms. In short, there is no single way of showing, modelling or mimicking *How Science Works*.

The following chapter takes up the discussion of *How Science Works*.

Points for reflection

- From your own observations and experiences, which types of investigation tend to be done in schools? Can schools really afford to let pupils carry out a truly open-ended investigation?
- How much guidance should pupils be given in carrying out investigations?
- A cynical view of investigational work in schools is that 'the investigations that are actually done tend to be those which are most easily organised and assessed'. Is this true in your experience?
- Can investigations in school science really reflect the way that science and scientists work? Is this too much to expect of them, given the constraints in school science, e.g. of time, resources, or management?

A glossary of terms and variables

Terms

Conceptual understanding/knowledge Concerned with the ideas and concepts of science, for example force, energy, magnetism, humidity, evolution, reaction.

Hypothesis A reasoned explanation put forward for an observed event or events. It should be testable (falsifiable) by investigation.

Procedural understanding/knowledge Concerned with the procedures of experimental, investigational work, i.e. identifying variables and understanding their importance; planning and designing an investigation; understanding ideas of measurement such as accuracy, reliability and 'repeatability'; recording, displaying and interpreting data.

Qualitative approach One that does not involve measurement, for example, using terms like quickly/slowly or large/small.

Quantitative approach One that involves measurements to make observations more precise and put numbers against them.

Variables

A variable is a quantity that can take different values. It can be categoric, discrete, continuous or derived.

Categoric A categoric variable is a classification, such as colour (red, green, yellow, etc.) or shape (square, oblong, round).

Continuous A continuous variable can have any value, such as mass, weight, volume, length, temperature, or time.

Control* Control variables are those that must be controlled and held constant by the investigator and which make the investigation a 'fair test'. (Sometimes the control variable is confused with 'the control' in an experiment, particularly in biology. A control, such as a plant which is not given any of the nutrients being tested, can be considered as one value of the independent variable.)

Dependent* The dependent variable is the effect or outcome of interest to the investigator. It is measured or judged in the investigation. In the example under *Independent* below it would be the length of the spring.

Derived A derived variable has to be calculated from more than one measurement, for example speed from distance travelled and the time taken; acceleration; work.

Discrete A discrete variable can only have an integer value, such as the number of layers of insulation or the number of germinated seeds.

Independent* The independent variable is the one which the investigator chooses to change systematically. For example, in an investigation into how different springs stretch, the independent variable is the mass chosen to hang on the spring.

Interacting Two independent variables whose effects on the dependent variable are not easily separated, such as the effect of water and air on rusting.

Key Key variables define an investigation. They are the independent variable and the dependent variable.

*'Independent' is the one you change; 'dependent' is the one you keep an eye on; 'control' is the one you keep the same.

References and further reading

Gott, R. and Duggan, S. (1995) *Investigative Work in the Science Curriculum*, Buckingham: Open University Press.

Laws, P.M. (1996) 'Investigative work in the science national curriculum', *School Science Review*, vol. 77, no. 281, pp. 17–25.

Osborne, J. (1997) 'Practical alternatives', *School Science Review*, vol. 78, no. 285, pp. 61–7.

Qualter, A., Strang, J., Swatton, P. and Taylor, R. (1990) *Exploration – a way of learning science*, Oxford: Basil Blackwell.

Watson, R. and Wood-Robinson, V. (1998) 'Learning to investigate', in Ratcliffe, M. (ed.) *ASE Guide to Secondary Education, Hatfield*: ASE/Stanley Thornes, pp. 84–91.

The ATLAS (Active Teaching and Learning Approaches in Science) materials contain many valuable ideas and useful guidance for teachers in doing investigations (from Collins Educational, London).

For a critical look at approaches to investigational work try:

Wellington, J. (ed.) (1998) *Practical Work in School Science: which way now?*, London: Routledge.

Woolnough, B. (ed.) (1991) *Practical Science* (various chapters), Milton Keynes: Open University Press.

Woolnough, B. and Allsop, T. (1985) *Practical Work in Science*, Cambridge: Cambridge University Press.

The AKSIS project, based at King's College London, looked closely at investigations in school science. One of several publications is:

Watson, R., Goldsworthy, A. and Wood-Robinson, V. (1999) 'What is not fair with investigations?', *School Science Review*, vol. 80, no. 292, pp. 101–6.

Various publishers produce resources for the classroom on investigational work. The Pupil Researcher Initiative (PRI) based at Sheffield Hallam University has been one of the best sources of new ideas and developments.

Chapter 9

How Science Works

Introduction

The Science National Curriculum for England was revised in 2006 for Key Stage 4 [14–16 year olds] and in 2008 for Key Stage 3 [11–14 year olds]. The implementation of these changes was 2007 and 2009 respectively. One of the key changes in both curriculum documents was a move from *content* to *process*. Within the move towards a greater emphasis on scientific process the notion of *How Science Works* was given top billing by the then Department for Education and Science (DfES, 2006).

Whatever your view of the balance between content and process, see Chapter 2, *How Science Works* proved difficult for teachers who now had to plan around ethical, political, cultural issues and management of risk and uncertainty in science. Some would argue that all of this is simply good teaching and should always have been part of the teaching narrative …

How Science Works – two key strands?

Developing ideas and theories to explain the world is at the heart of science. How science works focuses on the critical analysis and linking of evidence to support or refute ideas and theories. Effective enquiry work involves exploring questions and finding answers through the gathering and evaluation of evidence. Pupils need to understand how evidence comes from the collection and critical interpretation of both primary and secondary data and how evidence may be influenced by contexts such as culture, politics or ethics.

(DfES, 2006)

In developing the level and depth of enquiry suggested above, the process can be divided into two key strands:

1   explanations, arguments and decisions;
2   practical and enquiry skills.

Within the first key strand it is useful to think of three sub-strands:

* scientific thinking;
* application, implication and cultural understanding;
* audience-appropriate and purposeful communication.

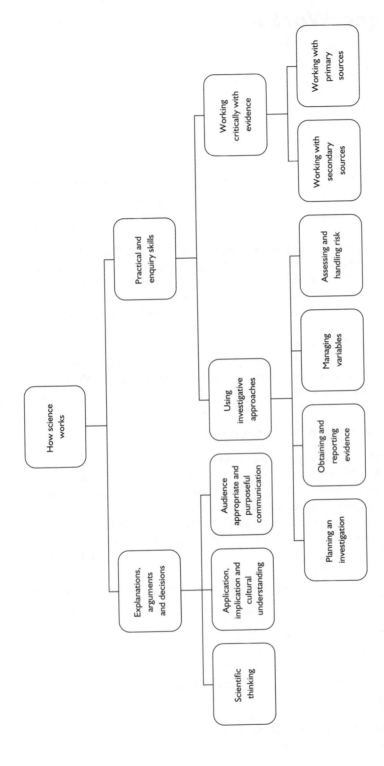

Figure 9.1 Key strands in *How Science Works*

The second key strand can be usefully broken down into two sub-strands:

* using investigative approaches;
* working critically with evidence.

As with all things, especially in science, the division and sub-division of a complex topic can be made ever more fine in its detail; Figure 9.1 offers our interpretation of the DfES guidance of *How Science Works*.

Ross *et al.* (2010) offer an analysis based on 'four key areas':

* data, evidence and enquiry skills;
* practical and enquiry skills;
* communication skills;
* applications and implications of science.

Looking at how *scientists* rather than *science* works, Williams (2008) offers the visual interpretation shown in Figure 9.2.

How Science Works – how to

How does science work? This is a very big question – have a go at answering it! We will not be offering *an answer*, not because we don't have an answer but because there is *no one answer*.

Figure 9.3 is an attempt to convey something of what it is to *do science* in the real world rather than the school laboratory. We argue that the importance of this is in the motivation and engagement of pupils, otherwise why should they want to learn a set of procedures or understand different cultural norms?

How Science Works – practical approaches

Taking the view that 'real-world science' is about asking questions of our observations then how could we, as science educators, give this experience to our pupils?

The idea of *cognitive conflict* was introduced in Chapter 4 and it could be argued that this approach lends itself to developing the skill set outlined in *How Science Works*.

One approach, then, is to engineer a situation in which pupils' thinking will be challenged, i.e. their current model will not be able to explain the observation. They are then set the task of designing an investigation to test their new ideas – if this leads to an outcome which does explain the observation then it will become part of their scientific thinking. This approach will also allow for the development of understanding that scientific thinking is often temporary and theories are transient.

In school physics it is now commonplace for a teacher to demonstrate Lenz's law by dropping a neodymium magnet down a copper tube and observing the extended fall time. In itself this can challenge pupils' thinking by virtue of the fact *they know* copper is a non-magnetic material. However, developing this into a *How Science Works* activity needs only a small adaptation:

Try dropping a stack of ten magnets down the copper tube and time the fall time. Repeat this with nine, eight, seven, six and five magnets. Now ask pupils to predict the fall time for four, three, two and one magnet. Finally measure the fall time for these magnets. Does observation match prediction?

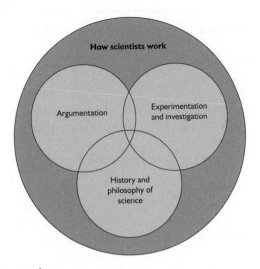

Figure 9.2 How scientists work

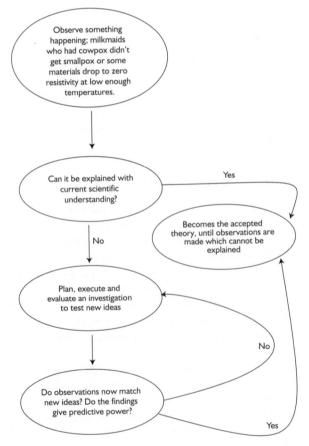

Figure 9.3 Real world science

In this particular case they will not match and a discussion can be developed around the pitfalls of making judgments based on limited data. This investigation is fully explained in Ireson and Twidle (2008a, b).

Staying with school physics an alternative could be to use cans of soft drink. Roll two cans down a gentle incline and ask pupils which will reach the end of the runway first. Now repeat the run but shake one of the cans; which will reach the end first now? Pupils can be challenged not only to collectively arrive at a theory but also to devise and carry out an investigation to test the theory. This investigation can be seen in Ireson and Twidle (2005).

How Science Works – in summary

This short chapter has raised your awareness of the place played by *How Science Works* in the English National Curriculum. However, more importantly, it should have highlighted the complexity of *real science* versus *school science*. You should also now be aware that, like many things in science education, the topic is complex and cannot be taken in isolation.

Revisiting Chapter 3 will help you place school science in context, whilst Chapter 14 looks at the nature of science. Chapter 16, on citizenship and sustainability in science education, also contributes to the debate and provides both background and potential resources for *How Science Works*.

Perhaps the answer is to allow several different models of scientific investigation that pupils in labs could follow for different types of work. This would certainly get round the problem of statutory guidelines presenting only one view of science – a view that teachers will inevitably adhere to due to the pressures of assessment and inspection. Therefore, pupils will receive the message that this is 'the nature of science' or 'how science works'. This would not be a useful, let alone a truthful, message. Despite the complexity and controversy in all the current debates on the history, philosophy and sociology of science, one message is clear: scientists have worked, do work and will work in a variety of different ways at different times in different disciplines for different reasons.

Points for reflection

- Where do you stand on the *process* versus *content* debate in science education?
- Where do you stand on the place for cultural and political aspects of science; should it be in school science?
- Should we, as a Nation, strive for some measure of scientific literacy to allow all citizens to engage with science in the news?
- Should it be the role of the science teacher to provide this literacy?

References and further reading

DfES (2006) *Secondary National Strategy* London: HMSO.

Golabek, C., Toplis, R. and Cleaves, A. (2010) 'Science curriculum change in England: How science works for pre-service teachers.' In M.F. Taşar and G. Çakmakcı (Eds.), *Contemporary Science Education Research: international perspectives* (pp. 467–72). Ankara, Turkey: Pegem Akademi.

Ireson, G. and Twidle, J. (2005) The rolling can investigation: towards an explanation, *International Journal of Mathematical Education in Science and Technology*, 36, 423–8.

Ireson, G. and Twidle, J. (2008a) Magnetic braking revisited: an activity for How science works. *Physics Education*, 43, 522–4.

Ireson, G. and Twidle, J. (2008b) Magnetic braking revisited: activities for the undergraduate laboratory. *European Journal of Physics* 29, 745–51.

Kind, V. (2008) *Teaching Secondary How Science Works*, London: John Murray.

Monk, Martin (2006) 'How science works: what do we do now?' *School Science Review*, vol. 88, no. 322, pp. 119–21; describes some valuable teaching strategies that can help teachers to deal with the section of the science national curriculum labelled *How Science Works* (which replaced Scientific Enquiry). This area of the curriculum will 'rely heavily' on teachers' own views of the nature of science, thus placing demands on teachers to reflect on and read in this area.

Ross, K., Lakin, L. and McKechnie, J. (2010) *Teaching Secondary Science*, London: David Fulton.

Toplis, R., Golabek, C. and Cleaves, A. (2010) 'Implementing a new Science National Curriculum for England: how trainee teachers see the How Science Works strand in schools'. *The Curriculum Journal*, 21(1): 65–76.

Williams, J. (2008) 'Science now and then: discovering *How Science Works*'. *School Science Review* 90, 45–6; from a special issue of *School Science Review* focusing on *How Science Works*.

Chapter 10

Safety in the science laboratory

Introduction

The issue of safety, particularly that of pupils, is not just a consideration when planning a lesson; it is probably *the* most important factor in science, or any other subject, that overrides all others.

However, a great number of practical activities that *could* be dangerous can, with forethought, be rendered safe. For example, the extraction of chlorophyll from leaves requires hot ethanol. Obviously using a Bunsen flame would be considered, we hope, unsafe while using a water bath filled from a hot kettle makes it suitable and safe for some pupils. This raises an important issue:

> it is not only the inanimate components of a lesson that need to be taken into consideration but also the organic ones, in the shape of the class being taught. What might be acceptable for a small, cooperative, high achieving, Year 11 class may not be suitable for younger, larger or less well behaved groups.
>
> (Ireson and Twidle 2006)

We would like to stress that this chapter is intended to serve as an introduction to the issue of health and safety, to raise an awareness of some of the important factors. It is not to be taken as guide to policy and it is no substitute for the numerous national and local publications available in both print and electronic format. To this end we would guide the reader to:

- *Hazcards*, CLEAPSS, 1995 (or later updates);
- *Topics in Safety*, ASE 3rd edition, 2001;
- *Safeguards in the School Laboratory*, ASE 11th edition, 2006a;
- *Safety Reprints*, ASE, 2006b
- *Safety in Science Education*, DfEE, HMSO, 1996.

Reflecting on risk

To many, science teachers included, school science laboratories may appear dangerous places. While we would never deny that the potential for danger exists within a school science laboratory it is our view, supported by the Health and Safety Executive, that careful planning makes the laboratory one of the safer areas of school; see Table 10.1.

Table 10.1 Accidents to pupils in schools by percentage

Sports activities	38.5
Gymnasium	27.0
Playground	12.1
Science laboratories	0.9

Source: Health and Safety Executive Statistics for 1991/2 (ASE, 1996)

Table 10.2 Most common school laboratory accidents by percentage

Chemicals in the eye	23
Chemical on the skin	21
Chemical in the mouth	4

Whilst annual data sets are not available on a national level, the data in Table 10.1 can be seen as consistent over time from 1991 to 1997 where the Health and Safety Executive report, of significant injury in school, shows only 0.8 per cent took place in the science laboratory (HSE 1997).

Given that relatively few accidents happen to pupils in science lessons, what then are the most common ones? Data here proves difficult to obtain with any degree of certainty but although rather dated, Tawney's report (1981) highlights, as may be seen in Table 10.2, chemicals as the greatest danger, accounting for almost half (48 per cent) of all school laboratory accidents to pupils.

Rules and regulations

Perhaps the most important piece of legislation in this area is the Management of Health and Safety at Work Regulations of 1992 (HSW Act). It is the employer's responsibility to ensure effective measures in planning, organisation, control and review of safety in order to provide a safe working environment for their *employees*. The use of the word 'employee' is very important since, as non-employees, pupils are not covered by the provision of the Act! However this does not exempt teachers from a duty of care since its neglect is a criminal offence. It is testament to the careful planning of UK science teachers that in the period 1975 to 1996 only two successful prosecutions were brought against them; both for 'blatant disregard of safety precautions' (ASE 1996). While the regulations under the HSW Act may seem onerous, further regulatory provision must also be kept in mind when planning for safe science education, for example:

- Control of Substances Hazardous to Health (COSHH) Regulations, which focuses on corrosive, harmful, irritant and toxic substances;
- Reporting of Injuries, Diseases and Dangerous Occurrences Regulations (RIDDOR), which addresses the legality for reporting serious injury;
- Electricity at Work Regulations, which covers the use, repair, installation and inspection of electrical services and equipment;
- Pressure Systems Safety Regulations, covering the safe installation, maintenance and operation of pressurised systems;
- Ionising Radiations in Educational Establishments in England and Wales Regulations, which focuses on the use of all ionising radiation in schools;

- Provision and Use of Work Equipment Regulations, which addresses the suitability, maintenance and inspection of equipment used in the place of work.

Whilst we would expect health and safety to become part of good practice for science teachers, the National Curriculum also places a statutory requirement on all teachers. The general guidance for the National Curriculum is explicit in stating:

Health and Safety
This statement applies to science, design and technology, information and communication technology, art and design, and physical education.
    When working with tools, equipment and materials, in practical activities and in different environments, including those that are unfamiliar, pupils should be taught: about hazards, risks and risk control;

- to recognise hazards, assess consequent risks and take steps to control the risks to themselves and others;
- to use information to assess the immediate and cumulative risks;
- to manage their environment to ensure the health and safety of themselves and others;
- to explain the steps they take to control risks.

(DfEE 1999)

It is interesting that this guidance was not in the Science document nor was it in the 2004 revision of the National Curriculum which was first taught in 2006.

Assessing risk

The basis for all health and safety legislation in schools is risk assessment. The legislation, as outlined above, applies to all school activities and not just practical work or teacher demonstrations in science. It could be argued that teachers were identifying *hazards* and assessing *risk* long before the phrase *risk assessment* was ever coined.
    What constitutes a hazard? What is risk? Borrows (1998) suggests the following, which we feel meets the needs of teachers in school:

A hazard is anything with the potential to cause harm. Hazards therefore include many chemicals, electricity at high voltages and such activities as carrying a tray of microscopes up and down stairs. Risk is the probability that harm will actually be caused by the hazard. There are two elements to risk:
- How likely is it that something will go wrong?
- How serious would it be if something did go wrong?

In addition to the two points above we would also add two more:

- Has the teacher a plan of action in case of an accident?
- Does the activity have a valid educational aim which makes the risk acceptable?

The Health and Safety Executive (HSE 2006) offer five steps to risk assessment:

1   Identify the hazards;
2   Decide who might be harmed and how;
3   Evaluate the risks and decide on precautions;
4   Record your findings and implement them;
5   Review your assessment and update if necessary.

Ross *et al.* (2010) reference General Risk Assessments (GRAs) giving six questions to be asked of an activity:

1   Is it educationally necessary?
2   Is there an alternative, less hazardous substance or procedure?
3   Is it a teacher demonstration or a pupil activity?
4   What are the age and experience of the pupils?
5   What personal protection or control measures are necessary?
6   How will residues be disposed of at the end?

Whilst the questions could be considered to be *good teaching* we would ask you one additional question: Did you answer each of these before, or during, the planning of your lesson?

Taking control measures

What are control measures? Any measure which reduces a risk is a control measure. These typically involve smaller quantities, more dilute solutions, protective equipment (though this should never be the first thought in reducing risk) or simply paying attention to advice given.

The approach to controlling the potential risks in science teaching is therefore just the same in principle as that which should be taken to control any other type of risk in schools. To teach practical science safely we need to look at the way in which materials and equipment are used and to consider how to reduce any risks to the health of pupils and teachers to an acceptably low level.

What if the risk is not zero? This, in our view, should not be a concern. Pupils are exposed to higher risks in many other school activities, see Table 10.1. In getting to school pupils cross roads, travel on buses or cycle. All of these activities have a non-zero risk but pupils, parents and teachers clearly judge the risk as *acceptable*:

> The task of carrying out a risk assessment may be delegated to an employee. However, as stated earlier, the responsibility still remains with the employer to ensure that such assessments are carried out before any hazardous activity takes place or hazardous chemicals and microorganisms are used. It is the responsibility of the employer to check that these tasks are delegated competently.
>
> (Ireson and Twidle 2006)

While having pointed out the nature of risk assessment we would not wish to inhibit teachers' use of practical work for fear of running foul of legislation:

> Contrary to popular impressions, there are in fact very few science activities and chemicals which schools might consider using which are banned at a national level. The major ones are benzene, and any mixture or solution containing more than 1% benzene, and various ozone depleters. In addition to these outright bans there are a number of complicated

restrictions on the dissection of eyes of various species, holdings of radioactive substances, making explosives, experiments involving cruelty to vertebrates and removal of protected species from the wild.

(Royal Society of Chemistry, 2005)

Although mechanistic in nature, Ireson and Twidle (2006) suggest a way in which risk assessment can be quantified using the two elements given by Borrows (1998). By rating 'how likely is it that something will go wrong?' and 'how serious would it be if something did go wrong?' on a scale of 1 to 5 the product of the two ratings gives an index from 0 to 25. The closer an assessment is to 25 the less appropriate it is. An example is given in Table 10.3, and as an alternative, a risk assessment for producing copper sulphate crystals is given in Table 10.4.

For a beginning teacher, or even an experienced one, it would be wise to make a record of risk assessments carried out in the lesson plan, scheme of work or worksheets. Some employers may have adopted a range of general or model risk assessments and these guidelines may form part of the department's policy documents. In such cases it is the employee's responsibility to ensure that the guidance is adhered to. However, on occasions the proposed activity involves a novel situation and in such circumstances the individual teacher would need to carry out a special risk assessment.

For the beginning teacher it would be wise to consult his or her head of department for advice in such situations or if they are at all unclear as to what the employer's requirements are. Reference to Table 10.4 highlights the importance paid to the teacher's past experience and the need to be alert.

It is important that pupils are taken through the processes involved in assessing risks and this will not only fulfil the requirements of the National Curriculum but also prepare them for the

Table 10.3 Risk assessment index: an example

Activity	Likelihood	Seriousness	Rating
Year 7, mean age 12, pupils dissolving sugar in water to create a saturated solution.	If using glass beakers danger from broken glass [1]. With plastic beakers [0]. Splashes into the eyes should be zero, all pupils wearing safety goggles, however still rate as [1].	Cut to pupils not serious, other than to the pupil of course [2].	In the worst case $2 \times 2 = 4$. Safe to proceed.
Year 13, mean age 18, liquid nitrogen for superconductivity investigations.	All wearing gloves and safety goggles. All liquid nitrogen in suitable Dewars which can vent to the atmosphere. Likelihood of spills or splashes on pupils [2], likelihood of large scale spill in a poorly ventilated room [1].	Spills onto person not serious if the liquid does not pool, danger of cryogenic burn if it does, [4]. Danger to all in the room from oxygen depletion following large scale spill and/or ventilation failure, [5].	In the worst case $2 \times 5 = 10$ Careful supervision or teacher demonstration.

Table 10.4 Example risk assessment for producing copper sulphate crystals

Hazardous chemical or microorganism being used or made, or hazardous procedure or equipment	Nature of the hazard(s)	Source(s) of information	Control measures to reduce risk
(1) Sulphuric acid	(1) Acid is corrosive if 1.5M or more: irritant if 0.5M or more.	(1) Bottle label: CLEAPSS Student Safety Sheets.	(1) Use lowest possible concentration, 0.5M; wear eye protection.
(2) Copper carbonate	(2) (a) The solid is harmful if swallowed and dust irritates lungs and eyes.	(2) (a) Bottle label: CLEAPSS Student Safety Sheets.	(2) (a) Avoid raising dust: wear eye protection.
	(b) When the reaction takes place, tiny bubbles of carbon dioxide are formed which may produce a spray of sulphuric acid as they burst.	(b) Text book; teacher	(b) Keep face well away from reaction; wear eye protection.
(3) Copper oxide	(3) (a) The solid is harmful if swallowed and dust irritates lungs and eyes.	(3) (a) Bottle label: CLEAPSS Student Safety Sheets.	(3) (a) Wear eye protection.
	(b) Unlike copper carbonate, copper oxide needs to be heated so the mixture may boil over, spill hot acid etc.	(b) Text book; teacher.	(b) Control Bunsen burner flame, stir to speed dissolving.
	(c) Hot tripods etc.	(c) Teacher; past experience.	(c) Pay attention.
(4) Copper sulphate	(4) Solid and solutions more concentrated than 1M are harmful.	(4) CLEAPSS Student Safety Sheets.	(4) Wash hands after activity. When solution is standing to crystallise label it carefully.
(5) Evaporating solution to form saturated solution.	(5) (a) Solution may boil over, or start spitting when nearly saturated.	(5) (a) Teacher; past experience.	(5) (a) Keep careful watch over Bunsen burner. Do not evaporate too much – allow to crystallise slowly. Wear eye protection.
	(b) Hot tripods etc.	(b) Teacher; past experience.	(b) Pay attention.
	(c) Process is slow, leading to rushing at end of lesson and accidents.	(c) Teacher; past experience.	(c) Use small volume, so it is quicker.

Source: CLEAPSS (2007)

hazards of home and work. To this end, CLEAPSS (2000) have produced pupil versions of teachers' safety sheets. In involving pupils in the process of risk assessment, particularly when planning their own investigations, they are able to contribute to their own safety. Having said that, such procedures do not absolve the teacher from his or her responsibility of ensuring that pupils' proposed activities are in accordance with the employer's risk assessments.

Points for reflection

- Has the planned activity been risk assessed in the last two years? What conclusions do you draw when you apply a risk assessment in the form outlined above?
- Can the potential risk outweigh the potential learning from a demonstration? If so what else could you do?
- Does removing risk prevent pupils from experiencing 'real science'?

References and further reading

ASE (1988) *Topics in Safety*, Hatfield: ASE.

ASE (1996) *Safeguards in the School Laboratory*, Hatfield: ASE.

ASE (1998) *Safety Reprints*, Hatfield: ASE.

ASE (1999) *Safe and Exciting Science*, Hatfield: ASE.

ASE (2001) *Topics in Safety* (3rd edn), Hatfield: ASE.

ASE (2006a) *Safeguards in the School Laboratory* (11th edn), Hatfield: ASE.

ASE (2006b) *Safety Reprints,* Hatfield: ASE.

Borrows, P. (1998) 'Safety in science education', in Ratcliffe, M. (ed.) *ASE Guide to Secondary Science Education*, Hatfield: ASE/Stanley Thornes.

CLEAPSS (1995) *Hazcards*, CLEAPPS: Brunel University.

CLEAPSS (2000) *Student Safety Sheets*, CLEAPSS: Brunel University.

CLEAPSS (2007) *Science Publications CD ROM*, CLEAPSS: Brunel University.

DfEE (1996) *Safety in Science Education*, Norwich: HMSO.

DfEE (1999) *The National Curriculum*, London: HMSO

Everett, D. and Jenkins, E. (1990) *A Safety Handbook for Science Teachers*, London: John Murray.

HMSO (1985) *Microbiology: an HMI guide for schools and non-advanced further education*, London: HMSO.

HSE (1997) *Health and Safety Executive 1996/7*, London: HSE.

HSE (2006) *Five Steps to Risk Assessment*, Sudbury: HSE Books.

Ireson, G. and Twidle, J. (2006) *Secondary Science Reflective Reader*, London: Learning matters.

Ross, K., Lakin, L. and McKechnie, J. (2010) *Teaching Secondary Science* (3rd edn), London: Routledge.

Royal Society of Chemistry (2005) 'Surely That's Banned? A report for the Royal Society of Chemistry on chemicals and procedures thought to be banned from use in schools', www.rsc.org.

Scottish Schools Science Equipment Research Centre (1981) *Hazardous Chemicals: a manual for schools and colleges*, Edinburgh: Oliver and Boyd.

Tawney, D. (1981) 'Accidents in school laboratories: a report of an investigation', *Education in Science*, vol. 95, pp. 32–3.

Chapter 11

Language in science teaching and learning

Children solve practical tasks with the help of their speech as well as their eyes and hands.
(Vygotsky 1978)

Although science is a 'practical subject', science teaching occurs mainly through the medium of language, both spoken and written. The aim of this chapter is to focus on that language and the way that teachers, texts and pupils use it. We start from three basic premises:

1   Language can be a major barrier in learning science;
2   We can identify the main sources of difficulty;
3   There are many teaching and learning strategies that can help to lower the language barrier in science.

Watch your language: the world of secondary science

In the school science lab pupils meet all sorts of strange objects and devices that they will never encounter elsewhere: they meet the world of the conical flask, the pestle and mortar, the Bunsen burner, the evaporating dish, the gauze and the watch glass, not to mention the pipette and the burette. To enter the lab is akin to Alice's passage down the rabbit hole into a new world. This is equally true of pupils' strange encounters with a new world of discourse.

Twas brillig and the slithy toves,
Did gyre and gimble in the wabe;
All mimsy were the borogoves,
And the mome raths outgrabe.
... Somehow it seems to fill my head with ideas – only I don't exactly know what they are!
(*Through the Looking-Glass and What Alice Found There*, Lewis Carroll, 1872)

How many pupils, confronted by a science textbook or by a whiteboard covered in scientific prose, are as confused as Alice was when she first read 'Jabberwocky'? Their heads may be full of ideas but they may not be quite sure what those ideas are, or where they came from. In many ways, the language of science resembles the language of Carroll's poem.

Classifying the words of science

Consider the random selection of words used in science textbooks and by science teachers below:

momentum inertia acceleration power photosynthesis gene
speed couple fruit wave electric current isotope parasite particle critical
angle trachea electron substance force meniscus neutron material
pressure mass proton photon work field amoeba velocity energy

Their only shared characteristic *could* be that each has a precision or 'fixedness' in its meaning. Science words *might* be considered to mean the same whatever the context and whoever the user. But do they? Certainly the 'fixed' meaning of science words has been questioned (Sutton 1992).

But it is the *difference between* the words of science rather than their *shared* features that we would like to concentrate on here, for the words in the above list do vastly different jobs. Take 'trachea' and 'inertia', for example. The word 'trachea' simply *names* a real object or entity: a windpipe; 'trachea', like many scientific words, is thus a synonym. It has meaning because it names or 'points to' a real entity. But how does a word like 'inertia' acquire meaning? It does not refer to an object or an entity. Surely then it must signify a *concept*. This concept is somehow derived from experience – the observation that 'heavy things tend to keep going', or a 'steamroller is hard to get started' or similar personal experiences.

Unfortunately, many concept words in science do not, and cannot, acquire meaning as easily as a word such as 'trachea'. Take the word 'atom', for example. Your, and our, meaning for this word can never be derived from experience. The same is true for other so-called unobservable entities. There are even greater problems for the meaning of many terms used in physics: 'frictionless body', 'point mass' and 'smooth surface', for example – not derived from experience, nor unobservable entities, but non-existent idealisations! The terms of Schrodinger's wave equation and De Broglie's statement of wave/particle duality present problems at an even higher level of abstraction. It is impossible to conjure up even a vague mental image of an *object* being a particle and a wave all at the same time.

This all indicates that it can be useful to divide the words of science into various types or categories. Through doing this, science teachers can become more aware of the language they use in classrooms. A classification or 'taxonomy' of the words of science is put forward in Table 11.1.

Each category of words acquires meaning in a different way, and it is this complexity that teachers of science need to be aware of:

- The first category can be called *naming words*. These are words that denote identifiable, observable, real objects or entities: words such as trachea, oesophagus, tibia, fibula, fulcrum, meniscus, vertebra, pollen, saliva, thorax, iris, larynx and stigma. Many of these are simply synonyms for everyday words already familiar to pupils, such as windpipe, backbone, or spit. Thus part of learning in science involves giving *familiar* objects new names. At a slightly higher level, some learning in science involves giving new names to *unfamiliar* objects, objects that pupils may never have seen before – perhaps because they cannot be seen with a naked eye, such as a cell, or because they belong to the world of school science laboratories, for example beaker, conical flask, Bunsen burner, spatula, gauze, and splint.

- The second category of *scientific words*, at a new level of abstraction, can be called *process words*. These are words that denote processes that happen in science: words such as evaporation, distillation, condensation, photosynthesis, crystallisation, fusion, vaporisation, combustion

Table 11.1 A taxonomy of the words of science

Level 1 Naming words

   1.1 Familiar objects, new names (synonyms)

   1.2 New objects, new names

   1.3 Names of chemical elements

   1.4 Other nomenclature

Level 2 Process words

   2.1 Capable of ostensive definition, i.e. being shown

   2.2 Not capable of ostensive definition

Level 3 Concept words

   3.1 Derived from experience (sensory concepts)

   3.2 With dual meanings, i.e. everyday and scientific, for example, 'work'*

   3.3 Theoretical constructs (total abstractions, idealisations, and postulated entities)

Level 4 Mathematical 'words' and symbols

* Such words are known as polysemic. A good place to start looking at polysemic words is Twidle (2003) Evaluating the benefit of replacing polysemic words by less ambiguous expressions, *School Science Review* 85 pp 109–16.

and evolution. Clearly, some of these process words acquire meaning for a pupil more easily than others. A teacher can point to a reaction on the front bench and say 'there, that's combustion', or demonstrate red ink losing its colour and say 'that's distillation'. Thus certain processes are in a sense visible, or at least 'showable'. Their meaning can be learnt by *ostensive definition* (from the Latin *ostendo*, 'I show'). Other processes belong to a higher level within this category. One cannot point to something happening and say 'that's evolution'. Through education and language development, 'evolution' may also become a concept, see Table 11.1, level 3.3.

- The third, and largest, category of words in science are *concept words*. These are words that denote concepts of various types: words such as work, energy, power, fruit, salt, pressure, force, volume, temperature, heat and so on. This area of learning in science is surely the one where most learning difficulties are encountered, for concept words denote ideas at gradually ascending levels of abstraction.
- Finally we should also note that many words can start as a name but, through language development in science, gradually be used as a concept. For example, fuel may be a name for petrol or paraffin, but gradually it acquires a general, conceptual meaning, such as 'a flammable material yielding energy'. Similarly with the terms salt and gas.

At the lowest level, certain concepts are directly derived from experience. Like certain processes, they can be defined ostensively by pointing out examples where the concept pertains. Colour concepts, such as 'red', are almost certainly learnt in this way. These can be neatly termed *sensory concepts*. The next category contains words that have both a scientific and (perhaps unfortunately) an everyday meaning: examples include work, energy, power, fruit and salt. The existence of the two meanings causes pupils difficulties and confusion. It also explains the seemingly strange yet often perceptive conceptions (alternative frameworks) that pupils possess of heat, plant nutrition, pressure, energy, work and so on. The same word is being used to denote two different ideas. In these cases the invention of totally new words (such as anode and cathode, coined by Faraday) might have made life easier for generations of school science pupils. Finally, concept words belonging to a third level are used to denote what we will call *theoretical constructs:* words such as element, mixture, compound, atom, electron, valency, mole, mass, frictionless body, smooth surface, field and so on. Some of these theoretical constructs, such as atom and electron, people may prefer to call unobservable entities because in a sense they exist. Others are simply idealisations, or total abstractions, that cannot possibly exist, such as point masses or frictionless bodies, except in the language of mathematics.

The language of mathematics, its 'words' and symbols, can be placed at the fourth and highest level of abstraction in a hierarchy of scientific words. The mathematical language used in advanced physics is neither derived from, nor directly applicable to, experience. Its meaning is so detached as to become almost autonomous. Indeed John von Neumann said of mathematics:

> Young man, in mathematics you don't understand things. You just get used to them.
>
> (Zukav 1979)

Using a taxonomy of words in science teaching

This hierarchy or classification is all very well, you might say, but of what possible use can it be to the science teacher? What implications does it have? We suggest four areas where it might be applied:

Beware of meaning at the higher levels

Different scientific words *mean* in different ways. The word 'iris' has meaning by labelling or pointing out an observable entity; similarly with many other words in level 1 of the taxonomy. But the meaning of words in higher levels is not as clear. At best they denote, or refer to, some mental image or abstract idea.

Words in the highest level of the taxonomy, such as 'electron', can *only* have meaning in a theoretical context. The meaning of 'electron' belongs to a theoretical world of nuclei, atoms, electric fields, shells and orbits – an imaginary, almost make-believe world to pupils starting science. Yet 'electron' can acquire meaning, just as the words in a far-fetched fairy tale do. The problem of meaning, or rather lack of it, at these higher levels of abstraction must be a major cause of failure in science education.

Are pupils 'ready'?

The lack of meaning for many pupils of scientific terms, particularly at level 3 of the taxonomy, may explain why many pupils fail to make sense of science. Perhaps they meet these words too soon – indeed the hierarchy in the taxonomy could be closely related to Piagetian stages of development. Is it possible, for example, for a pupil to acquire any meaning for a term denoting a theoretical construct before he or she has reached the formal-operational stage? (See Chapter 4.) More positively, can science teaching help achieve the required readiness and development?

Language development

A conscious awareness of gradually ascending development of meaning can often be useful to the science teacher in classroom teaching and lesson preparation. By developing word meanings for pupils – for example, from a word (say 'gas') being simply a name to becoming a concept – children's understanding, thought and language are enhanced. Word meanings can develop in a child's mind through both appropriate teaching and wider experiences.

Teaching for shared meaning

Science education must, to some extent, be initiation into a new language. With naming words this can be quite simple. But the more abstract a term becomes the more it must be taught by analogy or by the use of models. If there is no *entity* to which a term corresponds, then clearly meaning becomes more difficult to communicate. But there are dangers.

Encouraging children to make the words of science meaningful *to them* should not imply encouraging them to develop *their own meanings* for scientific words. As Wittgenstein pointed out (1958), there can be no such thing as a private language. Languages are, by definition, public. In short, meanings in science need not be *impersonal* but they must be *interpersonal*. We need to teach for shared meaning (Edwards and Mercer 1987).

These are just four areas where the taxonomy of Table 11.1 has relevance to science teaching. The taxonomy also has important uses in considering teachers' written material and in assessing the readability of science texts. These are both considered in later sections.

Teacher talk

Science teachers spend a lot of their time talking. Inspection reports in the past have shown that the dominant teaching style has been exposition from the teacher, and this is still common. It follows from this, and the discussion above on the complexity of scientific words, that teachers of science need to be especially careful of their spoken language.

One of the most valuable studies published on school language came from Barnes *et al.* (1969). The study identified three types of language used by teachers:

- *specialist language presented*: words and forms of language unique to the subject which teachers are aware of as a potential problem and therefore present and explain to their students;
- *specialist language not presented*: language special to the subject which is not deliberately presented either because it has been explained before or teachers are unaware that they are using it;
- *the language of secondary education*: terms, words and forms of language used by teachers that pupils would not normally hear, see or use except in the world of the school, i.e. not the language of the world outside.

This is an important classification and one of which all science teachers should be aware. It is invaluable as a framework for reflecting upon both teacher talk and teacher writing. Table 11.2 gives a summary of the categories, with examples from science; readers are invited to examine this table and see if they can add any further examples.

The right-hand column of the table, i.e. specialist language, can be further classified in terms of the taxonomy presented in Table 11.1. Which of the specialist terms are naming words, which are process words and which are concept words? It would seem that, in watching their language, teachers should be especially wary of those in level 3.3 of the taxonomy.

Table 11.2 Watch your language: could you add to the list?

Language of secondary education	Technical / specialist language
criterion	regular
relatively	equilibrium
factors	calibrate
specifically	proportional to
complex	uniform
assumption	force
ideally	work
initially	energy
related to	power
subject to	moment
recap	miscible
determines	random
distinguish between	diverges
effectively	exert
theoretically	secrete
becomes apparent	saturated
	mass
	trachea

Barnes and his colleagues went on to analyse some of the teacher and pupil talk that occurs in science lessons. Some of their extracts are superb. For brevity's sake we present just one below, said to be from a class for pupils who had recently moved into secondary education:

T: Now what we want is a method whereby we can take off this ... um ... green material ... this green stuff off the grass and perhaps one or two of you can suggest how we might do this ... yes?

P1: Boil it.

T: Boil it? What with?

P1: Some water in a beaker and ...

T: Yes, there's that method ... we could do it and ... um ... I think probably you could guess how we might be able to do it by what we've already got out in the laboratory. How do you think we might do it? *(Pestle and mortar are on bench.)*

P2: Could pound it ...

T: Pound it up with water and that's exactly what we're going to do.

T: We're going to cut the grass into small pieces and then we're going to put it into the ... what we call a mortar ... this is what we call a mortar ... this bowl ... and anyone know what we call the other thing which we're going to pound it in?

T: Now I don't know whether any of you could jump the gun a bit and tell me what actually is this green stuff which produces green colour ...

P: Er ¼ em ... water.

Table 11.3 Some 'hard' words in science

factor	average	concept
abundant	adjacent	contrast*
incident*	composition*	contract*
complex	component	rate*
spontaneous	emit	exert
relevant	linear	negligible
valid	random	sequence

Words marked* are potentially polysemic

T: No … have you heard of chlorophyll?
T: Put that into the distillation flask and then distil off and then we get thermometer recording the correct temperature which is the boiling point for acetone. Then we collect the acetone which came over as a distillate.

Look carefully at the talk here:

• Which words and terms can be classed as the language of secondary education?
• How is the specialist language being handled?
• It is also interesting to note the questioning going on here: is it closed or open?
• Is the teacher asking the pupil to 'guess what's in my head'? Barnes calls such questions *pseudo-questions*.

The Barnes study contains many similar extracts and is thoroughly recommended; little has changed since its publication. It would be a valuable activity for any teacher to record his or her discourse with a class in the same way and then to analyse it using the frameworks above.

In the forty years and more since Barnes' first work a number of important studies have been made of classroom language and the discourse of science in the UK, the USA and Australia. That research cannot be summarised here, see further reading, but our own analysis of it shows that certain words come up again and again. Table 11.3 shows our own potted summary of some of the difficult words identified in research on pupils' understanding.

Overcoming language barriers

Chapter 6, on inclusive science education, suggested several practical strategies for helping pupils to get to grips with some of the language of science; strategies such as wordbanks, and word games using laminated cards.

Other strategies for teachers are presented later in this chapter. One strategy that has been tried out in schools involves pupils using a glossary or a dictionary of all the scientific words they are likely to encounter in their pre-16 curriculum. Figure 11.1 shows one page from a science dictionary that contains explanations of 190 science words – there could be many more but these are a selection of the key words used in the curriculum of countries such as the UK, the USA and Australia. Each word is explained, rather than defined, and illustrations for each entry help to give it meaning. Many of the words are related and cross-referenced. A photocopiable

PRISM

A prism is a piece of glass in the shape of a 3D triangle that can do interesting things with light. Some prisms can split light into the seven colours that make up white light.

In a rainbow, raindrops act like tiny prisms and split sunlight into the colours of the spectrum: RED, ORANGE, YELLOW, GREEN, BLUE, INDIGO, VIOLET (remember: 'Richard of York gave battle in vain')

90° Right-angled prism

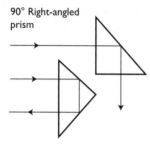

If the seven colours are painted evenly onto a disc and the disc is spun quickly, it appears to be white.

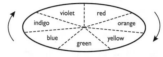

Prisms shaped so that one angle is 90° and the others are 45° can be used to reflect light, or change its direction completely. Prisms like this are called right-angle prisms and are used in cameras and binoculars.

PROTEIN

Protein is a body building food. It is used for growth (especially for young people or for pregnant women), or for repairing damaged or worn-out body tissue. Proteins can also be a source of energy. They are in foods such as meat, fish, eggs, cheese and soya beans, and also flour, rice and oatmeal.

Sources of protein

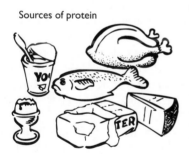

Vegetarians can get all of the proteins they need if they eat a wide variety of plant foods such as beans, peas, brown rice, pasta and nuts.

Proteins have very large molecules made up of lots of different amino acids joined together.

When a body digests proteins it breaks them down into amino acids. Like proteins, most of the human body is made up of the four elements: carbon, oxygen, hydrogen and nitrogen.

Figure 11.1 Entries from a science dictionary
Source: Wellington (2002)

glossary of this kind can be used in many ways in the classroom. For example, the entries can be copied and pasted on to laminated cards. These 'word cards' can then be kept in an index box for pupils to use when reading, revising, writing or discussing.

More specifically, teachers could use a glossary or dictionary of this kind:

*   to highlight new words which will occur in teaching a topic, e.g. electricity, energy, food, water, plant growth, etc. The words could be singled out, photocopied and made into a poster;
*   as refreshment. Many teachers are teaching outside their own subject specialism and it will be useful to them if they need 'refreshment', a reminder or in some cases a definition, if the word is completely new to them. A bit of pre-lesson revision is always useful (even in our *own* specialism) and also helps to remind us of the importance of language in science teaching.

Pupils can use the dictionary:

*   for revising or simply refreshing their memory;
*   when writing about science, e.g. a story, a description, an account of an investigation, a write-up of an experiment: the dictionary will help them to use words accurately and to stimulate new ideas and vocabulary to use in writing;
*   in reading about science, e.g. a science textbook, a story about science, a newspaper article or a piece in a magazine: the dictionary can help readers to understand the writing, to check its accuracy and to look for other words and ideas which connect with it;
*   in discussing or just talking about science, e.g. to clarify words; to look for new words, or to connect words and ideas together.

Teacher writing – for learning and understanding

One of the essential skills of the teacher is to present and explain the processes and the content of science in a palatable and interesting way. This is true of teacher talk but is equally applicable to teacher writing – whether it be on the interactive whiteboard or a worksheet. All the above cautions and frameworks for care in language apply to the written word perhaps even more than to the spoken word. Writing is in some ways more permanent, more open to scrutiny and less flexible and interactive. The aim of this section is to offer guidelines on writing material for pupils. Teacher writing is worthy of long discussion, see further reading, but for brevity here we begin simply by offering guidelines for writing, aimed principally at worksheet writing although many of the points apply equally to PowerPoint, whiteboard or writing for assessment; perhaps the latter is even more important. Table 11.4 offers our guidelines for *writing for learning and understanding in science.*

Readers are invited to look closely at these points – there may be guidelines here that you disagree with. If so, it is well worth drawing up your own list or adapting the one here: whichever guidelines you use, it is essential to have some pointers to clear and effective writing.

The language of science texts and the science textbook

In our view it is good practice for teachers to write some of their own material at least some of the time. It can help them, for example, to understand a topic more clearly themselves and to structure it and present it to pupils. Writing clear, readable material should be seen as one

Table 11.4 Writing for learning in science; guidelines and check list

Why write?
- To give experimental instructions
- To transmit information
- To structure a film, video, slides, etc.
- To ask questions, or to test (using, for example, all questions; information then questions; fill in the blanks; crosswords)
- To provide your audience with ready-made notes

Writing good material
- Write clearly and directly
- Do not present too much information or too little
- Try it out in rough first
- Make the reader think!
- Use plenty of structure such as an appetiser; headings that stand out; summary/key points
- Print neatly or type it – don't write
- Use a ruler
- Use graphs, diagrams and illustrations to break up the text where possible
- Do not write to a 'readability' formula

Watch your language
- Avoid long sentences, i.e. more than twenty words
- Try to keep to one idea per sentence
- Beware of technical terms which have not been introduced , such as 'mass', 'current', 'pressure', 'momentum', etc.
- Avoid the 'language of secondary education' (Barnes): terms like 'relationship with', 'recapitulate', 'exert', 'becomes apparent', 'derived from', etc.
- Avoid too many short, staccato sentences
- Address the reader as 'you', don't use the royal 'we'
- Keep language brief and concise (use a colleague as your editor)

Getting it right
- Have somebody from your target audience in mind as you write, for example, Jane Bloggs from Year 9
- If possible, try it out on a member of your target audience first
- Always ask a colleague or friend to check your writing before letting it loose, i.e. use a proof reader
- Misspellings and poor grammar are not acceptable

of the skills of a teacher. However, in the real world, teachers will commonly find themselves searching for, using and evaluating textual material written by others. The published scheme has proliferated and now is beginning to dominate – leading, unfortunately, to a reduced need for teachers to be able to write for pupils. The increased need now, however, is for teachers to be able to assess carefully, critically and to some extent objectively the texts, whether online or on paper, that they will be using and perhaps paying for. Many of the following features of a science text can be assessed fairly quickly and intuitively:

- its 'appeal';
- its structure and layout;
- the style of the writing;
- the use of illustrations both photographs and artwork;
- the use of colour where appropriate.

Subjective, intuitive judgement is valuable in looking at science texts. There are, however, also a number of tried and tested formulae for assessing quantitatively the 'readability' of a piece of text. These should not be seen as alternatives to the intuition of, especially, an experienced teacher with a critical eye for text, but they can be useful extensions and checks of subjective judgement. They are well worth trying on a range of texts, from *The Sun* newspaper to an A-level science text. They first became well known in a science context in the late 1970s and early 1980s (see Johnson 1979) when the commonly used textbooks of the time, such as Abbot's *O-Level Physics* and Mackean's *Biology* text, were shown to have reading ages of 18 and 19 respectively.

There are a number of readability measures with different features, all of which were discussed in full in Harrison (1980: 51–83). A summary of just three tests is given in alphabetical order; these have been chosen because they are fairly easy to apply, have reasonable validity and over the years have proved to be quite accurate. Generally, they look at sentence length and word length, judged by the number of syllables. The steps for applying each test are shown in Table 11.5.

Table 11.5 Four measures of readability

1. The Flesch formula

- Select at least three samples of 100 words;
- Count the average number of syllables in each 100 word sample (y);
- Calculate the average length of sentences in the samples (z);
- Calculate the Reading Ease Score [RES] from the Flesch formula:
- RES $= 206.835 - \{(z \times 1.015) + (y \times 0.846)$.

  Examples of typical RES:

  RES 90+   very easy, e.g. comics

  RES 60 – 70   standard, e.g. mass non-fiction

  RES 30 – 50   academic prose

  A US grade level [the Flesch-Kincaid grade level] and hence a reading age can be calculated using:
- US grade level $= (0.39 \times z) + (11.8 \times y) - 15.59$;
- Reading age is US grade level +5.

2. The FOG test

- Select a passage of exactly 100 words;
- Calculate the average sentence length (s);
- Calculate the percentage of polysyllabic words, words of three syllables or more, (p);
- The US grade level is then $0.4 \times (s + p)$;
- As before the reading age is then the US grade level +5.

3. The SMOG formula

- Select three sample passages, each of ten sentences; one from the beginning, one from the middle and one from the end of the text;
- Count the total number of words with three or more syllables in the thirty sentences (p);
- Find the square root of (p), $\sqrt{p}$;
- Reading age is then $8 + \sqrt{p}$.

These are all tests of readability which can be applied by teachers and have been shown to be reasonably valid and accurate.

A far easier way of finding a readability measure for your own text files is to use *Word,* or a similar word-processing package. This is outlined in Figure 11.2.

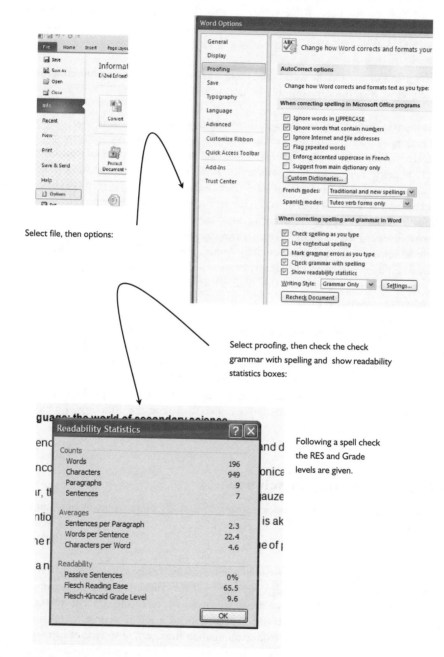

Select file, then options:

Select proofing, then check the check grammar with spelling and show readability statistics boxes:

Following a spell check the RES and Grade levels are given.

Figure 11.2 Readability using Word

Interestingly, it is possible to have a negative value for the Flesch–Kincaid grade score, e.g. if z and y were both 1, the US grade level would be -3.4 giving a reading age of 1.6 years! In our experience science texts never come close to this but in case you are wondering *Green Eggs and Ham* (Seuss, 1960) comes out at -1.3, giving it a reading age of 3.7 years.

Measurements of readability are largely preoccupied with counting syllables and sentence lengths and hunting for polysyllabic words. Is this the most accurate way of assessing the *difficulty* or 'transparency' of a text? An excellent example of lack of transparency in a sentence is given by T.H. Savory (1953):

> If there are more cows in the world than there are hairs in the tail of any one cow, there must be some cows with the same number of hairs in their tails.

It is extremely difficult to see *through* these words to the objects and facts involved. The sentence is almost opaque. Similarly with many of the words and terms of the physical sciences. Yet the 'opacity' of certain words is not taken into account by any measure of readability.

Opacity is partly related to the taxonomy in Table 11.1, although not wholly, as Savory's example shows. Naming words are most transparent because they point directly to their referent, usually an observable entity. Words in the higher levels, meanwhile, are the most opaque: it is far more difficult to 'see through' these words to any clear meaning or referent.

Consider the word 'oesophagus'. With its five syllables it will be judged less readable than the words 'electron', 'valency' and especially 'mole', indeed the word 'mole' has the same readability when used to refer to a little furry beast as it does when referring to the most difficult and discussed concept in chemistry. This is surely an unfair way of judging the difficulty or *understandability* of scientific prose.

Concentration in the past on the readability of science textbooks has certainly done a useful job in making them more *readable*. But surely a measure of 'understandability' is also appropriate for the pupil? As this is clearly related to the taxonomy in Table 11.1, some sort of weighting could be given to words depending on which level they belong to – the presence of a word in level 3.3, for example, could be given the added weighting of two extra syllables. At present, readability measures are unfair on biology texts, with their predominance of long naming words at level 1, yet give a deceptive underestimate of the difficulty of many physics texts (with their abundance of short words such as 'work', 'energy', 'field', and 'mass' belonging to level 3.2).

Reading for learning in science

> Since reading is a major strategy for learning in virtually every aspect of education … it is the responsibility of every teacher to develop it.
>
> (Bullock 1975)

Reading is by and large a neglected activity in science classes. Textbooks are often used to provide homework, to guide a practical, to keep pupils busy if they finish too soon or at worst to prop up a piece of apparatus. Traditionally science teachers have had little concern for text. This is unfortunate for many reasons: practising scientists spend a lot of their time reading; much science can be learnt more efficiently from reading than from, say, observing or listening; many pupils enjoy reading; and there is a wide range of reading on science available in children's books, magazines and newspapers.

Merkshire Community School – 'Reach for the Stars'

Year 7 Science – Elements, mixtures and compounds

Read the passage below and fill in the gaps. The words at the bottom of the page will help.

Elements, the simplest substances, are made from particles known as at_____. Each element contains atoms of only one type. Hydrogen is made only of hy_____ atoms, for example, and helium of only he_____ atoms. Different elements have different types of atoms.

A compound is a substance in which two or more el_____ are joined together. For example, the elements hydrogen and oxygen can combine to make water. The composition of water is always the same – every atom of oxygen is joined to two atoms of hydrogen. All compounds have a definite composition which we show by means of a fo_____. For water this is H_2O where H is the symbol for hydrogen and O is the symbol for oxygen, and the $_2$ shows that we have two atoms of hydrogen for every one atom of ox_____.

A mixture contains elements which are easily se_____. Mixtures do not always have the same composition. For example iron and salt is a mixture which can be easily separated with the use of a ma_____.

atoms	hydrogen	helium	elements
separated	magnet	formula	oxygen

Figure 11.3a Differentiated DART activities for a Year 7 (mean age 12) group: Activity A

The starting point in this section is that reading is an important but neglected activity in science education and that one of the responsibilities of science teachers is to teach pupils to read actively, critically and efficiently. This point is also followed up in a later chapter on using newspapers in education.

How can pupils be encouraged to read in science for longer periods? How can their reading become more active, reflective, critical and evaluative? A project described in Lunzer and Gardner (1984) suggested that passive reading occurs when reading tasks are vague and general, rather than specific; and when reading is solitary rather than shared. In contrast, active reading involves reading for specific purposes and the sharing of ideas and small-group work. The project therefore developed a number of strategies for use by teachers. These were called Directed Activities Related to Text, or DARTs (Lunzer and Gardner 1984; Davies and Greene 1984).

Merkshire Community School – 'Reach for the Stars'

Year 7 Science – Elements, mixtures and compounds

Read the passage below and fill in the gaps using the words at the bottom of the page.

Elements, the simplest substances, are made from particles known as _____. Each element contains atoms of only one type. Hydrogen is made only of _____ atoms, for example, and helium of only _____ atoms. Different elements have different types of atoms.

A compound is a substance in which two or more _____ are joined together. For example, the elements hydrogen and oxygen can combine to make water. The composition of water is always the same – every atom of oxygen is joined to two atoms of hydrogen. All compounds have a definite composition which we show by means of a _____. For water this is H_2O where H is the symbol for hydrogen and O is the symbol for oxygen, and the $_2$ shows that we have two atoms of hydrogen for every one atom of _____. Not all formulae are that simple however – insulin, which controls blood sugar levels, is $C_{254}H_{377}N_{65}O_{75}S_6$.

A mixture contains elements which are easily _____. Mixtures do not always have the same composition. For example iron and salt is a mixture which can be easily separated with the use of a _____.

atoms	hydrogen	helium	elements
separated	magnet	formula	oxygen

Figure 11.3b Differentiated DART activities for a Year 7 (mean age 12) group: Activity B

Directed reading activities make pupils focus on important parts of the text and involve them in reflecting on its content. They involve the pupils in discussion, in sharing ideas, and in examining their interpretations of a text. DARTs fall into two broad categories:

1 *Reconstruction (or completion) DARTs*: these are essentially problem-solving activities that use modified text – the text or diagram has parts missing (words, phrases or labels deleted) or, alternatively, the text is broken into segments that have to be re-ordered into the 'correct' sequence. These activities are game-like and involve hunting for clues in order to complete the task. Pupils generally find them very enjoyable and the results can feed in to pupil writing. Figures 11.3a and b give examples of DART activities for a Year 7 group.

Table 11.6 DARTS: a brief summary

Reconstruction DARTs using modified text	Analysis DARTs using unmodified text
1. Completing text, diagram or table	1. Marking and labelling
(a) Text completion Pupils predict and complete deleted words, phrases or sentences, cf. a Cloze task	(a) Underlining/marking Pupils search for specified targets in text, e.g. words or sentences, and mark them in some way
(b) Diagram completion Pupils predict and complete deleted labels and/ or parts of diagrams using text and diagrams as sources of information	(b) Labelling Pupils label parts of the text, using labels provided for them
(c) Table completion Pupils use the text to complete a table using rows and columns provided by the teacher	(c) Segmenting Pupils break the text down into segments or units of information, and label these segments
2. Unscrambling and labelling disordered and segmented text	2. Recording and constructing
(a) Pupils predict logical order or time sequence of scrambled segments of text, e.g. a set of instructions, then re-arrange	(a) Pupils construct diagrams showing content and flow of text using, for example, a flow diagram, a network or a continuum
	(b) Pupils construct and complete tables from information given in text, making up their own row and column headings
(b) Pupils classify segments according to categories given by the teacher	
3. Predicting Pupils predict and write part(s) of text, e.g. an event or an instruction, with segments presented a section at a time	(c) (i) Teachers set questions, pupils study text to answer them (ii) Pupils make up their own questions after studying text, either the teacher or other pupils then answer these questions
	(d) pupils list the key points made by the text or write a simple summary of the text

2   *Analysis DARTs*: these use unmodified text and are more study-like. They are about finding targets in the text. The teacher decides what the 'information categories' of the text are and which of these to focus on. These are the targets which pupils are to search for; this involves the pupils in locating and categorising the information in the text. When the targets are found they are marked by underlining and/or labelling. The search for targets can be followed by small-group and class discussion in which the merits of alternative markings are considered and pupils have a further opportunity to modify or revise their judgements.

In each case the text has to be prepared for pupils, or small groups of pupils, so that they can work with it. Many DARTs will involve marking or writing on the text itself. Table 11.6 shows a classification of the various DARTs that could be used with a piece of writing in science.

Notice that the analysis DARTs can be done with the straight, unmodified text – by, for example, underlining certain types of work; labelling segments of the text; or making up questions to ask about the text. Text from any source, such as government pamphlets, leaflets, newspapers or the internet could be used for this purpose. The reconstruction DARTs require modification before use by, for example, deleting key words from the text or labels from a diagram; or chopping up a passage into segments that need re-sequencing to make sense.

A note of caution when using newspapers

In the preceding text we have mentioned various forms of text but we also sound a note of caution. This caution applies to newspapers in the example given but can equally well apply to internet-based sources, see Chapter 13.

Consider the following, from a perceived expert, published in *The Sun* [17/11/10].

PUPIL: Can you explain what a black hole is?
PROFESSOR BRIAN COX (who was visiting the school):   When a star runs out of fuel it will collapse. There's nothing that can stop it collapsing but when it collapses it has still got all the mass in it. If it was as big as the sun when it started collapsing, it would be as massive as the sun when it finished collapsing. Even light can't escape from it, which is why it is called a black hole.

Thinking of what you have read regarding *readability* and *understandability* we ask you the following:

*   Does this answer the question asked by the pupil?
*   Are pupils likely to be confused by the interchangeable use of 'big' and 'mass'?
*   Does the answer imply, incorrectly, that a star the size of our Sun would collapse to form a black hole?

These sources, like others, need to be carefully read by the teacher since it is unlikely that any peer review process will have been followed. The danger is that celebrity status may carry a great deal of weight with pupils and as a teacher you must be aware of this.

The pupils' writing

The debate on pupils' writing in science is as long and important as that on reading. We cannot do it justice here but the main questions concern the style in which pupils should write and the purpose of their writing in science education.

Reasons for writing

Until quite recently there seemed to be general agreement in science teaching that the main reasons for writing in science lessons were either to take notes on the content/knowledge required or to write up a piece of practical work (Sutton 1989). On the latter there was also a consensus that it should follow the pattern: Aim ... Method/procedure ... Results ... Conclusions. This consensus has lasted for at least three reasons:

1   Generations of pupils, some of whom become teachers, feel familiar and comfortable with it.
2   It provides a convenient structure for reporting the kind of practical work that has often been done in schools, i.e. verifying or proving a law, fact or principle.
3   It was believed to reflect the nature of science and the way that scientists actually proceed and write up.

The latter two assumptions are now wide open to question. Practical work, see Chapter 7, is less commonly of the 'To prove …' or 'To verify …' or 'To demonstrate that …' kind. For example, investigational work, which requires a completely different structure in which to write it up, is now commonplace, see Chapter 8. Second, there have been a number of excellent, readable publications which show this kind of write-up is a false reflection of the way that scientists actually work and report. In short, a theory or 'conclusion' does not actually follow an experiment and the collection of results. On the contrary, it precedes and shapes the experiment: observation is theory-led. The reality is not a case of 'data first, theory later' (Sutton 1989). Experienced scientists such as Medawar (1979) showed a long time ago that reports that portray science in this clean, logical, methodical, inductive way are simply a fraud.

Thus changing views on the role of practical work and the nature of science mean that teachers need to rethink the 'writing up' that pupils do. There is also growing recognition that pupils can actually learn science through writing and therefore that modes and styles of writing other than either note-taking or write-ups of practicals should be tried.

Styles of writing and alleged reasons for each

There is a strong case for widening the range of writing that pupils do in science lessons, beyond the traditional formal report style. Writing could be broadened first of all to allow (on some if not all occasions) subjective and creative reporting – asking for experiences and feelings. Writing could be further extended by asking for imaginative and creative work based on the pupils' learning in science, such as a letter to an MP or the PM/the police/a pressure group, a newspaper report, or any other writing that might involve written role play. Pupils should use their science knowledge and 'specialist science language', see Table 11.2, in this kind of writing, for example, with teachers offering them key words or scientific terms to be included.

Figure 11.4 shows a 'project brief' to encourage pupils to write in groups on a range of topics relating to renewable energy sources, in this case on biomass.

The same resource is available with writing briefs on wind, hydroelectric, and geothermal sources. In short, three styles of writing, each with a different purpose, are summarised below:

1 the impersonal, the third person, i.e. the formal report, objective and factual;
2 the personal, the first-person report, i.e. subjective, creative, interpretative reporting of, for example, observations, experiences, feelings, impressions;
3 imaginative, expressive writing, for example 'a day in the life of …', 'a letter of complaint', 'how it feels to be …', 'a journey into …', 'shrunk to a millimetre …', which makes use of scientific knowledge and learning. This might also include imaginative drawing, as in Edward De Bono's well-known 'Design a dog-exercising machine/elephant-weighing machine' activity.

To encourage and stimulate different types of writing it will often be valuable to show pupils different models, such as writing from past scientists or past pupils, newspaper reports, or science stories. Different types of reading will enhance different styles of writing (Sutton 1989; Sheeran and Barnes 1991).

There are so many other issues impacting on pupils' writing that cannot be covered here that we finish with a brief mention of just four:

Renewable Energy Resources

BIOMASS

Project brief:

You are a government committee in a West African country. The country is facing an energy crisis. It cannot afford to build nuclear reactors to generate electricity nor can it afford to continue importing coal, oil and gas, which it uses in its power stations.

You are faced with the task of convincing the public that the way forward is to build and use small, community-owned biomass generators. The raw material is in plentiful supply.

To do this you need a publicity campaign to educate the people in the good sense of the idea and to provide the technical information (plans) to allow them to set up their own generators as a community group.

Your campaign should include:

• A leaflet
• A poster
• A report to the government Energy Ministry

If time permits:

• A short radio broadcast: many rural communities may have literacy (reading and writing) problems and use of radio could be very important.

Ideas Box:

Economic (cheap) to build and operate

Environmental, locally available raw materials

Figure 11.4 Writing brief for alternative energy resources

1   Writing has a range of purposes: it may be a way of keeping a record of content or practical work for future reference, such as revision; it may be used by a teacher to assist classroom control – pupils are almost as quiet when they write as when they eat; it may be a way, for pupils, of learning and clarifying; it can be a way of sharing, if pupils write in a small group. Teachers need to recognise these different purposes and use them.

2   The use of word-processors, on notepad, notebook, laptop, desktop, tablet or smartphone, can be a great aid to some people's writing, whether they have special needs or not. ICT can aid presentation, allow drafting and redrafting, encourage people to get started, allow spell-checking and encourage collaborative writing. In short, the use of ICT can change writing and marking quite radically. This is discussed further in Chapter 13.

3   There are various methods of note-making and note-taking that pupils can follow, ranging from the totally passive (straight from the teacher's head or the website to the pupil's notepaper) to the active. The continuum of possibilities is shown in Figure 11.5. Teachers should at least be aware of these different possibilities and examine the reasons why and when they might use them. For example, dictation might be a good means of classroom control but does it have any other value?

4   Why not start a lesson with some writing? This is an activity worth trying: give each pupil a small piece of blank rough paper as they walk in (small and rough because it is less daunting). Ask them to write on it one of the following:
   - a summary of what they did last lesson (perhaps with comment);
   - 'Everything you already know about …';
   - their views on …;
   - what they would like to know about X – for example, food, health, magnetism, nuclear energy, etc.;
   - the answers to five questions that you pose, such as on the previous lesson;
   - the key words, say five, that you will use today;
   - the plan for the day's lesson.

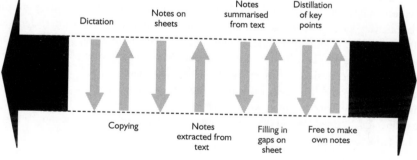

Figure 11.5 Ways of note-making and note-taking

You could also give them a sheet of drawings or diagrams on which they are asked to write or comment – for example, illustrating situations where forces are being used and asking pupils to mark in and describe the forces.

Activities such as this can be useful to start a lesson for a number of reasons: they are good for classroom control; they can help teachers to start 'from where the pupils are at'; they allow a recap and revision of the previous lesson; they can be a good source of feedback; they allow the use of open questions in a more manageable way than orally. They can also be enjoyable and amusing, especially if pupils write in twos.

Communicating science: more than words

What use is a book without words and pictures?

(*Alice in Wonderland*, Lewis Carroll, 1865)

Finally, we all need to remind ourselves that there is far more to science communication than verbal language, i.e. the spoken and written word. Words are important but in science more than any other subject we rely on a combination and interaction of words, pictures, diagrams, images, animations, graphs, equations, tables and charts. They all convey meaning in different ways and they all have their own importance and their own limitations. For example, the old saying that 'a picture is worth a thousand words' is probably true but it does not go far enough. There are certain meanings we wish to convey in science that cannot possibly be put across in words alone. Messages and meanings in charts and graphs, for example, can never be replaced by the written word, whether we use one thousand or two. The smells of science (which adults remember most vividly of all from their science lessons) or the touch and feel of practical work cannot be put into words. Gestures and other body language can convey scientific ideas more effectively and memorably than chalk and talk, or a passage in a textbook. In the jargon of linguists, there are a range of *semiotic modes* available to the science teacher (*semiotics* can be defined as the study of how we make meaning using words, images, symbols actions and other modes of communication). The onus on the good teacher is to employ these modes appropriately, i.e. in the right place at the right time for the right reasons. For example, chalk and talk might be fine for teaching some ideas, but others, e.g. change of state, may require animation (perhaps with multimedia or maybe simpler teaching aids such as marbles or ball bearings). The movement of plates in plate tectonics can be described in words but it may be better conveyed using gesture and hand movements.

Equations and mathematical symbols can sum up for some pupils in a nutshell some difficult ideas that are very lengthy in words (although symbols may not suit every learner). Ideas such as rate of change, proportionality and decay might best be shown on a graph. Cyclical processes, e.g. the carbon cycle, can best be shown using a diagram with arrows; while sequences, e.g. the manufacture of a chemical, can be seen visually with a flowchart.

We all know this and in some ways it is no more than common sense. But the art of good communication in science teaching would seem to involve at least three skills, some of which can be deliberately trained for and developed or coached, while others just seem to be part of the 'tacit', hidden knowledge and ability of the 'born teacher':

1   *The recognition that teaching does involve a range of modes of communication.* In science, we have at our disposal:
    *   the spoken and written word;
    *   visual representation;

- images, diagrams, tables, charts, models and graphs;
- movement and animation – either of physical models, e.g. a beach ball for the Sun and a pea for the Earth, or using multimedia, or using gesture or other body language; practical work with its feel, touch, smell and, of course, sounds;
- mathematical symbols, either as shorthand or in the form of equations to convey a connection.

2   *The awareness of these different modes and the recognition that different modes suit different learners*, i.e. learning styles vary. Some modes work best for some learners, other ways of conveying meaning work better with others.

3   *The ability* (which is often described as tacit or intuitive) *to switch from one mode to another when teaching*. If one way is not working then good teachers switch to another way according to the teacher's awareness of, and alertness to, the class. Even within a mode, e.g. the spoken word, one line of explanation or one analogy may not be working with a group of pupils. The teacher's knack is to move to a different approach within that mode ... or even a new mode completely, e.g. to use a physical model instead of talk or chalk. Each mode has its value and its limitations.

In summary then, once again science teaching presents both a challenge and an opportunity. It offers a range of ways of communicating (visual, verbal, graphical, symbolic, tactile) that can be exploited to engage with different learning styles or abilities and to provide a variety of teaching approaches. (We cannot expand further here but the work of Jon Ogborn and Gunter Kress, and Jay Lemke in the USA is particularly useful in this area.)

In summary ...

The ideas and findings of Barnes' work are still as important as ever for science education. Little has changed. Textbooks, and other sources of science text such as the internet, have become more 'readable', certainly in terms of standard readability tests (although we have heard teachers say that many of them look like colourful comics). In addition, teachers have become more aware of the language they use in speaking and writing. But for the pupil, the language barrier in science remains as real as ever and for many continues to be the main obstacle to their learning. Teachers still need to concentrate on how language is interpreted rather than just its 'delivery'. It is hoped that the practical strategies offered here will help in overcoming some of the language barriers in learning science.

Points for reflection

- In what ways is learning science like 'learning a foreign language'? How is it different?
- In your view, is the language of science the main barrier to learning science? What other 'main barriers' might there be?
- Do you feel the evolution of science textbooks has been of benefit to science education? How would you respond to the comment that 'science books are now more like comics than proper textbooks'?
- Is there (and should there be) any opportunity for extended reading in science? What sources could be (or should be) used for this extended reading?

References and further reading

General

Mercer, N. (1998) *Words and Minds*, New York: Routledge.

Mortimer, E. and Scott, P. (2003) *Meaning Making in Secondary Science Classrooms*, Maidenhead: Open University Press.

Wellington, J. and Osborne, J. (2001) *Language and Literacy in Science Education*, Buckingham: Open University Press; expands on many of the points made in this chapter.

Zukav, G. (1979) The Dancing Wi-Li Masters: An Overview of the New Physics, New York: William Morrow.

Arguing, talking and discussing in science

The March 2007 issue of *School Science Review* (vol. 88, no. 324) contains seven interesting articles on 'argument, discourse and interactivity', which cover topics such as online discussion; small group work in promoting argumentation; the importance of argument in presenting 'how science works'; and types of 'classroom talk'.

Mercer, N., Dawes, L., Wegerif, R. and Sams, C. (2004) 'Reasoning as a scientist: ways of helping children to use language to learn science', *British Educational Research Journal*, vol. 30, no. 3, June, pp. 359–77.

The words of science

Vygotsky, L. (1978) *Thought and Language*, Cambridge, MA: MIT Press.

Two excellent and influential pieces of research were carried out on pupils' understanding of non-technical words in science in the 1970s (words such as pungent, significant, average, propagate, and valid). They are still useful today.

Cassels, J.R.T. and Johnstone, A.H. (1978) *Understanding of Non-technical Words in Science*, London: Chemical Society Education Division.

Gardner, P.L. (1972) 'Words in science', part of the Australian Science Education Project, Melbourne.

Clive Sutton's work in this area is excellent, ranging from:

Sutton, C. (1980) 'Science, language and meaning', *School Science Review*, vol. 218, no. 62, pp. 47–56. to more recently:

Sutton, C. (1992) *Words, Science and Learning*, Milton Keynes: Open University Press.

One of the classics of twentieth-century philosophy that discusses the way language is used is:

Wittgenstein, L. (1958) *Philosophical Investigations*, Oxford: Blackwell.

In the science field, another classic from the same era is:

Savory, T.H. (1953) *The Language of Science*, London: Andre Deutsch.

The book that really opened up the language-in-education debate is:

Barnes, D., Britton, J. and Rosen, H. (1969) *Language, the Learner and the School*, Harmondsworth: Penguin.

Another important book is:

Stubbs, M. (1983) *Language, Schools and Classrooms* (2nd edn), London: Routledge.

An excellent general book on classroom language and ritual, drawing on the work of Vygotsky is:

Edwards, D. and Mercer, N. (1987) *Common Knowledge*, London: Methuen.

The ASE manual *Race, Equality and Science Teaching* (1991) Hatfield: ASE, gives a useful discussion on terms such as 'Third World', 'black', 'under-developed' and 'race' that are sometimes used thoughtlessly (see their Appendix 2, p. 176). It also contains activities for teachers on 'Language and learning in science' (pp. 85–8) and 'Children's writing' (pp. 89–93).

Three interesting studies of 'difficult words' from different parts of the world are:

Marshall, S., Gilmour, M. and Lewis, D. (1991) 'Words that matter in science and technology', *Research in Science and Technological Education*, vol. 9, no. 1, pp. 5–16.

Meyerson, M., Ford, M., Jones, W. and Ward, M. (1991) 'Science vocabulary knowledge of third and fifth grade students', *Science Education*, vol. 75, no. 4, pp. 419–28.

Pickersgill, S. and Lock, R. (1991) 'Student understanding of selected non-technical words in science', *Research in Science and Technological Education*, vol. 9, no. 1, pp. 71–9.

Writing, and teaching with text

Barlex, D. and Carré, C. (1985) *Visual Communication in Science*, Cambridge: Cambridge University Press; discussion and guidelines on using visual material in science teaching.

Chall, J. and Conard, S. (1991) *Should Textbooks Challenge Students?*, New York: Teachers' College Press; argues that textbooks should not be so hard that students cannot read and understand them, nor so easy that students are unchallenged and bored by them.

Lloyd-Jones, R. (1985) *How to Produce Better Worksheets*, Cheltenham: Stanley Thornes; a useful guide on producing classroom material with examples that can be photocopied.

Newton, D.P. (1990) *Teaching with Text*, London: Kogan Page.

Partridge, T. (1992) *Starting Science: Book J*, Oxford: Oxford University Press.

Shortland, M. and Gregory, J. (1991) *Communicating Science: a handbook*, Harlow: Longman.

Reading and readability

Bullock, A. (1975) A *Language for Life*, London: HMSO.

Carrick, T. (1978) 'Problems for assessing the readability of biology textbooks for first examinations', *Journal of Biological Education*, no. 12, pp. 113–21.

Harrison, C. (1980) *Readability in the Classroom*, Cambridge: Cambridge University Press.

Johnson, K. (1979) 'Readability', *School Science Review*, vol. 60, no. 212, p. 562.

Knutton, S. (1983) 'Chemistry textbooks: are they readable?' *Education in Chemistry* vol. 20, no. 3, pp. 100–5.

Long, R. (1991) 'Readability for science', *School Science Review*, vol. 262, no. 73, pp. 21–33.

Seuss, Dr. (1960) *Green Eggs and Ham*, New York: Random House.

Zakaluk, B. and Samuels, J. (1988) *Readability: Its Past, Present and Future*, Newark, NJ: IRA.

An excellent website, created by textbook author Keith Johnson, gives the reading ages and the 'human interest scores' of all the major science texts for 11–16 in the UK. The website is at: www.timetabler.com.

Encouraging active reading

Three accounts of active reading containing discussion and valuable classroom ideas are:

Bulman, L. (1985) *Teaching Language and Study Skills in Secondary Science*, London: Heinemann; this also includes useful sections on readability, pupils' writing, teacher talk and writing worksheets.

Davies, F. and Greene, T. (1984) *Reading for Learning in the Sciences*, London: Oliver and Boyd.

Lunzer, E. and Gardner, P.L. (eds) (1984) *Learning from the Written Word*, London: Schools Council/Oliver and Boyd.

See also:

Medawar, P. (1979) *Advice to a Young Scientist*, London: Harper & Row.

Sheeran, Y. and Barnes, D. (1991) *School Writing*, Milton Keynes: Open University Press; has an excellent chapter on 'Writing in science'.

Sutton, C. (1981) *Communicating in the Classroom*, London: Hodder & Stoughton; Chapters 1 and 2 on writing.

Sutton, C. (1989) 'Writing and reading in science', in Millar, R. (ed.) *Doing Science: images of science in science education*, pp. 137–59, Lewes: Falmer Press.

General, less recent

Henderson, J. and Wellington, J. (1998) 'Lowering the language barrier in learning and teaching science', *School Science Review*, vol. 79, no. 288, pp. 35–46.

Osborne, J. (1996) 'Untying the Gordian knot: diminishing the role of practical work', *Physics Education*, vol. 31, no. 5, pp. 271–8.

Wellington, J. (1998) 'Dialogues in the science classroom', in Ratcliffe, M. (ed.) *ASE Guide to Secondary Education*, Hatfield: ASE/Stanley Thornes, pp. 146–58.

Classroom resources

The *Science Wordbank*, in poster and A4 sheet form, can be obtained from: ASE Book Sales, College Lane, Hatfield, Herts AL10 9AA.

Wellington, J. (2002) *The Science Dictionary*, London: Continuum.

Chapter 12

Numeracy in science teaching and learning

Introduction

Most would agree that to be successful in science at any non-trivial level some understanding of basic numeracy is required. This is not to suggest that, for example, to study A-level physics a pupil must also study A-level mathematics (Ireson 1996) but rather that the ability to understand the required mathematics is needed. In science education the debate over the use of mathematics is not new; indeed it can be traced back to at least 1616 when Kepler made use of logarithms to speed up his calculations on planetary motion. His academic mentor, Michael Maestlin, chided him: 'It is not seemly for a professor of mathematics to be childishly pleased about any shortening of the calculations' (www.mathpages.com/rr/s8-01, accessed 14.01.06).

More recently a debate regarding the importance of numeracy in science focused on the use of calculators in both mathematics and science education. A collapse of the standards in pupils' ability to use number was predicted, with Duffin (1994) referring to the 'devastating impact on mathematical ability'.

Prior to Duffin's work a report for the Schools Mathematics Project (SMP 1976) stressed the importance of numeracy and asked: 'What will happen to those whose reliance on calculators becomes so strong that the understanding of basic mathematical operations is lost or never fully acquired?'

Such predictions appear not, in our view, to have come to pass. However this is not to play down the importance of numeracy and in 2001 the DfES published a report looking, in part, at numeracy in the world of work and drawing on the earlier work of the Basic Skills Agency (1997): 'We see signs here of an unexpected significance attached to numeracy in holding onto jobs. People without numeracy skills suffered worse disadvantage in employment than those with poor literacy skills alone.'

It could also be argued that science teachers can have a greater impact on numeracy than many other subjects. Indeed we suggest that pupils' numeracy and wider mathematical skills can be enhanced through the study and application of science.

Defining numeracy

The DfES, in 2001, proposed a definition of numeracy, in the National Numeracy Strategy, which sets out what pupils should be able to do by Year 9. This definition includes the following:

- Have a sense of the size of a number and where it fits into the number system;

- Use proportional reasoning to simplify and solve problems;
- Use simple formulae and substitute numbers in them;
- Measure and estimate measurements, choosing suitable units and reading numbers correctly from a range of meters, dials and scales;
- Collect data, discrete and continuous and draw, interpret and predict from graphs, diagrams, charts and tables;
- Give results to a degree of accuracy appropriate to the context.

(DfES 2001)

The same DfES publication also suggests how links between the departments of science and mathematics can operate together to enhance pupils' experience of numeracy. They suggest that departments should ask:

- To what extent does science teaching support the methods and approaches relating to aspects of calculation that are developed through the mathematics yearly teaching programmes?
- To what extent is the approach to the manipulation of algebraic expressions and solutions of equations in the Framework for teaching mathematics (DfES 2001) compatible with the needs of science?
- How does work in science link with using and applying mathematics in our school?

Ross *et al.* (2010) say that as a science teacher you should agree with mathematics teachers an approach to:

- the use of units and how to get a feel for them;
- how graphs are to be represented;
- mathematical notation and terms to be used;
- algebraic and other mathematical techniques, such as how algebraic expressions are to be simplified or how equations (especially simple proportions) are to be solved;
- how and when ICT resources such as graph plotters or graphical calculators will be used.

Muijs and Reynolds (2011) remind us, if reminding is needed, that numeracy:

- is based on the application of logic;
- means learning a conventional system.

Taking all of the above we offer a definition of numeracy across the curriculum, including in science, as:

> The ability to use number and simple mathematical functions to solve age-appropriate problems in a consistent manner throughout the school.

Obviously such a definition relies on cooperation between colleagues from all departments within the school. This cross-curricular emphasis is also stressed in the Ofsted inspection framework for mathematics across the curriculum, where the guidance for reporting on standards in mathematics (Ofsted 2001) says: 'inspectors are expected to give due attention to numeracy and pupils' competence in using their knowledge, skills and understanding of number, not only in mathematics, but also in other subjects.'

The guidance gives specific examples, some of which are more science specific, of evidence from other subjects and states that inspectors should look for the extent to which pupils can, for example:

- substitute numbers into formulae; and use and make sense of information presented in tables, charts and diagrams, and graphically;
- collect both discrete and continuous data, represent data pictorially and graphically, analyse data, make predictions; and
- explain their strategies and methods and use correct mathematical vocabulary.

Lenton and Stevens (1999) present a definition of numeracy based on the National Numeracy Project from 1995 that one can have little argument with. We all, surely, wish our pupils to be confident in:

> solving problems, having a sense of number, being able to calculate accurately and being able to suggest appropriate units.

This thinking was developed into the National Numeracy Strategy (see Hoult 2005) which has four key principles:

1   expectation;
2   progression;
3   engagement;
4   transformation.

Once again it is difficult to argue against pupils following this path.

Meeting the ideal

However, what is not as clear is the way in which these ideals are to be met both in general and specifically in science. Lenton and Stevens (1999) point to the mismatch between science and mathematics at Key Stage 3 (pupils aged 11–14). This again makes us question whether rather than a National Curriculum we have a number of national curricula operating in our schools.

Not only can we point to a mismatch between science and mathematics but also to the conceptual demand made of pupils at different levels within the mathematics curriculum. One such example is the fact that we have ratios being at higher level (Level 6) while percentages are at a lower level (level 5). If we accept that ratios are, indeed, a Level 6 skill then it is expected that at the end of Key Stage 3 pupils should be at Level 5/6 (DfEE 1999). It is worth stopping and thinking here about the structure of the National Curriculum and its stage-like approach. This approach echoes the work of Piaget, which would have the majority of 14-year-olds able to use ratio (Inhelder and Piaget 1958). However, work by Shayer and Adey, as long ago as 1981, suggests that only 30 per cent of 16-year-olds reach the early part of this stage. Should we then be surprised if many of our Key Stage 4 pupils (aged 14–16), let alone Key Stage 3 pupils, never get there?

Graphs are defined by DfES as a component of numeracy and they also have a number of problems associated with them. Again there is some mismatch between levels in science and mathematics and the ability to produce a line of best fit in order to reach Level 7. The notion of a graph is also clouded by the language used in subjects across the curriculum and beyond. A graph in some subjects may really be a bar chart, while software packages, for example Excel, not only tend to refer to all graphs and charts as 'charts' but also use the term 'column chart' for a bar chart, with 'bar chart' being a bar chart rotated through 90°. Little wonder pupils are confused! Literacy in science education has been addressed in the previous chapter, but let us look carefully at, for example, the use of the word 'weigh':

> How much does a pencil weigh? 0.4 g, 4.0 g, 40 g, 400 g

On the surface this is an excellent question that addresses a number of the aims of the National Numeracy Strategy. However in our eagerness to develop numeracy we must not forget literacy, see previous chapter and *polysemic* words, and think carefully about the use of 'weight' and 'mass'. The gram is a unit of 'mass' and hence 400 g cannot tell us how much something 'weighs'. Similar confusion exists when, in science, we talk of 'speed' and 'velocity' or 'heat' and 'temperature'.

If numeracy is to be developed in science we, as educators, must plan for it. What follows is an example of how this could be done.

Developing numeracy: an example

If you are teaching Key Stage 3 science then it is, perhaps, only safe to assume that the pupils have covered the Key Stage 2 mathematics curriculum. If you have a good liaison with your mathematics colleagues then the situation may be very different. Similarly at Key Stage 4 you can only be sure that pupils have covered the Key Stage 3 mathematics curriculum. Finally, of course, when teaching post-16 courses you can only be sure that your pupils have covered the foundation tier in GCSE mathematics.

For any topic you teach, the National Curriculum for both mathematics and science will detail the content for the two subjects and you can then build this into your planning; see Table 12.1.

Having decided what you feel is the required mathematics for successful teaching of the topic from the National Curriculum for science, or QCA scheme of work, the mathematics already covered by the class, prior to teaching the topic, can be elicited. This can be done partly by talking to the mathematics department and partly through diagnostic assessment. It is also worth remembering that the DfES definition of numeracy across the curriculum requires this cooperation. This allows the final column to be completed; if it has not been covered in mathematics, in this or an earlier Key Stage, then it will need to be covered in your science lesson.

Table 12.1 will allow you to ascertain what needs to be covered but the *how*, in the spirit of whole-school numeracy, will require you to observe how the content is taught elsewhere in the school. The aim here is to reinforce the methodology for the pupils and develop their transferable skills.

Developing graphical skills

While the topic of graphs may not immediately come to mind when one thinks of numeracy they are mentioned in definitions of numeracy given by the DfES as part of the Key Stage 3

Table 12.1 Planning for numeracy in science education

Topic: Pressure. Level: Key Stage 4

Science topic	Required mathematics	Key Stage 3 mathematics	Additional mathematics
The quantitative relationship between force, area and pressure leading to an understanding of $P = F/A$.	Use of algebra. Use of units. Simple computation. Degree of accuracy. Use of significant figures.	2.1 c. simplify the situation or problem in order to represent it mathematically, using appropriate variables, symbols, diagrams and models. 2.2 l. calculate accurately, selecting mental methods or calculating devices as appropriate. 2.2 m. manipulate numbers, algebraic expressions and equations and apply routine algorithms. 2.3 b. consider the assumptions made and the appropriateness and accuracy of results and conclusion.	

strategy. Returning to the DfES (2001) publication, the importance of developing pupils' graphical skills can be seen in:

> Does the teaching and interpretation of formulae and graphs support the expectations in mathematics? What use is made of different forms of graphs in science? Have we agreed with mathematics how graphs should be labelled and presented? Does the progression in graphical work in science support its development in mathematics?

However this does not offer guidance as to how pupils' understanding of graphs can be developed. Ross *et al.* (2010), when discussing numeracy in science, write of pupils and graphs;

> They need to experience the stories that graphs can tell ...

It is tempting to think that the use of ICT will help develop graphical skills and whilst *appropriate* use of ICT can have benefits, see Chapter 13, we would argue against assuming ICT develops *understanding* of graphs.

The importance of understanding graphs in the development of mathematical, or numeracy, skills has been investigated with undergraduates (Ireson and Gill 2002). Working with undergraduate students, Gill found that those students who performed well in end-of-year mathematics examinations were those who had scored highly on graph questions in the

Figure 12.1 An exercise for developing graphicacy

diagnostic test at the start of the year. Given that the end-of-year mathematics examination did not require graphical skills it would appear that questions involving graphs are a predictor of later mathematics success.

It is not proven that understanding graphs develops numeracy but, as educators, we should want our pupils to understand the meaning and construction of graphs given their common appearance in the science curriculum and in the media. The following is an exercise that could be used with Key Stage 3 pupils to develop their graphical understanding, giving some insight into the *stories graphs can tell*, or graphicacy (Ireson and Gill 2002):

- Take a sheet of A4 paper and measure the height and width.
- Cut the sheet into five strips, each with the same height but different width, see Figure 12.1, where each shaded area represents a strip.
- Calculate the area of each strip.
- Plot a graph of area, on the *y*-axis, against width, on the *x*-axis.
- What does the gradient of the graph tell you?
- Can you suggest an equation for the graph?

To assist pupils, Table 12.2 can be used and the explanation of first gradient and then equation can be used as a differentiated approach to this work.

Table 12.2 An exercise for developing graphicacy

Strip	Width, cm	Area, cm²
1		
2		
3		
4		
5		

Scales, units and significant figures

Whilst scales and units should be relatively simple in science, after all we use SI (*Système International*) units, things are not always as simple in the pupils' eyes.

Take pressure for example; we will in physics use the Pascal (Pa) as the unit of pressure but for any student looking at the equation Pressure = Force/Area it is also clear that the unit is newton per square metre (N/m^2 or Nm^{-2}). However, looking at a weather map, pupils will see pressure of the air in millibars (mbar), or if buying a watch may see *watertight to three atmospheres*. The use of units and scales of measurement needs careful introduction, and equivalences pointing out with, we would argue, the reason for the chosen scale and its units being made clear.

Similarly the use of significant figures needs careful introduction, especially if using calculators or spreadsheets; just because you can calculate to eight significant figures does not imply we can attach *meaning* to all of the figures. Pupils need to be taught, for example, the difference between quoting an answer as: 1.2 or 1.20 or 1.200 or even 1.2000001.

One final comment is made here regarding scales. Pupils may, depending on their course of study, be exposed to logarithmic scales (pH in chemistry or decibels in physics); these need additional careful handling. One of the authors has experience of a solicitor hoping to defend a client charged with releasing acidic waste into a river. The intended argument being that 4 is only a little less than 6 so the difference between the allowed and released value was small! Once the difference was known to be 100 times the case took on a different light.

In summary ...

This chapter has argued that science teachers should, due to the very nature of their subject, consider and develop pupils' numeracy. Numeracy has been broadly defined to include not only skills and knowledge such as ratio and estimation but also 'graphicacy': the ability to draw and interpret graphs and also to distinguish different types of 'graph' and 'chart' (and to choose the most appropriate for purpose). Planning for numeracy involves, of course, liaising with the Mathematics Department – but it also requires science teachers to teach some of the skills of numeracy themselves. Two practical exemplars of how this might be done have been given.

Finally attention has been drawn to the often overlooked issue of scales, units and significant figures.

Points for reflection

- We have defined numeracy in relation to school science, as: 'The ability to use number and simple mathematical functions to solve age-appropriate problems in a consistent manner throughout the school.' How far would you agree with this?
- How important do you think it is for a learner to understand the 'mathematics' as well as the 'science' being taught?
- Drawing on your classroom-based experience, do you feel that there is a gap between your students' mathematical and scientific understanding? How far is any mismatch a product of the curriculum being delivered, how far is it a product of differential demands made by teachers of the two disciplines and how far is it a product of the learners' development in the two disciplines progressing at different rates?

References and further reading

Basic Skills Agency (1997) *Does Numeracy Matter? Evidence from the national child development study on the impact of poor numeracy on adult life*, London: Basic Skills Agency.

DfEE (1999) *The National Curriculum for England: science*, London: DfEE.

DfES (2001) *Framework for Teaching Mathematics: years 7, 8 and 9*, London: DfES.

Duffin, J. (1994) *Calculators in the Classroom*, Liverpool: Manutius Press.

Hoult, S. (2005) *Achieving QTS. Reflective Reader: secondary professional studies,* Exeter: Learning Matters.

Inhelder, B. and Piaget, J. (1958) *The Growth of Logical Thinking*, London: Routledge.

Ireson, G. (1996) The effect of studying A-level mathematics on the A-level physics grade achieved, *School Science Review*, 72, pp. 116–19.

Ireson, G. and Gill, P. (2002) 'Physics and mathematics – the links', in Turlo, J., *Science and Materials Teaching for the Information Society*, Torun: Top Kurier.

Lenton, G. and Stevens, B. (1999) 'Numeracy in science', *School Science Review*, 80, pp. 59–64.

Muijs, D. and Reynolds, D. (2011) *Effective Teaching Evidence and Practice,* London: Sage.

Ofsted (2001) *Inspecting Mathematics 11–16 with Guidance on Self-Evaluation*, London: Ofsted.

Ross, K., Lakin, L. and McKechnie, J. (2010) *Teaching Secondary Science* (3rd edn), London: David Fulton.

Shayer, M. and Adey, P. (1981) *Towards a Science of Science Teaching*, London: Heinemann.

SMP (1976) *Calculators in Schools*, London: Schools Mathematics Project.

Enriching science learning and science teaching

Chapter 13

Using ICT in science education

Introduction

The use of ICT in science can involve word-processing and desktop publishing; database and spreadsheet use; communications; data-logging; simulations and modelling; multimedia of any kind including digital video and still cameras not forgetting camera phones; control hardware and software and more recently a move to 'minds-on' rather than 'hands-on' applications.

The main forms of ICT for school science have been summarised by Osborne and Hennessey (2003) as:

* tools for data capture, processing and interpretation;
* multimedia software;
* information systems;
* publication and presentation tools;
* computer projection technology.

Has this moved on? We would say yes, with the growth of availability of the technology. Pupils have smartphones with still and video capture, the ability to capture, store and edit audio files and a whole range of 'apps' which provide access to material previously controlled, through the use of CD-ROMs or DVDs, by the teacher. What once generated a 'Wow!' factor in pupils may now appear rather low tech in their eyes.

However, we can see some of the possibilities for the use of ICT in school summarised in Table 13.1. The list will grow as ICT itself progresses and becomes more readily available to schools, which also have staff who are better prepared to make use of the resources.

It can be seen that many of the applications cross 'packages' and we would wish to stress that, as with science itself, we cannot think in discrete boxes but rather we must take a more holistic view.

The first point to be made here is that science and especially school science, is often a very practical subject. It involves doing things, which is often one of its attractions to learners. It involves observing, measuring, communicating and discussing, trying things out, investigating, handling things, watching and monitoring, recording results; these are all things we see happening in the science classroom and ICT can help in virtually all of these activities.

However, as much as science is a practical discipline, it is equally a theoretical subject. It involves thinking, inferring, having good ideas and hunches, hypothesising, theorising, simulating and modelling, and always has done. Thinking and thought experiments are as

Table 13.1 Uses and applications of ICT in science learning and teaching

Package	Application(s)
Word processing and desktop publishing	Presenting information to learners; allowing learners to express their knowledge in a more creative way.
Databases and spreadsheets	Searching for patterns; testing hypotheses; recording and presenting data; assessing and organising data; plotting graphs; maintaining class records for evaluation and assessment.
Interactive media	Digital video and still cameras to emphasise teaching points; allowing learners to be creative in how they demonstrate their knowledge and understanding; use of interactive whiteboards; using smart phones and tablets [the iPad or Android].
Simulations and modelling	Predicting and searching for patterns; testing hypotheses; alleviating health and safety issues.
Data-logging	Collecting data; handling very rapid or very long time-base acquisition; recording data; use of sensors; linking to *How Science Works*.
Minds-on ICT	Building a simple data logger; using the data-logger to acquire data; understanding the features of a data communication system; understanding sensors; understanding data transfer.

important as hands-on activity. ICT can help as much in this aspect of science as it can in the practical aspect. Finally we must not forget that science can, and in our view should, be a design-and-make subject. This involves learners going beyond the hands-on and, by utilising both theory and practical moving towards a minds-on subject, discussed later. Again ICT can be a vehicle for moving learners down this road.

Second, we also need to see science from two different angles when we talk about learning and teaching it. The two viewpoints involve process and content. Both are equally important to science education. The content of science – its facts, laws, theories and understanding of them – needs to be taught alongside its processes. ICT can help in learning the content of science information sources such as the internet and material on CD-ROM can play a part (as can traditional books). ICT can also help in learning the content and facts of science by using it in revision or tutorial mode, discussed later. But equally, ICT can help in learning the processes of science – measuring, recording, processing data, hypothesising, and communicating. These skills and processes are vital to science itself, as well as to science education.

Table 13.2 sums up some of the areas of activity in science and the specific items of ICT that can enhance them. ICT in the process of science can be summarised as in Table 13.3.

Why use ICT in science teaching and learning?

We can start to answer this by first listing some of the things that modern IT systems, hardware and software, are good at:

- collecting and storing large amounts of data;
- performing complex calculations on stored data rapidly;
- processing large amounts of data and displaying it in a variety of formats;
- helping to present and communicate information;

Table 13.2 Overview of uses of ICT in science teaching and learning

Learning mode	Teaching purpose		Software tool	Software instrument
Receiver	Obtaining knowledge		Information storage	Database, browser
			Visual aid	
Reviser	Practice and revision		Simulation	
Creator	Exploring ideas		Modelling	Spreadsheet, modelling
Receiver	Collating and recording		Calculating	Spreadsheet, data-logging
Explorer	Presenting and reporting		Graphing	Spreadsheet, data-logging
			Measuring	Data-logging
			Publishing	Word processing, DTP, presentation packages, hypertext, graphics
Designer	Understanding knowledge			Spreadsheet, programming languages

Source; adapted from Newton and Rogers (2001)

Table 13.3 Process and ICT use in science teaching and learning

Process in science	ICT use
Measuring	Data-logging
Hypothesising	Simulations, spreadsheets
Recording and processing	Data-logging, spreadsheets, databases
Thinking	Simulations, modelling packages, design and make activities
Communication	Word processing, desktop publishing, email, internet, spreadsheets, interactive whiteboards, still and video cameras
Observing	Multimedia presentations, data-logging, projection software, digital microscopes

Source: adapted from Wellington (2000)

These capabilities all have direct relevance to the process of education, and they help us to address the key question of when to use ICT, and equally importantly, when not to. One issue concerns the use of computers as labour-saving devices. As listed above, computers can collect data at a rapid rate and perform calculations on it extremely quickly. But the question arises: should the computer, in an educational context, be used to collect, process and display rather than these being done by the learner? For instance, why should data-logging software plot graphs 'automatically', rather than a pupil using pencil, rule and graph paper? In other words when does the use of a computer in saving labour take away an important educational experience for the learner? A similar issue appears in the use of computers and electronic calculators to perform complex calculations rapidly. This may be desirable in some learning situations, e.g.

Table 13.4 Feedback from teachers on the impact of ICT on their teaching

Question	Very good	Good	Poor
Motivate interest	76%	15%	0%
Increase visual appeal	87%	7%	0%
Support different learning styles	46%	39%	4%
Assist class management	24%	57%	7%
Help students reach their potential	30%	52%	2%
Promote independent learning	28%	43%	28%
Prepare class work	56%	28%	0%
Assess students	.15%	35%	13%
Support STS (science, technology and society)	56%	22%	21%
Increase active learning	35%	39%	13%
Inform career choice	20%	28%	26%
Resources available	41%	33%	9%

Source: adapted from Regan (2010)

if the performance of a tedious calculation by human means actually impedes or 'clutters up' a learning process. But it can also be argued that the ability to perform complex calculations rapidly should be one of the aims of education, not something to be replaced by it.

The distinction between what counts as authentic, i.e. desirable and purposeful, and inauthentic, i.e. unnecessary and irrelevant, labour in the learning process is a central one in considering the use of IT in education. The notions of 'inauthentic' and 'authentic' labour should be remembered when we look at the added value of ICT in the examples later.

It is also worth noting that computers do exactly what they are instructed to do, very quickly, as many times as they are told to do it. On the one hand, this means that they are not, or at least not yet, capable of making autonomous or independent judgements, or personal interpretations. However it is also the case that they do not become tired, bored, hungry, irritable, angry or impatient, or liable to error. This may place them at an advantage in some situations as compared with teachers! It has been said that one of the reasons why children appear to enjoy learning with computers is precisely because of their impersonal, inhuman 'qualities'.

But what do teachers think about the uses of ICT in their teaching? Based on a sample of physics teachers, Regan (2010) offers feedback from teachers showing that the greatest impact of ICT is on visual appearance and motivation. The full results are shown in Table 13.4.

One final point on the 'abilities' of computers is worth stressing. Computers can, in a sense, speed up, or slow down, reality. As Kahn (1985) put it 'they operate outside the viscous flow of time in which humans perform tasks'. This is an important point that will be elaborated upon when the use of computer simulations in education is considered.

Why bother with ICT in the classroom?

It is worth noting that Betts (2003) presents evidence to support the case that ICT enhances the quality of learning in science. The conclusion reached by McFarlane and Sakellariou (2002) is that using ICT as a simulation of or alternative to laboratory-based practical work can aid students' theoretical understanding. Hence some measure of 'added-value' should be seen by the teacher.

The following benefits or 'added value' can be gained by trying and using IT in the classroom:

- motivation;
- excitement and pleasure;
- an improvement in pupils' self-esteem and perseverance;
- the opportunity for pupils to produce neater, more accurate work.

In science, in particular, the use of IT can extend and enhance learning in many other ways. For example:

- *Simulations* can show students phenomena and processes that may be too slow, too fast, too dangerous or too expensive to do in the school laboratory;
- *Data-logging* can assist in the recording of results, making results tables and plotting graphs so that students can spend more time on some of the 'higher order' skills such as interpreting, discussing and hypothesising;
- *Databases* on topics such as mammals, the planets or the periodic table can allow students to search through information in a fast, flexible way, to make connections and to try comparing one set of figures with another, e.g. wing span and speed of flight;
- *Spreadsheets*, in the same way, can offer the removal of drudgery, for example tedious, repetitive calculations such as taking the new length of a spring away from its original length every time, and allow students to get on to the more important things in science – asking 'What if …?' or 'Why don't we try …?';
- *Minds-on activities*: technology in terms of hardware and free software now makes it possible for pupils to build their own data-logger, which they program prior to taking readings, giving an understanding of data acquisition, data processing and data communication.

In the next section, we look at each use of ICT in science, with some illustrations of classroom possibilities. We start with computer simulations.

Types of simulation in science education

It is useful to make some fairly crude distinctions between types of simulation, which should act as a rough guide:

1 direct copies of existing laboratory activities, e.g. titrations;
2 simulations of industrial processes, e.g. the manufacture of sulphuric acid, bridge building;
3 simulations of processes either:
   - too dangerous
   - too slow, e.g. evolution, population growth, an ecosystem of any kind
   - too fast, e.g. collisions
   - too small, e.g. sub-atomic changes
   - to be carried out in a school or college environment;
4 simulations involving non-existent entities, e.g. ideal gases, frictionless surfaces, perfectly elastic objects;
5 simulation of models or theories, e.g. kinetic theory, the wave model of light or superconductivity.

238 Enriching science learning and science teaching

Why use computer simulations in science teaching?

The main advantages of using simulations can be summarised as follows:

1 *Cost*: money can be saved in directly copying some laboratory experiments, either by reducing outlay on consumables, e.g. chemicals, test-tubes, or by removing the need to buy increasingly costly equipment in the first place.
2 *Time*: using a computer simulation instead of a genuine practical activity may save time, although some teachers are finding that a good computer simulation in which pupils fully explore all the possibilities may take a great deal longer.
3 *Safety*: some activities simply cannot be carried out in a school setting because they are unsafe, e.g. modelling the operation of a nuclear reactor.
4 *Motivation*: there is a feeling, though with little evidence to support it, that computer simulations motivate pupils in science education more than traditional practical work. The familiarity with mobile technology and use of 'apps' by pupils would appear to strengthen this argument.
5 *Control*: the use of a simulation allows ease of control of variables, which traditional school practical work does not. This may lead to unguided discovery learning by pupils who are encouraged to explore and hypothesise for themselves.
6 *Management*: last, but certainly not least, computer simulations offer far fewer management problems to teachers than do many traditional activities.

Problems of handing out equipment, collecting it back again, and guarding against damage and theft are removed at a stroke. Problems of supervision, timing and clearing up virtually disappear.

Dangers of simulation

So much for the supposed advantages of computer simulations. What of the dangers in using computer simulations in science teaching and learning? The main dangers of using simulations lie in the hidden messages they convey, classified as follows:

1 *Variables*: simulations give pupils the impression that variables in a physical process can be easily, equally, and independently controlled. This message is conveyed by simulations of industrial processes, ecological systems, and laboratory experiments. In reality not all variables in a physical situation can be as easily, equally, and as independently controlled as certain simulations suggest.
2 *Unquestioned models*: facts and assumptions – every simulation is based on a certain model of reality. Users are only able to manipulate factors and variables within that model. They cannot tamper with that model itself. Moreover, they are neither encouraged nor able to question its validity. The model is hidden from the user. All simulations are based on certain assumptions. These are often embedded in the model itself. What are these assumptions? Are they ever revealed to the user? All simulations rely on certain facts, or data. *Where do these facts come from? What sources have been used?*
3 *Caricatures of reality*: any model is an idealisation of reality, i.e. it ignores certain features in order to concentrate on others. Some idealisations are worse than others. In some cases, a model may be used of a process not fully understood. Other models may be deceptive,

misleading or downright inaccurate; they provide caricatures of reality, rather than representations of it.

4   *Confusion with reality*: pupils are almost certain to confound the programmer's model of reality with reality itself – such is the current power and potency of the computer, at least until its novelty as a learning aid wears off. Students may then be fooled into thinking that because they can use and understand a model of reality they can also understand the more complex real phenomena it represents or idealises. Perhaps more dangerously, the 'micro world' of the computer creates a reality of its own. The world of the micro, the keyboard and the screen can assume its own reality in the mind of the user – a reality far more alluring and manageable than the complicated and messy world outside. The 'scientific world' presented in computer simulations may become as attractive and addictive as the micro worlds of arcade games as first noted by Weizenbaum (1984) and Turkle (1984).

5   *Double idealisations*: all the dangers and hidden messages discussed so far become increasingly important in a simulation which uses a computer model of a scientific model or scientific theory, which itself is an idealisation of reality, i.e. the idealisation involved in modelling is doubly dangerous in simulations that involve a model of a model. A simulation of kinetic theory, for example, is itself based on a model of reality.

Safeguards in using simulations

Given that science teachers will continue to use simulations, what safeguards can be taken to reduce these dangers? First, all teachers and, through them, pupils, must be fully conscious that the models they use in a computer simulation are personal, simplified and perhaps value-laden idealisations of reality. Models are made by man, or woman. Students must be taught to examine and question these models.

Second, the facts, data, assumptions – and even the model itself – which are used by the programmer must be made clear and available to the user. This can be done in a teacher's guide, or the documentation with the program. All sources of data should be stated and clearly referenced. Any student using a simulation can then be taught to examine and question the facts, assumptions and models underlying it.

Examples of simulation programs

A wide range of simulations is now available for school science ranging from simulations of chemical collisions, the manufacture of ethanol or the siting of a blast furnace to the simulation of electric and magnetic fields, electricity use in the home, wave motion, floating and sinking, a 'Newtonian' world of frictionless movement and the construction of bridges. For the life sciences, simulations are available on pond life, the human eye, nerves, the life of the golden eagle and predator–prey relationships.

Multimedia in science education

What is multimedia? We will take the view that to be multimedia the package should involve at least three of the following:

*   sound, including speech;
*   diagrams;

- animation;
- video;
- still photographs;
- text.

Value added or opportunity lost?

An ever growing number of CDs, DVDs, 'apps' and internet sites now allow pupils and teachers to carry out a number of 'virtual experiments'. This ensures that the investigation is both successful and repeatable and alleviates the need for expensive consumables, even if chemistry teachers tell us they 'miss the smell'. The key issue then becomes one of whether this devalues scientific activity by removing some of the real, hands-on, authentic business of science by placing it in the realm of multimedia.

Should investigations that can be done 'for real' in a laboratory be done on the screen? The questions we urge that teachers should ask before employing a multimedia approach are outlined in Table 13.5 and whilst this is aimed at an evaluation of a website the key questions can be asked of any multimedia application.

Home–school convergence

With the growth of multimedia systems and broadband internet applications in the home, many multimedia applications that, in the past, pupils only had access to in school are now common at home. This itself raises questions for the teacher: How do teachers respond, in a flexible way, to the pupil who is 'expert' at using the CD on which the next half term of study is based? How can equality of opportunity for multimedia and internet based learning be addressed when some homes will not have access? How will school ICT managers respond to the call for home media being used in school or school media at home? With home use, at times on systems way beyond those available in school, will multimedia lose its 'awe and wonder' effect in schools? These questions are limitless but teachers need to be aware they will be facing them. Later in this chapter we make reference to Virtual Learning Environments (VLE) which may allow schools to give greater equality of access, provided the pupil has home access to the internet.

Creating multimedia resources

It is now easy to create multimedia resources for school use through a number of authoring tools and interactive whiteboards.

What is an authoring tool? A multimedia authoring package enables you to design the links between the computer screen and the various computer-based multimedia resources, including whiteboards, and allows an interaction between the resources and the learner, so that topics can be explored in different ways in different situations. Multimedia authoring can be used to create a learning environment where students can have more autonomy and in which different styles of learning can be supported.

There are at least five key questions to consider before any form of teaching or learning material is created, be it paper-based, instructions on the whiteboard or a series of pages on the internet:

- What are the objectives?
- Who will the users be?

Table 13.5 Questions to ask of a website: five criteria for evaluating web pages

Evaluation of web documents	*How to interpret the basics*
1 Accuracy of web documents	Accuracy
• Who wrote the page and can you contact him or her? • What is the purpose of the document and why was it produced? • Is this person qualified to write this document?	• Make sure author provides email or a contact address/phone number. • Know the distinction between author and webmaster
2 Authority of web documents	Authority
• Who published the document and is it separate from the 'webmaster'? • Check the domain of the document, what institution publishes this document? • Does the publisher list his or her qualifications?	• What credentials are listed for the author(s)? • Where is the document published? Check URL domain.
3 Objectivity of web documents	Objectivity
• What goals/objectives does this page meet? • How detailed is the information? • What opinions (if any) are expressed by the author?	• Determine if page is a mask for advertising; if so information might be biased. • View any web page as you would an infommercial on television. Ask yourself why was this written and for whom?
4 Currency of web documents	Currency
• When was it produced? • When was it updated? • How up-to-date are the links (if any)?	• How many dead links are on the page? • Are the links current or updated regularly? • Is the information on the page outdated?
5 Coverage of the web documents	Coverage
• Are the links (if any) evaluated and do they complement the document's theme? • Is it all images or a balance of text and images? • Is the information presented cited correctly?	• If page requires special software to view the information, how much are you missing if you don't have the software? • Is it free, or is there a fee to obtain the information? • Is there an option for text only, or frames, or a suggested browser for better viewing?

Source: adapted from Kapoun (2005)

- What do they know already?
- What skills do they have?
- What do they understand?

Consider each of these in turn. What learning outcomes are intended for the activity or lesson? A clear statement of the intentions behind the learning activity will also provide the basis for evaluating the success or otherwise of the work you or others have planned. The audience for the resource or the participants in the activity also need to be well defined and understood. This will influence a number of characteristics including the level of language that is used and the way in which the resource is made purposeful and relevant. In the same way, any teaching or learning activity must take into account the existing or required knowledge, skills and understanding of the intended users.

Word-processing and desktop publishing (DTP): publishing tools

Why use word-processing in science education?

Most pupils and students still write by hand. Write-ups of experiments, evaluations, project work and so on are more likely to be handwritten than typed on a keyboard. Most people would argue that writing with a pen or a pencil is an essential skill and should be preserved. Few would disagree. A small minority would go further and suggest that the use of a keyboard to write words, a computer to process and store them, and a printer to print them, will actually hinder or stunt the development of handwriting and even writing generally.

Benefits of word-processing

The use of word-processing can provide the following enrichment and benefit:

1   Pupils are given the opportunity to draft and redraft their own work much more readily. This is well known, and all those who have used a WP system will have experienced it. It seems to affect different users in different ways. Some are much more inclined to actually make a start on a piece of writing, arguably the hardest part of the process, in the knowledge that it can easily be changed or edited. Some are actually much more inclined to keep going, just to get their thoughts down onto paper or the screen, knowing that they can easily be redrafted.

2   Pupils are able to collaborate, work cooperatively, on a piece of writing much more easily with a computer system than with pen and paper. Partnership in writing is encouraged. This occurs for perhaps two main reasons: first, the writing is up there on the screen for all partners to see. This enables them more easily to take an equal share in it. Second, the writing is actually physically done by a shared keyboard, there on the desk or bench. It often does not 'belong' to one person more than another as, say, a pen does.

3   The marking of work done on a word-processor can be so much more painless. This applies equally at all levels of education and writing. Writers are far more inclined to seek feedback and critical comment if they know that alteration, addition and editing are relatively simple. This is often said to apply especially to those most likely to make spelling or grammatical mistakes, which is certainly true: the use of word-processing does remove the need for marks and corrections all over a script. But it can have an influence on people's writing attitudes and habits at all levels.

4   The final product of a piece of writing can be so much better through the use of word-processing, as we will see later. This can produce a positive feedback loop, in turn influencing the earlier stages.

5   Finally, writing done with a word-processor can easily be stored and exchanged. On the one hand this may encourage malpractice with exam coursework, though we know of no cases. Its positive effect is to allow a person or a group to stop writing at a convenient point and take it up again more easily later.

Teachers' use of word-processing and desk top publishing

These are some of the main general points connected with the use of WP in science education. A further aspect of interest in the use of WP in schools is that teachers who are otherwise reluctant to use IT are often willing users of WP and DTP. Their activities tended to focus on the production of teaching materials such as worksheets, assignment sheets and tests, as well as general course and departmental documentation. The seemingly anomalous situation of a teacher owning several boxes of recordable CDs while never using a computer in a lesson seems to be not uncommon. One possible interpretation of this is that as WP is an extension of something familiar, namely typing, and the user is firmly in control of events, the technology is therefore relatively non-threatening to the user. It is accepted by IT sceptics because the pay-off outweighs the threat.

When used by teachers to produce teaching materials and professional documentation, WP can contribute to departmental teamwork (as can email). It is much easier to circulate draft copies to colleagues and accommodate their suggested changes when the document is stored electronically. In this sense, IT is an aid to management processes in schools, and within science departments.

Two key practical issues with WP

Over the brief history of ICT in schools, about twenty years, two key issues related to the use of WP have constantly surfaced and resurfaced:

1   Should pupils be taught keyboard skills, using the ubiquitous QWERTY layout at an early age? One of the barriers to the use of WP (and databases) has been pupils' slowness in typing in text. Should keyboard skills be taught to all pupils as a matter of course? Research shows that these skills are certainly one of the main requirements of employers in connection with IT (see Wellington 1989 for past research on this question).
2   A second barrier to use, as with many aspects of IT, is access to a computer system. What will be the effect of increased use of portable/laptop computers on the incidence and use of WP? Should they be introduced into science lessons on a wide scale, especially as pupils increasingly acquire their own laptops and have ICT at home?

Desktop publishing (DTP)

Word-processing programs are designed to manage text made up of letters, numbers and other symbols such as those found on typewriters. The layout of the text can be altered in several useful, but strictly limited ways. Desktop publishing (DTP) programs are more flexible. DTP can accommodate line drawings, artwork and photographs as well as data from other programs. The DTP user might utilise newspaper format in columns, text flowing round graphics, attractive data display such as a three-dimensional pie-chart, text enhancements including a variety of fonts, headings and borders. DTP programs can also operate as simple word-processors, which is not as retrograde as it appears because printing can be much quicker in this mode of use.

Pupils' presentation of work can be greatly enhanced with DTP and WP, which raises many issues for assessment.

The majority of the above points, regarding potential benefits of publishing tools, are summarised in Table 13.6, adapted from Newton and Rogers (2001).

An example of a writing frame used to allow pupils a more creative way to show their understanding of the work of Jenner is given in Figure 13.1.

Table 13.6 Potential benefits of publishing tools in science teaching and learning

Property of the publishing tool	Potential benefit(s)
Ease of presentation	Encourages writers of all abilities
Clarity of presentation	Improves self-esteem; focuses attention on the content rather than the presentation
Ease of editing	Pupils' develop thoughts in their own way; ease of editing encourages reflection
'Spell' and 'grammar' checkers	Pupils' knowledge of spelling and grammar can be developed
Graphics and images	Encourages creativity; alternative formats aid assimilation for information
Templates and writing frames	Easy to provide differentiated support; develops understanding of writing genres
Hyperlinks and hypertext	Develops understanding of the conceptual links between concepts

Source: adapted from Newton and Rogers (2001)

Spreadsheets

What is a spreadsheet?

A spreadsheet is a two-dimensional matrix of numbers, laid out in rows and columns. The on-screen page may show all, or just part, of the sheet and each location is described as a cell. Once you have entered numbers into the cells you can carry out certain operations. For example, the spreadsheet can add up the contents of a column of cells and arrive at a total.

At a more sophisticated level, you can link a number in one cell to those in other cells by the use of appropriate formulae. For example, a formula might involve specifying a sequence of operations to add the contents of two cells together and to put the result in a third cell. You could end up with an automatic large-scale calculator, with quite a number of formulae linking together different cells; hence, if the number in a particular cell is altered, this will cause changes to be made to all the other cells that relate to it. If you had a spreadsheet to calculate the monthly outgoings for your household, and then the price of milk went up, you could enter the new price and the spreadsheet could calculate the new daily, weekly and monthly total, the new total food bill, and the new total for outgoings – just after one alteration!

As a teacher, you might experience filling in a simple manual spreadsheet when you total the class attendance register on a Friday afternoon. The attendance sub-totals for each morning and afternoon for each weekday are set out in a matrix of rows and columns. Blank cells are available for the insertion of total attendances for the week, the number on roll in the class, the number of school sessions that week, the maximum possible attendance and finally the percentage attendance. Don't be deterred, a spreadsheet can offer much more than that!

What can I do with a spreadsheet?

A spreadsheet can support any kind of activity in which it is likely that calculations will be carried out upon numbers. Thus you could use a spreadsheet, for example, to plan a school or class educational visit. A suitable model could be set up to include such things as cost of transport, cost of meals, entrance costs etc. with one column containing a suitable formula to

THE OAK TREE TIMES

Issue 321 December 1797

NEW DISCOVERY BAFFLES PEOPLE

Is he genuine or is he a fraud? Dr Edward Jenner announced today that he has found a new wonder cure for smallpox. 'It is', he said, 'prevented by cowpox.'

He is calling his new preventative method vaccination.

James Phipps – the guinea pig.

James Phipps is an eight-year-old boy who was taken from his family for half a crown.

Dr Jenner was planning on conducting his experiments on the young lad.

The Experiment

Dr Jenner put a slit in Phipps' left arm and put the liquid from a cowpox blister in it, Phipps felt a bit sick but was otherwise all right.

Jenner then made a slit in Phipps' arm and put in the 'pus' from a smallpox victim.

'I didn't know what he would do so I was a bit scared of him at first.'

James soon recovered and was up and kicking a football around.

Continues on pages 60 to 65.

Figure 13.1 Example writing frame

calculate the charge per child. Any changes in costs would be reflected immediately in the charge cell. You could explore the effect of different transport quotes or entertainment options without having to rewrite anything.

The collection and manipulation of data, the formulation of a hypothesis and discussion of the results is only one application of a spreadsheet. Other applications include modelling, investigations, number pattern generation and problem solving. The spreadsheet is probably the best all-purpose mathematical tool currently available. However, although there is a relatively long learning curve before complete mastery, you can make a start at whatever level you wish.

You may use a spreadsheet to produce a range of graphs, or you may start by using the built-in functions to calculate totals, averages and standard deviations. We tend to use about a quarter of the features offered by a word-processor. Do the same with a spreadsheet, and when you need to know how to do something further, the motivation will get you through.

Spreadsheets in the classroom

If students are to see the potential applications for a spreadsheet, they need to use them over a number of years. They need to start in a modest way. They may begin by using the spreadsheet as a graph drawing tool, without using it for calculation purposes. It is an extremely quick and efficient tool for accepting data and displaying it in graphical format. As they gain in confidence, they may begin to play and experiment with numbers because calculations can be carried out with ease.

The use of the spreadsheet can give structure to abstract ideas. You can help the student to use a spreadsheet as a problem-solving tool, applying standard strategies, such as breaking a problem down into manageable bits. The use of a spreadsheet can shift the emphasis from number crunching to hypothesis formulation and it can set a real context for algebraic formulation. The spreadsheet offers the student an opportunity for mathematical discovery.

Using a simple spreadsheet to record marks for a class or year group will allow you to monitor both the student progress and the assessment instruments used.

The example in Figures 13.2 and 13.3 is an extract from a class in which a series of module tests are recorded. If a test has a very small spread or *standard deviation* then it should trigger interest; does the test fail to differentiate or were some elements poorly taught? The example is written in Excel® but any spreadsheet would do – you simply need to check how to use the formulae.

	A	B	C	D	E	F	G	H	I	J	K	L	M	N
1					Year 8 Science - Module Tests									
2					Test Results as percentage									
3	Name	Cells	Plants	Variation	Materials1	Materials 2	Patterns	Elec & mag	Forces	Light & sound	Energy	Earth & beyond	Mean	Std. Dev
4	Allen, J	34	32	56	45	43	38	87	31	23	18	34	40	19
5	Bostock, T	45	67	55	92	47	45	98	54	25	45	54	57	21
6	Carp, G	67	56	53	88	86	65	98	45	24	23	67	61	24
7	Deacon, C	23	45	50	67	62	43	98	23	67	67	81	57	23
8	Green, D	12	22	48	45	21	32	98	12	89	65	65	46	30
9														
10	Mean	36	44	52	67	52	45	96	33	46	44	60		
11	Std. Dev	21	18	3	23	24	12	5	17	31	23	18		
12														

Check this test - does it differentiate?

Figure 13.2 Using an electronic mark book

J	K	L	M	N
Light & sound	Energy	Earth & beyond	Mean	Std. Dev
23	18	34	=AVERAGE(B4:L4)	=STDEV(B4:L4)
25	45	54	=AVERAGE(B5:L5)	=STDEV(B5:L5)
24	23	67	=AVERAGE(B6:L6)	=STDEV(B6:L6)
67	67	81	=AVERAGE(B7:L7)	=STDEV(B7:L7)
89	65	65	=AVERAGE(B8:L8)	=STDEV(B8:L8)
=AVERAGE(J4:J9)	=AVERAGE(K4:K9)	=AVERAGE(L4:L9)		
=STDEV(J4:J8)	=STDEV(K4:K8)	=STDEV(L4:L8)		

Figure 13.3   Inserting the correct formulae

Spreadsheets: pros and cons

The use of spreadsheets can enhance students' learning in science, but what is the balance between pay-off and cost to the teacher? The cost, in its broader sense, involves acquiring and learning to use the software, at least so as to remain one step ahead of the students (or only one step behind!). It also involves building ICT into schemes of work and lesson plans, and booking a computer at the right time, in the right place. Finally the students must be shown how to use the software. The pay-offs from using spreadsheets must include the potential for improved student learning and motivation, otherwise they would have no place in the classroom. Additional advantages include the following:

- *Flexible learning*: students can work independently and at their own pace.
- *Working co-operatively in groups.*
- *Teacher–pupil relations*: pupils will notice and value the fact that the teacher has bothered to introduce a new and interesting activity.
- *Improved teacher competence in IT*: teachers may find uses for spreadsheets in their professional work other than with their classes. Departmental accounting and stocktaking, and collation of assessment schedules and examination results are two likely areas.
- *Increased teacher confidence in IT*: teachers who have hitherto been wary of computers may find that simple spreadsheets are much easier to use than they feared.
- *Emancipation*: spreadsheets can allow *modelling* and predicting to take place (the conjectural paradigm) while also taking away the drudgery of laborious calculations of rows and columns of figures.

Data-logging

Data-logging typically involves using a computer to record and process readings taken from sensors. Perhaps the simplest data-logging system is shown in Figure 13.4.

The sensor plays the part of a translator. It responds to some property of the environment and sends a message to the computer. The message, or signal, has the form of a voltage at one of the computer's input ports. The computer is programmed to record the value of the input signal. Temperature is an example of an environmental property which can be sensed in this way.

With modern data-logging systems, sensors can identify themselves, logging rates are automatically optimised, and interfaces match the type of information given by the sensor to the type which the computer can accept. Teachers should expect many of these features in new

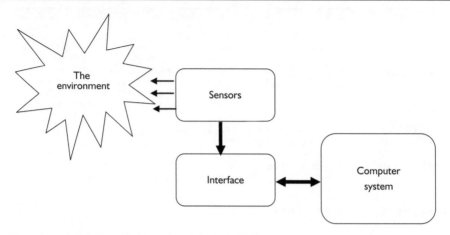

Figure 13.4 A basic data-logging system

data-logging equipment. The result should be that the 'inauthentic labour' of matching the computer to the environment is removed from the teacher and is incorporated in the hardware and software design of the system. Here are a few practical examples of using sensors in science:

- temperature sensors to study cooling curves or insulation, e.g. heat loss from the building;
- a light sensor to study the rate of the reaction where a precipitate forms;
- light and temperature sensors as simple meters to compare habitats;
- a data-logger to measure light, temperature and oxygen readings in an aquarium, pond or greenhouse;
- light gates to measure speed, time and acceleration;
- a position sensor to monitor the movement of a pendulum;
- sensors to study current–voltage relationships.

What added-value comes from data-logging?

The following advantages have been claimed:

- *Speed*: Computers can often log much faster and more frequently than humans.
- *Memory*: Computers have enormous capacity for retaining and accessing a large body of data in a compact form.
- *Perseverance*: Computers can keep on logging – they do not need to stop for food, drink, sleep or shelter.
- *Manipulation*: The form in which data are gathered may not be the form in which we want to communicate. Computers come into their own when it comes to fast manipulation of large bodies of data.
- *Communication of meaning*: Computers can present data when gathered, in real time, using graphic display to enhance the meaning which is communicated to the observer..

Some of these advantages are aimed at transferring 'inauthentic labour' from the human to the machine (see Barton's Chapter 14 in Wellington 1998). The change of emphasis away from the routine process of logging towards the use of interpreting skills can enhance scientific thinking,

Figure 13.5 A simple data-logger
Source: photograph Esmé Ireson

creativity and problem solving ability. However, this view is not universally shared by teachers. It has been pointed out that perseverance, ability to organise data systematically and calculating skills are part of science and that students should go through these processes in practical work.

We would like to move the agenda on from the current 'hands-on' view of data-logging to a more 'minds-on' approach. The advent of technologies and reduction in cost now makes it possible for pupils to build their own data-logger and program it, with no previous knowledge of either electronics or programming, prior to using it in an investigative setting. Not only will this give pupils a deeper understanding of sensors, data-acquisition and data processing but also the opportunity to forge links with Design and Technology.

Figure 13.5 shows a simple temperature sensor made from a 'bead' thermistor suitable for plotting a cooling curve and a humidity sensor. The data-logger was built by one of the authors at about one-fifteenth of the cost of a similar *commercial* logger and sensors. The data-logger is based on a Programmable Integrated Circuit or PIC chip.

Databases

What is a database?

In its simplest form a database is nothing more than an organised collection of information. Thus an address book, a telephone directory, a card index, and a school register are all examples of databases. They all contain data, which can convey information to people, and which is organised in a more-or-less systematic way, e.g. in alphabetical order. The advantage of organising data is partly for ease of use and access to information, but also well-organised and structured data can be used to show patterns and trends and to allow people to make and test hypotheses or hunches. Therein lies the *educational value* of a database. Having an organised and clearly structured collection of data allows and even encourages users to derive information and knowledge from it. The key skill to develop in pupils is the ability to *search* for information in a logical and systematic way. This is true for not only databases but also CDs, the Internet and spreadsheet use.

Searching skills and computer databases

The advantages of storing, organising and retrieving information from a computer system are worth considering briefly. First, using magnetic or optical media (e.g. floppy discs, 'laser discs', CDs, Flash cards (memory sticks) etc.), huge amounts of data can be stored in a relatively compact form. Second, data can be retrieved from a computer database quickly. Third, data retrieval from a computer database is relatively flexible. For example, to find a number in a paper-based telephone directory from a name and initials would be almost as quick as finding it from a computer-based directory: but consider the situation in reverse. How long would it take to find a person's name and initials with only their number? With a suitable computer database this could be done as quickly as a search in the other direction. Fourth, changes (editions, additions and subtractions) to a computer database can be made more easily and more painlessly than to, say, a card- or paper-based database – this is, in a way, similar to the use of word-processors in amending and redrafting text.

Important terms used with databases

A *file* is a collection of information on one topic, e.g. dinosaurs, planets, trees, birds. Files are organised into separate *records* (e.g. each type of dinosaur with its own name). Within each record, data might be stored on each kind of dinosaur and this can be organised into *fields*. One field might contain data on what the animal eats, another on its size, another on its weight, and so on. In setting up a file as part of a database, people can decide how many records they wish to include (e.g. how many different dinosaurs, and how many fields they wish to use in storing information on each animal). Of course, they can always add records (e.g. if we hear about more dinosaurs, or more fields or if we decide to store new or more complex data). Thus records and fields can be added to, edited, or even removed.

Why use databases in science education?

1 *For recording data collected during an investigation or an experiment.* Data can be entered directly onto the database and stored on a computer-based medium (e.g. a memory stick or even a mobile phone).
2 *In allowing students to sift or browse through their own, or someone else's data using the computer.* This kind of serendipitous learning (learning by browsing) can often be very valuable and is commonly underestimated. How much information do pupils assimilate through their own web-browsing?
3 *Students can explore data in a more systematic manner.* They can:
   - look for patterns
   - put forward hunches
   - make predictions
   - suggest and test hypotheses
   - draw and discuss interpretations.
4 *Better display.* With suitable software the computer system can be used to display and present data so that it conveys information in an attractive and clear way (cf. spreadsheets).

In summary the use of databases in science supports and enhances many of the so-called process skills in the science curriculum such as classifying, hypothesising and testing. It can also take away some of the 'inauthentic labour' or drudgery discussed earlier.

Using the Internet in science teaching

The value and potential of the Internet in science teaching

The Internet provides a way of:

- sharing and exchanging information
- communicating
- accessing information
- providing a local exchange of information on resources, e.g. for pooling
- linking with industry
- giving current information to pupils/students
- improving study skills and search skills
- giving pupils the excitement of on-line computer information
- allowing collaboration in science: between pupil and pupil, school and school, teacher and teacher (see ScI-Journal later)
- downloading material, e.g. data (particularly valuable for certain special needs pupils)
- setting up a forum for debate and queries amongst teachers of science.

Words of warning

Most people agree that the Internet is *potentially* a powerful resource for education – but as critical teachers we need to avoid being carried away by the hype which often surrounds it. It certainly has educational value, which lies in three areas: in exchanging and sharing ideas and information, e.g. between teacher and teacher, pupil to pupil or a mixture of both; in enhancing and facilitating communication, e.g. by e-mail; and third, in providing a source of information for learners and teachers on almost any topic from football to photosynthesis. The value of the first two uses for schools is beyond doubt. Initiatives such as ScI-Journal (see addresses below), for example, allow all sorts of ideas about investigational work to be shared and exchanged world-wide.

But use of the Internet as a vast source of information for schools is more problematic. Yes, there is a huge supply of data on every topic – but this is at once its potential and its downfall. How much of that information has been checked and edited, or even proofread? How accurate and reliable is the information? Who has written it and what were their motives? We should, quite rightly, treat all material on the Internet with a healthy scepticism, just as we would (or should) regard data in the national newspapers. This scepticism should be central to both the attitude of teachers and the message conveyed to learners. Refer back to Table 13.5 on the evaluation of websites.

Equally, the amount of information available is now so vast that it is extremely difficult for teachers to contain, or harness it, in order to meet the needs of a statutory curriculum. This is why so many teachers on courses which we run on multimedia always come up with three major, interconnected concerns: 'containing', vetting and drawing boundaries round material; similarly, structuring and guiding learners through material; and last but probably foremost, *curriculum relevance.* If learners are let loose on the Internet where will it all end? What relevance will it have to the 'delivery' of the curriculum which, in the twenty-first century, has become the classroom teacher's main driving force? And who can blame them, given the external pressures? The Internet does have *curriculum relevance.* The challenge for teachers is to 'map' Internet sources onto the curriculum and then their schemes of work – this takes time, but some of the links listed below may help as a pointer.

The teacher's role in using ICT in science

Matching learning and teaching objectives with ICT applications

One thing is certain: in the future the teacher's role will change as a result of ICT in school and in the home. Our argument here is that the teacher's role is an extremely complex one – it will require flexibility and reflection, and often a change of attitude. We look at the teacher's job closely in the next subsection.

But the first issue is to be clear about the teaching objectives in science and how they can be matched to, or *enhanced by,* the use of ICT. We have seen how several applications of ICT can help in learning and teaching science: spreadsheets, data-logging, word-processing, multimedia, and so on. The first job of the science teacher is to match these applications to their learning and teaching objectives. For example, data-logging can help pupils to observe, study and interpret data, and take away some of the drudgery of manual recording and processing, such as drawing a graph with pencil and graph paper. Spreadsheets can help to tabulate data clearly, and enable 'what if?' questions to be asked. Word-processors can help pupils to produce a well-presented report, e.g. of an investigation. Simulations, on a CD for instance, can allow people to do experiments that are either too dangerous, too fast or too slow to do in a school.

Teachers need to address the key question of what is the authentic or important learning objective. To take a crude example, if a teacher wants pupils to learn how to use a mercury-in-glass thermometer, then using a temperature sensor and a data-logger is not a good idea! There are numerous examples like this, which classroom teachers can reflect upon for themselves. The teacher's job, not an easy one, is to ask what ICT can do to help particular learning objectives in science and (as football managers say) to *take each one as it comes.*

The changed role of the teacher: observing, intervening, monitoring and supporting learning

The teacher's job is a tough one. As well as the educational question of matching objectives with ICT use there are plenty of practical issues to consider too. Some of these difficulties are hard to overcome, not least the issue of having the right resources available at the right time. Research shows that, even with the resources available, the teacher still has to decide: when to stand back and let the pupils get on with it, or when to intervene and steer them; similarly, how much structure and guidance should be given, e.g. worksheets to go with CDs, or free-rein learning.

The effective teacher's role seems to involve carrying out several demanding, complex and time-consuming tasks including:

* assessing proposed ICT for relevance and content (see next subsection);
* gaining a level of confidence and competence in using the material for oneself;

- organising access to the technology in an equitable way;
- organising access to other relevant material *away from the computer* to support children's learning;
- providing a structure or a framework within which the group will work – in many cases this will be an open-ended task and discussed with the group;
- assessing pupils' ability to teach others about the workings of the machine and making the need to hand over skills explicit to the pupil expert;
- assessing the work of the group and suggesting appropriate activities which may lead to progression in students' learning;
- reflecting on the activities of the class as a whole and acting on suggestions for amendments next time round.

Central to the teacher's facilitating role is the dialogue which goes on between the teacher and students working on the computer. This does not mean standing over the children at all times – such a task would be impossible – but it does mean engaging with learners at key moments and guiding their learning.

Assessing work done by ICT: additional demands and teacher expectations

Using ICT can improve pupils' work (especially those with special needs), but in assessing it teachers need to be aware of new issues which have cropped up as a result of ICT (both at home and at school).

Plagiarism, and giving references

A number of teachers have complained to me of science homework done with the aid of Encarta (or a similar CD-ROM, or the Internet) which has gone 'straight from the computer and onto printer paper without any intervention by the pupil's brain'. Teachers are rightly suspicious of such work, especially when the Microsoft copyright logo is still on the bottom of the page! Teachers need to demand that the work can be shown to be the pupil's own, even if a CD or the Internet was used as a source. Pupils must acknowledge the source of their work and *be taught the correct way to give references* (a skill which has rarely been taught in the past below undergraduate level).

Work enhanced by the use of ICT

Word-processed work can now be spell-checked and this becomes an additional issue for teachers, especially as few of their science pupils who use word-processors at home or school will be allowed to use them in the examination hall. Should some work also come in hand-written, e.g. reports of investigations? Similarly, with the ability of ICT (in the right hands and using a DTP package or similar) to make a pupil's work look highly professional, how should teachers view this and assess it? Scanning in images and drawing graphs with a computer package can make some pupils' work look superb. But is it all style and no substance?

Several pieces of research have indicated that word-processed work can be of most assistance for pupils with special needs, e.g. poor writers – those who have difficulty in writing by hand.

This is where ICT can be of great value to pupils who may be good at science, but whose writing ability does not do their scientific skill justice. But an issue at the other extreme for teachers assessing work is whether they can be 'conned' by superbly presented work.

The first question, raised above, is: whose work is it? The second question is: what is the quality of the *content* of work which has been presented in an all-singing, all-dancing style? Teachers (more and more in future with the growth in home use of ICT) will need to make careful judgements in these two areas, i.e.:

- Whose work is it? Are outside sources acknowledged?
- Is the quality of the *science* work being disguised – or enhanced – by the quality of the presentation?

Collaborative work

One of the excellent features of ICT is that it permits, or rather *enhances*, collaborative group work. Pupils can often write collaboratively using a computer whereas writing collaboratively with a pen is more difficult!

Increasingly, there will be assignments and coursework, at *all* levels of education, which have been done as a collaborative team effort. This trend will be fuelled by the demands of employers whose requirements of staff in new forms of employment always include 'team-work' and 'collaboration' near the top of the list. It is interesting to observe that collaborative work is commonplace in primary school and in Higher Education – but seems to be almost taboo in some secondary schools.

ICT will enhance collaborative work but the issue of how it should be assessed remains a controversial one:

- Should all partners receive equal credit, or the same mark?
- Have any pupils had a 'free ride'?
- Will pupils who (quite rightly) want a good mark avoid and exclude certain other pupils who might 'lower the grade'?

These issues will occur at all levels, from primary school to university. But they should not be allowed to prevent collaborative work from being done. Through careful observation of group work (who is doing what, when and for how long?), through record-keeping, and through discussion with pupils, teachers can ensure that collaborative work will be assessed fairly and individual pupils do not see it as a soft option.

A final note on access

We noted earlier that not all learners will have equal access to internet facilities and this needs due consideration when setting out-of-school activities. However, what is the situation in reality? The latest available figures we have been able to uncover are from the Office of National Statistics, 2009. Tables 13.7 and 13.8 show the access by household and usage by age respectively.

These tables show not only the lack of universal coverage of computer access but also the similarity of usage across the ages. It is not true that we can say, 'the young of today want everything on the computer'. As educators we need to take a much wider view of learning via ICT.

Table 13.7 Internet use in UK households

	2006	2007	2008	2009
Broadband	40%	51%	56%	63%
Dial up	17%	10%	9%	7%
No connection	43%	39%	35%	30%

Source: Adapted from Office of National Statistics (2009)

Table 13.8 Internet activity by age

	16–24	25–44	45–54	55–64	65+	All
Reading or downloading online newspapers or magazines.	46%	58%	52%	47%	44%	52%
Uploading self created content.	54%	44%	34%	29%	215	40%
Consulting the internet with the purpose of learning.	41%	39%	38%	32%	26%	37%
Looking for information about education, training or courses.	50%	33%	27%	12%	—	30%
Doing an online course.	—	9%	10%	—	—	8%

Source: Adapted from Office of National Statistics (2009)

Summary

We started this chapter by considering the nature of science and science education and then asking: 'How can ICT enhance and improve it?' By looking at what computers are good at it becomes clear that ICT can add value to learning and teaching in science. The chapter has outlined several applications of ICT which can be particularly beneficial (e.g. simulations, data-logging, the Internet).

One of the key jobs of the teacher is to ask what counts as authentic or appropriate use of ICT in science (as opposed to inauthentic or inappropriate use). This question can only be answered when we become clear on our learning and teaching objectives. For example, if our objective is to teach graph drawing with paper and pencil then a data-logging package is not appropriate. However, using a sensor with good data-logging and graph-plotting software can remove some of the drudgery and take pupils quickly to the higher order skills of discussing and interpreting graphical results. The chapter has also considered the important business of managing ICT in a school setting. This relates closely to the teacher's role in using ICT, including the important issue of taking account of and managing home use of ICT, which is growing at a rapid rate. The use of ICT at home and at school raises vital issues for the teacher's task of judging and assessing ICT work, including work done collaboratively. Key points in assessment were listed, with practical suggestions for teachers.

Finally, the teacher's role in reviewing and evaluating ICT as part of science education was discussed. The ability to review and evaluate software for its educational value and curriculum relevance is a key aspect of the teacher's repertoire of skills in using ICT. Ideas and a checklist for evaluation of ICT applications were put forward which should be valuable to teachers in critically considering ICT in education. Indeed, the main theme of this chapter is that teachers should look forward to the use of ICT in teaching and learning where it can give added value. There are enough examples available of 'value-added' activities – in data-logging, in simulations, in spreadsheet and database use, and in text processing – to show that ICT can genuinely enhance science education.

References and further reading

Betts, S. (2003) 'Does the use of ICT affect quality in learning science at Key Stage 3?' *Studies in Teaching and Learning*, pp. 9–17.

Blease, D. (1986) *Evaluating Educational Software*, London: Croom Helm.

Chapman, C. and Lewis, J. (1998) *IT Activities for Science: 11–14*, Oxford: Heinemann.

Collins, J., Hammond, M. and Wellington, J.J. (1997) *Teaching and Learning with Multimedia*, London: Routledge.

DfEE Statistical Bulletins (published annually).

Frost, R. (1998) *The IT in Secondary Science Book*, Hatfield: ASE.

Frost, R. (1998) *Software for Teaching Science*, Hatfield: ASE Publications.

Hoyles, C. (ed.) (1988) *Girls and Computers*. London: Bedford Way Papers.

Kahn, B. (1985) *Computers in Science*, Cambridge: Cambridge University Press.

Kapoun, J. (2005) 'Teaching undergrads WEB evaluation: a guide for library instruction', available at http://www.cbbnet.org/teaching/evaluation.html [accessed, 12 October 2011]

Loveless, T. (1996) 'Why aren't computers used more in schools?' *Educational Policy*, December, pp. 448–67.

McFarlane, A. (ed.) (1997) *IT and Authentic Learning*, London: Routledge.

McFarlane, A. and Sakellariou, S. (2002) 'The role of ICT in science education', *Cambridge Journal of Education* 32(1) pp. 219–32

Merali, Z., Blamire, R. *et al.* (1995) *Highways for Learning: An Introduction to the Internet for Schools and Colleges*, Coventry: NCET.

Newton, L. and Rogers, L. (2001) *Teaching Science with ICT*, London: Continuum.

Office of National Statistics (2009) *Internet Access Households and Individuals*, Cardiff: Office for National Statistics.

Osborne, J. and Hennessy, S. (2003) *Literature Review in Science Education and the Role of ICT: Promise, Problems and Future Directions*, FutureLab Report 6, Bristol: Futurelab.

Owen, M., Pritchard, J. and Rowlands, M. (1992) *Information Technology in Science*. Wales: MEU, Cymru. (A useful pack of ideas, information and case histories of IT use in science).

Regan, T. (2010) 'Embedding of ICT in the Learning and Teaching of Physics: What Teachers Say about the Use of Computers in Physics Lessons', *School Science Review*, 91 pp. 119–26.

Rogers, L. (1990) 'IT in science in the national curriculum', *Journal of Computer Assisted Learning*, no. 6, pp. 246–54.

Sanger, J. with Wilson, J., Davis, B. and Whittaker, R. (1997) *Young Children, Videos,and Computer Games*, London: Falmer Press.

Scaife, J. and Wellington, J.J. (1993) *IT in Science and Technology Education*. Buckingham: Open University Press.

Sewell, D. (1990) *New Tools For New Minds: A Cognitive Perspective on the Use of Computers with Young Children*, Hemel Hempstead: Harvester Wheatsheaf.

Turkle, S. (1984) *The Second Self: Computers and the Human Spirit*. London: Granada.

Underwood, J. and Underwood, G. (1990) *Computers and Learning*, Oxford: Basil Blackwell.

Weizenbaum, J. (1984) *Computer Power and Human Reason*, Harmondsworth: Penguin.

Wellington, J.J. (1985) *Children, Computers and the Curriculum*, London: Harper and Row.

Wellington, J.J. (1989) *Education for Employment: the place of information technology*, Windsor: NFER-Nelson.

Wellington, J.J. (1998) (ed.) *Practical Work in School Science: Which Way Now?*, London: Routledge, especially Chapters 14, 15 and 16.

Wellington, J.J. (2000) *Teaching and Learning Secondary Science: Contemporary Issues and Practical Approaches*, London: Routledge.

Useful sites for science

In science, there is now a wide range of sites in areas such as: the human body, space, mini-organisms, the periodic table, health, plants and biotechnology. The ASE journal, *School Science Review*, now has a regular section describing these sites and giving their addresses which is well worth looking out for.

The Science Museum also provides a rich source of educational materials for teachers at http://www.nmsi.ac.uk/education/stem.

One example of a site which meets curriculum requirements in several different areas is the Arthur C. Clarke website (www.acclarke.co.uk) which provides a comprehensive history of modern communications, computing and media, using text and images which are appropriate for Key Stages 3 and 4. In science, for example it covers large sections of the statements on electricity and magnetism and a good chunk on waves.

Worthy of a special mention is the Schools Online Project at http://sol.ultralab.anglia.ac.uk/pages/schools_online. This is a project with some excellent pages for science teachers, many containing good classroom ideas.

Other useful sites are:

ScI-Journal http://www.soton.ac.uk/~plf/ScI-Journal: an award-winning on-line publication. It gives science students the opportunity to publish their work so that other students around the world can read about it. Each edition consists of a number of science investigation reports written by students. They are mostly at KS4 level but cover a range of topics and approaches.

Pupil Researcher Initiative http://www.shu.ac.uk/schools/sci/pri/index.html

The ASE site http://www.ase.org.uk/

Finally a very special resource for teachers is:

Twidle, J., Childs, A., Dussart, M., Godwin, J. and Sorensen, P., (2005) 'Exploring the elements that make an effective web-based science lesson', British Education Communications and Technology Authority (BECTA) on behalf of the Department for Education and Skills.

Chapter 14

Exploring the nature of science

Conveying messages about the nature of science, and teaching about it directly, both present a challenge to science teachers. This chapter discusses what is meant by 'the nature of science' and presents strategies for, and classroom approaches to, teaching about the nature of science. Some of these involve using unplanned, spontaneous incidents in the classroom. Others involve planned learning and teaching. Many situations can involve the teacher in handling controversial issues in the classroom.

Exploring the nature of science cannot be divorced from *How Science Works*, see Chapter 9, indeed some authors may even put them together. We have separated them here in the hope it will generate a more reflective consideration on the part of the reader.

The 'nature of science' and the way it appears in the curriculum

Philosophers, historians and science educators have argued for decades on a definition of the nature of science (Lederman and Neiss 1997). Equally science educators have argued that the science curriculum in schools must address not only learning science, but also learning about the nature of science. The argument has been that it is not enough to simply 'know' science without understanding the 'how' and 'why' of theory, evidence and conclusion,

Driver *et al.* (1996) identify five rationales for teaching about the nature of science: a utilitarian argument, a democratic argument, a cultural argument, a moral argument and a science learning argument. Within these rationales we have the necessity of understanding the nature of science in order to make sense of socio-scientific issues (democratic argument) and to support successful learning in science (science learning argument). The form of these is addressed in Chapter 16, on citizenship and sustainability in science education, while the latter should be at the front of the reader's thinking. The need for an understanding of the nature of science is embedded in the science curriculum across the globe: in England and Wales, the nature of science is incorporated into the National Curriculum (NC) (Driver *et al.* 1996). Equally, the nature of science is a significant part of the US National Science Education Standards (NCR 1995) and appears as part of many state standards documents.

More recently the Science National Curriculum for England states that:

> Students should be taught: about the use of contemporary scientific and technological developments and their benefits, drawbacks and risks; to consider how and why decisions

about science and technology are made, including those that raise ethical issues, and about the social, economic and environmental effects of such decisions; how uncertainties in scientific knowledge and scientific ideas change over time and about the role of the scientific community in validating these changes.

(QCA 2006)

We agree that the nature of science should form part of any school-based science curriculum – hence the onus is on anyone preparing to teach secondary science to reflect on their own view of science first and to undertake their own study of the nature of science. So what is the nature of science and how might it be learnt and taught in the school science curriculum?

Some writers, for example Baker (2000), simply suggest that the nature of science is that set of characteristics which sets science apart from other modes of 'knowing', for example, instinct or faith. However others, for example Sagan (1987), suggest that science is different from other ways of knowing due to the discovery, modification and assimilation approach to the advancement of science; while Clough (2005) stresses the absence of dogma in science seeing it as an 'ongoing process of testing and evaluation' and Wuerston (2006) stresses the fact that science follows rules, but these rules are subject to revision following testing. For the purpose of what follows, we suggest that the nature of science can be taken to be 'a way of understanding natural phenomena which transcends the knowing of facts'.

Curriculum embodiments of the nature of science

In England, the National Curriculum sets out the following:

there are a number of *key concepts* that underpin the *study of science* and *how science works*. Pupils need to *understand* these concepts in order to *deepen and broaden* their knowledge, skills and understanding.

(QCA 2007 – our emphasis)

This apparently simple statement appears to embody the nature of science, especially when the National Curriculum document is explored further to reveal that the *key concepts* are listed as:

- Scientific thinking;
- Applications and implications of science;
- Cultural understanding;
- Collaboration.

(adapted from QCA 2007)

Given the potential complexity of the above, how can we approach teaching the nature of science in schools? First, we believe that new teachers need to learn and, where possible in their initial teacher education programme, be taught about the nature of science. Lipman *et al.* (1980) suggest that trainee teachers should 'be taught by the very same procedures as those they are expected to employ in the classroom'. Sorsby (2000) further suggests that: 'teaching and learning about the nature of science can be approached through philosophical contexts, especially using methodologies that involve argumentation'. Ratcliffe (1998) also stresses the use of argument and debate but offers the following advice: 'to ensure good practice in science lessons: clarify the purpose of the discussion; make the science base overt; emphasise the nature of the evidence;

use a framework for analysing discussion; value pupils' opinions; group pupils carefully; review the activity'.

In this chapter we offer an activity, followed by classroom strategies, which should enable teachers to reflect more deeply about the 'nature of science'; and we outline classroom activities which will help to develop teachers' own insights into how science works, again reflecting back on the material presented in Chapter 9.

Reflecting on your own view of the nature of science

We have seen some of the rationale given for why teaching about the nature of science is important. In this section, you will be asked to consider your own view of the nature of science. The following activity is taken from an article by Nott and Wellington (1993) in which they encouraged science teachers to explore their own understanding of the nature of science. Many of the terms used may be unfamiliar. In fact, many of these are problematic and a matter of debate.

Your nature of science profile

The aim of the activity that follows is to encourage readers to reflect upon their position. It is intended to be a way of getting you to think, learn and reflect rather than a valid measurement of your position on some sort of objective scale. So don't worry if, at the end of the activity, your profile is not as you expected. The thing to do then is to consider why – this is an important part of the process.

Please read each of these statements carefully. Give each one a number ranging from 'Strongly agree' (+5) to 'Strongly disagree' (−5) and place it next to the statement. A score of 0 will indicate a balanced view. For the moment, ignore the initials in brackets.

1. The results that pupils get from their experiments are as valid as anybody else's. (RP)
2. Science is essentially a masculine construct. (CD)
3. Science facts are what scientists agree that they are. (CD, RP)
4. The object of scientific activity is to reveal reality. (IR)
5. Scientists have no idea of the outcome of an experiment before they do it. (ID)
6. Scientific research is economically and politically determined. (CD)
7. Science education should be more about the learning of scientific processes than the learning of scientific facts. (PC)
8. The processes of science are divorced from moral and ethical considerations. (CD)
9. The most valuable part of a scientific education is what remains after the facts have been forgotten. (PC)
10. Scientific theories are valid if they work. (IR)
11. Science proceeds by drawing generalisable conclusions (which later become theories) from available data. (ID)
12. There is such a thing as a true scientific theory. (RP, IR)
13. Human emotion plays no part in the creation of scientific knowledge. (CD)
14. Scientific theories describe a real external world which is independent of human perception. (RP, IR)
15. A good solid grounding in basic scientific facts and inherited scientific knowledge is essential before young scientists can go on to make discoveries of their own. (PC)

16 Scientific theories have changed over time simply because experimental techniques have improved. (RP, CD)
17 'Scientific method' is transferable from one scientific investigation to another. (PC)
18 In practice, choices between competing theories are made purely on the basis of experimental results. (CD, RP)
19 Scientific theories are as much a result of imagination and intuition as inference from experimental results. (ID)
20 Scientific knowledge is different from other kinds of knowledge in that it has higher status. (RP)
21 There are certain physical events in the universe which science can never explain. (RP, IR)
22 Scientific knowledge is morally neutral – only the application of knowledge is ethically determined. (CD)
23 All scientific experiments and observations are determined by existing theories. (ID)
24 Science is essentially characterised by the methods and processes it uses. (PC)

Nature of science profile scoring instructions

Each statement has at least two letters in brackets after it – for example, PC; some have four – for example, RP, CD. Put your score for each question in the appropriate box(es) in Figure 14.1.

Some questions score twice. Some 'scores' must have their sign *reversed* before they can be used; this is indicated by a '–' next to the number, e.g. if your response to statement 1 is –3, then the score in the right-hand column on the RP box will be +3.

Add up the scores in the right-hand columns to give you a grand total for each grid. NB. Some statements score positive, some negative.

Transfer the marks from the columns to the position on each relevant axis in Figure 14.2. Join up the five marks. This is your profile at this moment.

RP		
Statement	Score	
1	(–)	
3	(–)	
21	(–)	
12	(+)	
14	(+)	
16	(+)	
18	(+)	
20	(+)	
Total		

ID		
Statement	Score	
5	(–)	
11	(–)	
19	(+)	
23	(+)	
Total		

CD		
Statement	Score	
2	(–)	
3	(–)	
6	(–)	
8	(–)	
13	(+)	
16	(+)	
18	(+)	
22	(+)	
Total		

PC		
Statement	Score	
7	(–)	
9	(–)	
17	(–)	
24	(+)	
15	(+)	
Total		

IR		
Statement	Score	
10	(–)	
21	(+)	
4	(+)	
12	(+)	
14	(+)	
Total		

Figure 14.1 Nature of science scoring grid

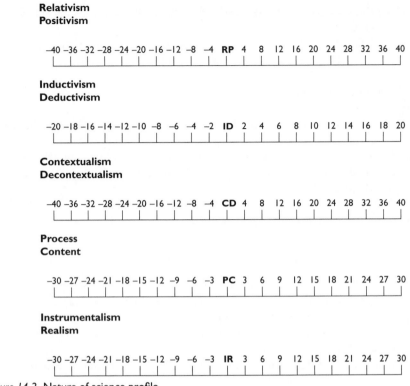

Figure 14.2 Nature of science profile

What does this all mean? Your nature of science

Are you a raving relativist? A proud positivist? Or a coy contextualist? What do all these terms mean anyway? Many of the terms used may be unfamiliar. In fact, many of them are problematic and a matter of debate. Their meanings change and shift and can be seen as insults or praise depending on whom you are talking to. Brief definitions for the meanings attached to the five axes are offered below.

Relativism/Positivism axis

Relativist: You deny that things are true or false solely based on an independent reality. The 'truth' of a theory will depend on the norms and rationality of the social group considering it as well as the experimental techniques used to test it. Judgements concerning the truth of scientific theories will vary from one individual to another and from one culture to another, i.e. truth is relative, not absolute.

Positivist: You believe strongly that scientific knowledge is more 'valid' than other forms of knowledge. The laws and theories generated by experiments are our descriptions of patterns we see in a real, external, objective world. To the positivist, science is the primary source of truth. Positivism recognises empirical facts and observable phenomena as the raw material of science. The scientist's job is to establish the objective relationships between the laws governing the facts and observables. Positivism rejects inquiry into underlying causes and ultimate origins.

Inductivism/Deductivism axis

Inductivist: You believe that the scientist's job is the interrogation of nature. By observing many particular instances, one is able to infer from the particular to the general and then determine the underlying laws and theories. According to inductivism, scientists generalise from a set of observations to a universal law 'inductively'. Scientific knowledge is built by induction from a secure set of observations.

Deductivist: In our definition this means that you believe that scientists proceed by testing ideas produced by the logical consequences of current theories or of their bold, imaginative ideas. According to deductivism (or hypothetico-deductivism), scientific reasoning consists of the forming of hypotheses which are not established by the empirical data but may be suggested by them. Science then proceeds by testing the observable consequences of these hypotheses, i.e. observations are directed or led by hypotheses – they are theory-laden.

Contextualism/Decontextualism axis

Contextualist: You hold the view that the truth of scientific knowledge and processes is interdependent with the culture in which the scientists live and in which it takes place.

Decontextualist: You hold the view that scientific knowledge is independent of its cultural location and sociological structure.

Process/Content axis

Process: You see science as a characteristic set of identifiable methods/processes. The learning of these is the essential part of science education.

Content: You think that science is characterised by the facts and ideas it has and that the essential part of science education is the acquisition and mastery of this 'body of knowledge'.

Instrumentalism/Realism axis

Instrumentalist: You believe that scientific theories and ideas are fine if they work, that is they allow correct predictions to be made. They are instruments that we can use but they say nothing about an independent reality or their own truth.

Realist: You believe that scientific theories are statements about a world that exists in space and time independent of the scientists' perceptions. Correct theories describe things that are really there, independent of scientists, such as atoms and electrons.

Points to reflect upon

Having had a chance to read the working definitions, consider the points below:

- How do you feel about your profile? Has it really 'measured' your views about science?
- Do you feel confident that you understand it all?
- Do you think your views/opinions have been challenged or changed by the exercise? Would you like to go back now and do it again?
- Would you like to try it out on your colleagues?

Whatever the shape of your profile, please do not worry and do not panic! There are many 'natures of science'.

Classroom strategies for the nature of science

School science in many countries is dominated by practical work. Although the value of this work has been questioned (see, for example, Hodson 1990; Wellington 1998), science teachers are used to organising demonstrations and practicals and to setting written work based on them and the theories they are meant to illustrate. However, the requirement that children learn about the 'nature of science' sets new challenges that some science teachers may not have tried: some may be willing to try, but some may be unwilling to recognise them as appropriate to science at all. Science teachers will need to organise and provide activities that include:

- structured discussion among small groups of children;
- structured reading or listening or watching of items that may involve some of the stories of science;
- drama and role play so that children can develop the qualities of sympathy and empathy with people in the past and from different cultures;
- experimental work where children have to engage with the models of science both to explain and predict.

This chapter will illustrate some of these strategies. First we consider incidents that arise spontaneously in science classrooms but which can all be used to convey messages about the nature of science.

Responding to 'critical incidents'

Lessons do not always go according to plan. The natural world, and the young people who inhabit it (pupils), do not always play ball. Over a number of years, Mick Nott and Jerry Wellington collected examples of critical classroom incidents that have either happened to us or that have been reported to us by experienced teachers. The list is long and still growing. Below we include a selection. They all force teachers into making on-the-spot decisions and often changing their plans. Teachers' responses to them, in the heat of the classroom, are often spontaneous. However, they are important in that the teachers' responses convey messages to pupils about the nature of science.

The selected incidents are divided up into those occurring during practical work, and those which raise moral questions or classroom discussion. Each incident evokes an on-the-spot decision which is informed by the teacher's views of the nature of science. The incidents below are critical because:

- they occur despite sound long-term planning;
- the way they are handled by the teacher can have a profound effect on pupils' views of science.

Please read each one carefully. For each one, think about: (i) what you *would* do in the heat of the classroom in responding to this incident; (ii) what you *could* do, e.g. given more time; (iii) what you *should* do, i.e. the moral course of action.

Practical incidents

A Heating magnesium

A class of 14–15-year-old pupils is heating magnesium ribbon in a crucible with a lid. The purpose of the lesson is to test the consequence of oxygen theory that materials gain mass when burnt.

At the summary at the end of the lesson four groups report a loss in mass, two groups report no difference and two groups report a gain in mass.

B Using microscopes

A class of 11–12-year-old pupils are working with microscopes and you want them to observe and draw onion skin cells. They set up the slides and you check that they have focused the microscopes competently and then they start to look and draw. You find their drawings to be nothing like your image of onion skin cells.

C Testing for photosynthesis

You have set up a demonstration of the production of oxygen by photosynthesis with Canadian pond-weed. Just before the lesson when the class are to look at the apparatus again, you notice that there is a small amount of gas in the test tube but not enough with which to do the oxygen test.

D Using circuit boards

Children are doing experiments with circuit boards. With two lamps in series, many find that one is brightly lit while the other appears to be unlit.

E Observing refraction

You are demonstrating wave phenomena using a ripple tank. The children are unable to observe refraction clearly, and frankly you find it hard to see with the apparatus available.

F Two more episodes from practical lessons

1   A teacher is doing the starch test on leaves. For inexplicable reasons the tests are indecisive.
2   A teacher is demonstrating the non-magnetic properties of iron sulphide. However, the freshly made sample sticks to the magnet.

In both instances, pupils say the following: 'But science experiments never work'; 'Anyway, we'll believe you. Tell us what should have happened.'

Non-practical critical incidents

G Explaining the universe

You are conducting a lesson on the big bang theory of the origin of the universe. A pupil at the front interrupts in the middle of your account of the big bang and says: 'My family believe that the Earth was created by God in six days. This is what it says in Genesis and we believe the Bible to be true.'

H Looking at life

You are well into a teaching unit on 'Life and Living Processes'. One of the pupils asks impatiently at the start of a lesson, 'When are we going to start cutting up rats then?'

I The unwilling chemist

You have a particularly reluctant learner in your chemistry class. The pupil is not aggressive but assertive, declaring that this work on chemistry is not something they like doing. When you ask why, the pupil says: 'Because if it hadn't been for chemists, we wouldn't have these chemicals ruining the Earth.'

J Contraception and Catholicism

You are teaching a group of 13–14-year-olds about contraception and the lesson is about different methods of birth control. One of the pupils asks: 'Do you believe it's right for the Catholic Church to say that only the rhythm method is acceptable? The rest are sinful?'

We have used these incidents with many groups of teachers, and asked them to respond by saying what they *would* do, *could* do and *should* do. The first question involves a kind of off-the-cuff, pragmatic reaction to the incident. The second involves a more divergent approach, as it asks what they could do if perhaps they had fewer constraints and more time to reflect. The third category of response leads into the area of what they really ought to do as science teachers (i.e. the moral area).

The incidents where laboratory activities 'go wrong' appear to elicit three categories of response. These are 'talking your way out of it', 'rigging' and 'conjuring' (Nott and Smith 1995). The majority of responses are in the first category of 'talking your way out of it' or, as we would like to say more positively 'talking your way through it'; when science teachers talk their way through practicals that have gone wrong they often engage the children in a critical evaluation of practical work. 'Rigging' is the use of strategies that teachers have learned over the years to ensure that the apparatus or procedure works. The last category, 'conjuring', is where the teacher fraudulently produces the correct result for an experiment by sleight of hand.

The 'conjuring' category, we must stress, is by far the smallest. But we have had the following responses from experienced teachers:

- 'I put my thumb on the scales to ensure that there is a gain in weight' (example A).
- '... spike it and it always works' (example C).
- '... cheat, use oxygen from a cylinder' (example C).

There appears to be a small set of experiments in the science repertoire that are *regularly* conjured. The pond-weed incident is a case in point: children are *not* told about how the result was produced. We have found that student teachers can start to conjure spontaneously or are inducted into it by science staff and technicians. We suggest that conjuring is a practice that student teachers should discuss and challenge (Nott and Wellington 1997). Others say that they resort to 'rigging' or 'tweaking' practicals, i.e. carefully adjusting the variables to achieve the 'correct result', e.g. in the pond-weed example teachers might dope the water with 'sodium bicarbonate' or use strong growlights.

But the majority of responses are in the category of 'talking your way through it'. The examples given below are all statements that teachers have actually made. We do not offer them all as examples of good practice, merely as illustrations of what often occurs. When science teachers talk their way through practicals that are going wrong they often engage the children in a critical evaluation of science practical work and therefore teach them about the nature of science.

- 'Blame the fact that the light bulbs aren't identical' (example D).
- 'Check the weighing procedures with the magnesium ribbon' (example A).
- 'Assume the experiment with pond-weed has been done wrongly' (example C).

But the talking can also involve explanations and interpretations of the reliability and replicability of practicals and the way that practical results are negotiated, as the following responses show:

- (With the magnesium strip) 'Stress the need to repeat experiments' (example A).
- (With the onion skin slide) 'Get the children to agree by consensus about what they see' (example B).
- 'Get them to see that negative results can be useful and significant' (example D).
- 'Get the class to discuss why it could have gone wrong with the magnesium ribbon' (example A).
- 'Analyse and average the results – perhaps average the data' (examples A and D).
- (With the onion skin slide) 'Show them a drawing of a slide and ask them if they can see something like that' (example B).
- '[I] would have to tell them the expected outcome otherwise they wouldn't learn anything [but] say if it's wrong for a reason.'

It is easy to be critical of science teachers who conjure experiments. But how many of us can honestly say we are totally innocent? The constraints of classroom life and the pressure of examinations force teachers into planning, tweaking, rigging or even conjuring practical work so that pupils are not confused by it and that they learn the 'right answer'.

However, it is only by 'talking their way through it' that teachers can use critical incidents of this kind to teach pupils about the nature of science. By discussing the incidents, teachers are conveying messages about real science, i.e. it is an activity:

- where practicals need to be evaluated and this involves repeating experiments;
- where the null result is as important as the positive result;
- that involves sharing results and collectively criticising, negotiating and deciding procedures;
- in which, to learn from and to do practicals, you need to have an idea in your head before you start;
- in which there are reasons why experiments go wrong, and that there is always a rational explanation;
- in which results need to match previously accepted knowledge.

The magnesium ribbon and pond-weed examples can illustrate the procedures that scientists use to check experimental results and show that experiments are as much the result of the experimenters' skills as they are a mirror of nature. The onion skin cells and ripple tank examples can show that the work of scientists is guided by other scientists' images and pictures of what is to be perceived – all observations are theory-laden and newcomers have to be trained to see in the ways of more experienced scientists.

Responding to non-practical critical incidents

In this way, events and demonstrations that don't always go according to plan can be used to illustrate the nature of science. Such critical incidents can be used to positive effect if teachers are alert and ready for them. In this way, much teaching about the nature of science can occur unexpectedly and spontaneously – as opposed to the planned teaching activities presented later.

What of the non-practical critical incidents shown earlier? They present teachers with equally difficult on-the-spot decisions – and they raise equally important questions about the nature of science and scientific activity. Students need to learn that scientists and scientific ideas are strongly influenced by the social, moral, spiritual and cultural contexts in which they live and work. Critical incidents such as examples G–J raise questions about the context of science and the controversies it provokes. In a crowded lesson, teachers rarely have the time to respond fully – hence the need for planned lessons on controversial issues, which is discussed in the next section. But groups of teachers we have discussed the incidents with have suggested possible strategies.

In response to the rat incident, one teacher said that she would point out that biology is the study of living things, not dead things, and would perhaps use the incident to prompt or plan a future class debate about the morality of dissection, and perhaps broaden it to discuss animal experimentation.

The big bang incident always prompts a lot of discussion, as does the connection between 'creationism' (or sometimes, 'intelligent design') and evolution. Several teachers said, in their responses, that the big bang theory should be presented as the 'accepted scientific explanation' but not the only possible explanation: 'It is a theory, not a fact.' Another tactic was to argue that: 'religious beliefs are religious beliefs, but scientists have theories which *explain* [the teacher's emphasis]: scientists have theories which are based on evidence'. Another response was that: 'theories change with time – they are not held on to for all time'. Thus the main thrust of this response is that religious beliefs are totally different from scientific theories, and that presumably they can exist alongside one another. Scientific knowledge is a way of explaining, but it is not the *only* way of explaining.

The student with 'an attitude' to chemistry elicited responses from teachers that promoted the benefits of chemistry to health and well-being, but there was also talk about scientists not always being in control of the products they create. Perhaps we should also convey the message that the application of knowledge is not the sole responsibility of scientists.

Increasingly, science teachers will be faced with controversial issues which arise spontaneously – one way of preparing themselves (and their pupils) for this is to plan and teach lessons which present a controversial issue and also teach some science content at the same time.

Handling controversial issues

Controversial issues, i.e. those for which there is no clear answer because they involve viewpoints and opinions, not just 'facts', will often appear spontaneously in science classrooms. In addition, by deliberately introducing and carefully handling controversial issues in the classroom, science teachers can motivate pupils and also portray many aspects of the nature of science.

Why include them?

There are at least three good reasons for including controversial issues in teaching and learning science:

1 They are a way of making 'content' more interesting, meaningful, exciting and relevant, i.e. engaging and motivating pupils.
2 They are a way of portraying the true nature of science, i.e. as an activity which is *not always* exact, clear, certain and unproblematic. Indeed, *not* to include controversial issues in the science curriculum would be a serious misrepresentation of the subject (see Wellington 1986a and Millar 1996) and lead to public misunderstanding of science.
3 Students can acquire important attitudes, *skills* and understanding of processes by examining controversial issues related to science.

Students can learn to weigh up evidence, to search for information, to detect bias, to question the validity of sources and to present their own considered viewpoint. The skills of communication, listening, working collaboratively and cooperating in group sessions can all be enhanced.

What are controversial issues?

Many aspects of science are not tentative or controversial. We would wager that in 50 years' time Newton's second law will still apply on Earth, metals will expand when heated, photosynthesis will still occur in the same way and caesium will react violently with water. Issues become controversial when there is either:

a) considerable scientific debate or disagreement about causes, theories and evidence, e.g. as in the case of cold fusion, BSE or GM foods;
b) debate and disagreement about the applications of science and its effects on the environment, on people or on animals, e.g. the use of nuclear energy and nuclear weapons; animal experimentation; cloning of animals or humans; the spread of GM foods.

Some issues in science are controversial for both the above reasons, i.e. both the science and its applications are controversial. These are perhaps the issues best suited to inclusion in the science curriculum.

Many current controversial issues, and several which have a longer shelf-life, relate closely to the knowledge and content of the science curriculum. For example:

* contraception
* creationism
* intelligent design
* religious beliefs
* food and diet
* pollution
* energy supplies
* the origin of the universe
* evolution
* the origin of life

- the paranormal
- smoking, alcohol and other drugs
- farming methods
- genetic engineering
- sex and reproduction.

All are subject to a lack of certainty (in both scientists and the public); a range of different views; different perspectives and responses according to a person's spiritual, moral or cultural standpoint.

The teacher's role

Traditionally, the science teacher has dealt with the 'facts' and left 'values' to the humanities staff. That approach will not do in the twenty-first century even if it ever did hold water. Many scientific issues now involve a complex mixture of facts, values, value-laden facts, and values dependent on people's perceptions of the 'facts'.

The science teacher's job is a difficult one. A teacher will be able to settle disputes on some factual points involved in controversial issues. For example, in a discussion on nuclear energy, a teacher can usefully correct the mistaken belief that a nuclear reactor could explode like an atomic bomb in the event of an accident. But should the teacher act as 'an authority' in settling matters of *value*? Clearly, a teacher who did so would not be acting objectively, neutrally or in a balanced way.

There is a legal requirement in some countries (including the UK) that teachers should present a balanced view when dealing with controversial issues. But how does this work in practice? Should the case *for* smoking be presented alongside the anti-smoking arguments? Should teachers balance the evidence against illegal drugs with the evidence for their benefits?

Most teachers are, quite justifiably, wary of exposing their own personal views and values to a classroom full of young people. They are often safer in adopting one or more of the following rules:

- *devil's advocate*: confronting individuals or groups by adopting (tongue-in-cheek) the opposite viewpoint;
- *the neutral chair*: ensuring that all views and values are given an 'equal airing', whilst not disclosing their own values;
- *the advocate role*: presenting all of the available viewpoints as objectively as possible, then concluding by stating his/her position.

The latter role is probably least safe, though it may be seen as safer than openly declaring a position at the outset or (more extremely) propagating a particular view on (say) drugs, contraception, food or nuclear energy (the various roles are presented in Plant and Firth 1995: 42).

However, it is often essential for a teacher to play some sort of advocate role, especially if (as is often the case in classroom discussion):

a) there is no divergence of view among participants, or the divergence is not equally distributed; or
b) some important viewpoints are not expressed at all.

Our own view is that teachers should challenge and confront different viewpoints, perhaps as a kind of devil's advocate, but they are on dangerous ground if they use the classroom as a platform from which to promulgate and promote their own personal views. Fortunately, there are accepted teaching strategies which can be used.

Practical classroom strategies for controversial issues

Obviously, discussion is likely to be the dominant approach rather than didactic teaching. However, simply asking, or expecting, students to read material on a controversial issue, and then discuss it, may not be appropriate in many classes. More active learning and involvement is often needed. The following activities offer a range of alternatives.

Brainstorming

Brainstorming is useful for starting open thinking on a new topic. This is likely to work best in a small group. It is an effective way of gathering people's ideas, associations and impressions of almost any topic. It will be most illuminating before discussion or teaching has begun. An open, non-evaluative session of this kind can form an excellent starting point for three main reasons:

• Interest and awareness are aroused.
• The teacher is provided with useful information on the views and prior knowledge of the students.
• People learn the attitudes and impressions of others in an enjoyable and non-argumentative way.

With larger or less manageable groups, individuals can be asked to write down the first three words or ideas that come into their mind in response to a given word; this can be done individually or in small groups. The responses can be collected and made into a large chart for display. Brainstorming is not a new idea and it may not work well for every teacher with all classes, but it is a good way of making an unbiased, open-minded start to a topic.

Another way of arousing interest is to ask members of a group to interview each other. This can be done in small groups or pairs. Interviewers can ask about peers' views, attitudes and opinions; about anxieties or worries; or even about their existing knowledge of a subject. Results can remain anonymous, and may prove as interesting to the teacher as to the group members themselves. The results may be collected and displayed. Teachers may wish to devise their own interviews to suit particular classes or, better still, ask the students to make up their own interviews to try out on the others. Questionnaires can also be used to raise consciousness and explore areas similar to those described for interviewing.

The questionnaires can be handed out to each student in the class, and once they are complete the results can be collated to form a 'class profile'. Histograms or pie-charts can be designed to display people's opinions and attitudes visually. Simple computer databases are ideal for collating and displaying results.

Examining pictorial material

Photographs, illustrations or projected slides can all be used as alternatives to written material for generating discussion and presenting evidence. Photographs, newspaper cartoons or topical pictures can be used to start a discussion or instigate written work.

To start discussion the teacher can:

- invite general comments from anyone in the group;
- focus on particular aspects of a picture, e.g. people's expressions, the likely time of the photograph, size and scale;
- ask for impressions or associations conjured up by the picture (rather like brainstorming);
- invite speculation on why the picture was made: What point it is trying to make? Why was a cartoon drawn?;
- invite discussion on what individuals might be saying or thinking.

Similar ploys can be used to promote written work. Students can be asked to write down three words or ideas which spring to mind when they see a picture, alternatively, students can write down what the characters in a picture might be saying, perhaps incorporating this into a comic strip. The suggested speeches can be compared and discussed. These, and other ploys, are all valuable starting points for using pictorial material to stimulate discussion and written work. Strategies for developing literacy in science are explored in Chapter 11.

Role play and simulation

Controversial issues are ideally suited to role play and simulation. The actual classroom practice will depend on the style, inventiveness and imagination of the teacher.

Active reading and writing techniques can also help students come to terms with the wide range of information presented in connection with controversial issues, see DART activities in Chapter 11. One activity to encourage reading and writing is to examine media coverage and controversial issues from different sources, e.g. the internet, newspapers, leaflets from pressure groups. Wall displays and collages could be made showing both the quantity and quality of newspaper coverage, and in some cases those of magazine articles. Different newspapers could be compared. If possible, old newspapers, or copies of parts of them, could be used to show coverage of present and past incidents.

All the activities described here are fairly simple, and can easily be adopted and adapted by class teachers for their own use. The value in many of the activities suggested is that the existing knowledge and prior attitudes of the group can be revealed, sometimes anonymously. This feedback is as essential to a teacher dealing with a contentious issue as it is in teaching other aspects of the curriculum, e.g. scientific concepts. In short, the teacher can start from where students are, both in their previous information and existing attitudes and use active learning strategies to go forward effectively and sensitively. Neither the teacher, nor any individual pupil in the class, need have their personal viewpoints or beliefs crudely exposed.

By introducing and carefully handling controversial issues in the classroom, science teachers can not only engage and motivate pupils, but also portray many aspects of the nature of 'real science'. They can also develop important critical skills and attitudes such as a healthy scepticism towards information and where it comes from. The next section describes a teaching approach which can be used to illustrate further aspects of the nature of science.

A case study – discussion work and role play: the story of Edward Jenner

The case study below concerns some curriculum materials called 'Jabs for James Phipps', which were first published in Solomon (1991). The specific topic is the story of Edward Jenner's work on vaccination. Teachers have slotted the materials in with units on topics such as microbiology or health.

A series of programmes was produced for schools called *Scientific Eye* (Yorkshire Television 1984). One particular programme, called 'Minibeasts and Disease', is a short, approximately five minutes, cartoon of the story of Edward Jenner and the famous vaccination of the small boy called James Phipps. The style is 'jokey', but this does not detract from the fact that the main points of this scientific episode are raised. The experimental procedure is described in a clear chronological order. A rationale is also provided for Jenner's actions. The cartoon suggests with its imagery that James was not necessarily a willing volunteer to an 'untested' procedure. This perhaps unintentionally raises ethical issues about this work. So here is a resource, common to many schools, which contains information about the introduction of a new idea, clearly describes the experiment and raises ethical and moral issues surrounding the procedure. It forms an ideal stimulus for some classroom activities about the nature of science.

The structure of the materials

The materials consist of the following:

Telling a story

The first part is an activity to process the information in the cartoon story in the video. The children are split into groups of approximately four. Each group is given an envelope with jumbled chunks of text that describe the story. The group task is to put the chunks of text in the right chronological sequence. (See Figure 14.3 for the ten chunks of text.) This could equally well be done as a 'drag and drop' activity using the interactive whiteboard or individually using a laptop or tablet.

If some blanks are included in the envelopes then the children can add any bits of information that they think are important. The children can take part in the 'ordering' and the telling of the story. When the pieces of paper are in the right order they can then be stuck onto a large piece of paper to make an 'instant' poster detailing the events of the story in the correct temporal sequence.

The purpose of this activity is to provide an alternative way of processing the information in the cartoon – in other words, to retell the story in a different manner. If done in mixed-ability groups it provides an opportunity for all children to contribute to the telling of the story.

Evaluating an experiment

The second part of the activity is to then open a second envelope containing pieces of paper with the phrases 'making a hypothesis', 'observing', 'prediction', 'reaching a conclusion' and 'doing an experiment', see Figure 14.4.

The children's task is then to match these words to the places where they think they occur in the story of Jenner's experiment that they have just put on the poster.

The purpose of this second activity is to help children to analyse the structure of the experiment. Teachers who have used these materials agree that the evaluation of Jenner's experiment happens, but it has also been reported that the analysis of the structure of the experiment has transferability across to other scientific investigations. The following is an extract from an interview with a teacher:

Jenner's experiment

Jenner puts cowpox pus into James' arm

Jenner sees that James doesn't get smallpox

JENNER HEARS THAT THE MILKMAIDS DON'T GET SMALLPOX

Jenner decides that having cowpox stops you getting smallpox

Jenner sees that James suffers from cowpox for a few days and then gets well

JENNER TAKES SOME PUS FROM A SMALLPOX VICTIM AND PUTS IT INTO JAMES'S ARM

Jenner thinks that if he gives someone cowpox first they won't get smallpox

JENNER HEARS THAT MILKMAIDS OFTEN GET COWPOX

JENNER TAKES COWPOX PUS FROM A MILKMAID

**Jenner thinks that having cowpox
might stop you getting smallpox**

Figure 14.3 Statements for Jenner's experiment

The amazing thing for me came in the next module along when the kids ... were planning an investigation ... One girl came back, she had a series of flow diagrams ... she had written on little boxes 'hypothesising here', 'testing here' and 'observing here' and I said, 'Where did you get all this from then?' She said she remembered it from the last unit that we did on the Jenner story. I went and had a chat with some of the other kids, and they had actually transferred the skills and ideas from ['Jabs for James Phipps'] to another [module], which to me is fairly successful ...

(Nott 1992: 222)

OBSERVING

Meaning: **To watch carefully what is happening.**

(As well as using your eyes you can observe by listening, smelling, touching and occasionally tasting.)

MAKING A HYPOTHESIS

Meaning: **To have an idea about why something happens.**

(You can use this idea to design experiments.)

DOING AN EXPERIMENT

Meaning: **When you design and carry out a test for your hypothesis.**

PREDICTION

Saying what you think is going to happen.

REACHING A CONCLUSION

Deciding what your experiment shows.

(You might be deciding if your hypothesis is right or wrong.)

Figure 14.4 Process words

It appears that the children, having analysed (and criticised) the structure of experimental work as exemplified in the Jenner story, learned something about the structure of experiments. That learning had then been transferred to the planning of their own benchwork experiments. It may be that learning 'processes' through stories is as important as learning them by doing experiments. The processes of experimental planning could be seen as the identical processes in the Jenner story.

Values and experiments

Lastly, the children can be invited to discuss whether they think Jenner's experiment was a 'fair test'. They can suggest improvements to Jenner's experimental design. They can be asked to discuss whether all improvements would be right and proper in terms of whether they would be allowed to do them, or whether they felt it would be right to do them.

The purpose of this activity is to encourage the children to evaluate the experiment and hence to consider whether there are any ethical and moral limits on the nature of the experiment and hence medical experiments in general.

Role play

When children watch the cartoon they do so with interest and feeling. The cartoon implies that the procedure involved some risk and possible hurt to James. This is done in a way that is amusing, albeit darkly amusing. The materials contain a role-play activity so that children can sympathise and empathise with the characters in the Jenner story.

The characters are the obvious characters in the cartoon – Jenner, James Phipps and Sarah Nelmes, the milkmaid. However, 'new' characters are also added. These are Mr and Mrs Phipps and James's aunt and uncle. These last two characters are fictitious; they are presented as two people who had James's interests at heart, and their views are constructed to represent contemporary arguments for and against Jenner's work.

A role card is available for each character, and questions at the end stimulate discussion among the children and make them start to build a character on the information they have, see Figure 14.5 for examples. A class can be split into small groups so that the roles can be built in groups and then one child from each group can act out the role – and even be prompted by her or his colleagues. A concise background to the organisation of role play in science is contained in Williams *et al.* (1992).

The pupils should spend time (approximately 15 minutes) 'getting into role' in groups. Then one child from each group can play the part of the character. The scenario suggested in the published materials is a press conference where those not playing a role can act as journalists. This format has been seen to work extremely well – children are familiar with press conferences from the news. It should also be noted that a press conference is an anachronism but the point is to play a role where feelings and values can be explored, not to play a drama that looks for historical authenticity.

Press conferences observed have covered a range of issues that the role cards raise, such as:

- fatalism, i.e. if God chose you to get smallpox then that was your fate versus the motivation of Jenner that God would be benign and want people to be saved;
- authority of experts on the risks of the experiment versus the risk of catching smallpox;
- the ethics of the experiment, including issues of experiments on animals;
- the influence of the employer–employee relationship between Jenner and the Phipps's household;
- the uncertainty whether the cowpox 'agent' would mutate into something more virulent inside James.

The materials can stimulate a broad coverage and, in some cases, expression of some subtle ideas. Teachers have been inventive and creative with it as well. One teacher reported creating

James

You are eight and three-quarters years old and love fishing. You have gone to Sunday school a few times but you usually manage to escape and go down to the river. You don't want to learn to read. You don't want to start work either, but you know you will have to as soon as you are nine.

When you were little you fell out of a tree and broke your leg. Your father got Dr Jenner to set the broken bone and it hurt very badly. You have always been scared of Dr Jenner from that time. Once he gave you a medicine to cure your fever which was made from bitter aloes. You couldn't get the taste out of your mouth for a week afterwards.

You don't know much about smallpox except that your aunt had it. Now her face looks horrible with large deep pits all over it. You cannot bear to kiss her.

Now decide:

Did you understand what Dr Jenner was going to do?
How would you feel about asking the doctor questions?
Now that you are safe from having smallpox would you advise friends to have the vaccination too?

James's Mum

You did not go to school but have worked with your husband in the fields for many years. Now that he is gardener to Dr Jenner things are much easier.

You have had nine children but two of them died when they were only babies. You have never forgotten that. Dr Jenner did come and give the babies some medicine but it did not help them. He was not able to help your sister either when she died in childbirth.

James is your youngest and you know you spoil him a little, but you can't help it. He is always out fishing when your husband wants him to help in the garden. A month ago your husband suggested that James should be given smallpox now to prevent him from getting it later. That seemed terribly dangerous. You didn't sleep for a whole week worrying about it.

Now decide:

How do you feel about doctors?
What did you think when Dr Jenner explained what he was going to do to James?
Did you talk it over with your husband? If so, what did you say to him?

Figure 14.5 Example role play cards

the scenario for the role play as 'the Phipps' family tea' – a familiar occurrence for children to use; and some children have worked the story up into 'the Jenner rap' (Nott 1992), and even a ballet!

The evidence appears to be that teachers have found this work to be very valuable both in exploring moral and ethical issues and in reprocessing the story and procedures of the experiment itself.

These materials deal only with a very narrow case, i.e. the experiment on James Phipps by Edward Jenner. It is important to add that the textbook impressions that it was solely Jenner who invented a safe technique of immunisation are wrong (see Smith 1987). The story of immunisation in England is one that involves other cultures and a determined woman, Lady Mary Wortley Montague (Alic 1986). There is also available some excellent classroom material, 'The long war against smallpox' (Science Education Group 1990), which adds to the historical dimension of the materials above and introduces the multicultural dimension. Both teachers and children learn about the nature of science from this.

In summary ... the nature of science and science as story-telling

This chapter has aimed to provide examples of classroom strategies that allow teachers and children to explore and investigate the nature of science in their classrooms. The intention has been to provide enough detail and information so that the reader can experiment with a range of teaching strategies that teach children science and the nature of science.

The above case is based on using a story of a scientist. How many stories of scientists does one need to know? The answer is: not many. A teacher only needs a small range of stories to convey the key ideas of the nature of science to children. Not every lesson is going to be, nor needs to be, based on historical information. An expectation that science teachers will be fully conversant with an accurate sociology, history and philosophy of science is unrealistic. The classroom resources cited and given in further reading below will provide any teacher with a good half-dozen ideas and stories to get going.

It is important to have some stories and to recognise that stories are an important part of the culture of science. As Peter Medawar said: 'Scientific theories are the stories that scientists tell each other.'

Points for reflection

- What do you feel should be the teacher's role when dealing with controversial issues (either pre-planned or spontaneous) in the classroom? Should a teacher ever divulge her/his views on a controversial issue? As examples, consider these: sexual behaviour; homosexuality; drug use; global warming; drinking alcoholic beverages; evolution; creationism and intelligent design; euthanasia; eating meat.
- How important do you think your own view of the nature of science is when teaching science?

References and further reading

Nature of science in the curriculum

Monk, Martin (2006) 'How science works: what do we do now?', *School Science Review*, vol. 88, no. 322, pp. 119–21; describes some valuable teaching strategies that can help teachers to deal with the section of the science national curriculum labelled *How Science Works*. This area of the curriculum will 'rely heavily' on teachers' own views of the nature of science, thus placing demands on teachers to reflect on it and read in this area.

Osborne, Jonathan and Ratcliffe, Mary (2002) 'Developing effective methods of assessing ideas and evidence', *School Science Review*, vol. 83, no. 305, pp. 113–24; suggests ways of assessing pupils' learning in *Ideas and Evidence* ('the processes and practices of science') and discusses how this may influence teaching in this area.

Rowcliffe, Stephen (2004) 'Story telling in science', *School Science Review*, vol. 86, no. 314, pp. 121–6; gives a good justification for using stories in science classes, not least to promote 'emotional involvement' in learning science; suggests practical ways of bringing stories into lessons and gives a guide to several sources of good stories.

Talbot, Chris (2000) 'Ideas and evidence in science', *School Science Review*, vol. 82, no. 298, pp. 13–22; discusses ways in which historical studies can be used to teach about ideas and evidence in the science curriculum and for the International Baccalaureate, using a range of examples such as atomic theory, the periodic table, N-rays, phlogiston and caloric theory.

Ideas and evidence: the June 2006 issue of *School Science Review* is devoted to discussions of 'ideas and evidence' in science learning and teaching, and its place in the national curriculum.

Main references

ACCAC (2000) *Science in the National Curriculum in Wales*. Accessed March 2006, at www.accac.org.uk/uploads/documents/23.pdf.

Baker, P. (2000) *Teaching Evolution Through Enquiry*. Accessed 12 April 2007, at www. nap.edu/readingroom/books/evolution98/contents.html.

Clough, M. (2005) *Teaching the Nature of Science to Secondary and Post-secondary Students*. Accessed 12 April 2007 at www.pantanteo.co.uk/issue25/clough.htm.

DfES (2004) *The Science National Curriculum for England*, London: DfES/QCA.

Driver, R., Leach, J., Millar, R. and Scott, P. (1996) *Young People's Images of Science*, Buckingham: Open University Press.

Lederman, N.G. and Neiss, M.L. (1997) 'The nature of science: naturally?', *School Science and Mathematics*, vol. 97, no. 1, pp. 1–2.

Lipman, M., Sharp, M. and Oscanyan, F. (1980) *Philosophy in the Classroom*, Philadelphia: Temple University Press.

Monk, M. and Dillon, J. (2000) 'The Nature of Scientific Knowledge', in Monk, M. and Osborne, J. (eds) *Good Practice in Science Teaching*, Buckingham: Open University Press, pp. 78–81.

NCR (1995) *US National Science Education Standards*. Accessed March 2006 at http://newton.nap.edu/html/nses/.

Nott, M. (1992) 'History in the school science curriculum: infection or immunity', *Proceedings of the Second International Conference on the History and Philosophy of Science Teaching*, Ontario: Queen's University.

Nott, M. and Wellington, J. (1993) 'Your nature of science profile: an activity for science teachers', *School Science Review*, vol. 75, no. 270, pp. 109–12.

QCA (2006) *Science Programme of Study*. Accessed March 2006 at www.qca.org.uk/downloads/10340_science_prog_of_study_from_2006_ks4.pdf.

QCA (2007) *The National Curriculum*, London: QCA.

Ratcliffe, M. (ed.) (1998) *ASE Guide to Secondary Science Education*, London: Stanley Thornes.

Sagan, C. (1987) 'The fine art of baloney detection', *Parade Magazine*, p. 1213.

Sorsby, B. (2000) 'The irresistible rise of the nature of science in science curricula', in J. Sears and P. Sorensen (eds) *Issues in Science Teaching*, London: RoutledgeFalmer, pp. 23–30.

Wellington, J. (ed.) (1998) *Practical Work in Science: which way now?*, London: Routledge.

Wuerston, E. (2006) *Teaching Evolution in Washington Schools*. Accessed 12 April 2007 at www.k12.wa.us/curriculuminstruct/science/Presentations/2.

General reading

Alic, M. (1986) *Hypatia's Heritage*, London: Women's Press.

Barlex, D. and Carré, C. (1985) *Visual Communication in Science*, Cambridge: Cambridge University Press.

Barrow, J. (1998) *The World Within the World*, Oxford: Oxford University Press.

Bentley, D. and Watts, M. (1988) *Teaching Science: Practical Alternatives*, Milton Keynes: Open University Press.

Brush, S. (1974) 'Should the history of science be rated X?', *Science*, 183: pp. 1166–72.

Chalmers, A. (1976) *What is This Thing Called Science?*, Buckingham: Open University Press.

Children's Learning in Science Project (CLISP) (1987) *CLIS in the Classroom: approaches to teaching*, Leeds: CSSME, University of Leeds.

Driver, R., Guesne, E. and Tiberghien, A. (1985) *Children's Ideas in Science*, Milton Keynes: Open University Press.

Futtock, K. (1991) *Louis Pasteur*, Nature of Science series, Hatfield: ASE.

Harrison, A.G. (2002) 'John Dalton's atomic theory: using the history and nature of science to teach particle concepts', paper presented at the Annual Meeting of Australian Association for Research in Education, Brisbane, 2–5 December 2002, available at: www.aare.edu.au/02pap/har02049.htm.

Hesse, M. (1973) 'Models of theory change', in Hesse, M. (1980) *Revolutions and Reconstructions in the Philosophy of Science*, Brighton: Harvester Press.

Hodson, D. (1990) 'A critical look at practical work in school science', *School Science Review*, March 1990, no. 71, p. 256.

Hunt, A. (1997) *The World of Science: New SATIS 14–16*, London: John Murray.

Millar, R. and Osborne, J. (1998) *Beyond 2000: science education for the future*, London: King's College.

Nott, M. and Wellington, J. (1997) 'Producing the evidence: science teachers' initiations into practical work', *Research in Science Education*, 27(3), 395–409.

Okasha, S. (2002) *The Philosophy of Science: a very short introduction*, Oxford: Oxford University Press.

Pedoe, D. (1976) *Geometry and the Liberal Arts*, London: Penguin.

Ratcliffe, M. and Grace, M. (2003) *Science Education for Citizenship: teaching socioscientific issues*, Maidenhead: Open University Press.

Rowland, M. (1991) 'The great Brownian motion swindle', *New Scientist*, 3 April 1991, p. 49.

Science Education Group, University of York (1990) *Science: The Salters' Approach. Key Stage 4. Unit Guide: keeping healthy*, London: Heinemann.

Shortland, M. and Warwick, A. (1989) *Teaching the History of Science*, London: BSHS/Blackwell.

Smith, J.R. (1987) *The Speckled Monster*, Chelmsford: Essex Record Office.

Solomon, J. (1991) *Exploring the Nature of Science*, Glasgow: Blackie.

Solomon, J. (1993) *Teaching Science, Technology and Society*, Buckingham: Open University Press.

Solomon, J., Hunt, A., Johnson, K. and Nott, M. (1989) *Teaching about the Nature of Science*, Hatfield: ASE.

Williams, S., Hudson, T. and Green, D. (eds) (1992) *Active Teaching and Learning Approaches in Science*, London: Collins Educational.

Yorkshire Television (1984) *Scientific Eye*, Leeds: YTV.

Critical incidents

Nott, M. and Smith, R. (1995) '"Talking your way out of it", "rigging" and "conjuring": what science teachers do when practicals "go wrong"', *International Journal of Science Education*, no. 17, pp. 399–410.

Nott, M. and Wellington, J. (1995) 'Critical incidents in the science classroom and the nature of science', *School Science Review*, no. 76, pp. 41–6.

Nott, M. and Wellington, J. (1996) 'Probing teachers' views of the nature of science: how should we do it and where should we be looking?', in Welford, G., Osborne, J. and Scott, P. (eds) *Science Education Research in Europe*, London: Falmer Press, pp. 283–94.

Handling controversial issues

Claxton, G. (1991) *Educating the Inquiring Mind: the challenge for school science*, London: Harvester Wheatsheaf.

Lock, R. and Ratcliffe, M. (1998) 'Learning about social and ethical applications of science', in Ratcliffe, M. (ed.) *ASE Guide to Secondary Education*, Hatfield: ASE/Stanley Thornes, pp. 109–17.

Millar, R. (1996) 'Towards a science curriculum for public understanding', *School Science Review*, vol. 77, no. 280, pp. 7–18.

Plant, M. and Firth, R. (1995) *Teaching Through Controversial Issues*, Nottingham: Nottingham Trent University.

Ratcliffe, M. and Fullick, P. (1996) (eds) *Teaching Ethical Aspects of Science*, Southampton: Bassett Press.

Ratcliffe, M. and Grace, M. (2003) *Science Education for Citizenship: teaching socioscientific issues*, Maidenhead: Open University Press.

Sheffield City Polytechnic (1992) *Active Teaching and Learning Approaches in Science*, London: Collins Educational (now Sheffield Hallam University).

Solomon, J. (1998) 'About argument and discussion', *School Science Review*, vol. 80, no. 291, pp. 57–62.

Stradling, R., Noctor, M. and Baines, B. (1984) *Teaching Controversial Issues*, London: Edward Arnold.

Wellington, J.J. (1986a) *Controversial Issues in the Curriculum*, Oxford: Basil Blackwell.

Wellington, J.J. (1986b) *The Nuclear Issue*, Oxford: Basil Blackwell.

Chapter 15

Using out-of-school sources

Many people equate learning in science with the formal science curriculum. Yet much, if not most, of children's learning about science takes place outside the confines of a timetable and a school. There is a mound of evidence to show that this 'informal' learning is both powerful and tightly held onto. Museums, newspapers, magazines, television and the internet can all be sources of learning outside school as can sport or music events. This chapter considers children's out-of-school learning and studies in detail three sources which teachers can make use of.

Formal and informal learning

All people learn science from a variety of sources, in a range of different ways, and for a number of different purposes. In other words, the reasons, sources and favoured modes for learning science vary from one individual to the next. There are two different sources of or areas of learning that must be considered in science education – these can be called *formal* and *informal* learning. The main features of the two areas are summed up in Table 15.1.

Table 15.1 Formal and informal learning in science

Informal learning	Formal learning
Voluntary	Compulsory
Often haphazard, unstructured, unsequenced	Structured and sequenced
Non-assessed, non-certificated	Assessed, certificated
Open-ended	More closed
Learner-led, learner-centred	Teacher-led, teacher-centred
Outside of formal settings	Classroom and institution based
Unplanned	Planned
Many unintended outcomes, more difficult to manage	Fewer unintended outcomes
Social aspect central, e.g. social interactions between visitors	Social aspect far less central
Low 'currency'	High 'currency'
Undirected, not legislated for	Legislated for and directed, controlled

Formal learning takes place largely through the medium of the curriculum. It is compulsory, highly structured and regularly assessed. In contrast, informal learning is voluntary, sometimes accidental, haphazard and unassessed. Therein lie its advantages as well as its drawbacks. It also has the advantage of being spontaneous, sociable, learner-led and open-ended but with the consequent drawbacks of being unpredictable, unsequenced and undirected. The distinction is not always clear-cut, however, nor should we assume that formal learning is always confined to school with informal learning always occurring outside. Much valuable informal learning takes place in school, while some formal learning occurs out of school.

One thing is clear: in future, informal and undirected learning in science will be of increasing importance – the so-called ICT revolution will ensure this. Learning will take place in a variety of contexts and through an increasing number of media. Learning outside of school is certain to be of growing importance in relation to the formal school curriculum. This will perhaps be as true in science, in our so-called 'scientific and technological society', as in any of the other curriculum subjects.

Using and understanding informal learning

Our view is that the realm of 'informal learning' in science is an under-used and under-studied area. If we knew more about it, or simply took more notice of it, children's science education could be greatly enhanced.

There is already evidence to suggest that 'factors outside of schools have a strong influence on students' educational outcomes, perhaps strong enough to swamp the effects of variations in education practices' (Schibeci 1989: 13). More knowledge of, and attention to, 'informally acquired ideas' (Lucas et al. 1986) could thus be used to enrich science education and the work of classroom teachers: 'If the process of acquiring these ideas were examined carefully, information could become available that would be of use to teachers in their day-to-day work' (Lucas et al. 1986: 341).

Lucas (1983) provided an excellent review of sources of informal learning and their influence on so-called 'scientific literacy'. His analysis offers valuable guidelines in considering out-of-school learning in science. He distinguished, for example, between intentional and unintentional sources of learning, and between accidental and deliberate encounters with learning sources. These distinctions present various interesting permutations, see Figure 15.1.

Thus a casual visit to a children's playground may be called an accidental encounter with an unintentional source of learning, for example a roundabout. Interestingly, this encounter may lead children to believe in the centrifugal force on an object that physics teachers later inform them is fictitious. Encounters with science may take place in an interactive, 'hands-on' science centre – these are likely to be deliberate encounters with an intentional source. There is clearly a huge variety of informal sources of learning that impinge on science education:

- everyday experiences, such as slipping on ice; fastening a seat belt; visiting Disneyland or Alton Towers; riding on a bus; eating, drinking, cooking; gardening; riding in a lift; sweating; boiling a kettle, etc., the list is endless;
- the media: television programmes, some deliberately educational, some providing 'accidental learning'; radio; newspapers; podcasts;
- access to multimedia at home, either via the internet, computer disk, or other media;
- visits to museums, science centres, workplaces, etc.

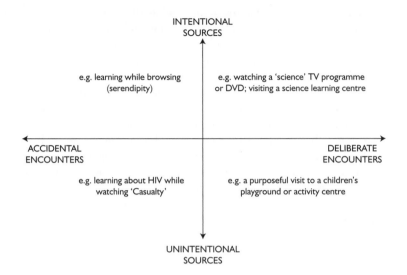

Figure 15.1 Classifying informal sources of learning

These and many others make up the so-called informal learning, which can sometimes support, but occasionally conflict with, the process of the formal science curriculum. In this chapter there is only room to consider briefly three sources of 'informal' learning in science: pupils' use of ICT in the home; text and print encountered out of school, be it supermarket, publicity leaflet, advert or news cutting; and interactive science centres of various kinds.

It is also worth noting that the Association for Science Education (ASE) offers a number of benefits of out-of-school learning, including:

- Provides opportunities for novel, unique and exciting learning experiences;
- Embeds science learning in a meaningful context;
- Can expand the science curriculum and give it purpose;
- Provides stimulus and motivation;
- Helps develop a pupil's identity.

(adapted from ASE 2006)

Example 1 Informal learning using ICT at home

The use of ICT in homes is growing faster than its use in schools – and there are already more systems in homes than in educational settings. We feel that teachers should take serious note of how, what, when and why children learn science via ICTs at home. However, this home access is not universal and the reader should refer to Chapter 13.

School-based ICT provides learners with a huge array of possibilities for learning science. Home-based ICT appears to be primarily used for two purposes: to access, prepare and present information (e.g. for a school assignment) or to follow-up some interest the student may have. In both cases, the 'discovery' of information is central to the endeavour. There is a great deal of excellent science content created by educational bodies and organisations but generally speaking, learners should be advised that they cannot always assume information on the internet has been carefully evaluated and will always be accurate and reliable. The website content of many sites has already been tried and tested by teachers, for example the BBC and Channel 4 sources, but the reality is that anyone can post content on the internet in an unvetted state. Pupils need to be aware of this just as they do when using an 'app' for their smart phone.

In summary ...

The use of ICT at home is a vitally important part of learning and an area ripe for school-based development. Home ICT can provide the possibility of quality time for the individual learner, which not every classroom can. Using ICT at home can play a vital role in the *affective domain of learning*, by developing enthusiasm, curiosity, interest and fascination for science. It can help to fulfil some of the requirements of the National Curriculum, in science and in ICT. But there are several issues and difficulties to be considered by teachers – not least those of access, equity, and the links between home and school in the use of ICT. For example:

- What are the implications of ICT use at home for science teaching and learning in school?
- What is 'appropriate use' of ICT at home?
- Do home systems interfere with school science education or can they be used to enhance it?
- How should teachers respond to, and assess, work done using home ICT?
- Is the home situation widening the gap between one set of pupils (the 'haves' of ICT) and another?

However we address these questions, one thing seems certain – science teachers cannot afford to ignore pupils' use of ICT, be it a computer or 'app', in the home environment.

Example 2 Using 'informal' sources of text in science teaching and learning

This section discusses the way in which print and reading from any outside source can be used in science education, although the main focus is on text from newspapers.

The science presented in newspapers can be of value in the school science curriculum but only if used carefully and critically. In addition, one of the aims of science education should be to develop in students both the will and the ability to read 'newspaper science' with a critical eye and with healthy scepticism. For a number of pupils the only science they will encounter in written form after leaving school will be in the tabloid newspapers – hence the necessity of learning to read with care and purpose. Finally, both newspaper science and the formal science curriculum act as 'media' between the scientific community at one level and the general public at the other; this idea is shown in Figure 15.2. Both contribute in some way to the public understanding of science, although their interaction may not always be productive.

Based on these premises, this section offers notes and suggestions related to the use of news cuttings and printed material from other sources in science lessons.

Why use material from newspapers in science education?

In addition to the general aim outlined above, using newspapers and other printed matter can help to meet the following objectives:

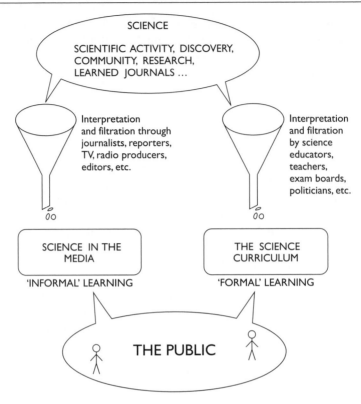

Figure 15.2 Media science and school science as filtering systems

1   To meet general curriculum requirements – for example to enable pupils to relate science to everyday life; to develop communication skill; to encounter a variety of sources from which they can gain information; to read purposefully an extended range of secondary sources; to engage in the critical evaluation of data; to use secondary sources as well as first-hand observation.

2   To provide material directly related to the content of the formal curriculum. Content analysis of the newspapers has shown that newspaper space is devoted to medical issues, the environment, space, food and diet, energy sources, pollution and waste management, and many other topics that relate to specific areas of science taught in schools (Wellington 1991).

3   To act as a starter in exploring some ideas about the nature of science, i.e. to distinguish between claims and arguments based on scientific considerations and those which are not; to study examples of scientific controversies and the ways in which scientific ideas change; to appreciate the tentative nature of conclusions and the uncertainty of scientific evidence. Current issues, and those from the recent past such as cloning, BSE, 'bird-flu' and cold fusion, can be used here as a complement to material from the history of science.

4   Newspaper material can also be related to cross-curricular themes such as health education, environmental education, citizenship and industrial and economic awareness.

5   To teach pupils to read critically and actively, and to develop an interest in reading about science; to allow group reading, analysis and discussion.

6   To raise awareness and interest in current issues related to science, many of which are
    controversial. By the same token pupils can become aware of some of the values and interests
    inherent in the development of science, and be enabled to see the limitations of science.

How can they be used?

Newspaper cuttings, and indeed other written material from magazines, supermarket leaflets and
even pressure groups (such as Greenpeace, Friends of the Earth) can be adapted for classroom
use. Table 15.2 provides a list of possible ideas for class and homework which we are sure could
be added to.

Finally for this section, we would stress the importance of the role of the teacher in encouraging
systematic analysis and careful criticism – teachers should not fall into the trap of seeing any of
the above as totally independent learning activities.

Which cuttings are best?

Classroom material using news cuttings drawn entirely from the so-called quality press and from
New Scientist can give the basis for good classroom activities, but they invariably have a reading
age higher than the pupils' chronological age and unless heavily edited or used in a very step-by-
step, structured way will be unsuitable, even at Key Stage 4. The quality papers, therefore, need
to be handled with care.

Table 15.2 Using newspapers in science teaching and learning

A: Possible ideas for class work

1. Issue raising/introducing an issue, for example, controversial issues

2. Starter activity, for example, for a new topic

3. Prompt/stimulus, for example, for discussion/role play; a stimulus to writing

4. Directed reading, for example, comprehension, examining keywords

5. Information/data extraction (and presentation and analysis), for example, making a graph
    from data in the text; interpreting a graph

6. Vocabulary/terminology study, for example, examining the language in an article; picking out
    difficult words

7. Poster making/collage/display creation, for example, on the environment; collections of
    headlines; articles from two papers on the same topic

B: Homework ideas

1. Content analysis, for example, pupils analyse one week of the paper taken at home (if there
    is one) for its 'science content' – this illuminates their interpretation of what 'science' is.
    Pupils then bring their analysis to the following week's lesson.

2. Making on activity for others, for example, selecting a cutting on science/a scientific issue and
    devising questions/activities on it for other pupils.

3. Searching for cuttings on a particular topic, for example, space, diet, environment, disease,
    flight, drugs, etc.

(NB: The pupils are probably the best source of newspaper material for the classroom!)

This is also true of the tabloids, though for different reasons. We would argue that cuttings from the tabloids (and that includes the *Sun* and the *Mirror*) should be used: first, these are the papers that the majority of school students and adults actually read; second, they present science and scientists in a way that needs to be challenged. Science in the media is so often presented as whiz-bang and dramatic, as certain, as an individual rather than a collective activity, as 'sudden' and unrelated to previous work, as carried out by crackpot and unorthodox discoverers (see Wellington 1991 for a fuller discussion of these points); third, from a purely practical point of view, they are more readable and often shorter and snappier than the quality coverage, which can sometimes go into inappropriate depth.

How should they be adapted for classroom use?

Certain rules can be followed in choosing and using text:

1 In line with the above comments, the cutting itself needs to be carefully chosen. The total text needs to be fairly brief (perhaps less than half of one A4 side) and, of course, readable. Diagrams, tables, pie-charts and other illustrations will help, especially if one of the aims is to interpret data and look at it critically.

2 If questions are directed at the text, a closed, simple question that merely asks for an item of information or a word from the passage should be placed first. It should be a question that every member of the class can answer. More difficult and perhaps open-ended questions can be left until later. This may seem an obvious point, but how many sets of questions in teachers' worksheets and even in textbooks start off with open-ended, difficult questions that half of a group struggle with and that act as a deterrent to continuing?

3 Questions that ask pupils to pick out and identify certain words in the passage can be used early on. Once they have found and highlighted important words, they can then be set the task of finding out (either from each other, a teacher, a textbook or dictionary) what those key words mean.

4 Open-ended questions that ask for an element of interpretation, discussion and evaluation should be left until the end, once pupils have got to grips with the passage. These questions can go *beyond* the text, and invite speculation and judgement.

To sum up points 2, 3 and 4, questions should be graded from simple to difficult and from closed to open – an obvious rule, but one which is surprisingly often ignored.

1 With more difficult passages, such as from *New Scientist*, teachers may choose to read through an article with a class, and then discuss its main points before embarking on the activities. With other material, teachers may simply let the class work in small groups, or individually, and then bring them together later to compare answers or points from discussion. In all cases we feel that some teacher intervention is needed to bring out the point behind the activity. This is particularly true in activities aimed at raising questions about the nature of science, such as: Why do scientists disagree? Are some scientists biased? What counts as a fair test? How are scientists portrayed in the media? and so on.

2 Finally, activities of this kind can very often be used as examples of the presentation of science, for example the way that data and statistics are presented in papers to make certain points or support certain arguments; the way in which science generally is presented to the public. Pupils can thus be encouraged to look critically at the presentation of science by the media – this is surely an essential prerequisite for participation as a citizen in a science-based democracy.

Example 3 Interactive science centres

What are interactive science centres?

A 'new generation' of science museums grew up in the 1960s in the USA with initiatives such as the New York Hall of Science in 1964 and the Exploratorium in San Francisco in 1969. The principles of the Exploratorium were based on the three Is, put forward by one of the driving forces behind it, Frank Oppenheimer (brother of Robert of atomic bomb fame): *innovation, interaction* and *involvement*. The new generation shifted museums away from 'objects in glass cases' to a stress on involvement, activity and ideas. Greatly influenced by this shift and by the success of children's museums and galleries, a new breed of stand-alone 'interactive science centres' (ISCs) grew up in the 1980s. In 1985 there were none in the UK. A decade later there were more than twenty, with centres such as the Exploratory in Bristol, and Techniquest in Cardiff leading the way, together with, in the London Science Museum, a self-contained hands-on centre called Launch Pad. Some of these were attracting up to 200,000 visitors per year and still do. In the following decade, up to 2005, some estimates suggest that a further billion pounds was spent on the ISC movement, largely with support from the UK National Lottery.

Interactive science centres, like elephants, are hard to define – but we all know one when we see one. Perhaps the first distinguishing feature is the general air of noise, enjoyment and activity that greets all those who enter.

Second, they contain activities or 'exploring stations' (McManus 1992) that visitors are invited to touch and do things with, i.e. to interact with. Typically a centre might have between 50 and 200 exhibits, most of which need to be hard-wearing and robust, and at least a few of which will be temporarily 'under repair'. The various centres will have certain exhibits (or 'plores' as they were first christened at the Bristol Exploratory) in common, partly because developers of plores have sold or shared their ideas with others and these have been transferred from one ISC to another. Our impression from visiting many of the centres is that most will contain a Bernoulli blower, a rotating turntable with a human on it holding a bicycle wheel, an echo tube, parabolic mirrors and many other exhibits with people doing things on them!

Third, science centres will have 'guides', 'pilots' or 'explainers' (as opposed to a uniformed attendant in earlier generations of museum) circulating around the centre to help visitors in any way, often showing them how to 'interact' with an exhibit although some may attempt to *explain* phenomena (often at their peril, if it involves concepts such as moment of inertia or gyroscopic motion). The key role of the explainer, in our view, is actually to get learners to *engage* with an exhibit, at whatever level. There might typically be four or five explainers 'on the floor', with perhaps about 180 visitors at any one time.

The centres each have their own distinctive flavour and emphasis, but they all have certain features in common:

*   All provide interactive, hands-on learning of science using a range of activities/events/ 'plores' rather than untouched exhibits in glass cases.
*   They all emphasise play and enjoyment as an essential element of learning.

The stress is on doing, seeing and experiencing rather than formal understanding and explanation. Although each 'event' carries a short explanation or caption, the evidence is that these are hardly ever read – in addition, the use of formal, structured worksheets in the centres is uncommon, if not discouraged.

How do they relate to the formal curriculum?

Our own observations, as independent observers having visited many of the ISCs in the UK and the USA, is that they do relate very closely to many of the areas of the formal school curriculum and even beyond. Some of the concepts being experienced though not explained, such as gyroscopic motion or human perception, extend to the realms of undergraduate science.

In addition, many ISCs can actually fill gaps in the curriculum coverage offered in a school setting. For example, expert demonstrations and 'science shows' can show phenomena that are either unsafe or impractical to do in a school lab, e.g. some examples of combustion or other dramatic chemical processes, while at primary level, centres can provide hands-on experiences in an enjoyable, 'free-range' environment that primary schools may not have the resources to offer.

It should also be noted that many exhibits go beyond the straitjacket of a formal curriculum and introduce learners to some difficult, but fascinating and important, topics such as human perception and chaos – the latter using examples from chaotic, unpredictable motion such as spinning magnets, Rott's pendulum, and other pendulum examples which learners are unlikely to see at school.

Learning in science centres ... and elsewhere

What do we know about learning? At the risk of annoying readers who have a background in psychology, we will attempt to sum up some of the key points about learning that have a bearing on what goes on in ISCs and also how teachers can best exploit them. Our potted version has three key points.

1 Learning depends on what the learner already knows. Learning is a process which involves interaction between what is *already* known and the *current* learning experience. For learning to be lasting and meaningful, it must connect with prior knowledge, prior conceptions and prior experience – otherwise it becomes rote or parrot-fashion learning. Learners construct knowledge on a foundation of what they already know.
2 Meaningful learning often occurs in a social context (though perhaps not always). Learners can help each other by talking and interacting – teachers can help learners by supporting, guiding, structuring and scaffolding their learning. Learners construct their own knowledge, but they often do it best socially. Other people are important.
3 Learning is *a situated process*. All of our knowledge is situated in a certain context or domain. It is often difficult for this to 'travel' or transfer – psychologists have searched in vain for over 70 years for conclusive evidence of transfer of learning or generalisable skills. Knowledge learnt in one context, e.g. a school science laboratory, does not always travel to another, e.g. rewiring your house. The street trader who can add up prices of fruit and vegetables in a jiffy may flounder when asked to do a written arithmetic test with paper and pencil, let alone a Maths GCSE paper.

These three potted points (derived largely from Vygotsky, Ausubel and Bruner – see Chapter 4 of this book) are all important in weighing up the role and the contribution of ISCs and comparing it with the function of formal, school curriculum-based science education. We must recognise that learning in the two contexts is different – formal school learning can contribute more to some aspects of learning in areas 1 to 3 above than the 'informal' learning in ISCs, and vice versa. It is important to compare and contrast the features of learning in the two contexts, i.e. ISCs and school (see Table 15.1 again).

Learning in formal settings is important. As Paulette McManus puts it:

> In formal educational situations, where you will learn, who you will learn with, whether you are qualified to learn, who you will learn from, what you will learn, how long you will be given to learn it and agreement on what you have learned and your level of understanding are matters largely out of the control of the individual learner. As a result of these restrictions on the individual, formal educational institutions are very efficient, admirable means of communicating knowledge throughout societies for the benefit of those societies and the individuals within them.
>
> (McManus 1992: 165)

Nevertheless, learning in less formal settings also has a role to play. Our argument is that learning science in ISCs is not a substitute for learning in a more formal, school context – but it can be an important complement to it. How?

Assessing the contribution of interactive science centres

Our own view is that ISCs make a significant contribution in three areas: the cognitive domain, the affective domain, and the important job of linking science and scientific concepts to real-world experiences. We will explain:

1   First, centres contribute indirectly to higher-order knowledge and understanding. One way is through what can be called the 'rubbing-off' effect of hands-on science. Children visit a centre, and do and see a large number of things in a short space of time. They often see or do something which rubs off and sticks, or 'sparks off' something in their mind which may resurface weeks, months, even years later. In other words, while hands-on science centres may not contribute immediately and directly to deep understanding, their indirect effect must not be forgotten.

2   A similar effect occurs through a second area of educational aims: the affective domain. This area involves the development of interest, enthusiasm, motivation, eagerness to learn, awareness and general 'openness' and 'alertness'. Interactive hands-on science centres can make a major contribution to the affective area. They may even begin to compensate for the neglect of this area in formal science education. Hands-on science centres generate activity, enthusiasm, adrenalin, excitement and interest. By developing motivation for science and technology they will, in many cases, ultimately contribute to understanding.

3   Finally, 'school science', as those of us who have been through the school system know, seems to have an existence of its own. It has its own apparatus, creating a world of conical flasks, test-tube racks, Pyrex beakers and all the other bits and pieces which remind adults instantly of school science. It has its own laboratories of a kind encountered nowhere else in the universe which by necessity combine working space with learning and teaching space. The world of 'school science' bears little relation to the world outside where science and technology abound. In playgrounds, in kitchens, on sports fields and golf courses, in shop windows, in the back garden or on rubbish tips there is enough science to keep people going for a lifetime. One of the achievements of hands-on science centres has been to relate science and technology to the things that most people (who don't go on to be research chemists) see and use. Lemonade bottles, bridges, incinerators, bricks, lifting jacks and giant see-saws can all be found in interactive centres but rarely in school science labs. Thus hands-on

centres can make a major contribution to a broad science education, and therefore scientific literacy, which school science in its unique world would not.

Research carried out in different parts of the world supports these claims. Stevenson (1992), for example, tracked a substantial number of visitors (many from family groups) to Launch Pad at different intervals after their visit. He discussed their memories of the visit as much as six months after the event. He found that family members were able to recall much of their visit in clear detail (how many pupils can do this six months after a school science lesson?). He concluded that a significant number of the memories reported to him showed that cognitive processing related to the activities during the visit had taken place. In addition, a substantial body of research conducted in Australia by Léonie Rennie supports the claim that both cognitive and affective learning do occur. She suggests that cognitive learning fades after a time (hardly surprisingly) but that affective outcomes are more resistant and long-lasting.

It seems that ISCs may be one means of providing the excitement and motivation for learners to continue with science post-16, which is clearly needed given the current depressing statistics on those who choose to follow sciences at advanced level.

In summary ...

A visit to a science centre is a complement to school learning, not a substitute for it. Science centres can enrich and broaden the formal science curriculum. Each offers a valuable contribution to science education. ISCs work for all ages of learner from one to 91 and beyond, and for all kinds of group ranging from the extended family to semi-formal groups such as Guides, Scouts and the Women's Institute. The ISCs have made a tremendous contribution to science education and the public understanding of science on an extremely low budget, with virtually nothing coming from the public purse. They deserve to be supported. Let us hope that the injection of large sums of money will not ruin them, will take account of their roots and will recognise the enormous and unique contribution they have made.

Bringing informal, outside learning into the classroom

We have considered just three examples of how 'informal' sources can be linked with formal science education. There are clearly many others that can contribute. One of the dangers, of course, is to try to over-exploit outside experiences or sources, resulting in what teachers call 'overkill', i.e. trying to make too much of a good thing. Given this qualification, however, there are several ways in which teachers can link the domains of informal, out-of-school learning and formal, structured learning:

- in introducing a lesson or a new topic, such as by starting with the pupils' experiences of that topic;
- in basing a lesson around an out-of-school activity, such as a visit, a TV programme, an advertisement;
- in providing ideas for project work and independent learning;
- by using 'everyday' materials (such as bleach, washing powder, food colourings) to replace or use alongside laboratory materials;
- in overtly valuing children's contributions to classroom discussions and everyday anecdotes about science experience;

- in displaying posters and adverts about the use of science in everyday life, for example plastics, chlorine, drugs;
- in placing practical problem-solving tasks in everyday, relevant contexts.

In summary ... looking to the future

One of the founders of the San Francisco Exploratorium, Frank Oppenheimer, argued for the value of informal learning in promoting science education, and against the dominance of formal, certificated education, see Table 15.1:

> no-one ever flunks a museum or a television program or a library or a park, while they do flunk a course – they do 'flunk out of school'. Only schools can certify students; only certified students can progress. As a result only schools are conceived as public education. I would like to suggest that the current mechanisms for certification are not only stifling to educational progress but that they are also extraordinarily costly and wasteful. Certification is an impediment.

> (Oppenheimer 1975)

Perhaps Oppenheimer was overstating the case for informal, out-of-school education as against the certificated, formal curriculum. But the importance of such learning is certain to grow in the future, not least due to the spread of ICT. Teachers need to be aware of it, to nurture it and to use it while avoiding over-exploiting it.

Points for reflection

- What types of valuable relevant experience do you feel that children could bring to the school classroom from home?
- How should you design learning tasks for individuals at home (if at all)? Is it fair to do this, e.g. if not all children have a home environment that is conducive to learning?
- How should you assess work done at home, possibly with ICT, perhaps involving small groups of pupils working together at someone's home?
- More generally, how can you and other teachers in your school achieve greater connection between home learning and school learning, so that the two domains complement and enhance each other rather than possibly conflicting or simply being unrelated to each other?
- Do you feel that the home situation is widening the gap between one set of pupils (the 'haves' of ICT) and another?

References and further reading

General

ASE (2006) *Safeguards in the School Laboratory*, 11th edn. Hatfield: ASE
Braund, M. and Reiss, M. (eds) (2004) *Learning Science Outside the Classroom*, London: RoutledgeFalmer.
Hein, G (1998) *Learning in the Museum*, New York: Routledge.
Sefton-Green, J. (2003) 'Informal learning: substance or style?' *Teaching Education*, vol. 13, no. 1, pp. 2–16.

ICT at home

Kerawalla, L. and Crook, C. (2002) 'Children's computer use at home and at school: context and continuity', *British Educational Research Journal*, vol. 28, no. 6, 751–71.
Wellington, J. (2001) 'Exploring the secret garden: the growing importance of ICT in the home', *British Journal of Educational Technology*, vol. 32, no. 2, 233–44.

Newspapers

Hyden, Fiona and King, Chris (2006) 'What the papers say: science coverage by UK national newspapers', *School Science Review*, vol. 88, no. 322, pp. 81–7; considers the content covered by UK newspapers and the areas that it favours (such as medicine and biology, at the expense of physics and chemistry); asks how this 'bias' might affect future science teaching.
Jarman, Ruth and McClune, Billy (2007) *Developing Scientific Literacy: using news media in the classroom*, Maidenhead: Open University Press; an excellent source of ideas on using the media to enrich science teaching and engage pupils; contains numerous ideas on using newspapers and other sources in science and how to encourage young people to read them carefully and critically.
Wellington, J. (1991) 'Newspaper science, school science: friends or enemies?', *International Journal of Science Education*, vol. 13, no. 4, pp. 363–72.

Formal and informal learning

Lucas, A.M. (1983) 'Scientific literacy and informal learning', *Studies of Science Education*, no. 10, pp. 1–36.
Lucas, A.M., McManus, P.M. and Thomas, G. (1986) 'Investigating learning from informal sources: listening to conversations and observing play in science museums', *European Journal of Science Education*, no. 8, pp. 41–52.
Schibeci, R.A. (1989) 'Home, school and peer group influences on student attitudes and achievement in science', *Science Education*, no. 73, p. 13.

Using 'outside' text or photographs in the classroom

Association for Science Education (ASE) (1991) *Race, Equality and Science Teaching*, Hatfield: ASE; contains an excellent section on choosing and using photographs in the classroom with examples that can be taken from newspapers, books, magazines, etc. The aims behind the activities include making science learners into 'critical observers' of the images of people and places presented by the photographs.
Wellington, J.J. (1986a) (ed.) *Controversial Issues in the Curriculum*, Oxford: Basil Blackwell.
Wellington, J.J. (1986b) *The Nuclear Issue*, Oxford: Basil Blackwell; both discuss the value of using controversial issues in developing certain skills, and suggest strategies for the classroom. *The Nuclear Issue* also contains examples that can be photocopied for classroom use.
Wellington, J.J. (1991) 'Newspaper science, school science: friends or enemies?', *International Journal of Science Education*, vol. 13, no. 4, pp. 363–72; contains an example of content analysis and a review of past news coverage.

Interactive science centres

Griffin, J. (1994) 'Learning to learn in informal science settings', *Research in Science Education*, no. 24, pp. 121–8.
Griffin, J. (1998) 'Learning science through practical experiences in museums', *International Journal of Science Education*, vol. 20, no. 6, pp. 655–63.

McManus, P. (1992) 'Topics in museums and science education', *Studies in Science Education*, vol. 20, pp. 157–82.

Moffat, H. (1991) 'Museums and the national curriculum', *Museums Journal*, vol. 91, no. 5, pp. 32–7.

Oppenheimer, F. (1975) 'The exploratorium and other ways of teaching physics', *Physics Today*, vol. 28, no. 9, pp. 9–13.

Quin, M. (ed.) (1989) *Sharing Science: issues in the development of interactive science centres*, London: Nuffield Foundation/COPUS.

Rennie, L.J. (1994) 'Measuring affective outcomes from a visit to a science education centre', *Research in Science Education*, no. 24, pp. 261–9.

Shortland, M. (1987) 'No business like show business', *Nature*, no. 328, pp. 213–14; a critical look at 'hands-on' science.

Stevenson, J. (1992) 'The long-term impact of interactive exhibits', *International Journal of Science Education*, vol. 13, no. 5, pp. 521–31.

Wellington, J.J. (1989a) 'Attitudes before understanding: the role of hands-on centres', *Sharing Science*, London: Nuffield Foundation/COPUS.

Wellington, J.J. (1989b) *Hands-on Science: 'It's fun, but do they learn?'*, video with notes, Sheffield: University of Sheffield Television Service.

Wellington, J.J. (1990) 'Formal and informal learning in science: the role of the interactive science centres', *Physics Education*, no. 25, pp. 247–50.

Full information on the UK science centres can be obtained from the British Interactive Group (BIG) at www.big.uk.com. Complimentary visits for teachers can be arranged to many centres – contact them direct to arrange a visit. The latest research and discussion on the centres can be found at: www.big.uk.com/knowledgebase/research/index.htm.

Chapter 16

Citizenship and sustainability in science education

Introduction

A number of aspects of the learning and teaching of science will contribute to the wider development of pupils in the school. Numeracy and Literacy are *whole-school issues* to which science can make a major contribution. The same view can be taken of both citizenship and sustainability, which can also be addressed through science. Issues of common debate which draw on science in the media, for example BSE, HIV, GM foods and more recently avian influenza impact on all members of society or citizens. Other issues that are rooted in science, for example animal experimentation, organ transplantation and nuclear weapons programmes raise ethical objections among a sizable minority (and in some cases a majority). With this in mind some may argue that *socio-scientific issues* is perhaps a better term than citizenship and *global issues* a better term than sustainability; whilst these terms may be even more wide-ranging than the areas to be discussed here, they both share a common view of being based in science and potentially impacting on society.

Citizenship has been a statutory part of the National Curriculum for England and Wales, from 2002 at Key Stage 3 and 2004 at Key Stage 4. However, unlike other statutory components of the National Curriculum, the eight-level scale is not in place but end-of-stage descriptors are available at Key Stages 3 and 4. In addition, for those schools and pupils who deem it appropriate, a short course GCSE is available that recognises pupil achievement. Sustainability can be seen as part of citizenship or even Personal, Social and Health Education (PHSE) but the Qualifications and Curriculum Development Authority (QCDA) see it as:

> Sustainable development is a cross-curriculum dimension. Like the other dimensions, it is a unifying theme that helps learners make sense of the world and their place in it. It can be integrated across subjects, and embedded in the routines, events and ethos of a school.
> (QCDA 2009)

All trainee teachers need to demonstrate competence in the standards, which include the National Curriculum framework and 14–19 pathways and assessments.

It is our contention, however, that best practice in science teaching will not be driven by any statutory mandate. Good lesson planning should, we argue, allow pupils to arrive at informed decisions in a supportive and unthreatening environment without the need for external pressures to drive them.

What is citizenship?

This is a difficult concept and one that many political leaders struggle with. Within science education, Ratcliffe and Grace (2003) say 'citizenship is a contested and slippery concept', while Heater (1999) suggests:

> Citizens need knowledge and understanding of the social, legal and political system(s) in which they operate. They need skills and aptitudes to make use of that knowledge and understanding. And they need to be endowed with values and dispositions to put their knowledge and skills to beneficial use.

Citizenship in schools or citizenship education is a fairly recent phenomenon, with the QCA (1998) stating that: 'Citizenship education must be education for citizenship. It is not an end in itself, even if it will involve learning a body of knowledge, as well as the development of skills and values.'

The approach to citizenship education that became part of the statutory orders for the National Curriculum began with the Crick Report (QCA 1998). The Crick Report identified three elements that should inform citizenship education:

- community involvement;
- political literacy;
- social and moral responsibility.

While it may not be immediately obvious that these three elements map onto the secondary school science curriculum, further analysis may make matters clearer.

Community involvement is being part of the school, tutor group or science class. Professional scientists (and science teachers) are part of their academic and professional communities. Research scientists are ever more involved in large-scale projects with multinational teams: these are part of a community. However we define community, pupils need to be aware that membership of the community brings with it responsibilities and duties (see Blandford 2006).

Political literacy need not be simply the understanding of the political system, be it democratic or not, since this could be seen as too narrow. Political literacy is perhaps better taken to be the development of those political skills of debate, decision making and critical and strategic thinking. Scientific research operates in this way as, indeed, do policy and curriculum developments in science education. Pupils in school can be engaged with scientific concepts via the use of mock debate, thus developing their personal political literacy.

Social and moral responsibility can also be addressed via science education. Typical examples could be environmental education, renewable energy and animal testing. The way in which we interact with each other, especially regarding these issues, is governed by our values. Did the development of the first atomic bomb ultimately save lives by bringing WWII to a swift end or cost lives by being detonated? Much depends on our values, or social responsibility, as does much of science. Indeed Robert Oppenheimer, who led the development of the atomic bomb, is often quoted as saying: 'Scientists cannot hold back progress for fear of what man may do with it.' A big question but one that, we argue, is open to secondary school science pupils.

What is sustainability?

This is a question much larger than a single chapter can address. However, Ofsted (2011) give us a working definition with direct relevance to schools:

> 'Sustainable development' means that as a society we have to live within the means of our natural resources, respect our environment, act on climate change, and work collectively towards an improved quality of life for our communities. This means that sustainable development is not just about environmental or green issues such as switching off unnecessary lights, recycling and buying locally grown fruit and vegetables. In schools it includes consideration of pupils' well-being, and the school's contribution to building a sustainable community.
>
> (Ofsted 2011)

A question of ethics?

Ethical issues, considering the above, cannot be divorced from citizenship or sustainability education. One could argue that moral decisions, and indeed social responsibility, are driven by our ethics. It could be further argued that both ethics and science share a similar definition. For example Fullick and Ratcliffe (1996) offer:

> Science: the process of rational enquiry which seeks to propose explanations for observations of natural phenomena;
> Ethics: the process of rational enquiry by which we decide on issues right (good) and wrong (bad) as applied to people and their actions.

Since science is a human construct then all science must apply to people and their actions hence science must involve the application of ethical processes.

Ethics often sparks the idea of a controversial issue. Wellington (1986) argues that a controversial issue must involve value judgements that cannot be settled by facts, evidence or experimentation alone and it must be considered important by an appreciable number of people. This is echoed by the Crick Report (QCA 1998) where controversial issues are defined as ones for which there is no universally held point of view, which commonly divide society and for which significant groups offer conflicting explanations and solutions. Is this not the way science evolves, for example the change from a heliocentric universe, the plum-pudding model of the atom or the corpuscular theory of light?

If we have science as a statutory requirement between the ages of 5 and 16 then it must prepare pupils, including those who do not study science post-16, for life. Social life is ever more dependent on science or its application and in order to play a full part in society members of that society need to be able to engage with the issues affecting it. Lord Dearing (2002) expresses this as:

> Democracy is more fragile than people realise. The quality of democracy depends on engagement by the people. If you look for ways of encouraging participation, it is in scientific contexts that you will find the issues which will really grab young people.

Ratcliffe and Grace (2003) explore the interest in applications of science rather than specific science content. The fact that adults draw on science knowledge they have 'gained through experience' in specific situations rather than from 'authoritative scientific' sources should suggest to us, as science educators, that providing the skills to enable them to do so effectively is at least as important as 'the mastery of fundamental science concepts'.

In listing the nature of socio-scientific issues, which, we argue, is an alternative term for citizenship or sustainability, Ratcliffe and Grace give nine reasons for including them in science education, arguing that such issues:

- have a basis in science, frequently at the frontiers of scientific knowledge;
- involve forming opinions, making choices at personal or societal level;
- deal with incomplete information because of conflicting/incomplete scientific evidence and inevitably incomplete reporting;
- address local, national and global dimensions with attendant political and societal frameworks;
- involve some cost-benefit analysis in which risk interacts with values;
- may involve consideration of sustainable development;
- involve values and ethical reasoning;
- may require some understanding of probability and risk;
- are frequently topical with a transient life.

A number of these reasons, in particular ones that address scientific enquiry, offer direct support for the National Curriculum. It is often the case, in the quest to complete the content, that dealing with incomplete data and dealing with probability and risk are often neglected in National Curriculum science and hence anything that assists pupils' understanding of these aspects must be an advantage.

A number of the points also feed into cross-curricular issues, for example: sustainable development links to design and technology or political and societal frameworks links to PHSE.

The Crick Report gave an expectation that 5 per cent of curriculum time would be given over to citizenship and that it could be facilitated in blocks, modules, tutor time, discrete periods, general studies programmes or through existing subjects.

What contribution can science make to the citizenship and sustainability curriculum?

Everington (2004) offers the following contribution science can make, not to citizenship but to spiritual, moral and cultural development:

- spiritual development: role of scientific discoveries in changing people's lives and thinking;
- moral development: why sustainable development is important;
- cultural development: relationship between culture and the nature of scientific exploration.

Giving a curriculum map and/or good advice however does not lead, naturally, to teaching resources for the classroom. Even when such material is provided it is not always taken up with enthusiasm. Ratcliffe and Grace (2003) suggest that teacher enthusiasm is driven by:

- their relevance to science teaching issues 'of the moment';
- their immediate applicability to classroom practice;
- their intrinsic interest.

However, our argument is that science teachers can make a unique offering to developing citizenship. Indeed, citizenship education will be incomplete in schools without the scientist's perspective and values. What do we mean by this?

Science teaching can help to develop some of the attitudes and values that contribute to citizenship. For example science can and should contribute to:

- pollution: for example in transport and energy production;
- use of materials: e.g. packaging, recycling;
- genetics: cloning, nature versus nurture, race;
- energy consumption and conservation: at home, outside, nationally, internationally;
- health and medicine: for example on smoking, diet, BSE, foot and mouth disease;
- the origin of the universe, evolution;
- reproduction.

Second, the skills and abilities that can be developed and enhanced through science education will include:

- personal, informed judgement (not just: 'That's my opinion and I'm sticking to it');
- communication;
- thinking skills, including being able 'to think for oneself';
- debating, discussing;
- listening to other people;
- taking action (legally);
- finding out, searching (including ICT);
- questioning and evaluating where information comes from, who put it there and how it is presented, e.g. graphs;
- respect for others – putting yourself in someone else's shoes.

The attitudes and values for citizenship and sustainability that can be developed in science education will include:

- healthy scepticism … but not cynicism;
- critical judgement … without being dismissive or scathing;
- careful evaluation and informed opinion;
- critical reading, watching and listening.

Many of these are known as the traditional scientific virtues and attitudes (Grinnell 1987). The immediate response, quite rightly, is: 'All very well … but how to do this in practice?' We do not have space here to consider this in full. But it should be noted that there are several, well-documented strategies that teachers can adopt in dealing with controversial issues, ethics and citizenship inside and outside the classroom. We can only list them here:

- using newspaper cuttings and other sources for group reading activity, see the chapters on literacy and using out-of-school sources;
- using DVD-based material in a structured way;
- bringing in guest speakers with a range of views on a variety of topics;
- setting up simulated TV/radio debates and press conferences in the classroom;

Table 16.1 Successful learners, confident individuals and responsible citizens

Successful learners	Confident individuals	Responsible citizens
Are creative, resourceful and able to identify and solve problems.	Have secure values and beliefs and have principles to distinguish right from wrong.	Sustain and improve the environment locally and globally.
Know about big ideas and events that shape our world.		Take account of the needs of present and future generations in the choices they make.
		Can change things for the better.

Source: adapted from QCA (2009)

- workplace visits and school audits, e.g. to assess their energy; conservation, impact on the environment (tactfully!);
- community projects, e.g. wildlife development (e.g. pond creation or preservation); conservation activity;
- looking at the school itself, e.g. heating and ambient temperature, lighting, transport;
- handling 'critical incidents' that involve ethical issues as and when they arise in the classroom (Nott and Wellington 1997);
- using SATIS and other past or current projects that have connected science, technology and society and produced classroom material on controversial issues.

To help teachers develop their own materials we can refer to the guidance given in *Citizenship: Scheme of Work for KS3 Teacher's Guide* (QCA 2001) where advantages, disadvantages and implications for delivery through the existing subjects are given, for example:

- *advantages*: integrated approach gives relevance for learning in the subject;
- *disadvantages*: coordination across departments;
- *implications*: extra time needed to meet both citizenship and subject objectives.

In addition teachers may wish to consult the guidance given in *Sustainable Development in Action* (QCA 2009) where the guidance for successful learners, confident individuals and responsible learner citizens is given, see Table 16.1.

This again highlights the common ground between citizenship and sustainability education. However, many would still argue that the disadvantages listed for citizenship education are only made more so by including sustainability.

We would argue that the advantages outweigh the disadvantages and that time may actually be saved through interdepartmental cooperation. If citizenship and sustainability are embedded into the subjects then curriculum time is not needed for discrete lessons. Not only do pupils receive a more holistic understanding of the issues being debated but, dare we suggest, the time gained may be given over to science!

In developing a lesson plan that will address citizenship, sustainability, ethical or socio-scientific issues through a science lesson, it is important that teachers ask themselves:

- What impact does your value system have on your views?
- What impact does your pupils' value system have on their views?
- How will you share the objectives of the lesson with your pupils?

(adapted from Ireson and Twidle 2006)

Theory into practice

From the above discussion, how can a lesson be constructed that addresses science content, allows pupils to express their views and addresses socio-scientific issues touching on ethics? In Figure 16.1 we offer a lesson plan for a Key Stage 3, age 11 to 14, science class that has been looking at blood as a transport mechanism.

Charles Drew developed the system of blood banking that undoubtedly saved numerous lives during the Second World War and continues to do so today. Having been made Director of the Red Cross Blood Bank he resigned when the US Army insisted that blood plasma collected from black and white donors be kept separate. On 1 April 1950 he was involved in a car accident that ultimately took his life. You will find a number of reports, both written and web-based, which talk of him being refused treatment due to his colour, but a number also referring to him having died from a broken neck.

It is our intention that the above lesson plan demonstrates how a number of socio-scientific issues can be addressed in school science while still addressing science content and hence answering the question, 'Doesn't it take too much time?'

An alternative approach, which requires less planning for the teacher, is to make use of well-produced resources that specifically link science content to socio-scientific issues. One such resource is based on a DVD produced by the Chemical Industry Education Centre at the University of York, *Without chemistry, what would we be left with?* Published in 2005 the DVD includes all the PowerPoint presentations, lesson plans and pupil worksheets for a number of Key Stage 3 and 4 citizenship lessons through science.

In summary ...

In this chapter we have discussed the meaning of the terms 'citizenship' and 'sustainability' and shown how they have become embodied in curriculum statements. It is our view that the line between citizenship and sustainability is rather blurred but the inclusion in the science curriculum is simply 'good teaching' and perhaps the term socio-scientific issues better draws these areas together.

Points for reflection

- What do you feel the teacher's role should be when presenting socio-scientific issues in the classroom? Can a teacher ever be 'neutral'?
- Do you think that socio-scientific issues, like citizenship, sustainability or ethics should be integrated into science teaching; removed from science teaching but taught elsewhere in the curriculum; or simply removed from the curriculum?
- How important do you consider media resources, from non-scientific sources, to be in a) teaching science and b) engaging learners in science?
- Having read the chapter and the example lesson based on the life and work of Charles Drew, consider how, at the time, you would have reacted had you been in his position. How would that reaction have been different had he lived in the 2000s rather than the 1940s? How would your reaction have differed as a scientist and as a human being?

Administration		NC reference	
• Register all pupils (have back-up for electronic system) • Have all resources to hand • Have pupil groups organised		• Sc2 2j, 2l • Citizenship KS3 2a, 2b, 3a • ICT KS3 3a, 3b, 3c	
Pupil learning objectives			Teacher objectives
By the end of the lesson pupils will be able to: • recall the development of blood banking and the use of plasma • discuss the ethical issues involved including religious objection and the myth regarding blood plasma from different races			• To organise and facilitate a science lesson which addresses socio-scientific issues
Time	Teacher/pupil activity	Feedback strategy	Organisation
08:45 08:50 08:55 09:00 09:05 09:15 09:25 09:40 09:45	Arrive prior to the class. Meet and greet, coats off, begin starter activity on the whiteboard. Call register while pupils work on starter. Go over starter activity Introduce the development of blood banking during World War II and the work of Charles Drew (first black American to receive a DSc). Split into groups, discuss the action of the US army in asking the Red Cross to separate blood from black and white donors – Drew's resignation. Use laptops to draft letter of resignation. Plenary questions, ethics Set research homework; the myth around Drew's death and religious objections to transfusions.	 Self assessment Intervention questions Use of science facts Open questions	Questions on whiteboard Discussion cards Laptops Homework sheets
Prompts: Equal Opps ✓ Cross-curricular links ✓ Continuity and progression ✓ Homework ✓ Safety NA Differentiation ✓			

Figure 16.1 Lesson plan example

The potential to explore socio-scientific, often controversial issues, in lessons is huge; this chapter and Chapter 14 have outlined many reasons for including them in science teaching and learning. The chapter has outlined some practical approaches for including socio-scientific issues in planning for learning, with numerous ideas for taking these further in the readings below.

References and further reading

Bell, D. (2004) 'Creating green citizens: political liberalism and environmental education', *Journal of Philosophy of Education*, 38, no. 1, February, pp. 37–51.
Blandford, S. (2006) *Remodelling of Schools*, London: Pearson.

Crick, Bernard, Solomon, Joan and Cartwright, Barry (2001) 'Citizenship and science; science and citizenship', *School Science Review*, vol. 83, no. 302, pp. 33–42; Crick explains the thinking behind the final report leading up to the introduction of citizenship into the National Curriculum, while the two other authors respond to this report.

DfEE/QCA (1999) *The National Curriculum for England: Citizenship*, London: The Stationery Office.

Donnelly, J. (2004) 'Ethics and the Science Curriculum', *School Science Review*, vol. 86, no. 315, pp. 29–32.

Everington, J. (2004) 'Spiritual, moral and cultural development', in Brooks, V., Abbott, I. and Bills, L. (eds) *Preparing to Teach in Secondary Schools*, Maidenhead: Open University Press.

Fullick, P.L. and Ratcliffe, M. (eds) (1996) *Teaching Ethical Aspects of Science*, Totton: Bassett Press.

Grinnell, F. (1987) *The Scientific Attitude*, Boulder, CO: Westview Press.

Heater, D. (1999) *What is Citizenship?*, Cambridge: Polity Press.

Ireson, G. and Twidle, J. (2006) *Secondary Science Reflective Reader*, Exeter: Learning Matters.

Jenkins, Edgar (2006) 'School science and citizenship: retrospect and prospect', *School Science Review*, vol. 88, no. 323, pp. 113–19; traces and discusses the varying connections between school science and citizenship education which have been present in the curriculum for over a century and have recently led to the introduction of *Twenty-first century science* in schools.

Lord Dearing (2002) Accessed March 2006, no longer available: www.wellcome.ac.uk/ node5930.html.

Lovelock, J. (2000) *The Ages of Gaia: a biography of our living Earth*, Oxford: Oxford University Press.

Nott, M. and Wellington, J. (1997) 'Critical incidents in the science classroom and the nature of science', *School Science Review*, vol. 76, no. 276, pp. 41–6.

Ofsted (2011) *Sustainable Development*, Manchester: Ofsted.

QCA (1998) *Education for Citizenship and the Teaching of Democracy in Schools*, London: QCA.

QCA (2001) *Citizenship: Scheme of Work for KS3 Teacher's Guide*, London: QCA.

QCDA (2009) *Sustainable development in action*, London: QCDA.

Ratcliffe, M. and Grace, M. (2003) *Science Education for Citizenship*, Maidenhead: Open University Press.

Wackernagel, M. (1996) *Our Ecological Footprint: reducing human impact on the Earth*, Island, BC: New Society.

Wellington, J. (ed.) (1986) *Controversial Issues in the Curriculum*, Oxford: Blackwell.

Wellington, J. (1987) 'A delicate balancing act', *Times Educational Supplement*, 22 May, p. 21.

Wellington, J. (2004) 'Ethics and citizenship in science education: now is the time to jump off the fence', *School Science Review*, vol. 86, no. 315, pp. 33–44.

The December 2004 issue of *School Science Review* contains a wide range of articles (16 in total) on ethics in science education; many of these contain useful, and often debatable, strategies for introducing socio-scientific issues into science lessons.

Index

ability 15, 16, 112
accommodation 66, 91–2, 153
active learning 30, 90–1, 236, 271–2
active reading 211–14, 221–2
adaptation 68
affective domain 15–18, 74–5
alternative frameworks 142, 200
alternative ideas 78–95
analogy 8, 52–3, 202, 219
assessing pupils' progress (APP) 86–7
assessment 11–14, 22, 84–9
assessment focuses (AFs) 87–8
assessment for learning (AfL) 12–13, 84–8, 112,
    123
Assessment of Performance Unit (APU) 78–81,
    113, 143
assimilation 66, 91, 244, 259
attention 93, 98, 101, 126, 131, 137
Ausubel, D. 12, 37, 72–3, 290
authentic labour 236

balanced science 46–55
behavioural approach 19, 81, 108–9, 130–4,
    137, 142
'big ideas' 49–50
Bloom's taxonomy 15–16
bouncing questions 98, 110
brain based learning 75–77, 125, 138
bridging 94
Bruner, J. 69, 71, 100, 290

children's ideas in science 78–81, 104
chunking 92–3
circuses 166
citizenship 33–5, 296–304
classroom management 119–39
CLIS (Children's Learning in Science) 25, 80, 104
closed questions 4–5, 96, 127–8
Cloze procedure 213
cognitive acceleration 100–2

Cognitive Acceleration through Science Education
    (CASE) 87, 101–3
cognitive conflict 91–2, 94, 101, 104, 110, 112,
    187
cognitive development 61, 66–7, 69, 101–2, 112
concept cartoons 98, 116
concept mapping 5–7, 24, 107
constructivism 68–9, 85, 113
continuity 14–18
control 130–4, 137
controversial issues 19, 268–78, 281
curiosity 35–6, 45, 51, 61, 69, 74, 90, 93, 99,
    107, 126, 164, 285
current developmental profile (CDP) 70
curriculum issues 31–5, 41–57

DARTs (directed activities related to text)
    150, 211–14
databases 10, 249–51
data-logging 100–1, 234, 247–9
demonstrations 165
desk-top publishing 242–4
development of ideas approach 94–5
diagnostic (teaching) assessment 12, 84–8, 101,
    107, 226–28
diagnostic questions/questioning 4, 80–4, 99
diagnostic teaching 76, 86, 99
dialogic teaching 94–5
differentiation 140–60
discovery learning 43, 69, 72–3, 169, 238
dyslexia 160

electronic voting 101
energy teaching 50–4
engagement 18–20, 74, 90–1, 99, 103, 107, 187,
    225, 298
ethics 298–9
Every Child Matters (ECM) 141–2
exclusion 156
explaining 5

'far-transfer' effect 102
feedback 12–14, 25, 30–1, 84–4, 100–1, 121–2, 126, 131, 134–6, 178, 218, 236, 242, 272, 303
formal operational thinking 67, 102
formative assessment 12–14, 84–6

gender differences 144–5
Glasersfeld, E. von 67–8, 89, 113
glossaries, use of 204–6
GNVQ 18
graphical skills 227–9

health and safety 191–7
higher-level thinking 97
homework 135–6
How Science Works 182, 185–90

ICT 10, 43, 100–1, 154–5, 233–57, 284–5
inauthentic labour 248, 251
inclusion 140–60
inclusive education 140–60
informal learning 282–95
information technology 233–57
interactive science centres 289–93
Internet 251–6, 272, 282–5
interviews 88, 114, 271
investigations 16, 171–84

language 3, 198–222
learning environment 71, 89–90, 109, 136, 240
learning styles 17–19, 75–6, 127, 136, 138, 219, 236, 123–5, 143–4
lesson planning 17–19, 119–23
lesson starters 93–4
literacy 198–222
lollipop sticks 87

marking 13–14, 86, 124, 134–5, 138, 213, 217, 242
meaningful learning 72, 91, 290
memory 9, 66, 73, 92, 155, 206
mentoring 30–1, 39
metacognition 103
metaphors 3, 8, 14, 25–8
mind mapping 107
motion sensor 100
motivation 3, 18–20, 23, 55, 74–5, 100, 143, 145–6, 150, 157, 162, 174, 187, 236–7, 238, 247, 284, 291–2
multimedia 8, 239–41
multiple intelligences 115, 124, 127, 138
multi-sensory approach 150–5, 218–9

National Curriculum 43–9, 189, 258–9, 296

nature of science 10–11, 34, 36–8, 168, 258–81
neuroscience 77–8, 112
'no hands up' 86–7
note-taking 217
numeracy 223–30

open questions 4, 96, 128–9, 218, 303

pausing 96
pedagogical knowledge 28–30
PEOR cycle 99, 101, 104, 110, 176
personalised learning 86
Piaget, J. 66–8, 71–2, 74, 77, 85, 89, 91, 93, 102, 109, 112–13, 115–19, 201, 225
plagiarism 253
planning 88, 103, 109–10, 112, 119–39, 149–50, 165–6, 176–7
post-16 science 18,48
practical work 8–9, 43, 161–84, 193–4, 214–15, 218–19, 236, 238, 249, 264, 266–7
predict-observe-explain (POE) 163–4
process science 42
professional development 25–40
progression 3, 13–17, 22, 85, 88–9, 107, 121, 148, 157, 175, 225, 227, 253, 303
pupils' writing 214–18

questioning 4–5, 96–9, 126–9

radical constructivism 68–9, 113
readability 208–10, 221
reading for learning 210–14
reception learning 73
reflective practice 28–30
retention of knowledge/understanding 81, 85, 101, 162
'right answerism' 72
risk assessment 193–7
role play 272–8
rote learning 72–91

safety 129, 167, 191–7
scaffolding 71, 100, 290
schemes of work 18–19, 119–20
scientific investigation 171–84
semiotics 218–19
simulations 10, 43, 127, 164–7, 234, 237–9
social and emotional aspects of learning (SEAL) 147–8
socio-scientific issues 268–72, 299
Socratic questioning 4, 99, 110
special needs 140–60
spelling 134, 151–2, 242
spreadsheets 10, 244–7
stages of development 66–7, 113, 201
story-telling 272–8

student-generated questions 103
subject knowledge 28–30
summative assessment 12–13, 18, 84
support teachers 149
sustainability 298–304

taxonomy of words 199–204
teacher development 25–40
teacher talk 202–4
teachers' science knowledge 28–30
teachers' writing 206–8
textbooks 9, 127, 152, 155, 199, 208, 210,
    219–21, 288
theories of learning 63
theory 62–3, 111, 112, 124, 162, 167–8, 176,
    189, 215, 234, 258, 268, 302
Thinking Science 62–3, 102–3, 114
thinking skills 61, 67, 87, 101–3, 112, 300

third party ideas 98–9
traffic lights 74, 86
transmission 90, 94, 99, 113

variables 183
virtual learning environments (VLE) 136, 240
visual, auditory and kinaesthetic (VAK) learning
    75–6, 123–5, 136, 138
Vygotsky, L. 69–72, 85, 95, 109, 112, 118, 220,
    290

wait(ing) time: see pausing 96, 129
web sites 241
wordbanks 152–4
wordprocessing 234, 242–3
wrong answers 21, 98, 110, 138, 176

zone of proximal development (ZPD) 70–2, 101,
    109, 110